Desperation Dinners!

by Beverly Mills *&* Alicia Ross

Illustrations by Mary Lynn Blasutta

Workman Publishing • New York

*Desperation Dinner*s is a registered trademark of Beverly Mills Gyllenhaal and Alicia Brady Ross

Library of Congress Cataloging-in-Publication Data
Mills, Beverly.
    Desperation dinners/by Beverly Mills and Alicia Ross; illustrations by Mary Lynn Blasutta.
        p.   cm.
Includes index.
ISBN-13: 978-0-7611-0481-0 (pbk.)
ISBN-10: 0-7611-1039-9 (hc)
    1. Quick and easy cookery. I. Ross, Alicia. II. Title.
TX833.5.M55 1997
641.5'12—dc21   97-28303
                                                  CIP

Cover design by Paul Hanson
Book design by Paul Hanson and Barbara Balch
Authors' photograph by Karen Tam
Cover food photographs by Kats Barry

Workman books are available at special discounts when purchased in bulk for premiums and sales promotions as well as for fund-raising or educational use. Special editions or book excerpts can be created to specification. For details, contact the Special Sales Director at the address below.

Workman Publishing Company, Inc.
225 Varick Street
New York, NY 10014-4381
www.workman.com

Manufactured in the United States of America

First printing October 1997
20 19 18 17 16 15

For our husbands, Anders and Ron,

who keep us sane

and for our children,

Sam and Grey, and Hannah and Rachel,
who provide the meaning and purpose
behind our constant desperation.

—*Beverly and Alicia*

MANY THANKS

During the two years we've spent writing this book, many people have shared their time, recipes, and insights. They have endured our busy schedules and kept us afloat with enthusiasm. These gifts grace this book like spices added at just the right moment, and we are deeply grateful.

We are particularly indebted to our editor, Suzanne Rafer, for her patience, careful crafting, and infallible instincts, and to our agent, Carla Glasser, for believing in our idea and for being our trusty guide and constant cheerleader.

Many thanks to one of the most incredible cooks we know, Liza Bennett, not only for generously lending many of her own recipes to this book but for supplying the inspiration for so many more. Still other recipes and inspiration came from Lynn Clark-Brady, Kathy Hart, Melanie Abbott, Pam Smith O'Hara, Felicia Gressette, Reta Ebanks, and Sandra Burnett.

A little friendship goes a long way, and we're received extra help from Denise Deen. She tirelessly tested our recipes and, best of all, spent every Friday afternoon over coffee listening to the details of how the book was coming.

Special thanks go to our recipe testers for their hard work, honesty, and attention to detail. Those friends who opened their kitchens and made room in their busy lives for our recipes are Florence Strickland, Cheryl Ross, Susan Cannon, Julie Realon, Terry Sullivan, Debi Williams, Melody Cobb, Marietta Wynands, Christine Klein, Diane Pearce, Rane Winslow, and Amy Dunn.

Without Marsha Johnson, Deena Smith, and Laura Vohs, who charmed our children and distracted their attentions from the kitchen, we could not have written this book. It certainly would not exist without the newspaper column that inspired it, and the column would never have made it off the kitchen counter without the editors who took a chance on a new idea. Thanks to all of them for their courage and encouragement, but especially to Debbie Moose of *The News & Observer,* Amy Carlile and Judy Walker of *The Arizona Republic,* and Kathy Purvis of *The Charlotte Observer.*

To Diana Loevy, Mary Anne Grimes, Lisa Wilson, and the entire staff at United Feature Syndicate, we owe a special thank-you. When the desperate life, writing this book, and handling the column seemed like it would surely bury us, they rescued us with their professional attention and care.

We will always be grateful to Peter Workman for his vision and for embracing the Desperation Dinners concept. To the many other people at Workman Publishing who brought this book to life, we offer special thanks—to Paul Hanson for the superb cover design, to Barbara Balch, who worked with Paul for the most beautiful and cook-friendly layout ever, to Nancy Murray in production, Steve Pesola in pre-press, Margery Tippie for her careful copy editing, and Lori Eisenkraft-Palazzola, Carrie Schoen, Emily Nolan, and Cathy Dorsey for their additional editorial work. We are also grateful for the energy and enthusiasm of Andrea Glickson in marketing and Ellen Morgenstern in publicity. A special thank-you to our publicist, Phyllis Heller, for a great tour. We thank Mary Lynn Blasutta for her delightful illustrations, Karen Tam for our cover portrait and Kats Barry for the cover food photos, as well as for adopting Desperation Dinners as part of her photo journalism career and real-life routine.

Finally, deep appreciation goes to our parents, Gayle and Jim Brady and Dot and Jay Mills, for their love and support. We also feel especially fortunate to have grown up with Josephine Young and Flonnie Hood, our respective grandmothers and wonderful cooks, around whose tables we have enjoyed so many fabulous meals.

To ours husbands and children—Ron, Hannah, and Rachel Ross, and Anders, Sam, and Grey Gyllenhaal—a thousand kisses for your enthusiastic appetites and for two years of sharing "Mom" with a 400-page baby that never stopped needing something.

Contents

Introduction: Leading the Desperate Life ix

The Desperation Dinners Promise xiv

Your Desperation Pantry xviii, *A word about:* **Desperation Symbols** xviii

CHAPTER ONE:

SOUPS 2

Easy, nourishing soups, packed with flavor, yet fast to prepare. Both steamy hot—Tangy Tomato Soup, Winter Corn Chowder—and refreshingly chilled—Beat-the-Heat Borscht, Cool California Bisque—there's a perfect soup here for any time of the year.

The Vim and Zing of Vinegar 14, *A word about:* **Cold Soups** 21

CHAPTER TWO:

STEWS 26

Even when your schedule is packed to the hilt, there's still time to concoct one of these fortifying stews and chilies. Serve up fragrant bowlfuls of Vegetable Veal Stew, Grandma's Chicken Stew, Super Chili, and Vegetable Hoppin' John.

A word about: **Onions** 31, *A word about:* **Calories** 35, *A word about:* **Garlic** 46

CHAPTER THREE:

SKILLET MEALS 48

With a decent skillet and a few quick tricks, you can pull off an entire dinner in no time flat—and with only one pan to wash afterwards. Fajitas in a Flash, Cuban Picadillo, Garlicky Potatoes and Sausage, and Blue Runners and Rice are just a few of the month's worth of recipes in this chapter.

A word about: **Spice Levels** 51, **The Right Skillet** 55, *A word about:* **Quick Rice** 59, *A word about:* **Cast-Iron Skillets** 64, *A word about:* **Cup Measures** 69, *A word about:* **Frozen Meat** 77, *A word about:* **Our Mu-Shu** 87

CHAPTER FOUR:
SALAD ENTREES 100

This selection of filling main-dish salads includes all our current favorites. There's a beef salad redolent with Thai flavors, a delicious Chicken Caesar good enough to serve your in-laws, plus a Picnic Pasta with Shrimp that's so easy, you can take it to a July Fourth celebration.

> **Salad in a Bag** 109, **The Refrigerator Pantry** 119, *A word about:* **Hard-Boiled Eggs** 125

CHAPTER FIVE:
PASTA 128

For all those who are already pasta converts and for those who need inspiration, here is a full selection of fast and fabulous recipes to help you noodle around your desperation. Try a particularly kid-friendly Real-Life Lasagna, a nontraditional but Oh-So-Easy Tetrazzini, and the Super-Stress Saving Pizza Pasta and Tuna and Fusilli Alfresco.

> **Measuring Pasta** 131, **How to Boil Water** 135, **Don't Just Stand There—Cook!** 139, **The Pasta Bowl** 147, *A word about:* **IQF Chicken Breasts** 151, *A word about:* **Milk Fat** 153, **Oil and Vinegar** 157, *A word about:* **Dairy Products** 171, *A word about:* **Stuffed Pasta** 175, *A word about:* **No-Cook Sauces** 179

CHAPTER SIX:
FOOD ON BREAD 188

Think Hungarian Goulash on Rye Toasts, Curried Lamb in Pita Bowls, Spanakopita in Pastry Cups and you'll get the idea of what we mean by food on bread. Hot and hardy open-face sandwiches—with plenty of gravy—makes a nice change from the usual rice or noodles.

> *A word about:* **Bread** 191, **Getting Some Help from the Butcher** 195

CHAPTER SEVEN:
BREAKFAST FOR DINNER 212

There are so many breakfast-style foods that are quick to prepare and make perfect Desperation Dinners. Who says Bacon and Tomato Pie, Brunch Rice Burritos, Seaside Eggs Benedict, or English Muffin "Pub Pie" has a time-of-day limit? Not us!

> *A word about:* **Leftover Rice** 223

CHAPTER EIGHT:

EASY ENTREES 232

Easy main dishes are basic to a desperate cook's repertoire. We've streamlined some favorites so you can make irresistible meat loaves, stuffed peppers, pork loin, and chicken piccata in 20 minutes or under. And a collection of wonderful grilled entrées as well.

A word about: **High Heat** 235, *A word about:* **Separating Eggs** 237, **Roll-Ups** 239, *A word about:* **Microwave Defrosting** 243, **Freeze Your Cheese** 245, **Burgers with Gravy** 247, *A word about:* **Quick Side Dishes** 258, *A word about:* **Buying Fresh Fish** 276, *A word about:* **Lemon Juice** 285, *A word about:* **Bottled Chopped Ginger** 287, *A word about:* **Grilling** 294

CHAPTER NINE:

QUICK SIDES 306

When there's a leftover roast or a store-bought prepared chicken in the offing, pair it up with one—or more—of these faster-than-fast sides. Great salads and slaws, Back-to-Burgaw Butter Beans, Cheddar Corn Cakes, and Mashed Potatoes with Onion and Basil. Plus Mexican Mini-Muffins, Feta Focaccia, and Fabulous French Bread.

A word about: **Tossed Salad** 308, *A word about:* **Fruit Salad** 315, *A word about:* **Quick Breads** 329

CHAPTER TEN:

DESSERTS 342

Treat yourself to dessert the no-fuss Desperation way. When you need something good and sweet and comforting, turn to Angel Biscuits with Blueberries, Practically Perfect Peach Crisp, and Amazing Apple Tart. When you need something sinfully rich and fast, then nothing but Magic Brownies fills the bill.

The Desperation Ice Cream Social 355

The Essential Shopping List 358
Organizing Your Pantry 361
Shelf Life 364
The Desperate Week 366
Conversion Table 368
Index 369

LEADING THE DESPERATE LIFE

From Beverly:

Most every night at six o'clock, I turn into a desperate woman. My children are hungry, I'm exhausted, and my husband is still at work. To make matters worse, there's a good chance I haven't been near a supermarket in three days. If any of this sounds familiar, you're reading the right book.

Desperation Dinners! is as much about real life as it is about recipes. It's part cookbook, part survival guide, and part culinary revolution. This book will teach you how to use what you have in the kitchen to put a healthy, home-cooked meal on the table in 20 minutes flat.

The idea for Desperation Dinners occurred to me seven years ago. At the moment it hit me, I was six months pregnant and waddling around the kitchen with an eighteen-month-old wrapped around one leg. There I was, the editor responsible for putting out the *Miami Herald*'s food section, plastering the refrigerator with menus from take-out joints. I was a culinary professional by day. By night, I was a wreck.

Cookbooks did little more than taunt me with picture-perfect food beyond the reach of my new reality. A box of macaroni and cheese just made me feel guilty. After all, my own stay-at-home mother never would have dreamed of feeding me elbow macaroni in orange pools of goo. Thanks to her, I learned not only to savor the comfort of simmering soup and warm yeast rolls, I learned to cook them, too. When I was a child and Mom's calls to dinner came, our family delighted in gathering around a table

> *"I was a culinary professional by day. By night, I was a wreck."*

laden with the results of her hours in the kitchen. I came to believe that food means love, and love tastes great.

Much of me yearned for my own children to have this, too. Wasn't there a middle ground between an hour-long stint as a stove slave and electrocuted hot dogs? I vowed to find it.

In the months that followed, I reexamined everything I believed about home cooking. What would happen if I didn't use homemade chicken stock that took hours to produce? What if I tried some dried thyme instead of picking those tiny fresh leaves off their twigs? I went on a scouting expedition to the supermarket and came back with a sack of convenience items I'd never noticed. I heated up a tablespoon of olive oil and dumped in a cup of chopped onions that came frozen in a plastic bag. In went some minced garlic scooped out of a jar. Next came a bottle of supermarket spaghetti sauce and a can of minced clams. I took a taste. Not bad. I threw in some dried herbs and a shot of Worcestershire sauce, and within minutes we were enjoying clam spaghetti (you'll find the exact recipe on page 159), and nobody at the table could tell I hadn't spent an hour cooking. Ingredient by ingredient, recipe by recipe, I discovered that dinner does not have to be so difficult after all.

The courage to share my ideas came four years later as the result of a friendship that developed between two three-year-old girls. Because our daughters became pals at preschool, I met Alicia Ross, a journalist and naturally gifted cook whose beliefs about food and family—and whose hectic lifestyle—matched my own.

My initial confession occurred late one summer afternoon, at a quarter of six. I was at Alicia's to pick up my daughter, and as I started to pull out of her driveway, Alicia glanced at her watch, then at two daughters already whining, "I'm hungry." A look of near terror crossed her face. Then a tangle of tension gushed out:

"This makes me crazy! My husband's on the way home, and I haven't even thought about dinner. There's not one thing in my house that's not in a solid block of ice. Why does fixing a simple family dinner have to be so hard? Tell me I'm not the only person who struggles with this!"

Without thinking, I blurted: "You need a Desperation Dinner."

From Alicia:

Little did I know that Beverly's one sentence that wild afternoon would change my life—and hers—so drastically. At my house, things veered out of control when I started back to work three years after my second child was born. As one part-time job turned into two, somehow the back stairs became littered with laundry. Then the whole family needed a haircut, a dentist appointment, and new shoes—all on the same day. At that time, I felt like I was on a trapeze, swinging between weekends. When the weekend finally came, I exhausted myself trying to catch up.

Standing there in the driveway, I had no idea what a Desperation Dinner was, but just from the sound of it, there was no doubt in my mind that a Desperation Dinner was what I needed.

In fact, I didn't need just one, I needed a whole recipe box full of them.

At its essence, Desperation Dinners are nothing more complicated than quick (20 minutes or under, start to finish), flavorful, nutritious recipes. Yet that's only part of it. Over the next few weeks, I kept asking Beverly questions and listened as she talked about stocking the pantry, organizing the freezer, and cooking up shortcuts. The more she talked, the more I realized what Desperation Dinners are really all about.

Desperation Dinners are grounded in the assumption that life tends to push us faster than we can go. At first I wondered whether, with all of her years of experience as a food editor and restaurant critic, Beverly worked some kind of magic in the kitchen that I could never duplicate. Before long, however, I found myself creating Desperation recipes of my own, and my kitchen will never be the same again.

Some changes came immediately. Suddenly I was keeping my knives sharp, my pantry was full, and I knew what to do with those frozen blocks of hamburger. As I experimented, I got a clearer idea of which convenience foods are really worth the extra expense and how to add a personal touch to boost their flavor. But what really surprised me was the fact that most days I wasn't

"There was no doubt in my mind that a Desperation Dinner was what I needed."

spending even half the time I used to in the kitchen, and we were eating just as well, if not better. Desperation Dinners became feeding my family without losing my mind.

Before long Beverly and I realized that if both of our families needed a whole recipe box full of Desperation Dinners, other people did, too. That's when the real work began.

From both of us:

A lot has happened in the three years since then. We teamed up and decided to put our tips and recipes down on paper. We started a weekly "Desperation Dinners" column, which now appears in dozens of newspapers around the country. Meeting weekly newspaper deadlines meant that we had to get really serious.

We each bought a digital stopwatch, and everything we cooked got clocked to the second. We also scrutinized every cookbook we could find that promised quick results. We tried dozens of recipes, only to find that often it would require a full kitchen staff to produce them in the time specified. We dabbled with the ways of chefs who swore by "fresh food and fresh only," and soon realized that three or four weekly grocery shopping trips and our time-starved lifestyles just wouldn't jibe.

Finally, we turned back to our own files and took a fresh look at our most cherished recipes. We found ourselves streamlining some recipes and creating others from scratch. At least once a week, we met in the kitchen for a giant cooking spree to try out ideas. One of us would suggest adding an ingredient to a dish that the other hadn't considered. That would spawn another idea, and before long the final recipe looked nothing like the original inspiration.

We expect that our recipes will most appeal to regular people leading regular, yet busy lives. If you're like us, ordinary life seems to include more desperation than you would prefer. The obstacles that stand between us, homemade yeast bread, and other gourmet feats most frequently involve our children. If one of them spikes a fever, baking time gets traded in for the doctor's office. And then

"So here it is— a book full of truly fast recipes."

there are homework assignments and car pools. Figure in nine-hour workdays, volunteer efforts, housework, gardening, and government studies urging us to get our daily exercise. Add any single unexpected thing, be it a long-distance call from an old friend or a flat tire, and we're automatically desperate.

On nights like those, don't talk to us about the joys of fresh thyme. The only thing we want to know about time is how to save it. By definition, saving time and avoiding stress in the kitchen require trade-offs. To the discerning gourmet, canned broth does not taste like simmered homemade. But we know without a doubt in this world that in 20 minutes or less, a Desperation recipe can take that canned broth and transform it into a savory soup that will sustain the body and soothe the soul. Suddenly, desperation doesn't seem so bad.

And so here it is—a book full of truly fast recipes, from soups to salads, pastas to desserts, that have come to seem to us like dear, reliable friends. We hope this book will help you to transform your kitchen into a sweeter and saner place to nurture yourself and feed the people you care for most. At its heart, that's what *Desperation Dinners!* is all about.

Beverly Mills and Alicia Ross

THE DESPERATION DINNERS PROMISE

When you're desperate, there's no room for failure. You need recipes you can count on. That's why every Desperation Dinner comes with certain promises, and here they are:

THESE RECIPES ARE NOT HARD

If you can flip a pancake, chop an onion, and stir with a wooden spoon, you can master every meal in this book. Don't be frightened of recipes that have more than five ingredients. Desperation Dinners are designed to maximize flavor, and that usually means bold seasonings. One of our goals is to keep peeling and chopping to a minimum, and most of our ingredients simply need to be thrown in. Okay, so you will have to do some prep work. But if the meal doesn't taste good, you're not going to eat it. And if you've spent even 10 minutes to produce something nobody wants to eat, you've wasted your time.

Friends who taste our 20-minute recipes before cooking them in their own kitchens often wonder aloud how we do it. "You write about cooking for a living, so *you* may be able to do this in 20 minutes," they say. "I bet I never could." That simply isn't the case. We are primarily busy mothers and overworked women who love food; we are not professional chefs. We gave up cooking from gourmet magazines about the same time we started subscribing to a diaper service. Even though there are two desperate brains behind the recipes developed for this book, when it came to testing them, there was always only one cook in the kitchen. So, if we can do it, so can you. And if you're like us, the second time you fix a recipe, you'll finish it even faster.

OUR RECIPES CAN BE MADE WITHOUT EXPENSIVE EQUIPMENT

Beverly is still using the Sunbeam mixer her mom gave her when she graduated from college. Alicia's food processor is a twelve-year-old Sears model that, at the time, cost $39. Beverly's kitchen is crowded, Alicia constantly fights counter clutter, and both of our refrigerators are crammed full. We'd have to work at not being embarrassed for you to see them. Still, out of this common ground, Desperation Dinners emerge.

A microwave oven for defrosting and occasional quick melting is the only big-ticket item we recommend. But what you really need to make most of the meals in this book is some basic equipment—a sharp butcher knife, a sharp paring knife, and a decent large nonstick skillet. If you didn't have any of these basics, a $50 investment would bring you up to speed.

THESE RECIPES DON'T LIE

Nothing is more annoying than a recipe with little white lies built in. Lots of recipes that claim to be quick don't count the time it takes to bake, peel, and chop. When we're exhausted, if the 20 minutes we bargained to spend cooking starts turning into 35, that's enough to finish us off. There are a couple of things you do need to know. Some recipes require you to *preheat* the oven. The time it takes to preheat is not counted in the 20 minutes. Some recipes requiring oven use tell you to *turn on* the oven or gas grill as a first step. In those recipes oven-heating time *is* included in the 20 minutes. When we call for thicker pasta (such as penne) that could take longer than 10 minutes to cook, we ask you to start with already-boiling water. The 9 minutes it takes to bring the water to a boil is not counted. We suggest boiling and preheating before starting after-work chores like changing clothes and check-

ing the mail. The recipes requiring preheated ovens and already-boiling water are clearly noted with little symbols placed near the recipe title. Three of our dessert recipes suggest optional time for cooling. By the time you finish your dinner, dessert can be ready.

THIS BOOK CAN TRANSFORM YOU INTO A 20 MINUTE COOK

If life were perfect, we'd either have a full-time cook or computerized appliances that would sense our distress and prepare dinner on their own. But for most of us, home-cooked food doesn't suddenly appear.

After extensive experimenting, we've found that 20 minutes is our magic formula. On average, it seems to be the least amount of time we can spend cooking and still turn out a really scrumptious meal, somewhere between lobster Thermidor and Hamburger Helper. And on desperate nights, 20 minutes is the most time we can bear to be in the kitchen. That's how our philosophy came to revolve around pushing the most flavor we can get into our recipes in one third of an hour. Every now and again we've hit the jackpot and come up with a recipe that takes less than our usual time and effort. We call these recipes Super Stress Savers, and they are earmarked as such.

With many of our recipes, you can expect to be moving steadily during the entire 20 minutes. But the reward is dinner, real food that pays back as much—or more—than you're required to invest.

That brings us to our final promise . . .

THESE RECIPES TASTE GOOD

For a Desperation Dinner to be a keeper, at the very minimum we must be willing to eat it ourselves once a week for a month straight. We've been delighted to find that not only are we happy to consume these meals, lots of other people have been raving, too. When we've carried our creations to neighborhood potlucks, church luncheons, and preschool parties, we've ended up being asked to share the recipes. At first we wondered if people were just being nice. Then the fan mail started arriving from around the country as people we didn't know—readers of our "Desperation Dinners" newspaper column—wrote to cheer us on.

We'd love to hear your opinions, desperate tales of woe, and everyday success stories. If you can ever find the time, write to us in care of Workman Publishing Co., 708 Broadway, New York, NY 10003-9555. Or by computer, send E-mail messages directly to us using this address: bev-alicia@desperationdinners.com

"On desperate nights, 20 minutes is the most time we can bear to be in the kitchen."

YOUR DESPERATION PANTRY

When you're desperate, you don't want to have to worry about grocery shopping. Our tips on how and when to shop and what to buy for the Desperate household start on page 358.

Obviously having a well-stocked cupboard is important, but if you spend 15 minutes searching for the can of chicken broth that's hiding behind a wall of cereal boxes, you'll never get your meal on the table in 20 minutes. We've suggested an organization plan on page 361 that works in our kitchens, and should in yours, too.

Whether you use our shopping list and pantry organization plan or devise your own is up to you. But do find a plan that works before the next moment of desperation strikes.

A word about: DESPERATION SYMBOLS

Throughout the book, you'll see that some recipes are accompanied by symbols. Located up by the recipe title, these are designed to help you select just the right recipe when desperation hits.

 When you need an especially kid-friendly recipe, look for recipes with this symbol.

 If you preheat the oven or put a pot of water on to boil as soon as you walk in the door, by the time you slip off your shoes, let out the dog, and flip through the mail, you'll be ready to prepare any of the recipes designated by one of these symbols.

 When life has you dangling at the end of your rope, turn to a Super Stress Saver. It'll be ready to enjoy in less than our usual 20 minutes.

Desperation Dinners!

CHAPTER ONE

Soups

On nights when we're ready for the loony bin, dinner often looks like this: a bowl of comforting soup, a tossed salad, and a slab of bread. It's the perfect solution when we're crazed, and nobody feels cheated.

Nothing is quite as cozy and nurturing on an icy day as a steaming bowl of your favorite soup. But soup is such a staple of our Desperation Game Plan that we can't give it up, even in the middle of an August swelter. That's when we switch to the classic cold soups—gazpacho, vichyssoise, or even a cold borscht.

We used to think the secret to magnificent soup was hours of simmering. We were wrong. You can make a surprisingly fine soup, start to finish, in just 20 minutes. All you need are a few streamlined strategies.

The basic trick is to get the ingredients into the pot as quickly as possible, crank up the heat, and let the broth boil like crazy for at least 10 minutes. That leaves 10 minutes for preparation, so you'll need to take advantage of every supermarket shortcut you can find. Already-sliced and already-peeled vegetables are widely available in most grocery stores, and in this case the extra expense is worth every penny.

Not having the luxury of a long simmer also requires a bolder hand when it comes to herbs and spices. You'll need an extra dash of hot pepper sauce and as much as an extra half-teaspoon of dried herbs and Worcestershire to make up for flavor that would otherwise develop during a slow simmer.

One of our favorite secrets is to use higher heat. We start most soups by flash-frying the onions and fresh vegetables to tenderize and release flavor. Once you add the broth, cover the pot and bring it to a boil as quickly as possible. Since most low-fat dairy products can't withstand boiling, think of them as flavorings to stir in just before serving.

Hard-line chefs would probably insist that you can't make soup without homemade broth. Ask yourself which is better—perfectly fine soup or no soup at all? The last time we had enough excess energy to make stock was . . . well, we can't even remember.

Luckily, we're growing less and less inclined to care. Canned broth and dried bouillon have come a long way since we were kids. You'll now find reduced-sodium and fat-free broth packed with flavor. Swanson carries a vegetarian broth and a delightful new Oriental flavor. The Knorr brand offers a fish-flavored bouillon cube that's the secret weapon behind our recipe for Almost-Dad's Clam Chowder.

When it comes to choosing broth and canned tomatoes, do spend a little extra money and stick with a brand name you trust. You won't be pleased with the outcome unless you start with quality products. We do agree with the hard-liners on one point: Broth ought to be more than colored water.

Finally, don't be afraid to substitute ingredients, particularly when the soup is served hot. For vegetarian meals, canned vegetable broth substitutes for beef or chicken broth. If the recipe calls for fresh tomatoes, high-quality canned tomatoes will work just as well. If you have plain yogurt but no sour cream, you probably won't be able to tell the difference. Part of the beauty of soups is that they are designed to be a jumble of flavors, so they are incredibly flexible. We've almost never met a well-seasoned soup we didn't like.

Here is a collection of some of our favorite Desperation soups that are so easy and flavorful, you may find the words "long simmer" starting to sound like a foreign language.

"The last time we had enough excess energy to make stock was . . . well, we can't even remember."

From Beverly:

Minestrone is one of my favorite quick soups to throw together on nights when I'm at a total loss for dinner ideas. Minestrone is low in fat, yet hearty enough to make a whole meal with a good loaf of bread. As a bonus, it really doesn't matter if you don't have exactly the right ingredients. My minestrone almost never turns out the same way twice. If there are no red beans in the cupboard, any color will do. No green beans? Just leave them out. As long as you have enough broth, spices, and tomatoes, plus some sort of beans and pasta, you're well on the way to a comforting dinner.

MINUTE MINESTRONE

1 cup (4 ounces) elbow macaroni
1 teaspoon olive oil
20 already-peeled baby carrots (for 1 cup sliced)
1 cup frozen chopped onions
2 teaspoons bottled minced garlic
1 can (14½ ounces) beef broth
1 can (14½ ounces) vegetable broth
1 can (14½ ounces) Italian-style stewed tomatoes
1 small can (8 ounces) tomato sauce
1½ teaspoons dried Italian seasoning
½ teaspoon sugar
1 cup frozen green beans
1 can (15 ounces) red kidney beans
1 small can (7¾ ounces) chickpeas
1 can (2¼ ounces) sliced black olives
Black pepper to taste
Already-grated Parmesan cheese, for garnish

1. Bring 5 cups of unsalted water to a boil in a covered 2-quart or larger pot over high heat. When the water reaches a rapid boil, add the noodles and cook 7 minutes (done but still firm).

2. Meanwhile, heat the oil in a 4½-quart Dutch oven or soup pot over medium-high heat. Begin slicing the carrots, adding them to the pot as you slice. Cook, stirring occasionally, for 1 minute. Add the onions and continue to cook 1 minute. Add the garlic and continue to cook until the carrots are crisp-tender, about 1 minute more.

3. While the vegetables cook, remove any visible fat from the beef broth. Raise the heat to high. Immediately add both broths, the stewed tomatoes, tomato sauce, Italian seasoning, and sugar. Cover the pot and bring the soup to a boil.

4. Meanwhile, place the green beans in a microwave-safe dish on high for 1 minute, uncovered. Also, rinse and drain the kidney beans and chickpeas; drain the olives.

5. When the soup is boiling, add the green beans, kidney beans, chickpeas, and olives. Let the soup boil for about 5 minutes more. The macaroni will be just done during this time. Drain it and in the last minute of soup boiling, add it to the soup pot. Season with black pepper to taste, stir, and serve with Parmesan cheese.

Serves 6

TANGY TOMATO SOUP

1 teaspoon olive oil
½ cup frozen chopped onions
1 teaspoon bottled minced garlic
2 cans (14 ounces each) pasta-style chopped tomatoes
1 can (15 ounces) tomato sauce
2 cans (14½ ounces each) fat-free chicken or
   vegetable broth
½ cup already finely-shredded sharp Cheddar cheese

1. Heat the oil in a 4½-quart Dutch oven or soup pot over medium-high heat. Add the onions and garlic and cook for 1 minute, stirring often. Add the tomatoes and their juice and the tomato sauce. Raise the heat to high, cover the pot, and bring to a boil.

2. Stir in the chicken broth. Cover the pot and bring the soup back to a boil. Reduce the heat to low and simmer for 10 minutes to develop the flavor.

3. Spoon the soup into individual serving bowls and sprinkle with cheese. Swirl it to leave ribbons of melted cheese in the soup.

Serves 6

From Alicia:

Deep desperation always hits when you least expect it. That's when you're better off heading back to the basics. I'm talking way back—say, grilled cheese sandwich and tomato soup basics.

Last fall I was in rush-hour traffic, with a broken-down car full of pre-schoolers, my husband was out of town, and it was nearly suppertime. By the time I got home, my kids were starving and chaos was about to erupt. I had hoped to just open a can of soup, but the shelf was bare. What I did have was canned tomatoes and frozen finely shredded cheese. In less than 20 minutes, we sat down to a surprisingly calm dinner of Tangy Tomato Soup and grilled cheese sandwiches.

What's the big deal about corn chowder, anyway? It's only a bunch of potatoes and corn floating around in a bland broth, right? Not with this recipe. Because corn and potatoes are rather plain, this soup relies heavily on the spices to liven it up.

The inspiration for this soup's rich flavor came from New Orleans chef Paul Prudhomme. We turned his 2-hour recipe into this 20-minute version. The chowder is hearty and inviting—the perfect end to a wintry day.

WINTER CORN CHOWDER

2 teaspoons olive oil
1½ cups frozen chopped onions
2 cups cubed frozen hash brown potatoes
Soup Seasoning Mix (recipe follows)
2 cans (14½ ounces each) fat-free chicken broth
3½ cups frozen corn kernels
2 tablespoons reduced-fat real bacon bits (not imitation)
1 teaspoon Worcestershire sauce
2 dashes hot pepper sauce (optional; see Note)
½ cup whole or low-fat milk, or half-and-half

1. Heat the oil in a 4½-quart Dutch oven or soup pot over high heat. Add the onions and potatoes, and cook until they start to brown and stick to the pot bottom, about 3 minutes. Stir occasionally.

2. Meanwhile, make the Soup Seasoning Mix.

3. When the onions and potatoes are brown on the edges, add 1 can of the chicken broth. Stir vigorously and scrape all of the brown bits from the pot bottom.

4. Add the second can of broth, Soup Seasoning Mix, corn, bacon bits, Worcestershire, and hot pepper sauce (if using). Stir to mix. Cover the pot and bring the soup to a boil. Boil 12 minutes to develop the flavor, stirring occasionally.

5. Reduce the heat to medium and add the milk. Re-cover and cook 1 minute to heat the milk through. Serve at once (or let stand off the heat until ready to serve).

Serves 6

Note: Omit the hot pepper sauce if serving children.

SOUP SEASONING MIX

1 teaspoon salt
¾ teaspoon onion powder
½ teaspoon garlic powder
½ teaspoon dried thyme
½ teaspoon dry mustard powder
¼ teaspoon paprika
¼ teaspoon dried marjoram

Combine all of the spices in a small cup or cereal bowl, stirring to mix well.

Makes about 1 tablespoon

Use this seasoning mix with Winter Corn Chowder or to season pork chops or chicken breasts.

TIME-SAVER

Remove the inside (shaker) tops from all spice jars. If you're like us, you rarely sprinkle, and the tops just get in the way of measuring out specific amounts.

From Beverly:

Homemade cream of mushroom soup is one of my favorite comfort foods, but I hadn't made it in more than a decade. All of my recipes required complicated hoop jumping. You either had to fiddle around with a roux or worry about egg yolks curdling. Not comforting at all. I couldn't help but wonder how mushroom soup would react to some Desperation cooking techniques. The result contained all of the fresh mushroom flavor and velvety texture I craved, but using plain old cornstarch as a thickener eliminated the bother.

Alicia and I developed this recipe with portobello mushrooms, an extremely flavorful, meaty variety that is becoming commonly available in grocery stores. A 6-ounce package of already-sliced portobello mushrooms costs about one dollar more than 8 ounces of already-sliced button mushrooms. If you can't find the portobellos or don't want the extra expense, the soup will turn out fine with two packages of sliced button mushrooms.

CREAMY WILD MUSHROOM SOUP

3 tablespoons butter
1 package (6 ounces) already-sliced portobello
    mushrooms
1 package (8 ounces) already-sliced fresh button
    mushrooms
½ cup frozen chopped onions
2 tablespoons dry sherry
1 can (14¾ ounces) fat-free chicken broth
3 tablespoons cornstarch
3 tablespoons water
2 cups half-and-half
Dash of hot pepper sauce, or to taste
Salt and black pepper to taste

1. Melt the butter in a 4½-quart Dutch oven or soup pot over medium-low heat. Meanwhile, chop the portobello mushrooms into bite-size pieces. Add them to the pot with the sliced button mushrooms. Cook until the mushrooms have released their liquid, about 4 minutes, stirring from time to time. Add the onions and sherry and cook for 1 minute to evaporate the alcohol.

2. Add the chicken broth, cover the pot, raise the heat to high, and bring the soup to a boil. Reduce the heat to low and continue to cook at a simmer for 3 minutes more to develop the flavor.

3. Meanwhile, combine the cornstarch and water in a small container that has a lid. Shake well until the lumps disappear, then set aside.

4. After the soup has simmered, raise the heat to medium-high, add the half-and-half, and stir. Shake the cornstarch mixture

again and add it to the pot, stirring constantly. Cook until the soup is thick, 3 to 4 minutes, stirring from time to time. Season with hot pepper sauce, salt, and pepper and serve.

Serves 4

STRESS-FREE POTATO SOUP

1 tablespoon butter or margarine
1 cup frozen chopped onions
1 can (14½ ounces) fat-free chicken broth
Already-boiled potatoes (for 4 cups small pieces) or
    1 package (1 pound 4 ounces) Simply Potatoes
    Diced Potatoes with Onions
2 cups (8 ounces) already-shredded sharp Cheddar cheese
1 cup (8 ounces) reduced-fat sour cream
¼ cup reduced-fat real bacon bits (not imitation)
⅛ teaspoon black pepper

1. Melt the butter in a 4½-quart Dutch oven or soup pot over medium-low heat. Stir in the onions and cook to melt off any ice, 30 seconds. Add the chicken broth, and packaged potatoes (if using), cover the pot, raise the heat to high, and bring the broth to a boil.

2. Meanwhile, if using leftover potatoes, cut them into bite-size pieces and set aside. When the broth boils, uncover the pot and whisk in the cheese. Reduce the heat to medium and continue to whisk until the cheese melts.

3. Stir in the leftover potatoes, sour cream, bacon bits, and black pepper. Simmer 5 minutes, stirring occasionally, then serve, or let stand off the heat until ready to serve.

Serves 6

If you're like us and always boil too many potatoes, here's the solution for leftovers. This rich soup takes only 10 minutes to throw together and contains all the flavors we love in a baked potato. We especially like to use red potatoes with the skins still on, which add nice flecks of color. If you make the soup using the packaged potatoes, the amount of frozen chopped onions should remain the same. The onions included with the packaged potatoes will only add to the flavor.

BEER-CHEESE VEGGIE SOUP

2 cups (8 ounces) cauliflower florets (see Box)
1 cup plus 3 tablespoons water
1 tablespoon margarine
½ cup frozen chopped onions
½ teaspoon bottled minced garlic
1 teaspoon Worcestershire sauce
1 can or bottle (12 ounces) light-bodied beer
1 can (14¾ ounces) fat-free chicken broth
3 tablespoons cornstarch
2 cups half-and-half
2 cups (8 ounces) already-shredded sharp Cheddar cheese
Reduced-fat real bacon bits (not imitation; optional)

1. Place the cauliflower and 1 cup water in a microwave-safe covered casserole and microwave on high until tender, about 5 minutes. Meanwhile, melt the margarine in a 4½-quart Dutch oven or soup pot over medium heat. Add the onions, garlic, and Worcestershire and stir well.

2. Add the beer. Raise the heat to high and boil 3 minutes to evaporate the alcohol. Add the chicken broth and bring the soup back to a boil. Lower the heat to medium and boil while you drain the cauliflower, chop it into bite-size pieces, and add it to the pot.

3. Combine the cornstarch and 3 tablespoons water in a small container that has a lid. Shake until the lumps disappear, then set aside. Add the half-and-half and cheese to the soup. Stir constantly until the cheese melts, then shake the cornstarch mixture again and add it to the pot. Stir constantly until the soup is thick, about 2 minutes. Serve garnished with bacon bits (if using).

Serves 6

There's something about the flavors of beer and cheese that seem made for soup. Throw in some cauliflower for texture, and you're got a balanced meal in a bowl. We prefer an American-style beer for this recipe, since some heavy imported beers can taste bitter. If you can find packaged cauliflower florets already cut in your supermarket produce section, this soup goes together in a snap. If not, just make quick work of whacking it off the stalk. Since the cauliflower will be chopped up eventually, appearance doesn't matter. This soup needs a buttery flavor, but at high heat, butter will burn. So, we suggest using margarine instead.

✳ *No cauliflower? Plain beer-cheese soup also makes a wonderful meal. It's a popular menu item in some of our favorite restaurants.*

PDQ BROCCOLI-CHEESE SOUP

1 teaspoon olive oil
1 cup frozen chopped onions
1 box (10 ounces) frozen chopped broccoli
1½ cups frozen broccoli pieces (see Box)
2 cans (14½ ounces each) fat-free chicken broth
1 teaspoon Worcestershire sauce
1 teaspoon low-sodium chicken bouillon crystals (optional)
¼ teaspoon dried tarragon
1 cup (4 ounces) already-shredded sharp Cheddar cheese
½ cup already-grated Parmesan cheese
½ cup reduced-fat sour cream
Salt and black pepper to taste

1. Heat the oil in a 4½-quart Dutch oven or soup pot over medium heat. Add the onions and cook for 1 minute, stirring often. Meanwhile, microwave all the broccoli 4 minutes, uncovered, on high, to begin defrosting.

2. While the broccoli defrosts, raise the Dutch oven heat to high and add the chicken broth, Worcestershire, chicken bouillon (if using), and tarragon. Cover the pot and bring the broth to a boil. As soon as it boils, add the broccoli. Cover the pot and bring the soup back to a boil, then reduce the heat to low.

3. Cook the soup at a simmer for 8 minutes to develop the flavor. Just before serving, stir in the Cheddar, Parmesan cheese, and sour cream. Add salt and pepper. Simmer without boiling just until the cheese melts, then stir, and serve at once, or let stand off the heat until ready to serve.

Serves 4

From Alicia:

On the spur of the moment one fall day, I decided to take a simple lunch to my daughter's preschool for the teachers to enjoy after class. Of course my most generous urges strike when I can least afford the time. Usually I'm forced to shrug them off and figure I'll do it another day.

Then I remembered Beverly's recipe for PDQ (Pretty Darn Quick) Broccoli-Cheese Soup. She always makes it for Saturday lunch when she's pressed for time. This soup is so quick and easy, I was able to throw it together in about 15 minutes. While the soup simmered, I heated some frozen bread sticks. Then I put the final touches on the soup and arrived with a steaming lunch just at the noon pickup time.

> ✱ *We use the frozen broccoli pieces to add texture, but two boxes of chopped will work just fine. Broccoli pieces are sometimes called "cutlets" and also come frozen in plastic bags.*

From Alicia:

It never fails. When my husband and I try to plan something special for Valentine's Day, catastrophe strikes. One year, our youngest came down with bronchitis. The year before, the baby sitter canceled that afternoon. The year before that, a business meeting ran later than expected and we missed our reservation. This year, Valentine's Day fell in the middle of the week, and I was afraid to even try and schedule something. So we planned our date for home.

On a special night out we'd normally go for a juicy steak with all the trimmings, most likely starting off with one of our favorite soups, French onion. Realizing the potential lateness of our home date, we decided to forgo the steak and just do the soup.

While my husband got the kids settled in bed, I spent less than 20 minutes preparing dinner. We lit a few candles, poured two glasses of wine, and sat down to our romantic dinner for two. It was one of the most memorable Valentine dinners we've ever had.

FAST FRENCH ONION SOUP

2 tablespoons margarine
3 extra-large onions (for 4½ cups slices)
2 cans (14½ ounces each) beef broth
1 can (14½ ounces) fat-free chicken broth
¼ cup dry sherry
2 tablespoons Worcestershire sauce
1 teaspoon dried minced onion
½ teaspoon bottled minced garlic
½ teaspoon onion powder
¼ teaspoon dried thyme
3 slices mozzarella cheese
3 cups plain or butter-flavored croutons
6 tablespoons already-grated Parmesan cheese

1. Turn on the broiler.

2. Melt the margarine in a 12-inch nonstick skillet over medium heat. Meanwhile, peel the onions, cut them lengthwise in half and then cut each half into ¼-inch slices, adding the slices to the margarine as you cut them. Raise the heat to high and cook uncovered, stirring from time to time, and reducing the heat to medium when the onions start to brown.

3. While the onions cook, remove any visible fat from the beef broth and pour it into a 4½-quart Dutch oven or soup pot over high heat. Add the chicken broth, cover the pot, and bring the broth to a boil, uncovering briefly to add the sherry, Worcestershire, dried onion, garlic, onion powder, and thyme.

4. While the soup is coming to a boil, place 3 ovenproof bowls on each of two baking sheets and set aside. Cut each mozzarella slice in half and set aside.

5. When the broth is boiling, add the onions to the soup pot and cover it. Reduce the heat to medium-high and boil for 1 minute to incorporate the onion flavor. Remove from the heat.

6. Ladle 1½ cups of soup into each bowl and sprinkle with ½ cup croutons. Place ½ slice of cheese over the croutons, then sprinkle each cheese slice with 1 tablespoon of Parmesan. Place 1 baking sheet at a time under the broiler for 1 minute or until the cheese melts. Serve at once.

Serves 6 (see Box)

> ✳ *If not planning to serve six at the outset, note that Fast French Onion Soup makes wonderful leftovers if you refrigerate it after step 5.*

SPEEDY BLACK BEAN SOUP ★★ ☺

1 teaspoon olive oil
¾ cup frozen chopped onions
2 cans (15 ounces each) black beans
1 can (14½ ounces) fat-free chicken broth
1 can (15¼ ounces) corn kernels, drained
1 can (14½ ounces) Mexican-style stewed tomatoes
3 bay leaves
1 teaspoon bottled minced garlic
1 teaspoon dried thyme
1 teaspoon balsamic vinegar
½ teaspoon ground cumin

1. Heat the oil in a 4½-quart Dutch oven or soup pot over medium heat. Add the onions and cook until slightly brown, stirring occasionally.

2. Meanwhile, pour 1 can of beans and their liquid into a large cereal bowl. Using the back of a serving-size spoon, mash the

Every trendy restaurant seems to have black bean soup on the menu these days, and we've sampled every one we've come across. Most of these soups seem packed with ingredients, yet we like this simple, straightforward recipe better than any we've tasted to date. Speedy Black Bean Soup is also one of the prettiest we've seen. Bits of corn and tomato peek out between the beans, making it colorful to look at as well as fun to eat.

Garnish this soup with just about anything you have on hand, from light sour cream and grated cheese to crumbled tortilla chips.

beans against the sides and bottom of the bowl until the beans are broken up and pasty.

3. Raise the heat under the pot to high and add the chicken broth, mashed beans, and the can of whole beans and its liquid. Stir well. Drain the corn and add it to the pot, then add the stewed tomatoes, bay leaves, garlic, thyme, vinegar, and cumin. Cover the pot and bring the soup to a boil.

4. Reduce the heat to low and simmer to let the flavors blend, 8 minutes, stirring often to prevent sticking. Remove from the heat and serve.

Serves 6

"We've almost never met a well-seasoned soup we didn't like."

THE VIM AND ZING OF VINEGAR

Spiking broths and soups with a hint of vinegar calls to attention the soup's differing flavors, emphasizing their presence. It's a good idea to keep a few bottles of vinegar in your pantry— say, rice wine for Asian soups, cider for fruit soups, balsamic for Mediterranean soups, and champagne, sherry, or ordinary red wine vinegar for any soup. Because wine vinegars are fermented, they vary in flavor, acidity, and quality. Be sure to taste your vinegar before using it to be certain that's the flavor and character you want to bring to the pot.

ALMOST-DAD'S CLAM CHOWDER

1 fish-flavored bouillon cube (Knorr brand)
1 cup water
2 teaspoons olive oil
1 large onion (for 1 cup chopped)
2 cans (14½ ounces each) sliced new potatoes, drained
2 cans (6½ ounces each) minced or chopped clams
1 bay leaf
1 tablespoon reduced-fat real bacon bits (not imitation)
1 teaspoon Worcestershire sauce
½ teaspoon dried thyme
¼ teaspoon black pepper
1½ cups low-fat milk or half-and-half

1. Cut off one third of the bouillon cube and drop it into the water in a microwaveable container. Microwave 3 minutes, uncovered, on high. (Wrap the remainder and refrigerate for later use.)

2. Meanwhile, heat the oil in a 4½-quart Dutch oven or soup pot over medium-low heat. Peel and coarsely chop the onion, adding it to the pot as you chop. Cook 3 minutes, stirring occasionally, while cutting the potato slices into halves or quarters. Add them to the pot.

3. Stir the fish bouillon to finish dissolving the cube. Add it to the pot and stir. Add the clams with their juice, the bay leaf, bacon bits, Worcestershire, thyme, and black pepper. Stir, cover, and bring to a boil. Reduce the heat to medium-low and boil slowly 10 minutes, to develop the flavor. Uncover frequently to stir.

4. Reduce the heat to low, add the milk, and stir. Cook until the milk is heated, about 2 minutes more. Serve at once.

Serves 4 generously

From Beverly:

I was born along the lower Outer Banks of North Carolina, and when I was growing up, Dad was always in charge of clam chowder. Soup making started early in the day, with Dad heading out across the bay to pry fresh clams out of a muddy bank on the other side. When he returned an hour or so later, Dad would dump his mollusks into a bucket of water. Then he'd sprinkle a little cornmeal over the water, a process he deemed necessary to purge the clams of grit. These and other rituals could stretch into the better part of an afternoon. When Dad finally brought his soup to the table, there was no finer place to be on all of Topsail Island.

In my family, seafood is serious business. Following in my father's footsteps, I, too, have always taken pride in making clam chowder. So when I decided to work on a Desperation version of the family soup, I kept the project under wraps. To be honest, my 20-minute rendition is not the same as Dad's all-day soup. But it comes pretty darn close.

From Alicia:

When my sister-in-law called to ask for an impressive soup recipe she could take to a party, this is the one I chose. She was braced to devote all day to simmering and was thrilled when our Pork Hot Pot took just 20 minutes. The combination of peppers makes this a colorful soup, but if you don't have all three, any combination will do.

✳ *The secret ingredients are the Oriental broth and Hoisin sauce. Swanson's Oriental broth is relatively new to the supermarket shelves and is a brilliant combination of soy and vegetable concentrates.*

Hoisin sauce, sometimes called Peking sauce, is a nicely balanced mixture of soybeans, garlic, chilies, and spices. It is a concentrated condiment and only a little is required. Luckily, bottled hoisin sauce, stored in the refrigerator, will keep indefinitely.

PORK HOT POT

¾ pound boneless center-cut loin pork chops (each ½ inch ˋthick), fresh or frozen
1 large onion (for 1 cup chopped)
1 teaspoon peanut oil
½ medium red bell pepper (for ½ cup pieces)
½ medium green bell pepper (for ½ cup pieces)
½ medium yellow bell pepper (for ½ cup pieces)
2 cans (14½ ounces each) Oriental-style broth
1 teaspoon bottled minced garlic
½ teaspoon hoisin sauce
Crushed hot red pepper to taste (optional)
1 can (5 ounces) sliced water chestnuts

1. If the pork chops are frozen, run hot water over them so you can remove any packaging. Place the chops on a microwave-safe plate and microwave 2 minutes, uncovered, on high, to begin defrosting.

2. Meanwhile, peel and coarsely chop the onion. Set aside. Heat the oil in a 4½-quart Dutch oven or large soup pot over medium-low heat. Begin trimming any visible fat from the pork (fresh or partially defrosted) and cut the meat into bite-size chunks, adding them to the pot as you cut.

3. Add the onion and raise the heat to medium-high. Cook, stirring occasionally to prevent sticking. While the onion cooks, seed the bell peppers and cut into bite-size pieces, then add them to the pot.

4. Add the broth, garlic, hoisin sauce, and crushed red pepper (if using). Cover the pot, raise the heat to high, and bring the soup to a boil. Drain the water chestnuts and roughly chop, adding them to the soup as you chop. Re-cover the pot and reduce the heat to medium-high. After boiling for about 3 minutes more to blend the flavors, remove from the heat and serve.

Serves 4

CHICKEN TORTILLA SOUP

2 skinless, boneless chicken breast halves (about ⅔ pound
  total), fresh or frozen
½ teaspoon olive oil
1 cup frozen chopped onions
1 tablespoon bottled lime juice
½ teaspoon bottled minced garlic
½ teaspoon chili powder
¼ teaspoon ground cumin
2 cans (14½ ounces each) fat-free chicken broth
1 cup bottled salsa
1 cup frozen corn kernels (optional)
4 ounces fat-free or regular tortilla chips (for 2½ cups crushed)
¼ cup already-shredded Monterey Jack cheese

1. If the chicken is frozen, run hot water over it so you can remove any packaging. Place the chicken on a microwave-safe plate and microwave 2 minutes, uncovered, on high, to begin defrosting.

2. Meanwhile, heat the oil on low in a 4½-quart Dutch oven or soup pot. Cut the chicken (fresh or partially defrosted) into bite-size chunks, adding them to the pot as you cut. Raise the heat to high and cook for 2 minutes, stirring occasionally. Add the onions, lime juice, garlic, chili powder, and cumin. Cook 2 minutes.

3. Add the broth, salsa, and corn (if using). Stir to mix. Cover the pot and bring the broth to a boil. Reduce the heat to medium-high and continue to boil 8 to 10 minutes to develop the flavor. Meanwhile, crush the tortilla chips slightly. Place the crushed chips in 6 soup bowls. Ladle the soup into the bowls. Sprinkle each portion with cheese and serve.

Serves 6

From Beverly:

This recipe was born out of true desperation. It was one of those nights when dinner was starting to look like salsa and chips—again. (We've been known to confuse dip with dinner on more than one occasion.) But while opening the jar, guilt intervened, and I decided to explore the pantry. I found some broth and a can of shredded chicken, and dumped the whole shebang into a soup pot along with some frozen onions and a few spices.

Ten minutes later, we sat down to Chicken Tortilla Soup—a virtual feast. The soup was a hit, and since first serving it, I have dressed it up a bit with frozen breasts instead of canned chicken.

❋ *Think of this recipe as the soup version of chicken nachos. Optional garnishes include sour cream, chopped avocado or a dollop of guacamole, chopped tomato, and sliced black olives and jalapeños.*

CHINA IN A POT

This soup packs in a lot of ingredients, but it's not a lot of work because you only chop the chicken and onions. The mélange results in an authentic, complex flavor. Our thanks to Beverly's sister-in-law, Liza Bennett, for sharing this original recipe.

✳ *This recipe uses the relatively new Swanson brand of Oriental broth, but if you can't find it, substitute a second can of chicken broth.*

2 skinless, boneless chicken breast halves, (about ⅔ pound total), fresh or frozen
1 can (14½ ounces) fat-free chicken broth
1 can (14½ ounces) Oriental broth (see Box)
1 cup already-sliced fresh mushrooms
1 cup frozen corn kernels
2 tablespoons rice wine vinegar or distilled white vinegar
1 tablespoon dark sesame oil
2 teaspoons reduced-sodium soy sauce
1 teaspoon sugar
1 package (3 ounces) chicken-flavored ramen soup
1 package (6 ounces) frozen snow peas
3 scallions (green onions; for ¼ cup chopped)

1. If the chicken is frozen, run it under hot water so you can remove any packaging. Place the chicken on a microwave-safe plate and microwave 2 minutes, uncovered, on high, to begin defrosting.

2. Meanwhile, pour both cans of broth into a 4½-quart Dutch oven or soup pot. Cover, and bring to a boil over high heat. Slice the chicken (fresh or partially defrosted) into ¼-inch wide strips. Cut the longest strips in half. When the broth boils, stir in the chicken, mushrooms, corn, vinegar, sesame oil, soy sauce, and sugar. Crumble the ramen noodles into the pot and add the flavor packet. Stir. Cover the pot and bring the broth back to a boil.

3. When the broth boils, uncover the pot and add the snow peas, raise the heat to high, and bring the broth back to a boil. Reduce the heat so that the soup simmers.

4. Meanwhile, slice the scallions, using all of the whites and enough of the tender green tops to make ¼ cup. To serve, ladle the soup into 4 bowls and sprinkle with the scallions.

Serves 4

PRESTO PESTO CHICKEN SOUP ★★

2 skinless, boneless chicken breast halves (about ⅔ pound total), fresh or frozen
½ teaspoon olive oil
¾ cup frozen chopped onions
2 cans (14½ ounces each) fat-free chicken broth
1 can (14½ ounces) diced tomatoes
1 teaspoon Worcestershire sauce
½ teaspoon bottled minced garlic
½ cup half-and-half (see Box)
¼ cup commercially prepared pesto
Salt and black pepper to taste

1. If the chicken is frozen, run hot water over it so you can remove any packaging. Place the chicken on a microwave-safe plate and microwave 2 minutes, uncovered, on high, to begin defrosting.

2. Meanwhile, heat the oil in a 4½-quart Dutch oven or large soup pot over medium-low heat. Cut the chicken (fresh or partially defrosted) into bite-size chunks, adding them to the pot as you cut. Raise the heat to medium, add the chopped onions, and cook 2 minutes, stirring from time to time.

3. Add the broth and raise the heat to high. Cover, and bring to a boil. Drain the tomatoes and add them to the pot, along with the Worcestershire and garlic, keeping the lid closed as much as possible. When the soup boils, reduce the heat to medium-low. Continue to cook at a slow boil until the chicken is no longer pink but is still tender, about 6 minutes. Remove from the heat.

4. Stir in the half-and-half, pesto, and salt and pepper. Let the soup rest off the heat for 1½ minutes, then serve.

Serves 4 generously

From Beverly:

Everybody has an off day, even the most reliable chefs. I got the idea for this soup after eating an unfortunate version of it that happened to be served at one of my favorite restaurants in town. It sounded so good on the menu—cream of chicken soup with tomatoes and basil—but how could such a lovely combination be so bland? I left the restaurant not only baffled, but craving the soup I thought I should have eaten for dinner. A couple of days later, this is the soup I stirred up. Not only is it full of flavor, it goes together easily in less than 20 minutes.

> ✳ *To save on calories, substitute low-fat milk for the half-and-half.*

From Beverly:

Almost a decade ago, during a vacation to the Andalusia region of southern Spain where gazpacho originates, I couldn't get enough of this refreshing cold soup. I ordered it at lunch and dinner in every restaurant we visited. My intense craving—plus some fairly uncharacteristic mood swings—tipped my husband off that something was up. Once we returned to the States, a trip to the doctor confirmed what my spouse suspected: Our first child was on the way.

My appetite for gazpacho did not diminish, and I spent the following months trying to come up with the perfect recipe. This is the closest to an authentic version I could devise based on my memories of our last childless hurrah on the Costa del Sol. It's one of the few before-kids recipes I often repeat because it goes together in 18 minutes flat.

BEVERLY'S PERFECT GAZPACHO

1 French-style dinner roll or 2 slices bread
1 small onion
1 large tomato
1 medium cucumber
1 large green bell pepper
1½ teaspoons bottled minced garlic
3 cups vegetable juice, such as V-8, refrigerated if possible
¼ cup red wine vinegar
2 tablespoons extra-virgin olive oil
2 teaspoons Worcestershire sauce
1 teaspoon honey
½ teaspoon hot pepper sauce
Salt and black pepper to taste

1. Put the bread in a blender or food processor and process to make fine-textured bread crumbs. Measure out ½ cup of the crumbs and set aside. (Reserve any extras for another use.)

2. Peel the onion and set aside. Core and halve the tomato, peel and halve the cucumber, and halve and seed the bell pepper. Set half of each vegetable aside and cut the remaining halves into large chunks. Place the chunks in the blender or food processor along with the whole peeled onion, the garlic, and 1 cup of the vegetable juice. Process on high until the vegetables are practically liquid.

3. Pour the soup into a 2-quart serving bowl. Add the vinegar, oil, Worcestershire, honey, hot pepper sauce, bread crumbs, and remaining 2 cups vegetable juice. Add the salt and black pepper and stir to mix.

4. Refrigerate the soup while coarsely chopping the remaining vegetable halves into bite-size cubes. Stir into the soup and adjust the seasonings to personal preference. Serve at once or refrigerate until ready to serve.

Serves 4

> ✳ *Keep cans of vegetable juice in the refrigerator for instantly cold soup.*

A word about:
COLD SOUPS

Soup is still soup, even when it's cold. Cold soups are refreshing and simple to make, plus they add a whole new dimension to quick summer meals. So, if you've never tasted cold soup, suspend all preconceived notions, be bold, and take the 20-minute plunge.

Regardless of what many recipes would have you believe, only minimal cooking is necessary for most cold soups. Our Vite! Vite! Vichyssoise (page 22) is a prime example. A classic French vichyssoise (pronounced *vishy-swahz*) takes considerable preparation time, requiring peeling potatoes and rinsing the sand from layers of leeks. The Desperation version, however, is ready to serve in 15 minutes. All you have to do is fry one onion and dump the other ingredients into the blender or food processor.

There is one trick. If you need to put your soup on the table fast, you won't appreciate having to wait around while it chills. So you have to think of your refrigerator as if it were a pantry. Keep a few cans of potatoes and beets, a jar of V-8, and assorted flavors of broth at the back of one shelf. Then, on a hot night when you just can't face another salad, you'll be ready.

> "*In the middle of an August swelter is when we switch to the classic cold soups.*"

This soup goes down like liquid velvet. If your potatoes and broth are not already cold (see Box, page 21), chill the soup for 20 minutes in the freezer, stirring once after 10 minutes. If you happen to have any left over, this soup tastes even better the second day. To make it even more special, garnish each serving with bacon bits, snipped chives, chopped parsley, or a dash of paprika.

VITE! VITE! VICHYSSOISE

1 tablespoon butter
1 large onion (for 1 cup chopped)
2 cans (14½ ounces each) sliced new potatoes, refrigerated if possible
2 cans (14½ ounces each) fat-free chicken broth, refrigerated if possible
1 cup whole milk or half-and-half
½ teaspoon Worcestershire sauce
¼ teaspoon salt (optional)
Black pepper to taste

1. Melt the butter in an 8-inch or larger nonstick skillet over medium heat. Peel and coarsely chop the onion, adding it to the skillet as you chop. Cook until translucent, 4 minutes, stirring occasionally and taking care not to brown the onion. (Reduce the heat to low, if necessary.)

2. Meanwhile, drain the potatoes and put them and 1 can of broth into a blender. Puree until smooth (see Note).

3. Add the onions to the blender and process until pureed, about 45 seconds, then pour the mixture into a 3-quart or larger serving bowl. Stir in the remaining broth, the milk, Worcestershire, salt (if using), and pepper. Serve at once or refrigerate until ready to serve.

Serves 6

Note: You can use a food processor for this as well, but add only half a can of broth, to prevent overflow. Add the remaining half can of broth in step 3.

BEAT-THE-HEAT BORSCHT ★★ ☺

1 clove garlic

1 can (15 ounces) sliced beets, refrigerated if possible

1 can (14½ ounces) fat-free chicken broth,
*   refrigerated if possible*

1 jar (16 ounces) sweet-and-sour red cabbage,
*   refrigerated if possible*

⅓ cup reduced-fat sour cream

1 teaspoon lemon juice, from frozen concentrate

¼ teaspoon dried dill

¼ teaspoon celery salt

⅛ teaspoon ground cardamom

1. Crush the garlic cloves with a flat side of a chef's knife blade to loosen the skin. Remove the skin and drop the cloves through the feed tube onto the moving blade of a food processor or blender and process to mince them fine, about 20 seconds. Add the drained beets and about half the can of chicken broth to the workbowl. Process until the beets are pureed.

2. Pour the beet mixture into a 3-quart or larger serving bowl. Add the remaining chicken broth, cabbage with its juice, sour cream, lemon juice, dill, celery salt, and cardamom. Stir well and serve at once, or refrigerate until ready to serve.

Serves 4

If you like pickled beets, you'll love this soup. The wonderful sweet-and-sour combination seems particularly nice on a very hot day. Jarred sweet and sour red cabbage is responsible for a good portion of the flavor in this recipe, plus it means you don't have to cook the cabbage as you would in a traditional borscht. We developed this recipe using the Greenwood brand, which is manufactured by Comstock. If your supermarket doesn't carry it, ask the manager to place a special order. If your ingredients are already cold, you can stir this soup together in only 10 minutes.

From Beverly:

My theory, sexist though it may be, is that men, in general, are suspicious of cold soup. I happened to be going to a potluck supper on the evening after Alicia and I tested this recipe. We agreed this was a perfect opportunity for field research, so I whipped up another batch. Of the half-dozen men at the party, only one volunteered when the offer came to try some cold cucumber soup.

When I explained my theory, all of the men experienced a sudden change of mind. One man shoved crackers in the soup and ate it like dip. Another declared that if the soup were only a bit thicker, it would make a nice salad dressing. Each one said he was surprised that it tasted so good, and they all proceeded to finish the entire bowl.

COOL CALIFORNIA BISQUE

2 cloves garlic
2 large cucumbers
1 very ripe California avocado
1 can (14½ ounces) fat-free chicken broth, refrigerated
*   if possible*
½ cup reduced-fat sour cream

1. Crush the garlic cloves with a flat side of a chef's knife blade to loosen the skin. Remove the skin and drop the cloves onto the moving blade of a food processor or blender and process for about 20 seconds to mince them fine.

2. Peel the cucumbers, cut them in half, and use a spoon to scoop out the seeds. Finely dice one of the cucumbers and set it aside. Cut the other cucumber pieces into fourths and place them in the processor workbowl.

3. Cut the avocado in half and discard the pit. Using a spoon, scoop the flesh into the workbowl. Add about ½ cup of the chicken broth and process on medium-high until the vegetables are pureed. Stop midway to scrape down the sides of the workbowl if necessary.

4. Pour the puree into a 3-quart or larger serving bowl and stir well. Add the remaining broth and sour cream and whisk vigorously to blend. Add the reserved diced cucumber and stir well. Serve at once.

Serves 4

JUST PEACHY YOGURT SOUP

1 bag (16 ounces) frozen sliced peaches
2 cups orange juice
2 tablespoons honey
1 carton (16 ounces) vanilla-flavored low-fat yogurt
1 cup blueberries, fresh or frozen

1. Pour half the peaches, the orange juice, and honey into the container of a blender. Process on high, stopping to stir if necessary, until the peaches are a smooth puree. Add the remaining peaches and blend on high, stopping frequently to stir, until all the peaches are smooth.

2. Add the yogurt and pulse until just blended.

3. If using frozen blueberries, pour them into a colander and run cool water over them for 1 minute to defrost slightly.

4. To serve, pour the soup into bowls and sprinkle ¼ cup blueberries on top of each serving.

Serves 4

This delicious soup is perfect for the end of a hot and hurried day. It's flexible, too. You can use pineapple or tropical blend juices instead of orange juice. Or garnish with any small fresh or frozen fruit in place of the blueberries.

This makes a filling summer meal served with muffins smeared with peanut butter or assorted crackers and mild cheese.

CHAPTER TWO

Stews

From Alicia:

I t was a bitterly cold December day several years ago when my attitude toward stew took a decided turn. I had just come home from fighting the holiday crowds at the mall to find that my youngest child had spiked a fever. The freezing temperatures had numbed my feet, and the overly eager crowds at the mall had numbed my usual holiday cheerfulness.

One look at my family told me I was not the only one who could use a little old-fashioned comforting. What we needed was a big bowl of one of my grandmother's stews. Maw-Maw, our affectionate nickname for her, would simmer concoctions of vegetables, meats, and wonderful seasonings all day in a huge pot atop her stove. The aromas would permeate the entire house, drawing the whole family around her table.

But whether I'm shopping, caring for sick children, or just trying to get through a regular week, my too-packed schedule almost never allows for an all-day simmer. Yet when I need the healing effect of Maw-Maw's stew, I need it now. Could the rejuvenating stews and chilies of my childhood be re-created to fit my current level of desperation?

Although we all made it through that dreary night successfully, though stewless, it made me realize I needed to include
these comfort foods in my routine. I was reminded that there's
something inherently healing about a steaming bowl of thick, rich
stew or chili. Beverly and I looked at some of our favorite recipes
and decided they could use an update to bring them into the
realm of possibilities for frantic nights. Tender cuts of meat, bags
of frozen vegetables, and canned chicken and beans have all
played a role in our 20-minute recipe remakes. Our technique is
based on the same premise as that of our Desperation soups—put
your ingredients in the pot as quickly as possible and crank the
heat up to high.

Proud of our success in the "old-fashioned" camp, we
decided we could do a little trimming of time in some other
favorites, too. We've stretched the definition of stews and chilies
to include Deceptively Simple Fish (our version of Jamaican
brown-stewed fish) and a meatless version of the traditional
Southern Hoppin' John.

These dishes are no-nonsense foods that just seem to be
able to melt away the stress with the cold. We hope they work the
same magic for you.

"A stew that would ordinarily require hours of simmering is ready to serve in just 20 minutes."

STEAK STEW

2 tablespoons vegetable oil
½ cup all-purpose flour
½ teaspoon salt
½ teaspoon black pepper
1¼ pounds boneless sirloin, already cut into 1-inch cubes
1 can (14½ ounces) beef broth
1 large onion (1 cup chopped)
1 cup hearty red wine, such as burgundy or cabernet sauvignon
1 package (8 ounces) already-sliced fresh mushrooms
¼ cup reduced-fat real bacon bits (not imitation)
1 bay leaf
1 teaspoon garlic powder
½ teaspoon dried thyme
¼ cup water

One of these days, someone from the supermarket is going to volunteer to come home and cook dinner for you. They're getting closer to it all the time, and it's especially evident in the meat department. We've noticed more ready-to-cook meats with names like "beef for stew" or "beef for stir-fry."

This recipe takes advantage of already-cut beef cubes, but the trick is to spend enough money to ensure that the meat is tender. An advantage to slow cooking is that it will make even tough cuts of meat fork-tender. But when you live life on the flash-fry, you've got to use the good stuff. Sirloin cuts should work fine.

If there's nothing suitable in the case already, ask the butcher to help you select a tender steak and to cut it while you continue shopping. They probably won't come home and cook for you, but cutting meat is a service most supermarkets gladly provide to those who are willing to ask.

1. Heat the oil in a 4½-quart Dutch oven or soup pot over medium heat. Meanwhile, pour the flour, salt, and pepper in a large zipper-top plastic bag and shake to mix. Add the meat and toss to coat with flour. Remove the meat from the bag and shake off the excess flour. Reserve the flour in the bag. Add the meat to the pot and raise the heat to high. Cook, stirring frequently, until it begins to brown about 3 minutes.

2. Meanwhile, skim the fat from the beef broth. Peel and chop the onion, adding it to the pot as you chop. Add the beef broth, wine, mushrooms, bacon bits, bay leaf, garlic powder, and thyme. Cover, and bring to a boil.

3. Meanwhile, combine ¼ cup of the reserved flour and the water in a small container that has a lid. Shake well until the lumps disappear. When the stew boils, reduce the heat to medium-high, and drizzle the flour-water mixture over it, stirring constantly. Cook until thick, 3 minutes, stirring often. Serve at once.

Serves 4

VEGETABLE VEAL STEW

1 tablespoon vegetable oil

½ cup all-purpose flour

½ teaspoon black pepper

1¼ pounds boneless veal for stew, already cut into 1-inch cubes

1 can (14½ ounces) beef broth

1 can (14½ ounces) stewed tomatoes

½ cup water

1 bag (24 ounces) frozen mixed stew vegetables

1 package (8 ounces) already-sliced fresh mushrooms (optional)

2 tablespoons (½ packet) Lipton Onion Soup Mix

1 tablespoon Worcestershire sauce

1 tablespoon ketchup

1 teaspoon bottled minced garlic

½ teaspoon dried thyme

½ teaspoon dried basil

1. Heat the oil in a 4½-quart Dutch oven or soup pot over medium heat. Meanwhile, pour the flour and pepper into a large zipper-top plastic bag and shake to mix. Add the meat and toss to coat with flour. Then, shake off the excess flour, add the meat to the pot, and raise the heat to medium-high. Cook, stirring frequently, until it begins to brown, about 3 minutes.

2. Meanwhile, skim the fat from the beef broth, then add the broth to the pot. Stir well to remove any brown bits from the bottom. Add the stewed tomatoes, water, stew vegetables, mushrooms (if using), soup mix, Worcestershire, ketchup, garlic, thyme, and basil.

3. Raise the heat to high, cover the pot, and bring the soup to a boil. Boil to thicken the stew, uncovering often and stirring to prevent sticking, about 5 minutes. When thick, serve the stew.

Serves 6

A stew that would ordinarily require hours of simmering is ready to serve in just 20 minutes, thanks to cubes of tender veal. There's nothing to cut or chop in this recipe. Several companies make bags of frozen "stew vegetables," a mixture of carrots, onions, potatoes, and celery cut in larger chunks than "soup vegetables." If your meat is frozen, defrost it according to your microwave's instructions before beginning to cook.

Here's a traditional stew that is usually made with tougher cuts of lamb such as shoulder and shank. With these cuts, the stew requires up to 2 hours of slow simmering until the meat falls apart. Using ground lamb, a hearty, comforting dinner is ready in just 20 minutes.

✳ *If you can't find ground lamb at the supermarket, choose lamb kebabs or a small lamb roast and ask the butcher to grind it for you. Or you can substitute ground beef.*

LAMB AND WHITE BEAN STEW

1¼ pounds ground lamb, fresh or frozen (see Box)
2 teaspoons olive oil
2 cups frozen chopped onions
1 tablespoon bottled minced garlic
2 teaspoons dried rosemary
1 teaspoon Worcestershire sauce
1 teaspoon concentrated beef broth (see Box, facing page)
½ teaspoon dried thyme
¼ teaspoon black pepper
2 cans (19 ounces each) cannellini beans
1 can (14½ ounces) stewed tomatoes
1 cup white wine

1. If the meat is frozen, run hot water over it so you can remove any packaging. Place the meat on a microwave-safe plate and microwave 3 minutes, uncovered, on high, to begin defrosting.

2. Meanwhile, heat the oil in a 4½-quart Dutch oven or soup pot over medium heat. Add the onions and let cook, stirring from time to time.

3. Add the lamb (fresh or partially defrosted) to the skillet and raise the heat to high. Stir in the garlic and cook, turning and breaking up the meat occasionally. Add the rosemary, Worcestershire, concentrated beef broth, thyme, and black pepper.

4. Continue to cook, stirring frequently, until all the lamb is crumbled and browned, 5 to 6 minutes. Meanwhile, rinse and drain the beans and set aside.

5. Stir in the tomatoes and wine. Cover the pot and bring the stew to a boil. When the pot boils, uncover it and cook at a rolling boil for 5 minutes. Gently stir in the reserved beans and cook for 2 minutes to heat the beans through. Remove from the heat and serve.

Serves 4

✳ *We use the Knorr brand of concentrated beef broth (a liquid version of a bouillon cube) for this recipe. If you can't find it, crumble in 1 reduced-sodium beef bouillon cube.*

A word about:
ONIONS

Our friend Amy never chops a fresh onion. For her, the first fumes are blinding. She weeps, she coughs, her eyes remain red for hours. Frozen chopped onions revolutionized her kitchen. Before we told Amy about this relatively new product sold in plastic bags in the frozen foods section of the supermarket, Amy substituted dried onion flakes in all of her recipes.

Frozen chopped onions taste infinitely better than dried flakes, but they aren't quite as assertive as the real thing. However, there are lots of recipes in which the convenience of frozen onions makes them a life-saving substitute. Several Desperation recipes, like the one for Lamb and White Bean Stew, call for frozen chopped onions. We use them when time is *really* an issue or if a recipe calls for a lot of ingredients and onion is more a subtle undertone rather than a major presence.

Turkey kielbasa sausage is one of our favorite secret weapons. It stores for weeks unopened in the refrigerator and takes literally just minutes to cook. The garlic-infused sausage is wonderful plain, but also improves the flavor of just about anything that cooks with it.

This meal is practically mindless. Kielbasa, potatoes, and cabbage steam in one pot, making cleanup a breeze. If you can stand a few extra calories, the Mustard Butter Sauce that follows adds a wonderful zip to the vegetables.

KIELBASA, CABBAGE, AND POTATOES

1½ cups water
4 medium red potatoes (about 1½ pounds total)
1¼ pounds turkey kielbasa sausage
1 medium green cabbage (about 1½ pounds)
Mustard Butter Sauce (optional, recipe follows)

1. Pour the water into a 4½-quart Dutch oven or soup pot and bring to a boil, covered, over high heat.

2. Meanwhile, wash the potatoes well but do not peel; cut them into halves or thirds, for pieces about an inch thick. Cut the sausage into 4 pieces, and cut the cabbage into 4 wedges. Remove the outer leaves and core from each quarter.

3. When the water is boiling, place the potatoes, cut side down, in a single layer in the pot. Lay the sausage pieces on top of the potatoes and place the cabbage wedges on the very top. Cover the pot and cook at a rolling boil for 15 minutes, or until the potatoes are tender.

4. Meanwhile, make the Mustard Butter Sauce (if using).

5. Remove the pot from the heat. Using a slotted spoon, divide the cabbage wedges, sausage pieces, and potatoes among four serving bowls. Discard any water from the pot. If using the sauce, drizzle it over the vegetables and serve.

Serves 4

MUSTARD BUTTER SAUCE

3 tablespoons butter
1 tablespoon German-style or Dijon mustard

Place the butter in a small microwave-safe bowl and cover with a paper towel to prevent spatters. Microwave on low until melted, about 45 seconds. Add the mustard and stir until the sauce is smooth.

Makes ¼ cup

This quick butter sauce is perfect for the preceding Kielbasa, Cabbage, and Potatoes, but it's also great on plain baked or mashed potatoes and over any steamed vegetable.

From Alicia:

This is a twist on traditional tomato-based chili. It started as a personal challenge to see if I could make a chili without tomatoes and chili powder but with plenty of flavor. My first attempt was so fiery that I had to back off considerably. Who would have thought a teaspoon of white pepper or quarter teaspoon of cayenne could make such an impact? Beware of the mild appearance of this chili. It's anything but bland.

WHITE BEAN AND CHICKEN CHILI

3 skinless, boneless chicken breast halves (about 1 pound total), fresh or frozen
1 teaspoon olive oil
1 large onion (for 1 cup chopped)
1 tablespoon bottled minced garlic
1 can (15 ounces) Great Northern white beans
1 can (19 ounces) cannellini beans
1 can (4½ ounces) chopped green chilies
1½ teaspoons ground cumin
1 teaspoon pepper, preferably white
⅛ teaspoon cayenne pepper
1 can (14½ ounces) fat-free chicken broth
2 tablespoons cornstarch
2 tablespoons water
½ cup already-shredded Monterey Jack cheese (optional)
¼ cup reduced-fat sour cream (optional)

1. If the chicken is frozen, run it under hot water so you can remove any packaging. Place the chicken on a microwave-safe plate and microwave 2 minutes, uncovered, on high, to begin defrosting.

2. Meanwhile, heat the oil on medium in a 4½-quart Dutch oven or soup pot. Peel and coarsely chop the onion, adding it to the pot as you chop. Stir occasionally to prevent sticking.

3. Cut the chicken (fresh or partially defrosted) into bite-size chunks, add them to the pot and stir occasionally. Add the garlic and continue to cook, stirring occasionally.

4. While the chicken cooks, rinse and drain both of the beans and drain the chilies. Add the chilies to the pot along with the cumin, white pepper, and cayenne pepper. Raise the heat to high and add the broth and drained beans. Cover the pot and bring the chili to a boil.

5. Meanwhile, combine the cornstarch and water in a small container that has a lid. Shake well to remove any lumps.

6. When the chili boils, the chicken should be cooked through (even if you began with partially defrosted). Add the cornstarch mixture a little at a time, stirring constantly. Continue to boil until the chili reaches the desired thickness.

7. Remove from the heat and serve, or let the chili rest until you're ready to eat. Garnish with cheese and sour cream (if using).

Serves 4

A word about:
CALORIES

While this is not a low-fat cookbook, we realize many people are concerned about cutting calories. That's why most of the recipes in this book take advantage of reduced-fat ingredients and cooking techniques. You'll see lots of our recipes requesting skinless chicken breasts, nonstick pans, and skim milk.

When we started our "Desperation Dinners" newspaper column, we invested in computer software used by professional dieticians and began analyzing our recipes to learn more about how to cut fat and calories without scrimping on flavor. The majority of the recipes in this book are more healthy because of that research.

When you find yourself in a rice rut, it's time to break with boredom and pull out the couscous. We've never known anyone who didn't like couscous. Of course, we've never met that many people who've actually eaten it. That's a shame, because couscous—tiny grains of durum wheat—is tailor-made for busy cooks. Couscous (rhymes with "goose-goose") not only has a marvelous nutty flavor, it cooks in 5 minutes flat. Serving a bed of couscous under stew—or on the side as a pilaf—suddenly adds a touch of the exotic to a meal without being too weird. We like to make this recipe for company. Guests never fail to be intrigued, and they'll never suspect the entire dinner goes together in just 20 minutes.

AFRICAN CHICKEN STEW

Basic Couscous (recipe follows; see Box, facing page)
3 skinless, boneless chicken breast halves
(about 1 pound total), fresh or frozen
2 teaspoons olive oil
1 large onion (for 1 cup sliced)
10 already-peeled baby carrots (for ½ cup sliced)
2 teaspoons bottled minced garlic
1 can (14½ ounces) stewed tomatoes
½ teaspoon ground cinnamon
½ teaspoon ground cumin
¼ teaspoon ground turmeric (optional)
Black pepper to taste
1 teaspoon honey
1 cup frozen zucchini or yellow squash
1 cup frozen red, yellow, and green bell pepper stir-fry mix,
such as Birds Eye
1 small can (7¾ ounces) chickpeas
½ cup raisins (optional)

1. Prepare step 1 of Basic Couscous. While the liquid comes to a boil, if the chicken is frozen, run it under hot water so you can remove any packaging. Place the chicken on a microwave-safe plate and microwave 3 minutes, uncovered, on high, to begin defrosting.

2. Meanwhile, heat the oil in a 4½-quart Dutch oven or soup pot over medium heat. Peel and slice the onion into ¼-inch rings, adding them to the pot as you slice. Slice and add the carrots. Stir occasionally.

3. If the liquid for the couscous is boiling, proceed with step 2 of the Basic Couscous recipe.

4. Slice the chicken (fresh or partially defrosted) into ½-inch-wide strips. Cut the longest strips in half. Add the chicken and garlic to the pot, cover, raise the heat to high, and cook 2 minutes.

5. Uncover, stir well, and immediately add the stewed tomatoes, cinnamon, cumin, turmeric (if using), black pepper, honey, zucchini, and bell peppers. Stir again. Cover and boil for 10 minutes to fully cook the chicken, uncovering occasionally and stirring to prevent sticking.

6. Drain the chickpeas and stir in, along with raisins (if using). Cook 1 more minute to combine flavors, then serve over a bed of the couscous.

Serves 6

BASIC COUSCOUS

1 can (14½ ounces) fat-free chicken broth
1¼ cups water
1½ cups quick-cooking couscous

1. Bring the broth and water to a boil in a covered 2-quart saucepan over high heat.

2. Stir in the couscous, re-cover the pan, and remove from the heat until the liquid is absorbed, about 5 minutes. Set aside until ready to serve; fluff with a fork and serve.

Makes about 4½ cups

* *Couscous originated in northern Africa, where young girls spent years learning to make it from scratch. Today, harried cooks can dash into most any supermarket and whiz out with the convenient, quick-cooking variety. Look for it in the rice aisle.*

Replacing part of the couscous cooking water with broth gives a richer flavor, much like the effect of a rice pilaf. This basic recipe can be topped with any kind of stew you choose. Or throw frozen vegetables in during step 1 to make a pilaf of sorts.

From Alicia:

Maybe it's my southern heritage showing, but I crave this stew. Good Brunswick stew needs to be hearty and thick. Years ago, the meat base was squirrel. Nowadays, chicken works well for most people. The choice of vegetables varies from cook to cook, but one thing is still true: the stew must be low on broth and high on vegetables and meat.

This recipe is so good, I was asked to make it for three hundred people at a Thanksgiving feast following a children's music program. With just corn muffins and a small salad, it was a perfect meal.

❋ *Leftover stew refrigerates well for 3 days, or you may want to turn it into vegetable soup by adding another can of tomatoes and enough chicken broth to reach the desired consistency.*

OUR BRUNSWICK STEW

2 teaspoons vegetable oil
1½ cups cubed, frozen hash brown potatoes
1 cup frozen chopped onions
1 can (14½ ounces) fat-free chicken broth
1 cup frozen corn kernels
1 can (15 ounces) lima beans
1 can (15 ounces) black-eyed peas
1 can (14½ ounces) stewed tomatoes
3 cans (5 ounces each) white-meat chicken
1 tablespoon reduced-fat real bacon bits (not imitation)
1 teaspoon sugar
1 teaspoon Worcestershire sauce
½ teaspoon black pepper
½ teaspoon dried basil
½ teaspoon dried thyme

1. Heat the oil in a 4½-quart Dutch oven or soup pot over high heat. Add the potatoes and onions. Cover and cook for 4 minutes, uncovering to stir about every 30 seconds. (The potatoes will stick to the pot bottom.) Add the chicken broth and stir and scrape the brown bits from the pot bottom.

2. Add the corn, then cover and cook while opening the cans. Rinse and drain the lima beans and black-eyed peas and add them to the pot, then add the tomatoes and the chicken with its juice.

3. Stir in the bacon bits, sugar, Worcestershire, pepper, basil, and thyme, then re-cover and bring to a boil, uncovering occasionally and stirring. Reduce the heat to medium-high and continue boiling, stirring occasionally, for 8 minutes. Serve at once.

Serves 6

GRANDMA'S CHICKEN STEW ☻

2 cans (14½ ounces each) fat-free chicken broth
1 can (14½ ounces) vegetable broth
¾ cup already-shredded carrots
8 ounces (about 4 cups) wide egg noodles
1 large can (10 ounces) white-meat chicken
1 tablespoon all-purpose flour
2 tablespoons cold water
Black pepper to taste

1. Bring the chicken broth and vegetable broth to a boil in a covered 4½-quart Dutch oven or soup pot over high heat. This should take 8 to 10 minutes. When the broth boils, add the carrots, noodles, and the chicken and its juices. Cover the pot and bring the broth back to a rolling boil.

2. Uncover the pot and stir, breaking up any chicken chunks slightly. Continue to boil, uncovered, over high heat until the noodles are tender, about 6 minutes.

3. Meanwhile, combine the flour and water in a small container that has a lid. Shake well until the lumps disappear.

4. When the noodles are just tender, add the flour mixture and stir constantly until the stew is slightly thick, about 2 minutes. Season with pepper and remove from the heat. Serve in large soup plates or bowls.

Serves 4

From Alicia:

A lot of my favorite childhood meals were eaten in my grandmother's kitchen. Maw-Maw, as we call her still, seemed to cook her hugs into everything she prepared.

Whether it was a warm and nourishing stew or pretty-as-a-picture straw-berry cake, it was sure to leave everyone around the table satisfied.

When Beverly and I developed this recipe, I was taken back to that yellow Formica table where every-thing tasted so wonderful. Full-bodied and filling, your family will think you've cooked your love right into this lovely, old-fashioned stew.

From Beverly:

This is my favorite chili, and it's a hit every year when we invite friends over to watch the Super Bowl. Pitted oil-cured olives are listed as optional because they are a bit pricy and may not be available in some supermarkets. (Check the imported or Greek foods section.) However, these little gems are worth seeking out because they add a lovely exotic flavor. They really do make this chili worthy fare for a gathering of special friends.

> ✸ *This chili is mild enough even for most children. If you prefer chili that sounds an alarm, increase the chili powder to a tablespoon and add hot pepper sauce to taste.*

SUPER CHILI

1 pound ground turkey, fresh or frozen
1 teaspoon olive oil
1 large onion (for 1 cup chopped)
1 large green bell pepper (for 1½ cups chopped)
1 cup frozen carrot slices
1 can (15½ ounces) red kidney beans
1 can (15 ounces) black beans
2 cans (14½ ounces each) chili-style stewed tomatoes
2 teaspoons chili powder (see Box)
1 teaspoon garlic powder
1 teaspoon ground cumin
14 already-pitted oil-cured olives (optional)
Salt and black pepper to taste

1. If the turkey is frozen, run hot water over it so you can remove any packaging. Place the turkey on a microwave-safe plate and microwave 2 minutes, uncovered, on high, to begin defrosting.

2. Meanwhile, heat the oil in a 4½-quart Dutch oven or soup pot over medium heat. Peel and coarsely chop the onion, adding it to the pot as you chop. Stir occasionally.

3. Add the turkey (fresh or partially defrosted) to the pot and raise the heat to high. Cook, turning and breaking up the meat from time to time. While the meat cooks, seed and coarsely chop the bell pepper, adding it to the pot as you chop. Add the carrots.

4. While the turkey cooks, rinse and drain both of the beans. Add them to the pot along with the stewed tomatoes, chili powder, garlic powder, cumin, and olives (if using). Stir well.

5. Cook on high, stirring frequently, until all the meat is crumbled and browned. Reduce the heat to medium and cook about 5 minutes more. Season with salt and pepper and serve.

Serves 6

DECEPTIVELY SIMPLE FISH

⅓ cup all-purpose flour

2 tablespoons vegetable oil

1½ pounds firm, white skinless, boneless fish fillet,
    such as mahi mahi, flounder, or cod

½ teaspoon seasoning salt (see Box)

½ teaspoon black pepper

12 already-peeled baby carrots

1½ cups water

1 tablespoon red wine vinegar

1 teaspoon Worcestershire sauce

1 medium onion (for ¾ cup slices)

1 large green bell pepper (for 1½ cups strips)

1 large fresh, ripe tomato

1. Spread the flour on a plate. Heat the oil in a 4½-quart Dutch oven or soup pot over medium-high heat. Working quickly, cut the fish fillet crosswise in half. Sprinkle ¼ teaspoon seasoning salt over one side of each fish half. Sprinkle ¼ teaspoon black pepper over the other side. Dip each piece into the flour to coat on both sides. Shake off any excess and discard the remaining flour.

2. Place both fish pieces in the hot oil and fry for 3 minutes on the first side. Turn and fry 2 minutes on the other side. While the fish cooks, slice each baby carrot into 4 long strips. After you have finished browning the fish on the second side, add the water, carrots, vinegar, and Worcestershire. Cover the pot, turn the heat to high, and bring the water to a boil.

3. Peel the onion and cut it into ¼-inch slices. Add the onion to the pot, separating the slices into rings. Seed the bell pepper, slice into ¼-inch strips, and add. Cut the tomato into wedges, and add. Re-cover the pot between additions.

From Alicia:

Brown stew fish is Jamaican cooking at its best. I first sampled it while overlooking the bay at a small restaurant in Ocho Rios, Jamaica. I came home raving about the delicate fish combined with the perfect spices and textures and knew I had to learn how to make it at home.

When Beverly and I first attempted a version of the Jamaican classic, we expected the fish fillet to fall apart as it boiled. But the fillets hold their shape nicely. We asked a friend to try it out, too. She got the same great results, and suggested substituting white wine for half of the water, as a variation. She also added a shot of hot pepper sauce for a true Jamaican kick. "My husband loved this," our friend reported, "and the cats had to be asked off the table four times."

> ❋ *Try to choose a brand of seasoning salt that's free of MSG and artificial colors. We tested this recipe using the Lawry's brand.*

4. Continue to boil the mixture, covered, until the vegetables are soft and fragrant and the liquid reduces to a gravy, about 7 minutes. Serve at once, cutting each fish piece in half and spooning some of the vegetables and gravy over the top.

Serves 4

SUMMER'S RATATOUILLE

2 tablespoons olive oil
2 medium onions or 1 extra-large (for 1½ cups chopped)
1 pound fresh tomatoes (for about 3 cups chopped)
1 teaspoon salt
2 teaspoons dried oregano
2 tablespoons dried basil (see Box)
1 teaspoon sugar
Pinch of cayenne pepper
1 medium eggplant (about 8 ounces)

1. Heat the oil in a 4½-quart Dutch oven or soup pot over medium heat. Peel and coarsely chop the onions, adding them to the pot as you chop. Raise the heat to high and cook the onions 4 minutes to soften, stirring often.

2. Meanwhile, dice the tomatoes (with the peels still on). When the onions are soft, add the tomatoes and their juice to the pot with the salt, oregano, basil, sugar, and cayenne. Cover and bring to a boil.

3. Meanwhile, cut the unpeeled eggplant into 1-inch-thick slices. Stack the slices, cut them into 1-inch chunks, and add to the pot. Cover, and cook until the eggplant is tender, 8 to 10 minutes, stirring occasionally. Remove from the heat and serve.

Serves 4

From Alicia:

It never seems quite fair that after months of not having one tomato fit to consume, we are suddenly inundated with them during the summer months. I have them on my window sill, my screened-in porch, even lined in rows in my basement. I just can't let them go to waste.

After pots of tomato sauce and salads of every description, I hit on a terrific recipe for ratatouille.

This versatile Mediterranean stew has many different forms. My recipe is a simplified version bursting with flavor. I always serve it with rice, a green salad with light dressing, hard rolls, and good iced tea.

✳ *If you happen to have fresh summer basil in the garden, substitute ¼ cup chopped for the dried.*

VEGETABLE HOPPIN' JOHN

2 teaspoons olive oil
1 large onion (for 1 cup chopped)
1 medium green bell pepper (for 1 cup chopped)
2 teaspoons bottled minced garlic
2 cans (14½ ounces) vegetable broth
1 vegetable bouillon cube
1 teaspoon Worcestershire sauce
½ teaspoon dried basil
½ teaspoon black pepper
2 cans (15 ounces each) black-eyed peas packed without pork
1 package (14 ounces) quick-cooking (10-minute) brown rice
1 can (14½ ounces) Cajun-style stewed tomatoes

Don't be fooled into thinking this version of Hoppin' John is bland because there's no meat. Our twist on the traditional Southern favorite confidently relies on vegetable broth and the vegetarian vegetable bouillon cubes (we use Knorr brand) to pack the flavor punch.

1. Heat the oil in a 4½-quart Dutch oven or soup pot over medium heat. Peel and coarsely chop the onion, adding it to the pot as you chop. Seed and coarsely chop the bell pepper. Add it to the pot and stir.

2. Add the garlic and broth, and raise the heat to high. Add the bouillon cube, cover the pot, and bring the broth to a boil. Uncover to add the Worcestershire, basil, and black pepper, and immediately re-cover after each addition.

3. While the broth is coming to a boil, drain and rinse the peas. Set aside. Uncover the pot, add the rice, and stir. Cover again, reduce the heat to medium, and let the rice cook until the broth is just absorbed, about 8 minutes. Add the tomatoes and drained peas and stir to mix. Continue to cook, covered, until heated through, 1 to 2 minutes. Remove from the heat and serve.

Serves 6 generously

From Alicia:

Vegetarian chili has always been a favorite way to use small amounts of vegetables I find in my refrigerator. It can be made hundreds of ways. I used to use bulgur to add body, but the time it took to soften was annoying. I recently discovered a marvelous ingredient that took care of that problem. It's called TVP (texturized vegetable protein), and it's made from processed soy protein. TVP has long been used by vegetarians to replace meat in recipes like chili and sloppy joes. It adds a chewy texture without all of the fat and cholesterol. TVP looks a lot like puffed rice cereal (only brown and more flaky). If you don't find it at the supermarket, check health food stores.

> ✳ *This recipe calls for the usual onions, peppers, carrots, and mushrooms, but it's very flexible. Throw in extra squash or zucchini, red or yellow peppers, or most any vegetables you happen to have.*

VERY VEGETARIAN CHILI

1 cup TVP (texturized vegetable protein)
1 cup water
1 teaspoon olive oil
1 cup already-sliced fresh mushrooms
1 cup already-shredded carrots
1 large onion (for 1 cup chopped)
1 medium green bell pepper (for 1 cup chopped)
1 teaspoon bottled minced garlic
2 cans (15 ounces each) red kidney beans
2 tablespoons chili powder
1 teaspoon dried oregano
2 cans (14½ ounces each) diced tomatoes
⅓ cup wine, red or white
1 tablespoon Worcestershire sauce
Salt and black pepper to taste
Hot pepper sauce to taste
Already-shredded sharp Cheddar cheese (optional)
Reduced-fat sour cream (optional)

1. Place the TVP and water in a 2-cup glass measure and microwave, uncovered, on high, until the water boils, about 2 minutes. Set aside to soften.

2. Heat the olive oil in a 4½-quart Dutch oven or soup pot over medium heat. Add the mushrooms and carrots. Peel and coarsely chop the onion, adding it to the pot as you chop. Seed and chop the bell pepper, adding it as you chop. Add the garlic. After all of the vegetables are added, stir, then cook until the onions and peppers are tender and the mushrooms have released their liquid, about 3 minutes.

3. Rinse and drain the beans. Add to the pot along with the chili powder, oregano, and tomatoes with their juice, stirring well. Stir in the wine and Worcestershire. Stir in the softened TVP.

4. Cover the pot and raise the heat to high, bringing the mixture to a boil. Then reduce the heat to low and simmer, stirring occasionally, for 5 minutes or until ready to serve. Before serving, season with salt, black pepper, and hot pepper sauce. Serve garnished with Cheddar cheese and sour cream (if using).

Serves 6

INDONESIAN CURRIED VEGETABLES

2¼ cups water
2½ cups quick-cooking (10-minute) brown rice
1 tablespoon olive oil
1 cup already-cut broccoli florets
1 cup already-sliced fresh mushrooms
1 medium green bell pepper (for 1 cup strips)
1 cup already-shredded red cabbage
1 cup already-shredded carrots
2 cups frozen chopped onions
1 tablespoon good-quality imported curry powder
2 teaspoons bottled minced garlic
1 teaspoon ground cumin
1 teaspoon bottled chopped ginger
2 cans (14½ ounces each) diced tomatoes
3 tablespoons peanut butter

From Alicia:

I first sampled an Indonesian dish similar to this one at a restaurant in Chapel Hill, North Carolina, called Pyewacket. The chef there creates his own curry with a lovely blend of whole cumin seeds, coriander, fenugreek, cinnamon, cardamom, turmeric, and, well, the list seems to go on and on.

Although this recipe relies on an imported curry powder mix, the ingredients list still seems long. Don't let this intimidate you. Because most of the ingredients are already shredded or chopped, it takes no time at all to put the dish together.

1. Bring 2¼ cups water (this amount is correct; there is more rice than water) to a boil in a 2-quart saucepan. Meanwhile, begin step 2. When the water boils, add the rice, cover the pan, reduce the heat to low, and simmer for 5 minutes. Remove from the heat until ready to serve.

2. Heat the oil in a 4½-quart Dutch oven or soup pot over medium heat. Add the broccoli and mushrooms and cook, stirring occasionally, while seeding the bell pepper and cutting it into thin strips. Add the pepper, cabbage, carrots, and onions. Raise the heat to medium-high and stir occasionally.

3. Stir in the curry powder, garlic, cumin, and ginger. Stir in the tomatoes and their juice. Raise the heat to high, cover the pot, and bring the stew to a boil. Uncover the pot and boil, stirring from time to time, for 3 minutes more to blend flavors.

4. Reduce the heat to low and stir in the peanut butter, blending well. Serve over the brown rice.

Serves 4

A word about:
GARLIC

If you're the sort of person who never objects to peeling garlic, you can always substitute 1 medium clove of fresh garlic for every ½ teaspoon of bottled garlic in our recipes. But when you're rushed, bottled minced garlic becomes addictively simple. Unless garlic remains raw in the finished dish or is a prominent rather than just flavoring ingredient, reach for the bottled.

BEANS AND GREENS

1 tablespoon olive oil
2 medium onions or 1 extra-large (for 1½ cups chopped)
2 cans (15.8 ounces each) chopped mustard greens or collards
2 tablespoons plus 2 teaspoons bottled minced garlic
2 cans (14½ ounces each) Great Northern beans
2 teaspoons balsamic vinegar
1 teaspoon Worcestershire sauce
Salt and black pepper to taste
1 or 2 bottled roasted red peppers (optional)

1. Heat the oil in a 4½-quart Dutch oven or soup pot over medium-low heat. Peel and coarsely chop the onions, adding them to the pot as you chop. Cook for 2 minutes. Meanwhile, drain the greens and set aside.

2. Add the garlic to the onions and cook for 30 seconds, stirring often. Add the drained greens and raise the heat to medium-high. Drain the liquid from one can of beans only, then add both cans of beans and the remaining liquid to the pot, along with the vinegar, Worcestershire, and salt and black pepper. Stir gently to mix well. Raise the heat to high and bring the mixture to a boil, then reduce the heat to medium.

3. Continue to cook, uncovered, at a slow boil for another 5 minutes to allow the flavors to blend. Meanwhile, if roasted peppers are desired, cut them into strips.

4. To serve, spoon the stew into bowls and garnish with the roasted red pepper strips (if using).

Serves 4

From Beverly:

This adaptation of a classic Italian recipe comes from my friend Sally Hicks, a newspaper reporter whose unpredictable work schedule means she must rely on what's in her pantry more often than not. I made her Beans and Greens during an ice storm when going to the store was out of the question. I garnished this hearty dish with bottled roasted red pepper to add color. Although it's a hearty vegetarian meal alone, my leftovers were yummy as a side dish with baked pork chops.

CHAPTER THREE

Skillet

Forget complicated side dishes. Forget sinks piled high with dirty dishes. With a decent skillet and a few tricks from this chapter, you can pull off an entire dinner in 20 minutes with only one pan to wash. Stovetop skillet meals are so convenient, we're practically addicted. There are saucepans in our cupboards we haven't touched in months.

Traditional skillet meals tend to be filling entrées that mix a starch, vegetables, and meat and bind it all together with some sort of sauce or broth. You'll find lots of these recipes, such as Southwestern Chicken on the Spot, Flexible Jambalaya, and French Peasant Supper in the following pages. A few of the recipes call for cooking the rice or noodles in a separate pot, but whenever possible we eliminated that step.

We also experimented with recipes that aren't usually prepared in a skillet just to see what would happen. Shepherd's pie in a skillet? Delicious. What about barbecued chicken? You won't believe how good it is. Fajitas? "We loved this recipe!" our taste testers told us.

All in all, the results surpassed even our most optimistic hopes. For the next few months, we put every meal we ate to the Desperation Skillet Test. We even examined our favorite casseroles, and several of them, like lasagna, Greek moussaka, and chicken tetrazzini, ended up working equally well in a skillet.

This chapter also includes recipes for stir-fries. We figure most desperate cooks are more likely to stir-fry in a skillet on a day-to-day basis than they are to drag out the wok. Of course

meals

you'll want the right skillet, and we cover everything you need to know about buying one on page 55.

One of the nice things about most skillet recipes is their flexibility. If you're missing an ingredient, chances are you can substitute a close second and the dish will turn out just fine. And if, like us, you realize you forgot to defrost the meat, a skillet can be a lifesaver. All you need is a quick shot in the microwave and the frying action of the skillet, and your family will never know you haven't been planning dinner for days.

Finally, one of the secret ingredients we can't live without is the relatively new, improved "instant" rice now available in supermarkets. Simply dump this rice in the skillet toward the end of the recipe and it finishes off your meal in just five minutes. All the necessary information can be found on page 59.

You'll find a month's worth of skillet recipes in this chapter. By the time you're finished, you may find, as we did, that it gets harder to make yourself cook any other way.

"Your family will never know you haven't been planning dinner for days."

From Beverly:

I've always loved Thai food, but it was during my first pregnancy that I found myself on a first-name basis with the staff of the Thai House II in North Miami Beach. Every Friday before heading home from work, I'd phone in my take-out order: seafood soup for two, pad thai noodles, string beans with ground pork, and whatever curry dish happened to strike my fancy. Then I'd wheel by the restaurant, race home, and consume the entire feast myself.

Now we live in a town without a true Thai restaurant and I'm not pregnant, but my cravings can still rage out of control. I have been forced to discover how fast and easy it is to make my own Thai curry. That's especially true now that canned unsweetened coconut milk is available in many regular supermarkets (don't confuse this with sweetened cream of coconut). The steak for this recipe must be already-defrosted or fresh.

CRAVIN' BEEF CURRY

2½ cups "instant" (5-minute) rice
½ teaspoon vegetable oil
1 large onion (for 1 cup strips)
10 already-peeled baby carrots
1 large green bell pepper (for 1½ cups chopped)
1 tender beefsteak, such as New York strip
   (1 inch thick and about 12 ounces)
1 can (14 ounces) unsweetened coconut milk
1 teaspoon bottled minced garlic
1 teaspoon bottled chopped ginger
1 teaspoon curry powder
1 teaspoon ground coriander seed
1 teaspoon crushed hot red pepper (see Box, facing page)
½ teaspoon ground cumin
¼ teaspoon ground cardamom
¼ teaspoon ground turmeric
¼ teaspoon salt, or to taste

1. Bring 2½ cups water to a boil in a 2-quart saucepan. Meanwhile, begin steps 2 and 3. When the water boils, add the rice, cover the pan, and remove from the heat until ready to serve.

2. Heat the oil in a 12-inch nonstick skillet over medium heat. Peel the onion and cut it into strips about ¼ inch wide, adding them to the skillet as you cut. Reduce the heat to low and cook while you prepare the remaining vegetables, stirring occasionally to prevent the onions from browning.

3. Cut each carrot lengthwise into 4 strips, adding them to the skillet as you cut. Seed the bell pepper, cut it into thin lengthwise strips, and add them to the skillet. Continue to cook, stirring occasionally.

4. Meanwhile, trim the excess fat from the steak and slice it thin. Add all of the meat to the skillet at the same time and raise the heat to high. Stir-fry until the steak is pink only in the middle, 2½ to 3 minutes. Add the coconut milk and stir to mix.

5. Reduce the heat to medium and add the garlic, ginger, and all the remaining seasonings. Stir well, then reduce the heat to low and simmer for 3 to 4 minutes to blend the flavors. Serve over a bed of the rice.

Serves 4

> ❋ *If you don't like spicy food, reduce the crushed red pepper to ½ teaspoon, or to taste. If you're feeding children, simply serve their portions before adding the red pepper at the last minute.*

A word about:
SPICE LEVELS

One of the hardest aspects of committing our recipes to an official book has been coming to terms with what we call the Spice Level. In random recipe taste-tests, we quickly ran up against a wide range of personal preferences on distinct flavors like curry spices, garlic, hot pepper, salt, and sugar. Extremes of "too much garlic" and "too bland" could be heard about the exact same recipe.

Rather than veer to the middle, we decided to stick with what we like. But the most important advice we'd offer about using this book is this: Taste as you go. And remember, it's a recipe, not a rule. You salt addicts and garlic fiends know who you are, so be prepared to add more. For the timid of tongue, our maxim is this: You can always add but you can't subtract, so sprinkle in strong spices gradually.

This is our basic Desperation stir-fry recipe, and it is endlessly flexible. You can make it with 3 skinless, boneless chicken breast halves and chicken broth in place of the beef and beef broth, and you can substitute just about any vegetable you have on hand for the carrots, mushrooms, and broccoli. The same goes for the sauce: In place of the sesame oil, play around with any of the bottled Asian sauces you find at the supermarket, such as hoisin sauce, plum sauce, chili oil, stir-fry sauce, black bean sauce, lemon sauce, and so on.

> ✳ *Be sure to buy frozen broccoli florets in a plastic bag for this recipe so that the florets will thaw in the skillet.*

BEAT-THE-CLOCK STIR-FRY

1 can (14½ ounces) beef broth
2½ cups "instant" (5-minute) rice
12 ounces lean beef, such as round steak, fresh or frozen
2 teaspoons vegetable oil
1 large onion (for 1 cup wedges)
1 can (8 ounces) sliced water chestnuts
12 already-peeled baby carrots
1 cup already-sliced fresh mushrooms
1 cup frozen broccoli florets (see Box)
¼ cup dry sherry or red or white wine (optional)
2 teaspoons bottled minced garlic
1 teaspoon bottled chopped ginger
1 teaspoon reduced-sodium soy sauce
1 tablespoon cornstarch
2 teaspoons dark sesame oil

1. Skim the fat from the beef broth. Bring 1½ cups water and 1 cup of the broth to a boil in a 2-quart saucepan. Meanwhile, begin steps 2 and 3. When the water boils, add the rice, cover the pan, and remove from the heat until ready to serve.

2. If the beef is frozen, run it under hot water so you can remove any packaging. Place the beef on a microwave-safe plate and microwave 2 minutes, uncovered, on high, to begin defrosting.

3. Heat the vegetable oil in a 12-inch nonstick skillet over medium heat. Peel the onion and cut it lengthwise in half, then cut each half into 4 pieces. Add the onion to the skillet and cook 2 minutes, stirring occasionally. While the onion cooks, drain the water chestnuts.

4. Cut the carrots in half lengthwise and add them to the skillet. Add the mushrooms. Cut the beef (fresh or partially defrosted)

into thin strips, then raise the heat to medium-high and add the beef to the skillet. Stir-fry 3 minutes. Add the drained water chestnuts, broccoli, sherry (if using), garlic, ginger, and soy sauce, and stir-fry 2 minutes more.

5. Add ½ cup of the remaining broth to the skillet. Combine the remaining ¼ cup broth with the cornstarch in a small container that has a lid and shake well until the lumps disappear. Add the mixture to the skillet along with the sesame oil. Stir and cook until the liquid thickens slightly, about 3 minutes. Serve over a bed of the rice.

Serves 4

FAJITAS IN A FLASH

1 pound boneless steak, such as skirt steak, sirloin, or rib-eye
    (about ½ inch thick)
1 large onion (for 1 cup strips)
2 teaspoons vegetable oil
⅓ cup red wine or beef broth
2 tablespoons molasses
1 tablespoon Worcestershire sauce
1 tablespoon lemon juice from frozen concentrate
Juice of ½ lime
1 teaspoon bottled minced garlic
1 medium green or red bell pepper (for 1 cup strips)
8 (10-inch) flour tortillas
Salt and black pepper to taste

From Beverly:

Just because it's thirty degrees outside and I don't feel like grilling doesn't mean I don't feel like eating fajitas. Fajitas are one of my favorite southwestern meals, and I crave them at the most inconvenient times. It was just such a moment that encouraged me to cut my steak into strips and toss them in a skillet. With the optional toppings suggested in the box on page 54, you'll hardly miss the singe of the grill. This recipe calls for an already-defrosted or fresh steak.

❋ *Optional toppings
for fajitas include:
Bottled salsa
Already-shredded
   Cheddar or Mexi-
   can blend cheese
Reduced-fat sour
   cream or plain
   yogurt*

1. Using a very sharp knife, cut the steak into strips about ¼ to ½ inch wide. Peel the onion and cut it lengthwise in half, then cut each half lengthwise into strips the same width as the meat. Set the onion aside.

2. Heat the oil in a 12-inch nonstick skillet over high heat. Add the beef and stir-fry for 2½ to 3 minutes for medium-rare (or to desired doneness). Turn the beef out onto a platter and set aside.

3. To the skillet add the wine, molasses, Worcestershire, lemon and lime juices, and garlic. Bring to a boil over high heat, stirring, then add the onion and cook while you seed the bell pepper and cut it into strips about ¼ to ½ inch wide. Add the bell pepper to the skillet and continue to cook on high until the vegetables are tender and about half the wine sauce has evaporated, about 3 minutes. Stir from time to time.

4. While the vegetables cook, set out the salsa, cheese, and any other toppings (if using; see Box). Wrap the tortillas in wax paper or paper towels and warm them in the microwave for about 40 seconds on high.

5. When the vegetables are tender, return the meat and any juices to the skillet. Toss the meat for about 1 minute to warm through and coat with sauce, then season with salt and black pepper.

6. To serve, return the meat and vegetables to the platter and let everyone build 2 fajitas to personal preference.

Serves 4

THE RIGHT SKILLET

To pull off some of the recipes in this chapter without worrying about your food leaping out of the pan, you'll want to have the right kind of equipment.

Although most of these recipes work perfectly well in a standard 12-inch frying pan with a lid, you'll face less hassle if you use what we call an extra-deep 12-inch nonstick skillet. On the label, most manufacturers call this sort of pan a chicken fryer or chef's pan. The distinguishing factor is the deep sides, which stand 2 inches or even higher. Typical nonstick sauté skillets tend to have more sloping, shallow sides, while traditional frying pans have sides of 1½ inches. It's hard to believe, but that extra half-inch of side gives you room to stir easily when you're dealing with a recipe that serves 6 people. Extra-deep skillets will hold from 4 to 5 quarts of food.

Extra-deep skillets are also almost always sold with a lid. Lids for sauté skillets are not always available, and when they are, they're usually sold separately. Some extra-deep skillets have a regular handle on one side and a small loop handle on the opposite side. This is helpful for balancing. We've found the price on these skillets listed from $20 to $145. Discount "mart" stores carry national brands for around $25. Be sure to buy a pan with a nonstick surface. Not only is cleanup a breeze, it lets you cut down on the amount of oil needed.

Some of the more expensive skillets are made entirely of metal and can go straight from the stovetop into the oven. However, many of these have maximum temperature restrictions, and we've found that the extra expense is not worth the implied convenience. For the recipes that require top browning under the broiler, a cast-iron skillet is the best choice. A 12-inch cast-iron skillet will cost from $15 to $20 at discount stores.

"At our houses, it's a choice: four hours in the kitchen vs. clean underwear, our kids' soccer games, and bargain-hunting for back-to-school clothes."

From Alicia:

For my mom, shepherd's pie was an economical way to use leftover potatoes and roast beef or country-style steak. A quick shepherd's pie was one of the first meals Beverly and I created together, and we wanted a version that didn't depend on leftovers but could be pulled together from the pantry and freezer. We had no idea we were starting with the hardest recipe we could have picked. Using extra-lean ground beef turned out to be our biggest obstacle. Without fat, there's no base for making gravy. We finally solved that dilemma with a flavorful combination of beef broth, spices, and sour cream. A dozen shepherd's pies later, we finally achieved what went on to become one of my favorite recipes.

SKILLET SHEPHERD'S PIE

1 pound extra-lean ground beef, fresh or frozen
2 teaspoons vegetable oil
1 large onion (for 1 cup chopped)
2 tablespoons ketchup
1 tablespoon Worcestershire sauce
2 teaspoons bottled minced garlic
1 cup frozen green peas
1 beef bouillon cube
½ cup water
1 tablespoon cornstarch
1 package (20 ounces) refrigerated mashed potatoes,
    such as Simply Potatoes brand
1 tablespoon butter or margarine
½ cup reduced-fat sour cream
¾ cup (3 ounces) already-shredded sharp Cheddar cheese

1. Turn on the broiler.

2. If the beef is frozen, run hot water over it so you can remove any packaging. Place the beef on a microwave-safe plate and microwave 3 minutes, uncovered, on high, to begin defrosting.

3. Meanwhile, heat the oil in a 12-inch cast-iron or other heat-proof skillet (see Note) over medium heat. Peel and coarsely chop the onion, adding it to the skillet as you chop.

4. Add the beef (fresh or partially defrosted) to the skillet and raise the heat to high. Cook, turning and breaking up the meat until it is crumbled and browned and the onion is tender, about 5 minutes. While the meat is browning, stir in the ketchup, Worcestershire, and garlic.

5. When the meat is browned, stir in the peas. Reduce the heat to medium-low and let simmer.

6. Meanwhile, combine the bouillon cube and water in a 1-cup glass measure. Microwave 1 minute, uncovered, on high, to dissolve the cube. Stir the cornstarch briskly into the bouillon until well blended. Pour the cornstarch mixture into the skillet and stir well. Continue to simmer, stirring occasionally.

7. Meanwhile, microwave the potatoes according to package directions, adding the butter. While the potatoes warm, stir the sour cream into the thickened beef mixture. Spoon the potatoes over the beef mixture, spreading them to within 1 inch of the skillet sides. Sprinkle the cheese over the potatoes and broil until the cheese is melted and bubbly, 2 minutes. Serve at once.

Serves 4

Note: If you don't have a skillet that can withstand broiling, transfer the meat to a 9-inch square casserole dish before broiling in step 7.

TIME-SAVER

Buy frozen vegetables in family-size plastic bags for more control in measuring. Vegetables that come in bags thaw much faster than in boxes. Whack the bag on the countertop to loosen frozen clumps.

From Alicia:

What is it about cream of mushroom soup that turns simple beef and rice into a magical combination the whole family craves? When Beverly let me sample this casserole, I knew immediately what I would be fixing for dinner that night. And that's the lovely thing about this simple one-pot meal: You can decide to throw it together at the last minute, and all of the ingredients are likely to be right in your kitchen.

I've fixed this homey and satisfying meal several times since Beverly first shared her recipe with me. It's one of those meals that's easy to fall back on when it's time for dinner and I haven't got a clue what to make.

HEARTLAND RICE AND BEEF

1¼ pounds extra-lean ground beef, fresh or frozen
1 teaspoon olive oil
1 large onion (for 1 cup chopped)
2 teaspoons bottled minced garlic
¼ teaspoon black pepper
1 package (8 ounces) already-sliced fresh mushrooms
1 medium green bell pepper (for 1 cup chopped)
2 teaspoons Worcestershire sauce
1 can (14½ ounces) beef broth
1 can (10¾ ounces) reduced-fat cream of mushroom soup
2¼ cups "instant" (5-minute) rice
Salt to taste (optional)
½ cup already finely shredded sharp Cheddar cheese,
    or more to taste

1. If the beef is frozen, run hot water over it so that you can remove any packaging. Place the beef on a microwave-safe plate and microwave 3 minutes, uncovered, on high, to begin defrosting.

2. Meanwhile, heat the oil over medium heat in an extra-deep 12-inch nonstick skillet that has a lid. Peel and coarsely chop the onion, adding it to the skillet as you chop.

3. Add the beef (fresh or partially defrosted) to the skillet and raise the heat to high. Add the garlic, black pepper, and mushrooms and cook, turning and breaking up the meat from time to time.

4. Seed and coarsely chop the bell pepper and add it to the skillet. Add the Worcestershire. Continue to cook, stirring frequently, until all of the meat is crumbled and browned, 5 to 6 minutes. Meanwhile, remove any visible fat from the beef broth.

5. When the meat is browned, stir in the beef broth, mushroom soup, and rice. Cover the skillet and bring to a boil. Boil until the rice is tender and absorbs most of the broth, about 5 minutes. Stir from time to time, keeping the skillet covered as much as possible.

6. Season the mixture with salt (if using), then sprinkle with the cheese. Cover and cook just until the cheese melts, 1 to 2 minutes more. Serve at once.

Serves 6 generously

A word about:
QUICK RICE

If you've been turned off in the past by the texture of 5-minute rice, it's time to try again. Uncle Ben's makes a relatively new "instant" rice that offers a significant improvement over the other brands we've tried.

The difference is obvious even by looking at the uncooked grains, which are more plump than the quick rice of old. While the finished product still isn't as fluffy as traditional 20-minute rice, Uncle Ben's Instant Rice also doesn't turn to mush like many other brands do.

"Instant" rice gives the best results if you cook it with broth instead of plain water. Or you can jazz it up with other assertive flavors and spices. And that's an added benefit to many of our skillet recipes, which call for cooking the rice along with everything else.

On nights when we have slightly more time, we also enjoy experimenting with the new brands of "instant" brown rice that cook in 10 minutes and with the "instant" white and wild rice mixes that cook in 7 to 10 minutes.

MOUSSAKA IN MINUTES

The traditional Greek moussaka is a layered casserole, usually made with lamb, that's baked for over an hour. In order to get the same great flavor in a third of the time, we prepare our moussaka in a skillet and serve it over orzo, a rice-shaped pasta commonly used in Mediterranean cooking. Another secret to our speedy version involves using an already-prepared "light" Alfredo sauce. These are commonly found in the supermarket refrigerator case next to the pesto and fresh pastas.

2 cups (12 ounces) orzo pasta
1¼ to 1½ pounds extra-lean ground beef,
*   fresh or frozen*
2 teaspoons olive oil
1 large onion (for 1 cup chopped)
1 large eggplant (12 to 16 ounces; for 4 cups cubed)
1 small can (8 ounces) tomato sauce
¼ cup ketchup
¼ teaspoon ground nutmeg
⅛ teaspoon ground cinnamon
1 container (10 ounces) reduced-fat Alfredo sauce
¼ cup already-grated or already-shredded
*   Parmesan cheese*

1. Turn on the broiler.

2. Bring 2½ quarts of unsalted water to a boil in a covered 4½-quart or larger pot. When the water reaches a rapid boil, add the orzo and cook 7 minutes.

3. If the beef is frozen, run hot water over it so you can remove any packaging. Place the beef on a microwave-safe plate and microwave 3 minutes, uncovered, on high, to begin defrosting.

4. Heat the oil over medium-high heat in a 12-inch cast-iron or other heatproof skillet (see Note, page 57). Peel and coarsely chop the onion, adding it to the skillet as you chop. Begin cutting the eggplant into 1-inch squares, leaving the peel on. Set aside.

5. Add the beef (fresh or partially defrosted) to the skillet. Cook, turning and breaking up the meat, until most of the meat is crumbled and browned, about 3 minutes. Finish cutting the eggplant while the meat cooks.

6. Add the eggplant, tomato sauce, and ketchup to the skillet and stir to mix. Cover, and boil until all the meat is no longer pink and the eggplant is soft, about 6 minutes. Stir frequently to prevent sticking, taking care not to make the eggplant mushy.

7. Meanwhile, add the nutmeg and cinnamon directly to the container of Alfredo sauce. Stir well. Drizzle the sauce evenly over the skillet. Sprinkle the Parmesan cheese evenly over the meat mixture and place under the broiler until the top is bubbly and just begins to brown, 2 to 3 minutes. Drain the orzo and serve the meat over a bed of orzo.

Serves 6

CUBAN PICADILLO

2½ cups "instant" (5-minute) rice

1¼ pounds extra-lean ground beef, fresh or frozen

1 teaspoon olive oil

1 medium onion (for ¾ cup chopped)

1 teaspoon bottled minced garlic

½ teaspoon black pepper

½ teaspoon ground cumin

⅛ teaspoon ground cinnamon

⅛ teaspoon ground cloves

½ cup frozen green peas (optional)

1 can (14½ ounces) stewed tomatoes

¼ cup raisins

¼ cup sliced pimiento-stuffed green olives

¼ cup white wine (optional)

From Alicia:

I t's a struggle to find meals that satisfy adults and my picky kids at the same time. So when I find a recipe we all enjoy, I'm thrilled.

When I first served Cuban Picadillo to my family, I braced for the usual "I don't like this" before the first bite even reached their lips. Instead I got, "Cool, sloppy joes on rice." I don't care what they call it so long as we're all eating the same meal.

TIME-SAVER

Chop an onion in a flash by cutting both ends off and slicing top to bottom only through the outermost layer of skin. Peel off this outer layer and cut the onion in half from top to bottom. Then place the flat side on a cutting board and cut into small "wedges" determined by the size you wish to chop the onion (i.e., ½ inch for coarsely chopped, ⅛ inch for fine). Then holding the wedges together, chop perpendicularly to the wedge cuts. The layers of the onion will make the third cut for you. Repeat with the second half of the onion.

1. Bring 2½ cups water to a boil in a 2-quart saucepan. Meanwhile, begin steps 2 and 3. When the water boils, add the rice, cover the pan, and remove from the heat until ready to serve.

2. If the beef is frozen, run it under hot water so you can remove any packaging. Place the beef on a microwave-safe plate and microwave 3 minutes, uncovered, on high, to begin defrosting.

3. Heat the oil in a 12-inch nonstick skillet over medium heat. Peel and coarsely chop the onion, adding it to the skillet as you chop. Add the meat (fresh or partially defrosted) to the skillet and raise the heat to medium-high. Cook, turning and breaking up the meat until it is crumbled and browned. While the meat browns, stir in the garlic, black pepper, cumin, cinnamon, and cloves.

4. When the meat is nearly done (after 8 to 10 minutes), add the peas (if using), stewed tomatoes, raisins, olives, and wine (if using). Stir well to mix and bring to a boil. Reduce the heat to medium-low and simmer until the liquid has nearly evaporated, about 5 minutes, stirring occasionally. Picadillo should be moist, but not soupy. Serve over a bed of rice.

Serves 4

FIERY CHINESE BEEF ★★ ☺

1 can (14½ ounces) Oriental broth or fat-free chicken broth

2½ cups quick-cooking (10-minute) brown rice

2 teaspoons peanut or other vegetable oil

12 ounces to 1 pound tender beefsteak, such as boneless sirloin,
*   already cut into thin, 2-inch-long strips*

1 package (16 ounces) frozen stir-fry vegetables with broccoli

2 tablespoons cornstarch

2 teaspoons bottled minced garlic

1 teaspoon sugar

1 teaspoon bottled minced ginger

1 teaspoon Asian black bean sauce, or to taste

½ teaspoon crushed hot red pepper, or to taste

1. Bring 1 cup of the broth and 1¼ cups water to a boil in a 2-quart saucepan (you will have more rice than liquid). Meanwhile, begin steps 2 and 3. When the liquid boils, add the rice, cover the pan, reduce the heat to low, and simmer for 5 minutes. Remove from the heat until ready to serve.

2. Heat the oil in a 12-inch nonstick skillet over medium-high heat. Add the meat and stir-fry for 2 minutes. Raise the heat to high and add the frozen vegetables. Cook, stirring occasionally.

3. Meanwhile, combine the cornstarch with the remaining broth in a small container that has a lid. Shake well until the lumps disappear, then set aside.

4. Add the garlic, sugar, ginger, black bean sauce, and hot pepper to the skillet. Shake the cornstarch mixture again, stir it into the mixture in the skillet, and bring to a boil. Stir frequently until the sauce is thick, 3 minutes. Serve over a bed of the brown rice.

Serves 4

This is the ultimate in super-quick stir-fry recipes. The meal only takes 10 to 12 minutes to make if you buy meat already cut from the butcher and use the frozen vegetable stir-fry mix. If you can't get tender meat precut, you'll have plenty of time to prepare your own and still put dinner on the table in 20 minutes. Do use steak that's already-defrosted or fresh for this recipe.

The nutty flavor of brown rice works well here. Since you don't need a whole can of broth to make the stir-fry sauce, we've used what remains to cook the rice.

Feel free to add more crushed red pepper if you're a fan of fiery foods. Or leave it out altogether. At half a teaspoon, this dish is moderately hot.

☀ *Asian black bean sauce is found in the supermarket near the soy sauce. Oyster sauce, hoisin sauce, or bottled stir-fry sauce can be substituted.*

A word about:
CAST-IRON SKILLETS

Many cooks shy away from cast iron because it has to be seasoned before it's used, and that sounds so temperamental. But seasoning a cast-iron skillet really translates into simply using it. Granted, you do need to start somewhere, but pulling the pan out and cooking with it is what perfects the surface.

Most cast-iron products come with initial seasoning instructions, but don't let them throw you. Just two things are necessary for seasoning your pan: oil and heat. First, wash your new pan and dry it thoroughly. Then oil the inside and out with solid vegetable shortening or a mild salad oil. (If you oil the outside of the pan, it will help prevent rust from forming during the long lifetime of your skillet.) Bake the empty pan in a preheated 350°F oven for at least an hour. (If you are already cooking something else, just pop the pan on the unused rack.) Carefully remove the pan from the oven (it's very hot), let it cool to room temperature, and wipe off the excess oil with paper towels. Now you're ready to cook.

For everyday cleaning, hand wash, using a plastic scouring pad to loosen any tough spots. (Avoid abrasive pads, and never put the pan in the dishwasher.) The more you use the pan, the easier cleanup will be, and to keep the pan in top shape, dry it well before storing.

If you notice rust on the pan after long periods of inactivity, gently remove the spots with a plastic scouring pad and then wash and dry. Oil the spot and rebake it in the oven. Cool and store the skillet. Before your next use, wipe the oil off and cook as usual.

BAYOU STROGANOFF

4 boneless center-cut loin pork chops (each ½ inch thick; about 1 pound total), fresh or frozen
1 teaspoon vegetable oil
1 medium onion (for ¾ cup chopped)
1 teaspoon Creole or Cajun seasoning blend, or more to taste
1 can (14½ ounces) fat-free chicken broth
1½ cups "instant" (5-minute) rice
1½ cups frozen broccoli pieces
½ cup reduced-fat sour cream

1. If the pork chops are frozen, run hot water over them so you can remove any packaging. Place the chops on a microwave-safe plate and microwave 2 minutes, uncovered, on high, to begin defrosting.

2. Meanwhile, heat the oil over medium heat in a 12-inch non-stick skillet that has a lid. Peel and coarsely chop the onion, adding it to the skillet as you chop. Cook until soft, stirring occasionally. While the onion cooks, slice the chops (fresh or partially defrosted) into ¼-inch strips, adding them to the skillet as you cut. Stir occasionally as you add the strips.

3. Sprinkle the Creole seasoning over the pork and onions. Cook, stirring often, until the pork is no longer pink, 4 to 5 minutes. Raise the heat to high, add the broth and rice, and stir well. Cover the skillet, bring the broth to a boil, then reduce the heat to medium. Simmer until most of the broth is absorbed, 5 minutes.

4. Meanwhile, place the broccoli in a microwave-safe dish and microwave, covered, on high, for 3 minutes to defrost.

5. Uncover the skillet and stir in the broccoli and sour cream to blend well. Cook until heated through, 30 seconds, and serve.

Serves 4

This recipe is based on an idea from the Rice Council, the folks who make their living trying to get us to eat more of you-know-what. It was such a delightful twist on the traditional stroganoff that we couldn't resist the temptation to adapt the recipe to fit the Desperation lifestyle. The original recipe calls for leftover cooked rice, but our instructions use quick-cooking rice in case you don't have any leftover on hand. If your pork chops are frozen, we've included defrost instructions. We also trimmed the fat, with no detectable change in flavor, by calling for reduced-fat sour cream and fat-free broth.

✳ *In spite of the Cajun seasoning, this dish is mild enough for children. If you like spicy Cajun food, increase the seasoning to 2 teaspoons.*

This is one of those recipes that's too easy to taste so good. A couple of long simmers leave plenty of time to throw together a simple salad. If you're not pressed for time, you can substitute 3 cups of sliced fresh zucchini, 2 cups of diced fresh tomatoes, and 2 teaspoons of Italian seasoning for the canned zucchini. Add the fresh vegetables along with the rice. Fresh is always nice, but we couldn't tell much of a difference in flavor between the two versions when we tested them.

✻ *Many brands of sausage refer to a pork-turkey blend as "light" or "lite" sausage. Bulk sausage means sausage not contained in casings or links. If you can't find bulk sausage, buy links and remove the meat from the casings.*

SAUSAGE AND ZUCCHINI SKILLET

1 package (12 ounces) "light" breakfast-style bulk sausage (see Box)
¾ cup frozen chopped onions
1 can (14½ ounces) fat-free chicken broth
¼ cup water
2¼ cups "instant" (5-minute) rice
2 cans (16 ounces each) zucchini with Italian-style tomato sauce
¼ cup already-grated or -shredded Parmesan cheese

1. Fry the sausage over high heat in a 12-inch nonstick skillet that has a lid, turning and breaking up the chunks constantly for 2 minutes. Continue to cook until most of the sausage is browned, about 5 minutes, reducing the heat if the sausage begins to burn. Add the onions, broth, and water. Cover the skillet and bring the liquid to a boil.

2. As soon as the liquid boils, add the rice and stir to moisten well. Cover the skillet and cook until the rice absorbs most of the moisture but not all of it, about 4 minutes. (Electric stoves may require reducing the heat to medium.)

3. Add the zucchini and stir gently to combine. Sprinkle evenly with the Parmesan, cover, and cook until the cheese has melted and the zucchini is hot, 3 to 4 minutes more. Serve at once.

Serves 6

GARLICKY POTATOES AND SAUSAGE

1 tablespoon olive oil

4 to 6 medium red potatoes (for about 4 cups cubed)

5 cloves garlic

1 package (12 ounces) "light" breakfast-style bulk sausage
   (see Box, facing page)

1 teaspoon dried rosemary

1 teaspoon sugar

1 can (14½ ounces) diced tomatoes

1. Heat the oil over medium heat in an extra-deep 12-inch non-stick skillet that has a lid. Meanwhile, scrub the potatoes (leave the skins on) and cut into roughly ¾-inch cubes, adding them to the pan as you cut. Raise the heat to high, then cover and cook for 3 minutes to brown the cubes slightly, uncovering occasionally to stir. While the potatoes cook, begin to peel and chop the garlic.

2. Add the sausage to the skillet and stir constantly for 2 minutes with a fork or spatula to break up the chunks. Once the sausage is broken up, cook until the potatoes are golden brown and the sausage is brown, 7 to 9 minutes more, stirring occasionally. (If the sausage begins to burn, lower the heat for a minute or so.)

3. Meanwhile, finish chopping the garlic and add it to the pan. Add the rosemary and sugar and stir well.

4. When the sausage is done, stir in the tomatoes with their juice and cook until about half of the juice evaporates, 2 to 3 minutes more, and serve.

Serves 4

From Alicia:

One of my favorite side dishes has always been potatoes with fresh garlic and tomatoes in the Provençal style of southeastern France. The rustic appearance of the unpeeled potatoes is so down-home, it reminds me of hash browns North Carolina style, with lots of garlic and a little rosemary thrown in for good measure. One night when a craving for those wonderful potatoes struck about the same time as my nightly desperation, I threw in some sausage, and heated some store-bought sourdough bread. Dinner was served in 20 minutes.

This recipe is inspired by the French cassoulet, a dish with many regional variations that can spark endless arguments over which is best. Some cassoulets contain preserved duck and others partridge, some call for bread crumb toppings and some do not. The consistent ingredients for cassoulet are pork and fat—and plenty of both—and as for time, some cassoulets require up to 5 hours of work spread over 3 days.

If the French argue so passionately about the authenticity of their own cassoulets, our quick and easy version would surely give them a stroke. Their versions, however, contain enough cholesterol to give *us* a heart attack. Therefore, we feel perfectly justified in offering up our lightened, 20-minute rendition of this hearty peasant supper. Begin this one with already-defrosted or fresh boneless pork.

FRENCH PEASANT SUPPER

½ teaspoon olive oil
20 already-peeled baby carrots (for about 1 cup sliced)
2 boneless center-cut loin pork chops (each about ⅜ inch thick; about ½ pound total)
8 ounces turkey kielbasa sausage
1 large onion (for 1 cup chopped)
½ cup water
¼ cup white wine
2 tablespoons ketchup
1 tablespoon honey
1 tablespoon bottled minced garlic
3 bay leaves
½ teaspoon dried thyme
¼ teaspoon black pepper, or more to taste
Pinch of ground cloves
2 cans (15 ounces each) navy beans
½ cup plain dry bread crumbs

1. Turn on the broiler. (Or use the toaster setting of a toaster oven.)

2. Heat the oil in an extra-deep 12-inch nonstick skillet over medium-high heat. Meanwhile, slice the carrots into circles, adding them to the skillet as you slice.

3. While the carrots cook, cut the pork chops into ½-inch cubes, adding them to the skillet as you cut. Slice the sausage into ¼-inch circles, adding them as you cut. Stir occasionally to prevent sticking.

4. Peel and coarsely chop the onion, adding it to the skillet as you chop. Stir in the water, wine, ketchup, honey, garlic, bay leaves, thyme, black pepper, and cloves and cook until the pork cubes are no longer pink, about 4 minutes, stirring frequently. (Reduce the heat to medium if the pork begins to burn.)

5. Meanwhile, rinse and drain the beans and set aside. Toast the bread crumbs under the broiler or in the toaster oven until crisp and light brown. Set aside.

6. Stir the beans into the pork mixture and simmer just long enough to mix well and heat through, about 2 minutes. Scatter the toasted crumbs on top and serve.

Serves 6

A word about:
CUP MEASURES

When you're cooking in a rush, you've got to keep moving. That's why you'll keep seeing words like these over and over in the instructions to our recipes: "adding as you chop" or "adding as you slice." What that means is that after you've chopped a good handful, go ahead and throw it in.

Why, then, you might wonder, do we specify a cup measure for onions and other vegetables? The truth is, it really doesn't matter in Desperation recipes whether or not you have exactly a cup of onions. The important thing is to grab an onion and get it in there. If you're adding as you chop, there's no way you can measure anyway.

The only reason we specify a cup measure is to give you a ballpark idea of the amount we're aiming for. After all, one cook's large onion may be another cook's jumbo. But again, in a typical soup or skillet meal, it really won't matter. Chop, cook, and enjoy.

When the leaves start to fall, it's hard to get enough apples. I'd put them in every dish at every meal if it were possible. This recipe came about after a particularly greedy apple forage at the local farmers' market. The contrasting combination of tart apples, sweet cabbage, and pork is particularly nice. It's best eaten in front of a roaring fire—use the packaged instant fire logs to get one going quickly!

HARVEST PORK CHOPS

1 can (14½ ounces) fat-free chicken broth
1½ cups water
2½ cups "instant" (5-minute) rice
4 boneless center-cut loin pork chops (each about ⅜ inch thick;
    about 1 pound total), fresh or frozen
1 tablespoon butter or margarine
1 medium onion (for ¾ cup slices)
Black pepper to taste
1 large tart apple, such as Granny Smith
    (for 1 cup slices)
½ cup apple juice, white wine, or water
1 tablespoon dark or light brown sugar
2 tablespoons Dijon mustard
1 tablespoon cider vinegar or distilled white vinegar
1 bag (8 ounces) cabbage coleslaw mix
2 tablespoons cornstarch
3 tablespoons water

1. Combine 1 cup of the chicken broth and the water in a 2-quart saucepan and bring to a boil. Meanwhile, begin step 2 (if necessary) and step 3. When the liquid boils, add the rice, cover the pan, and remove from the heat until ready to serve.

2. If the pork chops are frozen, run hot water over them so you can remove any packaging. Place the chops on a microwave-safe plate and microwave 2 minutes, uncovered, on high, to begin defrosting.

3. Meanwhile, melt the butter over low heat in an extra-deep 12-inch nonstick skillet that has a lid. Peel the onion, cut it in half lengthwise, and cut each half into 4 crescent-shaped slices, adding the slices to the skillet as you cut them. Raise the heat to medium and cook for 2 minutes, stirring occasionally.

4. Add the pork chops (fresh or partially defrosted) to the skillet, pepper them to taste, and cook until brown on the first side, about 3 minutes.

5. Meanwhile, cut the unpeeled apple in half, core it and cut it into ¼-inch-thick slices. Turn the pork chops and add the remaining ¾ cup chicken broth, the apple juice, brown sugar, mustard, and vinegar. Stir well. Immediately add the apple slices and coleslaw mix. Stir to coat the slaw with sauce. Cover the pan, raise the heat to high, and bring the liquid to a boil. Then reduce the heat to low and simmer, covered, just until the chops are no longer pink in the center, about 8 minutes.

6. Meanwhile, combine the cornstarch and 3 tablespoons water in a small container that has a lid. Shake well until the lumps disappear, then set aside.

7. When the chops have simmered for 8 minutes, uncover the skillet, shake the cornstarch mixture again, and add it to the skillet, stirring constantly. Stir until the sauce is the desired consistency for gravy, about 2 minutes.

8. To serve, place a chop on a bed of rice on each serving plate and top with some onions, apples, cabbage, and gravy.

Serves 4

"A freezer stocked with the right kinds of meat means you can be a spur-of-the-moment cook."

From Beverly:

From Beverly:

My college roommate introduced me to this dish, which was created by her family's Japanese housekeeper. I never met Misako, but I felt I knew her well, since Mary often grew homesick for the exotic and wonderful dishes she created. Misako would express a care package by Greyhound bus from time to time, and it was a happy day when a box of her homemade egg rolls arrived at the dormitory.

Misako made these pork chops with thick slices of fresh tomato, but for desperate cooks, canned tomatoes work just as well. The mushrooms and ginger are my own additions. Make this with already-defrosted or fresh boneless pork.

MISAKO'S PORK CHOPS

1 teaspoon vegetable oil
4 boneless center-cut loin pork chops
  (each about ⅜-inch thick; about 1 pound total)
1 large onion (for 1 cup rings)
1 can (14½ ounces) Oriental broth or fat-free chicken broth
1½ cups "instant" (5-minute) rice
1 can (14½ ounces) stewed tomatoes
1 teaspoon Worcestershire sauce
1 teaspoon bottled chopped ginger
1 teaspoon garlic powder
¼ teaspoon onion powder
¼ teaspoon dried basil
¼ teaspoon salt (optional)
¼ teaspoon black pepper
1 medium green or red bell pepper (for 1 cup rings)
1 cup already-sliced fresh mushrooms
3 tablespoons water
2 tablespoons cornstarch

1. Heat the oil over medium heat in a 12-inch nonstick skillet that has a lid. Add the pork chops and sauté, turning once, until they are golden brown on both sides, 3 minutes. While the chops cook, peel and slice the onion into thin rings, scattering them evenly over the chops as you slice.

2. Add the broth, rice, stewed tomatoes, Worcestershire, and ginger, stirring well to moisten the rice. Turn the heat to high, cover the skillet, and bring the broth to a boil. Measure the garlic powder, onion powder, basil, salt (if using), and black pepper into a small dish. Uncover the skillet and add all of the spices at once, stirring well.

3. Re-cover the pan and let cook while you seed the bell pepper and slice it into ¼-inch rings. Add the pepper slices and mushrooms to the skillet, distributing them evenly over the chops. Cover again and continue to boil the mixture on high for about 8 minutes, until the chops are just done (no longer pink in the center).

4. Meanwhile, combine the water and cornstarch in a small container that has a lid. Shake well until the lumps disappear, then set aside.

5. When the chops have simmered for 8 minutes, uncover the skillet, shake the cornstarch mixture again, and add it to the skillet. Stir constantly until the liquid reaches the desired thickness, 1 to 2 minutes.

6. Spoon out a bed of rice and vegetables onto each serving plate. Top with a pork chop and serve.

Serves 4

> **TIME-SAVER**
>
> Store your knives on a magnetic strip close to your work space. It's a thrill to only have to reach up and grab that chef's knife instead of digging through the drawer. The strips cost about $10 at kitchen shops and department stores.

This dish is inspired by *arroz con pollo,* the Spanish and Latin American dish that is usually made with bone-in chicken and takes an hour or more of preparation. The rice is often yellow, which comes from the addition of saffron or annatto. Since saffron is extremely expensive and hard to find, and annatto is even more elusive, we've simply left it out. If you happen to find saffron in your supermarket, add 6 to 10 threads along with the chicken. With or without saffron, this is an exotic dish that will add a little olé to a plain old night.

CHICKEN OLÉ

4 skinless, boneless chicken breast halves (1⅓ pounds total), fresh or frozen
2 teaspoons olive oil
1 extra-large or 2 medium onions (for 1½ cups chopped)
2 large green bell peppers (for 3 cups chunks)
1 can (14¾ ounces) fat-free chicken broth
½ cup white wine
1 can (14½ ounces) diced tomatoes
2½ cups "instant" (5-minute) rice
½ cup sliced pimiento-stuffed green olives
½ cup frozen green peas (optional)
1½ teaspoons bottled minced garlic
2 bay leaves
1 teaspoon dried oregano
½ teaspoon ground cumin
¼ teaspoon salt, or more to taste
¼ teaspoon black pepper

1. If the chicken is frozen, run it under hot water so you can remove any packaging. Place the chicken on a microwave-safe plate and microwave 3 minutes, uncovered, on high, to begin defrosting.

2. Meanwhile, heat the oil, over medium heat, in an extra-deep 12-inch nonstick skillet that has a lid. Peel and coarsely chop the onion, adding it to the skillet as you chop.

3. Cut each breast into 3 strips about an inch wide, then add the chicken (fresh or partially defrosted) to the skillet and raise the heat to high. Cover the skillet and cook while seeding the bell peppers and cutting them into 1-inch-wide strips. Cut the strips crosswise in half, and add the peppers to the skillet all at once.

4. Add the broth and wine. Cover the skillet and bring the liquid to a boil. Meanwhile, drain the tomatoes. Keeping the pan covered as much as possible, add the drained tomatoes, rice, olives, peas (if using), garlic, bay leaves, oregano, cumin, salt, and black pepper. Stir well.

5. Cook at a rolling boil until the rice is tender, 5 minutes more. Remove the bay leaves, stir well, and serve.

Serves 4 generously

DRUNKEN CHICKEN

2½ cups "instant" (5-minute) rice
4 skinless, boneless chicken breast halves
    (about 1⅓ pounds total), fresh or frozen
1 can (6 ounces) pineapple juice (¾ cup)
¼ cup reduced-sodium soy sauce
¼ cup light or dark rum
1 teaspoon bottled minced garlic
1 teaspoon bottled chopped ginger
1 tablespoon peanut or other vegetable oil
2 to 3 bunches scallions (green onions; for 1½ cups sliced)
3 tablespoons cornstarch
¼ cup water
1 can (5 ounces) sliced water chestnuts

1. Bring 2½ cups water to a boil in a 2-quart saucepan. Meanwhile, begin step 2. When the water boils, add the rice, cover the pan, and remove from the heat until ready to serve.

From Alicia:

My college roommate and I used to spend whole Saturdays preparing a feast for that night's dinner. One of our favorite meals was an Asian chicken dish cooked in foil. It was labor intensive, but uniquely flavorful.

I still crave that chicken, not to mention the lazy Saturdays required to pull it off.

The marinade for that long-ago dish inspired this recipe. Pineapple juice and rum bring a sweet highlight, and the salty soy sauce gives the proper contrast. It has an incredible flavor, and yet I can put it on the table in less than 20 minutes.

2. If the chicken is frozen, run it under hot water so you can remove any packaging. Place the chicken on a microwave-safe plate and microwave 2 minutes, uncovered, on high, to begin defrosting. Meanwhile, make a marinade in a medium-size bowl by combining the pineapple juice, soy sauce, rum, garlic, and ginger. Stir with a whisk to blend.

3. Cut the chicken (fresh or partially defrosted) into bite-size pieces and add them to the marinade. Stir to coat and set aside. Start heating the oil in a 12-inch nonstick skillet over low heat, while you slice the scallions, using all of the whites and enough of the tender green tops to make about 1½ cups. Set aside.

4. Raise the heat under the skillet to high. Using a slotted spoon to reserve the marinade, lift the chicken into the skillet and cook, stirring from time to time, for 3 minutes. Meanwhile, combine the cornstarch and the water in a small container that has a lid and shake well until the lumps disappear. Add the mixture to the reserved marinade.

5. Add the scallions to the skillet, stir, and continue to cook until the chicken is no longer pink, 3 to 4 minutes. (Reduce the heat to medium-high if necessary.) While the chicken cooks, drain the water chestnuts.

6. Add the water chestnuts and marinade to the skillet and stir to mix well. Cook until the sauce is thick, about 2 minutes, stirring constantly. Serve at once over a bed of the rice.

Serves 4

A word about:
FROZEN MEAT

Afreezer stocked with the right kinds of meat means you can be a more flexible cook on the spur of the moment. But you can't do anything in 20 minutes with an iceberg. The trick is to think thin and small. Here are some ideas:

• Buy several 1- to 1½-pound packages of extra-lean ground beef or turkey. Wrap the entire package (still wrapped in its store wrapping) in a sheet of heavy-duty aluminum foil. Use a permanent marker to label the contents and date right on the foil.

When you're ready to cook, take off the foil and run the frozen meat (store wrapper and all) under comfortably hot tap water for 30 seconds. Remove the plastic wrap, pry off the plastic tray, put the icy block on a microwave-safe plate, and pop it into the microwave on high for 2 or 3 minutes. This thaws the meat just enough so you can brown it quickly for Desperation recipes.

• The same procedure works for boneless chicken breasts, steaks, and chops (pork, veal, lamb)—so long as they're thinly sliced, about ¼ to ⅜ inch.

• When it comes to chicken, we recommend buying "individually quick-frozen" boneless chicken breast halves. These are a relatively new item to many groceries. The breast pieces are glazed with ice, which means they don't stick together and can be used conveniently one or two at a time. The breasts are usually sold in a 4-pound, resealable plastic bag (see Box, page 151, for more about IQF chicken).

On unpredictable days, stocking thin meats in your freezer means you won't have to worry about dinner until the last possible minute.

Just two special ingredients, honey-spiked mustard and orange slices, transform plain chicken and rice into an exotic meal. Because you don't have to peel the oranges, the whole dish goes together in a snap.

> ✷ Look for jars of "fresh-packed" orange segments under the brand name SunFresh in the supermarket produce section. If you can't find these bottled fresh-tasting oranges, ask the manager to order them. Substitutes include the segments of 1 tangerine (cut in half, seeds removed), a cup of drained pineapple chunks or a cup of drained, canned mandarin oranges.

CITRUS CHICKEN

3 skinless, boneless chicken breast halves
     (about 1 pound total), fresh or frozen
1 teaspoon vegetable oil
1 medium onion (for ¾ cup chopped)
1 teaspoon bottled minced garlic
Savory Rice (recipe follows)
¼ cup sliced or slivered almonds
1 cup fat-free chicken broth remaining from the
     Savory Rice recipe
¼ cup honey mustard, or more to taste
1 teaspoon balsamic vinegar
1 cup bottled orange segments (see Box)
1 tablespoon cornstarch
2 tablespoons water

1. The oven or toaster oven should be already heated to 325°F.

2. If the chicken is frozen, run hot water over it so you can remove any packaging. Place the chicken on a microwave-safe plate and microwave 2 minutes, uncovered, on high, to begin defrosting.

3. Meanwhile, heat the oil over medium heat in a 12-inch non-stick skillet that has a lid. Peel and coarsely chop the onion, adding it to the skillet as you chop. Add the garlic and stir from time to time.

4. Slice each breast half (fresh or partially frozen) into strips about 1 inch wide. Push the onion to the sides of the skillet and add the chicken. Cook the chicken, stirring frequently, until it turns white and barely begins to brown, about 5 minutes.

5. While the chicken cooks, start the Savory Rice. Toast the almonds in a small baking pan in the oven until light brown, about 5 minutes, and set aside.

6. When the chicken is white, add the remaining 1 cup chicken broth to the skillet. Add the honey mustard and vinegar and stir until the mustard dissolves. Cover the pan and bring the broth to a boil. Reduce the heat to low and simmer 5 minutes. Taste the sauce. If you prefer a stronger mustard flavor, add 1 to 2 tablespoons more honey mustard and stir.

7. Add the orange segments to the skillet. Raise the heat to medium. Combine the cornstarch and water in a small container that has a lid and shake well until the lumps disappear. Add the cornstarch mixture to the skillet a little at a time, stirring constantly. Simmer until thickened, about 2 minutes more.

8. To serve, place a chicken cutlet on a bed of rice, and top with some sauce and orange segments. Garnish with the almonds.

Serves 4

SAVORY RICE

2 cans (14½ ounces) fat-free chicken broth
2½ cups "instant" (5-minute) rice
1 cup frozen green peas

1. Pour 1 cup chicken broth into a glass measure and reserve for use in Citrus Chicken.

2. Bring the remaining 2½ cups broth to a boil in a 1-quart or larger saucepan over medium-high heat. Add the rice and peas, stir, cover the pan, reduce the heat, and simmer 5 minutes.

3. When the rice is done, remove the pan from the heat until the chicken is cooked. Just before serving, stir to incorporate the peas.

Serves 4

This easy rice pilaf pairs nicely with Citrus Chicken, but you can use it anytime you wish to serve rice with poultry or pork.

Barbecued chicken is one of my family's favorite meals, and I usually make my own barbecue sauce because I don't care for the artificial smoke flavoring contained in many commercial brands. Although it's easy to whip up a ketchup-based sauce and pop the chicken into the oven, there are many nights when I just can't wait long enough for the chicken to bake. This recipe is my compromise. The barbecue sauce goes right into the skillet and turns the rice into a flavored pilaf. With green peas added, it's a convenient one-dish dinner.

> ✳ It's okay if all the chicken hasn't taken on color when you are ready to add the broth. Just add the broth—the flavor of the dish doesn't depend on the chicken getting browned.

STOVETOP BARBECUED CHICKEN

4 skinless, boneless chicken breast halves
(about 1⅓ pounds total), fresh or frozen
Cooking oil spray
1 medium onion (¾ cup chopped)
1 can (14½ ounces) fat-free chicken broth
1½ cups "instant" (5-minute) rice
¼ cup ketchup
1 tablespoon light or dark brown sugar, firmly packed
1 tablespoon lemon juice from frozen concentrate
1 tablespoon distilled white vinegar
1 teaspoon Worcestershire sauce
1 teaspoon garlic powder
½ teaspoon onion powder
½ teaspoon dry mustard powder (or 1 teaspoon
prepared mustard)
Black pepper to taste
1 cup frozen green peas

1. If the chicken is frozen, run hot water over it so you can remove any packaging. Place the chicken on a microwave-safe plate and microwave 3½ minutes, uncovered, on high, to begin defrosting.

2. Meanwhile, spray with cooking oil spray a 12-inch nonstick skillet that has a lid and heat it over medium heat. Peel and coarsely chop the onion, adding it to the skillet as you chop. Let cook, stirring frequently.

3. Meanwhile, slice each breast (fresh or partially frozen) into ¾-inch wide strips, adding them to the skillet as you slice. Raise the heat to high and add the broth and rice (see Box). Stir well

and bring the broth to a boil, meanwhile adding the "barbecue" seasonings (ketchup, brown sugar, lemon juice, vinegar, Worcestershire, garlic powder, onion powder, mustard, and pepper). Stir well, then cover the skillet.

4. When the broth boils, reduce the heat to medium-high and cook for 4 minutes.

5. Uncover the skillet and stir in the green peas, then re-cover and continue to cook until almost all the broth is absorbed and the rice is tender, about 3 minutes more. Serve.

Serves 4

SOUTHWESTERN CHICKEN ON THE SPOT ★★

4 skinless, boneless chicken breast halves
(about 1⅓ pounds total), fresh or frozen
1 teaspoon olive oil
½ large green bell pepper (for ¾ cup strips)
½ large red bell pepper (for ¾ cup strips)
1 teaspoon chili powder
½ teaspoon ground cumin
1 teaspoon bottled minced garlic
½ cup frozen chopped onions
1 can (14½ ounces) crushed or diced tomatoes
⅓ cup bottled salsa
⅔ cup fat-free chicken broth or water
1 cup "instant" (5-minute) rice
1 can (15 ounces) black beans
½ cup already-shredded Cheddar, Monterey Jack, or
Mexican blend cheese

Bottled salsa replaces part of the liquid required for the rice, which absorbs the tomato flavor as it cooks. Since this dish contains rice and vegetables, a generous serving with bread on the side makes a satisfying meal. But if you feel inclined, serve it with a simple side dish of shredded lettuce topped with chopped tomato (taco style). A dab of reduced-fat sour cream makes a nice garnish.

❋ *Really, really desperate? Substitute 1½ cups of frozen green, red, and yellow bell pepper stir-fry mix for the fresh and add them to the skillet along with the rice. Bags of the pepper mix can be found in the supermarket freezer case.*

1. If the chicken is frozen, run hot water over it so you can remove any packaging. Place the chicken on a microwave-safe plate and microwave 2 minutes, uncovered, on high, to begin defrosting.

2. Heat the oil over medium-high heat in a 12-inch nonstick skillet that has a lid. Slice the chicken (fresh or partially defrosted) into ½-inch strips, adding them to the skillet as you slice. Seed both the bell peppers and cut into ¼-inch strips, adding them to the skillet as you cut.

3. Stir the chili powder and cumin into the chicken and peppers and continue to cook for 3 minutes, stirring from time to time. Add the garlic, onions, tomatoes with their juice, salsa, and chicken broth. Cover the skillet and bring the mixture to a boil.

4. When the liquid boils, add the rice and stir well. Cover the skillet, reduce the heat to medium, and cook for 5 minutes. Meanwhile, rinse and drain the beans.

5. When the rice has absorbed the broth, remove the skillet from the heat, stir in the beans, and sprinkle evenly with the cheese. Cover and let the dish rest for 2 minutes until the cheese melts, or until you are ready to serve.

Serves 4

FRENZIED FRIED RICE

2 skinless, boneless chicken breast halves
 (about ⅔ pound total), fresh or frozen
Cooking oil spray (optional)
2 large eggs (optional)
2 tablespoons peanut or other vegetable oil
1 large onion (for 1 cup chopped)
1 cup already-sliced fresh mushrooms
¼ cup dry sherry
3 tablespoons reduced-sodium soy sauce, plus
 additional for serving (optional)
1 tablespoon bottled minced garlic
4 cups leftover cooked rice (regular long-grain or
 quick-cooking brown)
1 to 2 bunches scallions (green onions; for ¾ cup chopped)
1 can (5 ounces) sliced water chestnuts
1 cup frozen green peas
1½ tablespoons dark sesame oil

1. If the chicken is frozen, run it under hot water so you can remove any packaging. Place the chicken on a microwave-safe plate and microwave 2 minutes, uncovered, on high, to begin defrosting.

2. Meanwhile, if you're using the eggs, spray a 12-inch nonstick skillet with cooking oil spray and set it over medium heat. Beat the eggs lightly, pour them into the skillet, and cook without stirring (as you would an omelet) until they are almost dry. While the eggs cook, cut the chicken (fresh or partially defrosted), into bite-size chunks. When the eggs are ready, remove them to a plate and set aside.

3. Heat 1 tablespoon of the peanut oil in the 12-inch skillet over high heat. Add the chicken and cook, stirring occasionally. As it

Don't you just hate it when you overshoot on the rice? Here's the perfect solution. In fact, we like this dish so much we often cook too much rice on purpose, giving us a head start on a meal later in the week. Traditional fried rice always calls for egg, but since neither of us really cares for it, we leave it out. With or without the egg, this fried rice is hearty enough for a light supper.

> ✳ *For frenzied flexibility, try 10 ounces of a tender cut of pork or shrimp in place of the chicken.*

cooks, peel and coarsely chop the onion, adding it to the skillet as you chop. Cook 1 minute. Stir in the remaining 1 tablespoon peanut oil, the mushrooms, sherry, 3 tablespoons soy sauce, and garlic, then add the rice and cook about 3 minutes, stirring frequently.

4. Slice the scallions, using the white and enough of the tender green tops to make ¾ cup. Add them to the skillet and stir well. Drain the water chestnuts and roughly chop, adding them as you chop. Add the peas and sesame oil. If using the egg, cut it into thin strips, add to the skillet, and stir. Stir-fry 1 minute more to heat the water chestnuts and peas. Serve, passing extra soy sauce at the table (if using).

Serves 4

L o mein is more or less the Chinese version of spaghetti. The secret to lo mein is a good stir-fry sauce. Ours offers a balance between soy sauce and oyster sauce, which is sold alongside soy sauce in most supermarkets. Ketchup is a surprising addition, but it neutralizes the acid in the dish and binds the sauce. Bottled minced garlic and bottled chopped ginger give the sauce an authentic Asian flavor without the hassle of peeling and mincing fresh.

LAZY LO MEIN

8 ounces Chinese lo mein noodles (see Box, facing page)
2 skinless, boneless chicken breast halves
    (about ⅔ pound total), fresh or frozen
Stir-Fry Sauce (recipe follows)
1 tablespoon vegetable oil
1 large onion (for 1 cup chopped)
1½ cups already-shredded carrots
1 cup already-sliced fresh mushrooms
1 can (14 ounces) bean sprouts
Unsalted dry-roasted peanut halves (optional)

1. Cook the noodles in already-boiling water according to package directions. Meanwhile, continue with the recipe, and when the noodles are done, drain and set aside.

2. If the chicken is frozen, run it under hot water so you can remove any packaging. Place the chicken on a microwave-safe

plate and microwave 2 to 3 minutes, uncovered, on high, to begin defrosting. Meanwhile, make the Stir-Fry Sauce and set aside.

3. Heat the oil in an extra-deep 12-inch nonstick skillet over medium heat. Peel and coarsely chop the onion, adding it to the skillet as you chop. Stir from time to time. While the onion cooks, slice the chicken (fresh or partially defrosted) into strips about ¼ inch wide. As you finish each breast, add the slices to the skillet. Raise the heat to medium-high and stir occasionally.

4. While the chicken cooks, add the carrots and mushrooms and stir to mix. Drain the sprouts, rinse them under cold water, and drain again.

5. Stir-fry the mixture until the chicken is no longer pink. Immediately add the sprouts, Stir-Fry Sauce, and noodles. Raise the heat to high and cook until the noodles and chicken are heated through and coated with sauce, 2 to 3 minutes, stirring constantly. Serve, garnished with peanut halves (if using).

Serves 4

> ☀ *Chinese lo mein noodles are available in Asian markets and in some large supermarkets but regular linguine pasta, cooked until barely tender, works just fine.*

STIR-FRY SAUCE

3 tablespoons reduced-sodium soy sauce
2 tablespoons oyster sauce
1 tablespoon bottled minced garlic
1 tablespoon rice wine vinegar or distilled white vinegar
1 tablespoon ketchup
2 teaspoons bottled chopped ginger
1 teaspoon dark sesame oil

Whisk all of the ingredients together in a 1-quart bowl.

Makes ½ cup

This sauce would also be good for stir-frying a mélange of fresh vegetables.

From Alicia:

My husband loves mu-shu and orders it nearly every time we visit our favorite Chinese restaurant. I'd never tried to fix it at home because the thought of shredding and chopping all those vegetables made me shudder. One day, though, when I was mixing my favorite Desperation coleslaw, I got a brain flash. Since already-shredded cabbage and broccoli slaw mixes have taken an hour out of making a huge bowl of slaw, I figured they could speed me through mu-shu, too.

My husband loved the result so much, he asks for it regularly. Now the recipe has become a family favorite, and I turn to it again and again.

MINDLESS MU-SHU

2 skinless, boneless chicken breast halves
(about ⅔ pound total), fresh or frozen
1 tablespoon peanut or other vegetable oil
1 to 2 bunches scallions (green onions; for ¾ cup chopped)
1 package (8 ounces) cabbage coleslaw mix
½ cup already-sliced fresh mushrooms
¼ cup dry sherry or fruity white or blush wine
2 teaspoons cornstarch
¼ cup reduced-sodium soy sauce
½ teaspoon bottled minced garlic
1 package (8 ounces) broccoli coleslaw mix
(see Box, facing page)
1 cup already-shredded carrots (optional)
1 tablespoon dark sesame oil
8 small (8-inch) flour tortillas
4 to 8 teaspoons hoisin sauce or plum sauce to taste

1. If the chicken is frozen, run hot water over it so you can remove any packaging. Place the chicken on a microwave-safe plate and microwave 2 minutes, uncovered, on high, to begin defrosting.

2. Meanwhile, heat the peanut oil in a 12-inch nonstick skillet over medium heat. Slice the scallions, using all of the whites and enough of the tender green tops to make about ¾ cup. Immediately add them to the skillet, along with the shredded cabbage mix and mushrooms. Raise the heat to high and cook to soften the vegetables, stirring occasionally.

3. Meanwhile, cut the chicken (fresh or partially defrosted) into ¼-inch-wide strips, adding them to the skillet as you slice. Combine the sherry and the cornstarch in a small container that has a

lid and shake well until the lumps disappear. Add the mixture to the skillet along with the soy sauce and garlic. Stir well. Add the broccoli slaw and carrots (if using) and stir. Continue to cook, stirring frequently, until the chicken is no longer pink, 5 to 7 minutes. Toward the end of cooking, add the sesame oil and stir well.

4. Just before serving, put the tortillas on a microwave-safe plate, cover with wax paper, and microwave on high for 1½ minutes to warm through. To serve, spread hoisin sauce to taste on each tortilla (½ to 1 teaspoon), then top with ½ cup of the filling. Roll up, burrito style (one end tucked in), and serve at once.

Serves 4 generously

> ✺ *Broccoli slaw is made from shredded raw broccoli stalks and is sold in plastic bags in the supermarket produce section.*

A word about:
OUR MU-SHU

There are just a few things you should know about our mu-shu recipe, beginning with why we call for tortillas. Special mu-shu pancakes are available in Asian markets, but the small flour tortillas found in the dairy case at most grocery stores make a fine substitute. Also, we've noticed that hoisin sauces from the grocery store are sometimes stronger than the ones served in most restaurants, so beware. If you can't find hoisin sauce, substitute plum sauce.

Finally, authentic Chinese mu-shu dishes contain eggs for symbolic reasons. The yellow color is reminiscent of yellow cassia blossoms, and in Chinese that's what the word *mu-shu* means. Since most people are more worried about cholesterol these days than symbolism, we decided to leave the eggs out. They don't really contribute to the flavor, and adding them just makes more work.

From Alicia:

Really just a simple stir-fry, this fabulous recipe has the depth of some of the most difficult and exotic Thai recipes I've tasted. For several years, I've enjoyed marinating my chicken for kebabs and then serving them with a peanut "dip," a combination known as *satay* to lovers of Thai food.

After my children were born, what was once one of my standby recipes got banished to the few weekends when I had hours to marinate, and peel and mince fresh ginger. Then our friend Julie Realon shared this recipe. It blew us away. The secret is bottled chopped ginger, found in the supermarket produce section, which gives a remarkably bright taste without all the peeling.

The chicken is thinly sliced and sautéed in a robust sauce, then a spicy peanut sauce is added near the end of cooking for a taste of Thailand in just 20 minutes.

TEMPTING THAI CHICKEN

2½ cups "instant" (5-minute) rice
4 skinless, boneless chicken breast halves (about 1⅓ pounds),
  fresh or frozen
Spicy Peanut Sauce (recipe follows)
2 teaspoons vegetable oil
1 tablespoon bottled minced garlic
1 tablespoon bottled chopped ginger
1 to 2 bunches scallions (green onions; for ¾ cup chopped)
1 can (8 ounces) sliced bamboo shoots
⅓ cup unsalted peanuts
1 tablespoon reduced-sodium soy sauce
1 tablespoon dry sherry
1 teaspoon sugar

1. Bring 2½ cups water to a boil in a 2-quart saucepan. Meanwhile, begin step 2. When the water boils, add the rice, cover the pan, and remove from the heat until ready to serve.

2. If the chicken is frozen, run it under hot water so you can remove any packaging. Place the chicken on a microwave-safe plate and microwave 2 minutes, uncovered, on high, to begin defrosting. Meanwhile, make the Peanut Sauce and set aside.

3. Heat the oil in a 12-inch nonstick skillet over high heat. Cut the chicken into short strips about ½ inch wide, adding them to the skillet as you cut. Add the garlic and ginger and cook until the chicken is no longer pink, 5 to 7 minutes, stirring frequently.

4. While the chicken cooks, cut the scallions into ¼-inch slices, using the white and enough of the tender green tops to make ¾ cup; drain the bamboo shoots, and chop the peanuts. Set each aside.

5. When the chicken is no longer pink, add the scallions, bamboo shoots, peanuts, soy sauce, sherry, and sugar. Stir well, then add the Peanut Sauce and stir well again. Cook until heated through, 2 minutes. Serve over a bed of the rice.

Serves 4

SPICY PEANUT SAUCE

1½ tablespoons creamy peanut butter
2 tablespoons vegetable oil
2 tablespoons reduced-sodium soy sauce
2 tablespoons sugar
2 teaspoons rice wine vinegar or distilled white vinegar
½ teaspoon dark sesame oil
⅛ teaspoon ground cayenne pepper (see Box)

Combine all the ingredients in a small bowl and whisk until well combined.

Makes about ½ cup

This peanut sauce would also make a good dipping sauce for grilled chicken or pork.

✳ *Control the level of spicy heat in the Spicy Peanut Sauce by adding or deleting the ground cayenne pepper. For those who really like it hot, throw in some crushed hot red pepper to taste.*

From Alicia:

Back when the Cajun food craze was sweeping the nation, I got caught up in the frenzy. Cajun cooking is really just regional country cooking. Since I was raised on country cooking, I figured I could handle it. I soon found myself dedicating hours to reading cookbooks and experimenting with different recipes.

One of my first attempts was a two-hour jambalaya. It drew raves from the whole family. Problem was, I knew I'd never find two hours to make it again. I headed back to the drawing board to apply some Desperation cooking techniques. Voilà! By substituting some convenient items such as canned beans, bottled garlic, and fast-cooking rice, we can now enjoy a robust jambalaya in just 20 minutes.

> ✻ *Small shrimp that come bagged and frozen are sometimes called "salad shrimp." They are always peeled and usually cooked. If you find them raw, it won't throw off the timing in this recipe.*

FLEXIBLE JAMBALAYA

1 teaspoon vegetable oil or margarine
1 medium onion (for ¾ cup chopped)
8 ounces turkey kielbasa sausage
1 teaspoon bottled minced garlic
1¾ cups "instant" (5-minute) rice
1 can (14½ ounces) fat-free chicken broth
¼ cup white wine
½ teaspoon onion powder
½ teaspoon dried oregano
½ teaspoon dried thyme
½ teaspoon black pepper
Ground cayenne pepper or Tabasco sauce to taste (optional)
1 can (15 ounces) white beans, such as Great Northern
1 can (15 ounces) black beans
1 can (14½ ounces) stewed tomatoes
½ cup frozen small shrimp (see Box)

1. Heat the oil over medium heat in a 12-inch nonstick skillet that has a lid. Peel and coarsely chop the onion, adding it to the skillet as you chop. Cut the sausage into ¼-inch-thick slices, adding them to the skillet as you slice.

2. Increase the heat to medium-high, add the garlic, and cook for 2 minutes, stirring from time to time. Add the rice, chicken broth, and wine. Bring to a boil, then reduce the heat to medium, cover the pan, and cook 5 minutes.

3. Meanwhile, combine the onion powder, oregano, thyme, black pepper, and cayenne pepper (if using) in a small bowl or cup. Drain and rinse both of the beans.

4. Add the spice mixture to the skillet and stir. Stir in the beans, stewed tomatoes, and shrimp.

5. Cover the skillet, reduce the heat to medium-low, and cook, stirring occasionally, until the rice has absorbed most of the liquid, the shrimp have heated through, and the flavors have blended, 8 to 10 minutes. Remove from the heat and serve.

Serves 6

WILD TURKEY SKILLET ★★ ☺

2 packages (4 to 6 ounces each) quick-cooking wild rice blend
1 cup frozen green peas
12 ounces leftover cooked turkey or chicken
(for about 3 cups chopped)
1 can (10¾ ounces) reduced-fat cream of mushroom soup
½ cup reduced-fat sour cream
1 teaspoon Worcestershire sauce
½ cup already finely shredded sharp Cheddar cheese

1. Pour the required water, rice, and any seasonings into an extra-deep, 12-inch nonstick skillet that has a lid. Bring the mixture to a boil over high heat and cook according to package directions, about 10 minutes. Add the peas to the skillet in the last 2 minutes of cooking.

2. Meanwhile, chop the turkey into bite-size pieces and set aside. When the rice has cooked, reduce the heat to low, and add the turkey, soup, sour cream, and Worcestershire to the skillet. Stir well to moisten the rice with the soup and sour cream.

3. Evenly distribute the rice in the pan, and sprinkle the cheese on top. Cover the pan and simmer until the cheese melts and the casserole bubbles around the edges, about 5 minutes. Serve at once.

Serves 4

From Beverly:

When I'm not in a hurry, I'll roast a turkey breast to have on hand for the weekend. On Friday night, we'll have it sliced with rice and gravy and a steamed vegetable. There's always plenty left for sandwiches at Saturday lunch and then some. It's the "then some" part that gives me trouble. I don't want to waste good meat, but I also don't want to bore my family. That's where this recipe comes in handy. It's a quick way to use leftover turkey that's definitely not boring.

Any quick-cooking wild rice blend will do. Just use the amount of water specified in the package instructions. If you should want to use a boil-in-the-bag rice, use 3 cups of water for the skillet, pour the rice out and discard the bag.

In New Orleans restaurants this dish comes with a bib. You're expected to peel your own shrimp, heads and all, and keep the sauce from dripping down your elbows as best you can. Our version isn't quite so messy. If your shrimp come with the tail portion of the shrimp peel intact, it would be perfectly proper to leave it attached, but if sauce on the fingers isn't appealing, go ahead and remove the tails before cooking. Buying the largest shrimp you can find makes the job easier.

❊ We tested this recipe using Heinz bottled chili sauce, which is found in the supermarket near the ketchup.

If you can't find already-peeled raw shrimp, substitute already-cooked peeled shrimp. Add cooked shrimp in step 3, but cook only until heated through, 1 minute.

BARBECUED SHRIMP ON SPICY RICE

Spicy Rice (recipe follows)
1 tablespoon olive oil
1 tablespoon butter
1½ teaspoons bottled minced garlic
1 cup fat-free chicken broth remaining from
   the Spicy Rice recipe
½ cup bottled chili sauce (see Box)
1 teaspoon Cajun seafood seasoning blend
   (see Box, facing page)
1 teaspoon Worcestershire sauce
½ teaspoon dried thyme
Tabasco sauce to taste (optional)
1 pound (16 to 20) already-peeled large raw shrimp
   (see Box)

1. Make the Spicy Rice.

2. Heat the oil and butter in a 12-inch nonstick skillet over medium heat. Add the garlic and cook 30 seconds. Add the chicken broth and raise the heat to high. Add the chili sauce, Cajun seasoning, Worcestershire, thyme, and Tabasco sauce (if using). Boil for 1 minute, stirring well to blend.

3. Add the shrimp and cook until they just turn pink, about 3 minutes, stirring frequently. Remove from the heat and serve over a bed of the rice.

Serves 4

SPICY RICE

1 tablespoon butter
1 medium onion (for ¾ cup chopped)
1 medium green bell pepper (for 1 cup chopped)
2 cans (14½ ounces) fat-free chicken broth
1 teaspoon Cajun seafood seasoning blend
2½ cups "instant" (5-minute) rice

1. Melt the butter in a 2-quart saucepan over medium heat. Peel and coarsely chop the onion, adding it to the pan as you chop. Seed and coarsely chop the bell pepper, adding it to the pan as you chop. Cook for 1 minute to soften the vegetables slightly, stirring occasionally.

2. Measure out 1 cup of the broth and set aside for use in the shrimp recipe or for another use. Add the remaining 2½ cups broth and Cajun seasoning to the onions and peppers. Raise the heat to high, cover the pan, and bring the broth to a boil.

3. When the broth boils, uncover the pan and stir in the rice, then re-cover and remove the pan from the heat. Set aside until ready to use.

Serves 4

This is especially nice with Barbecued Shrimp, but it also makes a good all-purpose pilaf.

※ *There are lots of Cajun spice blends on the market, and although any of them can be used in this recipe and the others in the book that call for the product, we've had good results with Paul Prudhomme's brand, Seafood Magic.*

From Beverly:

This colorful dish, as pleasing to the eye as it is to the palate, is one of my husband's favorite meals. It's reminiscent of a stir-fry, and the wine finish makes more of an au jus, or collection of pan juices, than it does a sauce. The result is a light meal bursting with flavor.

✱ *For variety, serve this dish atop orzo, pasta that looks like rice. Use 1½ cups uncooked orzo in step 1 and proceed with the recipe.*

ITALIAN SHRIMP AND VEGETABLES

2½ cups "instant" (5-minute) rice
2 teaspoons olive oil
20 already-peeled baby carrots (for 1 cup sliced)
1 medium onion (for ¾ cup sliced)
½ cup already-sliced fresh mushrooms
1 medium red or green bell pepper (for 1 cup strips)
2 cloves garlic
½ cup white wine
2 teaspoons balsamic vinegar
1 teaspoon Worcestershire sauce
1 teaspoon dried Italian seasoning
1 pound already-peeled medium raw shrimp
Salt and black pepper to taste

1. Bring 2½ cups water to a boil in a 2-quart saucepan. Meanwhile, begin step 2. When the water boils, add the rice, cover the pan, and remove from the heat until ready to serve.

2. Heat the oil in a 12-inch nonstick skillet over medium heat. Slice the carrots into ⅛-inch circles and add them to the skillet. Cook, stirring occasionally to prevent browning, as you prepare and add the remaining vegetables. Peel the onion and slice it into somewhat large pieces by cutting it into lengthwise quarters and then slicing through the quarters at ½-inch intervals. Add the onion to the skillet and stir, then immediately add the mushrooms and stir.

3. Seed the bell pepper and slice it into ¼-inch strips. Add them to the skillet and stir. Peel and chop the garlic and add it to the skillet, along with the wine, vinegar, Worcestershire, and Italian seasoning. Raise the heat to medium-high and stir well.

4. Immediately add the shrimp and cook, stirring constantly, until the shrimp just turn pink, about 3 minutes. Do not over-cook.

5. Season with salt and black pepper. Serve over a bed of the rice, spooning some pan juices over each serving.

Serves 4

AUNT FLO'S SHRIMP CREOLE

2½ cups "instant" (5-minute) rice
1 tablespoon olive oil
2 medium onions (for 1½ cups chopped)
1 medium green or red bell pepper (for 1 cup chopped)
1 medium rib celery (for ½ cup chopped)
1 tablespoon Worcestershire sauce
2 teaspoons bottled minced garlic
1 teaspoon Cajun or Creole seasoning blend
1 bay leaf
½ teaspoon dried thyme
¼ teaspoon Tabasco sauce
1 can (14½ ounces) diced tomatoes
1 small can (8 ounces) tomato sauce
1 Knorr fish-flavored bouillon cube (see Box, page 96)
Black pepper to taste
1 pound already-peeled medium raw shrimp

1. Bring 2½ cups water to a boil in a 2-quart saucepan. Meanwhile, begin step 2. When the water boils, add the rice, cover the pan, and remove from the heat until ready to serve.

Traditional shrimp Creole recipes call for making the sauce a day ahead with fresh tomatoes. By substituting convenient canned tomatoes, you can whip up a surprisingly robust sauce in just 20 minutes.

Our thanks to Florence Ann Strickland for the inspiration for this recipe. "I always try to keep Creole sauce, without the shrimp, in the freezer to have on hand when guests come," Beverly's Aunt Flo says. "For a quick seafood dinner, just cook the rice, add the shrimp to the thawed sauce, and make a green salad. Bingo, you have a great meal with little time spent in the kitchen."

2. Heat the olive oil in a 12-inch nonstick skillet over medium heat. Peel and coarsely chop the onion, adding it to the skillet as you chop. Seed and coarsely chop the bell pepper and add it, stirring, to the skillet. Chop the celery into bite-size pieces and add it to the pan, then raise the heat to medium-high.

3. Stir the vegetables well, then add the Worcestershire, garlic, Cajun seasoning, bay leaf, thyme, and Tabasco sauce, and stir well again. Reduce the heat to medium and add the tomatoes with their juice and the tomato sauce. Cut off one half of the fish bouillon cube and crumble it into the skillet, then season with black pepper. Simmer the sauce for 2 minutes, stirring from time to time.

4. Add the shrimp, raise the heat to medium-high, and cook just until the shrimp turn pink, 2½ to 3 minutes, stirring frequently. Serve at once over a bed of the rice.

Serves 4

From Alicia:

Who would think that seafood marries so well with cabbage? Not me. I couldn't believe it when I saw this dish described on the menu of a popular French restaurant in Raleigh. What pulls it all together is the classic butter sauce. The restaurant version was made in stages and required three pans. We've simplified the method so it requires just one skillet.

FRENCH SCALLOP SAUTÉ

2 tablespoons olive oil
2 packages (8 ounces each) cabbage coleslaw mix
2 cups already-shredded carrots
1 small onion (for ½ cup diced)
¼ teaspoon salt
¼ teaspoon black pepper
4 tablespoons (½ stick) butter
¼ cup white wine
1½ pounds bay scallops (see Box)
2 tablespoons half-and-half

1. Heat the oil in an extra-deep 12-inch nonstick skillet over medium heat. Add the slaw mix and carrots. Raise the heat to high and cook, stirring frequently, until the cabbage is tender but not browned, about 5 minutes. Meanwhile, finely dice the onion and set it aside.

2. When the cabbage is tender, remove the skillet from the heat. Season the vegetables with the salt and pepper, and pour onto a serving platter. Set aside, covered with aluminum foil.

3. Wipe the skillet clean with several layers of paper towels. (Watch out, it'll be hot!) Add the butter and diced onion and cook over medium heat until the butter melts, stirring frequently. Cook to soften the onion, 1 minute more. Add the wine, raise the heat to high, and boil the mixture for 2 minutes to evaporate the alcohol and reduce the liquid slightly.

4. Add the scallops and cook until they are just opaque, about 2 minutes, stirring frequently. Uncover the platter with the vegetables; using a slotted spoon, remove the scallops from the skillet and arrange them over the vegetables. Cover the platter again with the foil.

5. Continue to boil the liquid in the skillet to reduce it slightly, about 2 minutes. Reduce the heat to low, add the half-and-half, and rotate the skillet in a circular motion to mix it in. Cook 1 minute more to heat through.

6. Pour the sauce over the scallops and vegetables and serve.

Serves 4

> ✳ *We like to use small bay scallops rather than the larger sea scallops for this dish. Only about ½ inch in diameter, they cook quickly and their small size ensures scallops in each mouthful.*

SALSA BEANS AND RICE

2½ cups "instant" (5-minute) rice
1 teaspoon olive oil
1 large onion (for 1 cup chopped)
1 can (15½ ounces) red beans
1 can (15½ ounces) white beans
1 can (2¼ ounces) pitted sliced black olives (optional)
1 can (15 ounces) black beans
2 cans (14½ ounces each) salsa-style diced tomatoes (see Box)
1 cup frozen corn kernels
1 teaspoon chili powder
1 teaspoon ground cumin
1 teaspoon garlic powder
¾ cup already-shredded Cheddar or Monterey Jack cheese

Red, white, black, and yellow—this rainbow of ingredients carries the vegetarian staple of beans and rice to a whole new spectrum. The flexibility of this dish makes it one of our favorites. If you have a little more time, you can bake it in a 350°F oven, and without the rice it becomes a hearty side dish. Use any variety of beans or Mexican-friendly cheese you like.

❋ *If salsa-style toma-toes are not available, substitute 1 jar (16 ounces) salsa and 1 can (14½ ounces) diced tomatoes, drained.*

1. Bring 2½ cups water to a boil in a 2-quart saucepan. Meanwhile, begin step 2. When the water boils, add the rice, cover the pan, and remove from the heat until ready to serve.

2. Heat the oil over medium heat in an extra-deep nonstick 12-inch skillet that has a lid. Peel and coarsely chop the onion, adding it to the skillet as you chop. Let cook while you drain the red and white beans and the olives (if using).

3. Raise the heat to high and add the drained beans and olives, the black beans with their liquid, tomatoes, corn, chili powder, cumin, and garlic powder. Stir well to mix. Cover the skillet and bring to a boil. Lower the heat to medium, uncover, and cook for 3 to 4 minutes more. Stir occasionally.

4. Lower the heat to a simmer and sprinkle the cheese over the bean mixture. Cover and cook until the cheese melts, 2 to 3 minutes. Serve the beans over a bed of the rice.

Serves 6

BLUE RUNNERS AND RICE

2 teaspoons olive oil

1 large onion (for 1 cup chopped)

2 medium ribs celery (for 1 cup chopped)

½ large red or green bell pepper (for ¾ cup chopped)

2 teaspoons bottled minced garlic

½ teaspoon dried thyme

½ teaspoon dried basil

½ teaspoon dried oregano

½ teaspoon black pepper

½ teaspoon Tabasco sauce, or more to taste (optional)

2 bay leaves

1 can (14½ ounces) fat-free chicken broth

1 pound turkey kielbasa sausage

1 can (15½ ounces) red kidney beans

1¾ cups "instant" (5-minute) rice

½ cup water, if needed

1. Heat the oil over medium heat in a 12-inch nonstick skillet that has a lid. Peel and coarsely chop the onion, adding it to the skillet as you chop. Chop the celery and bell pepper, adding them to the skillet. Cook the vegetables until crisp-tender, about 4 minutes, stirring frequently. Stir in the garlic, thyme, basil, oregano, black pepper, Tabasco (if using), and bay leaves.

2. Raise the heat to high, add the broth, cover the skillet, and bring the broth to a boil. Meanwhile, cut the sausage into slices about ¼ to ½ inch thick and set aside. Rinse and drain the beans.

3. When the broth boils, stir in the sausage, beans, and rice. Reduce the heat to medium-low, cover the pan, and cook until the rice is tender, 5 to 10 minutes. (If the broth disappears before the rice is tender, add ½ cup water.) Serve.

Serves 6

From Beverly:

A friend of mine who grew up in New Orleans loves to tell the story of his next-door neighbor and her summer version of red beans and rice. In winter, this staunch grand dame of "Old New Orleans" society would spend half a day soaking and simmering to make red beans in the traditional manner. But in hot weather, when the family moved to its more casual summer home on the shore, all formality gave way. From time to time, the matriarch would declare it a day for "Blue Runner beans."

"It took me years to figure out what Blue Runner beans were," my friend says. "Finally I asked, and it seems Blue Runner was the brand name of the canned beans the family preferred. It turns out nobody in the family could tell the difference between canned Blue Runner beans and the kind that took three hours to make. Right then I decided that if canned red beans are good enough for old Old New Orleans, they're good enough for me."

Here's the version of red beans and rice made with the help of a can.

CHAPTER FOUR

Salad

Go ahead. Serve salad for dinner. It's easy, and not a soul at the table need feel deprived. Main-dish salads can be as hearty or as light as you want them to be. Sometimes we like to stuff our salads with pastas and meats, but we always pay penance with low-fat dressings. Turkey Salad with Grapes and Pecans or Ham-Cheese Pasta Salad can bring new life to leftover meats. Let our Anti-Stress Antipasto rescue you from a steamy kitchen some muggy night. Easy Chef Salad might even spur you on to clean out the vegetable bin.

But we don't need an excuse to eat salad, and neither should you. Salad, in its many and varied forms, is one of our favorite meals. Some salads provide a lighter alternative and some, like Warm Potato Salad Dijon with Ham, are hearty and comforting.

To put together a Desperation salad, you need to know some useful tricks, and we've discovered a few of them. Bags of already-washed, mixed salad greens from the supermarket produce department will cut your preparation time by at least 5 minutes. For best flavor, be sure to buy a brand that does not add preservatives (for more information, see Box, page 109).

To serve a cold pasta salad on a moment's notice, cook the pasta until barely done, then rinse it in a colander for several minutes under cold running tap water until it cools. You can throw in

entrées

a couple of ice cubes to speed cooling. Then drain and shake the colander to get rid of as much water as possible, removing any unmelted ice cubes.

Especially in warmer months, we use our refrigerator as part pantry. Switching a few cans from your cupboard to the bottom shelf of your fridge will provide several other cool salad possibilities for dinner on those sweltering summer nights. Details are described on page 119.

Salads are not just for those of us on the latest diet. Main-dish salads are filling, delicious, and unbelievably fast.

"We both love big platters of salad brimming with meats, lettuce, and vegetables."

Traditional recipes for this salad call for grilled marinated steak, but using rare deli roast beef means you can prepare an exotic meal without having to cook a thing. The fresh herbs are a particularly refreshing addition if you happen to have them on hand. Be sure to choose a lettuce blend that does not contain preservatives, or substitute a large head of romaine lettuce.

The inspiration for this recipe comes from our friends Scott and Kathryn Higham of Baltimore.

THAI BEEF SALAD WITH RED-HOT DRESSING

Red-Hot Dressing (recipe follows)
1 pound thinly sliced rare deli roast beef
2 bags (10 ounces each; 7 cups) European-blend salad mix
  (see Note)
3 small Kirby (pickling) cucumbers (for 1¼ cups sliced)
¼ cup fresh mint leaves, tightly packed (optional)
¼ cup fresh cilantro leaves, tightly packed (optional)

1. Make the Red-Hot Dressing. It'll take you about 5 minutes.

2. Slice the beef into ½-inch-wide strips and place in a 1-quart or larger bowl. Pour ½ cup of the dressing over the beef and stir until the beef absorbs most of the dressing. Reserve the remaining dressing.

3. If the lettuce is not prewashed, rinse it, drain, and spin or pat dry. Place the lettuce in a 3-quart or larger serving bowl. Slice the cucumbers. Add them to the bowl. Chop the mint and cilantro (if using) and add to the bowl.

4. Add the marinated beef to the bowl. Pour the remaining dressing over, toss well to mix, and serve.

Serves 4

Note: European-blend includes romaine, escarole, endive, and radicchio, but any mixed salad greens, or a large head of romaine alone, will do.

RED-HOT DRESSING

1 lemon

1 lime

6 cloves garlic

2 tablespoons Thai-style fish sauce (nam pla)

2 tablespoons reduced-sodium soy sauce

2 tablespoons Worcestershire sauce

4 teaspoons sugar

2 teaspoons Dijon mustard

1 teaspoon crushed hot red pepper, or to taste

2 tablespoons peanut or vegetable oil

1. Halve the lemon and lime and squeeze the juice into a 1-quart or larger bowl. Peel the garlic and squeeze it through a garlic press into the bowl. Add the remaining ingredients except the peanut oil and whisk until well combined.

2. Add the oil slowly in a thin stream, whisking constantly until it is thoroughly blended in. Use right away or refrigerate until ready to eat.

Makes 1 cup

Our favorite Thai recipes are those that combine sour and sweet with a lot of fire. Devotees of authentic Thai food wouldn't be without a bottle of *nam pla,* the salty fish sauce that can be found in Asian groceries or the Asian food sections of many large supermarkets. The brand A Taste of Thai calls it "seasoning sauce," while the Kame brand labels it "fish sauce." No matter the name, this typical Thai condiment provides a subtle, yet distinct depth to the dressing.

ANTI-STRESS ANTIPASTO

1 package (10 ounces; 3½ cups) Italian-style lettuce mix
4 slices hard salami
4 slices mozzarella cheese
1 small can (7¾ ounces) chickpeas
1 small can (3¼ ounces) pitted black olives
1 large cucumber (for 1 cup sliced)
4 ripe Roma (plum) tomatoes
8 small pepperoncini
Lemon-Balsamic Vinaigrette (recipe follows)

In Italy, the term *antipasto* refers to food eaten as a first course, whether hot or cold. But in the United States, antipasto often means a large composed salad with multiple ingredients as found on most old-fashioned Italian menus. We both love big platters of salad brimming with meats, lettuce, and vegetables. Alicia calls it "grazing food." By the time we finish them, neither of us can think of eating anything more. So we just go ahead and call it dinner. Serve your salad platter with our Italian Herb Breadsticks (see Index) or with assorted crackers. And, if you don't have a large platter, compose the salad on individual dinner plates.

The ingredients included are our favorites, but feel free to substitute any meats, vegetables, or Italian pantry staples you have on hand. Each diner should add salt and pepper to taste at the table.

1. If the lettuce is not prewashed, rinse it, drain, and spin or pat dry. Place the greens on a 14-inch-wide or larger serving platter.

2. Stack the salami slices on top of each other and cut each of them into quarters. Scatter the wedges evenly over the greens. Using the same method, cut the cheese into bite-size squares and scatter them evenly over the plate.

3. Rinse and drain the chickpeas; drain the olives. Scatter both over the salad. Peel and thinly slice the cucumber and arrange them over the platter. Cut each tomato into quarters and space them evenly around the outer edge of the plate. Place the pepperoncini at even intervals.

4. Make the Lemon-Balsamic Vinaigrette, and drizzle it evenly over the plate. Serve at once.

Serves 4

LEMON-BALSAMIC VINAIGRETTE

1 lemon
2 tablespoons balsamic vinegar
½ teaspoon dried oregano
1 clove garlic
½ cup extra-virgin olive oil

1. Cut the lemon in half and squeeze the juice into a nonreactive 2-cup or larger bowl. Add the vinegar and oregano. Peel the garlic and squeeze it through a garlic press into the bowl. Whisk until well combined.

2. Add the olive oil slowly in a thin stream, whisking constantly until it is thoroughly blended in and the mixture is thickened. Use right away or refrigerate, covered, up to 1 week.

Makes about ¾ cup

This tart dressing is especially well suited to our antipasto, but it would also complement any Italian-style salad.

Here's a salad that's rich, hearty, and served slightly warm. The tricky part of this recipe is getting the water on to boil. As soon as you feel the urge for dinner, throw a quart of water into a Dutch oven and crank up the heat. With hot water to the rescue, the rest of this salad is a snap.

❋ *If your kids won't touch beets, just leave them out and add them to the adults' plates later.*

WARM POTATO SALAD DIJON WITH HAM

1 pound small red potatoes
8 ounces fresh green beans
Half 10-ounce package prewashed fresh spinach
1 can (15 ounces) quartered beet wedges (see Box)
2 slices (about 4 ounces each and ¼ inch thick) deli ham,
    such as baked Virginia ham
Creamy Dijon Dressing (recipe follows)

1. Scrub the potatoes (leave the skins on) and cut them into quarters. Drop them into 1 quart of already-boiling water and boil, covered, for 7 minutes over high heat.

2. Meanwhile, rinse the green beans, trim off the tough ends, and set aside. If the spinach is still gritty, rinse it, drain, and spin or pat dry. Pull off any tough stems, tear it into bite-size pieces, and place on a large serving platter or in a large salad bowl. Drain the beets and scatter them over the spinach. Set aside.

3. As soon as the potatoes have boiled 7 minutes, add the green beans to the pot. Continue to boil, covered, until the beans and potatoes are tender, 4 minutes. Meanwhile, cut the ham into long strips about ¼ inch wide and scatter them over the spinach and beets. Begin to make the Creamy Dijon Dressing.

4. Pour the beans and potatoes into a colander and allow cold water to run over them for about 2 minutes to cool. Let them drain while finishing the salad dressing. Scatter the potatoes evenly over the greens and arrange the green beans on top in a spiral pattern. Drizzle the dressing evenly over the salad and serve.

Serves 4

CREAMY DIJON DRESSING

1 clove garlic
½ cup extra-virgin olive oil
1 tablespoon red wine vinegar
¼ teaspoon salt
¼ teaspoon black pepper
1 tablespoon Dijon mustard
1 tablespoon reduced-fat mayonnaise

Peel the garlic and chop well by dropping it through the feed tube of a blender or food processor with the motor running. Add the olive oil slowly in a thin stream. With the motor still running, add the remaining ingredients and process for about 15 seconds until thoroughly blended. Use right away or refrigerate up to 2 weeks.

Makes about ½ cup

This dressing would be just as wonderful on an ordinary tossed salad. A touch of mayonnaise is the surprising ingredient. It tames the garlic and provides a wonderful silky texture. The dressing can also be prepared in a bowl with a wire whisk and a healthy measure of elbow grease.

From Beverly:

This was the first meal I ever prepared for a soon-to-be sister-in-law, and I knew, whether spelled out or not, that this was a test. I passed. "That was the best Caesar salad I ever ate," she later reported. Here's the recipe, guaranteed to impress the most discriminating in-laws (or anyone else).

> ✳ *If you don't have leftover grilled, sautéed, or roasted chicken breasts, leftover (or deli bought) turkey breast, grilled fish, or cooked shrimp make for a terrific Caesar salad.*

CHICKEN CAESAR SALAD

1 large head romaine lettuce (for 8 cups torn)
½ cup already finely shredded Parmesan cheese
1 cup Caesar-style croutons
2 leftover cooked skinless, boneless chicken breast halves
   (about ⅔ pound total; see Box)
Caesar Dressing (recipe follows)

1. Core the lettuce, then rinse it, drain, and spin or pat dry. Tear the leaves into bite-size pieces and place in a 3-quart or larger bowl. Sprinkle the cheese over the lettuce; then scatter the croutons on top of the cheese.

2. Slice each chicken breast lengthwise into 8 pieces. Set aside.

3. Make the dressing and pour over the salad, and toss well to coat. Divide the salad among 4 serving plates. Top each serving with 4 slices of chicken and serve.

Serves 4

From Beverly:

This dressing is adapted from a recipe given to me a dozen years ago by my then next door neighbor Joanne Vitelli. We've left out the traditional raw egg for health reasons, but the creaminess of the Dijon mustard means you don't really miss it.

CAESAR DRESSING

1 lemon
2 tablespoons red wine vinegar
2 tablespoons Dijon mustard
2 teaspoons anchovy paste, or to taste (see Box, facing page)
¼ teaspoon black pepper
1 clove garlic
½ cup extra-virgin olive oil

1. Cut the lemon in half and squeeze the juice of the lemon into a 2-cup or larger bowl. Add the vinegar, mustard, anchovy paste,

and pepper. Peel the garlic and squeeze it through a garlic press into the bowl. Whisk until well combined.

2. Add the olive oil slowly in a thin stream, whisking constantly until it is thoroughly blended in and the mixture is thickened. Use right away or refrigerate, covered, up to 3 days.

Makes about ¾ cup

> ✸ *If you have a tin of anchovy fillets on hand, you can substitute 1 finely minced fillet for the paste. But the paste is a great way to get the classic anchovy flavor without having to worry about leftovers from the tin.*

SALAD IN A BAG

Produce companies have made it easier for us to eat more salad. How? Knowing that we hate the time it takes to prepare one, they now market 10-ounce bags of grit-free greens of every sort, from baby spinach to combinations of romaine, red leaf, and radicchio. Several companies offer these blends, usually with fancy names like Italian or European mix. In our supermarket, one European mix includes romaine, escarole, endive, and radicchio, while the Italian mix is simply a toss of romaine and radicchio.

When we first encountered these bags of lettuce with price tags between $2 and $3, we thought, "No way. They're too expensive." It wasn't long before we were hooked on the speed and convenience. After a while, we realized the price is actually very economical. You're getting a mixture that would cost up to three times as much to put together yourself if you bought the individual, whole heads, and you don't have the waste of leftover lettuce wilting in your fridge.

In our recipes that call for bagged salad mix, we list our suggested favorite, but you can substitute any lettuce combination you happen to have on hand. The 10-ounce bags are plenty greens for four side salads.

We call for an already-prepared salad mix here, but you can use any combination of lettuces and greens that you happen to have on hand for this hearty main dish. We like to dress it up from time to time with a little of the fancy field-greens mix from the local health-food supermarket. When our friend Rane Winslow tested the recipe for us, she added fresh strawberries to it and said it was a hit with her family. The drumsticks and wings aren't needed for the salad, so save them to serve to the kids at another meal.

ROASTED CHICKEN ON GREENS

1 purchased roasted chicken (about 1¼ pounds)
Raspberry Vinaigrette (recipe follows)
2 bags (10 ounces each; 7 cups) Italian-blend salad mix
   (see Note)
4 tablespoons already-crumbled blue cheese

1. Remove the drumsticks and wings from the chicken and reserve for another use. Remove and discard the skin from the breast portion. Cut and pull the breast meat away from the bone in chunks, using a knife and your fingers. Repeat with the thigh portions. Cut the meat into bite-size chunks and set aside. (You should have about 2 cups.)

2. Make the Raspberry Vinaigrette. This should take you about 5 minutes.

3. If the salad greens are not prewashed, rinse them, drain, and spin or pat dry, then tear them into bite-size pieces. Pile 1½ cups greens in the center of each serving plate. Top with ½ cup of the reserved chicken and 1 tablespoon crumbled blue cheese. Drizzle 3 tablespoons vinaigrette, or to taste, over each salad and serve.

Serves 4

Note: Italian-blend mixes usually include romaine and radicchio greens, but any mixed salad greens, or 2 large heads of romaine alone, will do.

RASPBERRY VINAIGRETTE

3 tablespoons seedless all-fruit raspberry jam
⅓ cup red wine vinegar
¼ teaspoon salt
¼ teaspoon black pepper
1 cup vegetable oil

Put the jam into a 2-cup glass measure and microwave on high for 15 seconds or just until the jam melts. Add the vinegar, salt, and pepper and whisk until well combined. Add the oil slowly in a thin stream, whisking constantly until it is thoroughly blended in. Use right away or refrigerate until ready to eat.

Makes about 1½ cups

B e sure to choose a seedless jam for this slightly tart, fruity vinaigrette. It keeps well refrigerated for several weeks and is just as wonderful with plain tossed salad as it is with slightly fancier fare.

From Alicia:

If you've always thought chicken salad had to be cold, here's a recipe that will surprise you. Intended to be served warm or at room temperature, this autumn chicken salad offers a welcome twist on an old favorite. Beverly came up with this dish to take to a Labor Day picnic and ended up spending the better part of the meal scribbling down the recipe for neighbors who requested it. A week later, I carried it to a lunchtime gathering at my church, and the same thing happened to me.

While most dishes lose their impact as they cool to room temperature, this blend of chicken, walnuts, raisins and apples, with its hint of mango chutney and curry, just improves.

A FALL SALAD

4 skinless, boneless chicken breast halves (about 1⅓ pounds),
* fresh or frozen*
⅓ cup reduced-fat mayonnaise
2 tablespoons bottled mango chutney
½ teaspoon curry powder
Cooking oil spray
1 teaspoon bottled minced garlic
½ tart apple (for ½ cup chopped)
4 large lettuce leaves (optional)
⅓ cup raisins
¼ cup already-chopped walnuts

1. If the chicken is frozen, run hot water over it so you can remove any packaging. Place the chicken on a microwave-safe plate and microwave 3 minutes, uncovered, on high, to begin defrosting. Meanwhile, combine the mayonnaise, chutney, and curry powder in a 2-quart or larger bowl. Stir well to mix.

2. Lightly coat a 12-inch nonstick skillet with cooking oil spray and heat over medium heat. Cut the chicken breasts (fresh or partially defrosted) into bite-size chunks, adding them to the skillet as you slice.

3. When all the chicken is added, add the garlic and continue to cook, stirring occasionally, until the chicken is no longer pink, 6 to 10 minutes (do not overcook). While the chicken cooks, core the apple half and dice it into bite-size pieces, leaving the peel on. If using lettuce, rinse it, drain, and spin or pat dry and place a leaf on each serving plate. Remove the chicken from the heat.

4. Stir the apple, raisins, and walnuts into the mayonnaise mixture. Add the chicken and stir well to coat with sauce. Serve warm or at room temperature, spooned over the lettuce (if using).

Serves 4

TURKEY SALAD WITH GRAPES AND PECANS

4 large lettuce leaves
½ cup reduced-fat mayonnaise
2 tablespoons reduced-fat sour cream
1 tablespoon lemon juice from frozen concentrate
¼ teaspoon salt
⅛ teaspoon black pepper
4 cups refrigerated cooked turkey breast
½ pound seedless red or green grapes (for 1 cup halved)
3 scallions (green onions; for ¼ cup sliced)
½ cup chopped pecans

1. If the lettuce is not prewashed, rinse it, drain, and spin or pat dry. Place a lettuce leaf on each serving plate.

2. Combine the mayonnaise, sour cream, lemon juice, salt, and pepper in a 2½-quart or larger bowl, and whisk to blend well.

3. Cut the turkey into bite-size chunks and add to the bowl. Using a small serrated knife, cut the grapes in half and add them to the bowl. Cut the scallions into thin slices, including enough tender green tops to make ¼ cup, and add to the bowl. Stir gently but thoroughly to mix with the dressing.

4. Top each lettuce leaf with 1 cup of salad, garnish with 2 table-spoons pecans, and serve.

Serves 4

From Alicia:

This is a quick and especially easy way to use leftover turkey. But I've also cooked a 4-pound turkey breast with the sole purpose of making this salad later in the week.

A couple of tablespoons of chopped fresh basil leaves make a nice addition if you have any on hand. With leftover turkey breast, this salad goes together in less than 15 minutes.

EASY CHEF SALAD

When the last little bits of everything start to pile up in your vegetable bin, it's time to make Easy Chef Salad.

This recipe includes the ingredients we commonly have on hand. Feel free to substitute any vegetables or anything else you find available. From apple slices to zucchini cubes, practically anything works in a chef salad. If you don't typically keep deli meats in the fridge, good pantry substitutes include canned tuna or chicken and tins of smoked oysters, mussels, or clams.

Finally, we like to spread the ingredients out on the counter and allow each person to custom-build a salad to taste. (Using paper plates or sheets of wax paper for this cuts down on cleanup.) Top the salad off with your favorite fat-free bottled dressing or whip up our herbed vinaigrette on page 309.

½ cup frozen green peas
3 bags (10 ounces each; 10½ cups) salad mix of choice
12 already-peeled baby carrots (for ⅔ cup sliced)
1 large rib celery (for ½ cup chopped)
1 medium bell pepper, any color (for 1 cup strips)
4 ounces deli-roasted turkey breast, or more to taste

Optional Toppings

¼ cup reduced-fat real bacon bits (not imitation)
½ cup already-shredded sharp Cheddar cheese
16 cherry tomatoes
1 can (11 ounces) mandarin oranges, drained

1 cup salad dressing of choice

1. Rinse the peas in a small colander or strainer to partially defrost and set aside to drain, then place in a small bowl. If the lettuce is not prewashed, rinse it, drain, and spin or pat dry.

2. As each of the following ingredients is prepared, place it on a paper plate or sheet of wax paper, or in a small bowl, and set aside. Slice the carrots into thin circles. Coarsely dice the celery. Seed the pepper and cut it into thin strips. Slice the turkey into long, thin strips.

3. Compose the salads: Place 2½ cups lettuce on each plate and top with the peas, carrots, celery, and pepper and turkey strips. Add the optional toppings as desired. Serve at once and pass the dressing.

Serves 4

SAILOR'S SALAD

4 large lettuce leaves
½ cup reduced-fat mayonnaise
1 tablespoon sweet pickle relish
1 teaspoon ketchup
¾ teaspoon seafood seasoning, such as Old Bay
1 package (8 ounces) flake-style imitation crabmeat
  (surimi; see Box)
3 large ribs celery (for 1½ cups coarsely chopped)
1 medium green or red bell pepper (for 1 cup coarsely chopped)
1 small onion (for ½ cup finely diced)

1. If the lettuce is not prewashed, rinse it, drain, and spin or pat dry. Place a lettuce leaf on each serving plate.

2. Combine the mayonnaise, relish, ketchup, and seafood seasoning in a 3-quart or larger serving bowl, and stir well to mix.

3. Coarsely chop the crabmeat and celery into bite-size pieces and add them to the bowl. Seed and chop the bell pepper into roughly ½-inch pieces and add it to the bowl, then peel and finely dice the onion and add it as well. Stir gently but thoroughly to mix with the dressing. Top each lettuce leaf with salad and serve.

Serves 4

From Beverly:

If you grew up along the coast as I did, imitation crabmeat is not the usual fare. When you want to make something with crab, you just bait a wire mesh trap with chicken necks, throw it off the end of the dock, and wait a couple of hours. A good friend from the Midwest introduced me to imitation crab, or surimi, as it is officially named. Made mostly from pollock, a firm, white-fleshed fish, the biggest advantage of surimi is, of course, the price, but I found I liked the flavor, too, so long as I didn't think of it as crab. I just call it surimi, which gives me a different set of expectations, and everything turns out fine.

❋ *The key to enjoying surimi is buying a good-quality brand. Surimi grew a couple of notches in our esteem when we discovered that it is very low in fat and cholesterol. It also keeps for weeks unopened in the refrigerator.*

This salad was inspired by a recipe for a hot shrimp and asparagus Mexican appetizer shared with us by a friend. The cool color combination of greens and pinks was so lovely, we decided to turn it into a salad for a Cinco de Mayo celebration. It's pretty enough for a party, yet simple enough for a mid-week evening meal, since it goes together in 15 minutes.

CINCO DE MAYO SALAD

1 pound fresh asparagus
Southwestern Harvest Dressing (recipe follows)
1 large head romaine lettuce (for 8 cups torn leaves)
Ice cubes
1 pound already-cooked-and-peeled shrimp
¼ cup already-shredded Colby-Jack cheese

1. Pour water to a depth of 1 inch into a 4½-quart Dutch oven or soup pot and bring it to a boil over high heat. Meanwhile, wash the asparagus and snap off the tough ends. When the water boils, add the asparagus and cook, uncovered, until just tender, 4 to 5 minutes.

2. Meanwhile, make the Southwestern Harvest Dressing and set aside.

3. Core the lettuce, then rinse it, drain, and spin or pat dry. Begin tearing the leaves into bite-size pieces, placing them in a 3-quart or larger bowl.

4. When the asparagus is done, drain it in a colander. Throw in a handful of ice cubes and allow cold water to run over the spears for about 2 minutes to cool. Meanwhile, finish tearing the lettuce.

5. To serve, pour half of the dressing over the lettuce and toss. Place 2 cups of the dressed greens on each serving plate. Use paper towels to dab any excess moisture from the asparagus, then top the greens with 4 to 6 spears per portion and a quarter of the shrimp. Sprinkle 1 tablespoon cheese over each serving and drizzle on additional dressing to taste.

Serves 4

SOUTHWESTERN HARVEST DRESSING

1 small onion
⅓ cup low-sodium vegetable juice, such as V-8
1 tablespoon vegetable oil
2 tablespoons red wine vinegar
¼ teaspoon ground cumin
¼ teaspoon chili powder
¼ teaspoon black pepper
¼ teaspoon sugar

1. Peel the onion. Using the finest side of a four-sided grater, grate enough onion to make 1 teaspoon with juice. Wrap and refrigerate the remaining onion for another use.

2. Combine the grated onion with the remaining ingredients in an 8-ounce or larger jar that has a lid. Cover and shake well to blend. Use right away or refrigerate up to 1 week.

Makes about ½ cup

Here's a south-of-the-border version of our Harvest Vinaigrette (see Index). You get the same low-calorie satisfaction with its own unique twist. Try it on your favorite tossed salad combination, as well as on spinach salad.

TUNA WITH RED BEANS AND AÏOLI

Making use of your already-cold assortment of staples in the refrigerator (see box, facing page for how-tos), this recipe can be ready to eat in 10 minutes. Aïoli is just a fancy French name for garlic-flavored mayonnaise that perfectly accents the simple combination of tuna and beans. Aïoli goes together in no time if you use your food processor, but you can finely mince the garlic by hand and then stir together the rest of the ingredients.

Spoon this salad over lettuce leaves, serve with marinated artichoke hearts on the side, and you've got a meal scrumptious enough even for company.

4 large lettuce leaves
4 cloves garlic
2 teaspoons olive oil
½ teaspoon dried tarragon (optional)
½ cup reduced-fat mayonnaise
1 can (15½ ounces) refrigerated red kidney beans
1 can (8 ounces) refrigerated sliced water chestnuts
1 large can (12 ounces) refrigerated white tuna packed in water
Black pepper to taste

1. If the lettuce is not prewashed, rinse it, drain, and spin or pat dry. Place a lettuce leaf on each serving plate.

2. Peel the garlic and drop it through the feed tube of a food processor, with motor running. Pour the olive oil and tarragon, (if using) through the feed tube and process to combine with the garlic. Turn off the motor, remove the lid, and add the mayonnaise. Scrape down the sides. Process until blended, 45 seconds. Scrape the mixture into a 2-quart or larger serving bowl, stirring to make sure all of the oil and garlic is incorporated.

3. Pour the kidney beans into a colander, rinse under cold running water, and drain thoroughly. Add to the bowl with the garlic mayonnaise. Drain the water chestnuts, then coarse chop the slices. Add to the bowl. Drain the tuna and add it as well. Flake the tuna with a fork, then stir well to mix with the other ingredients. Season with black pepper. Spoon the salad onto the lettuce and serve.

Serves 4

THE REFRIGERATOR PANTRY

We keep wishing for an appliance that'll zap food instantly cold—sort of a microwave for summertime. When the weather turns muggy, nobody feels like eating hot food. But if you need to put a meal on the table now, chilling time is a luxury you just don't have.

The obvious solution is to start with food that's already cold. To accomplish this, we recommend shifting a good portion of your pantry cans to the refrigerator for the summer months.

At the very least, your fridge pantry should contain several cans of your favorite salad toppers. We like to chill crushed pineapple, olives, tuna, water chestnuts, and jars of marinated artichoke hearts. We also include assorted beans for hearty main-dish salads, such as Tuna with Red Beans and Aïoli on the facing page. Good bean staples include red kidneys, black beans, cannellini, and chickpeas.

If you like quick cold soups, such as our Vite! Vite! Vichyssoise on page 22, keep a couple of cans of chicken broth in the refrigerator, too. For making chilled borscht in a flash, you'll also need a cold can of beets and a jar of sweet-and-sour red cabbage (Beat-the-Heat Borscht is on page 23).

With an already-cold assortment of staples, your spur-of-the-moment options for summer simply multiply.

"Especially in warmer months, we use our refrigerator as part pantry."

BLACK BEANS AND COUSCOUS SANTA FE STYLE

Our friend Pam Smith O'Hara first gave us the idea to combine couscous and black beans. The author of a vegetarian cooking column, Pam often takes a similar salad to cookouts. On several occasions, she reports, even the chief burger chef decided to forgo the beef and make a meal of black beans and couscous instead.

We use extra-sweet frozen corn in this recipe to add to the vibrant flavor. The corn should be just defrosted, not hard but still crunchy, before adding it to the salad. Although fresh herbs are optional, do use some for an extra zip, if you happen to have them on hand.

This makes a large amount, but leftovers will keep well in the refrigerator for several days.

1 package (10 ounces) quick-cooking couscous
6 lettuce leaves
1 large fresh lime or lemon
3 tablespoons extra-virgin olive oil
1 teaspoon red wine vinegar
½ teaspoon ground cumin
1 to 2 bunches scallions (green onions; for ¾ cup chopped)
1 medium red or green bell pepper (for 1 cup chopped)
¼ cup fresh cilantro or parsley leaves, tightly packed (optional)
1 cup frozen corn kernels, preferably extra-sweet
2 cans (15 ounces each) black beans
Ice cubes
Salt and black pepper to taste
Blue corn chips (optional)

1. Bring 2¼ cups unsalted water to a boil in a 2-quart or larger saucepan and stir in the couscous. Cover the pot and remove from the heat. Let stand for 5 minutes.

2. Meanwhile, if the lettuce isn't prewashed, rinse it, drain, and spin or pat dry. Place a lettuce leaf on each serving plate.

3. Cut the lime in half and squeeze the juice into a 3-quart or larger serving bowl. Add the oil, vinegar, and cumin and whisk to blend well. Chop the scallions, including enough of the tender green tops to make ¾ cup. Add to the bowl with the dressing. Seed the bell pepper and chop it into bite-size pieces, adding it to the bowl as you chop. Chop and add the cilantro (if using).

4. Place the frozen corn in a colander and rinse under cold running water to defrost slightly. Shake vigorously to drain well and add to the bowl. Drain the black beans in the colander and rinse under cold running water. Shake to remove as much water as possible, then add the beans to the bowl. Stir to mix the vegetables and dressing.

5. Pour the couscous into the colander, throw in 2 handfuls of ice cubes, and rinse under cold water, tossing with the ice cubes until the couscous reaches cool room temperature, about 2 minutes. Drain well, removing any unmelted ice cubes and fluffing the couscous thoroughly with a fork to break up any chunks. Then add the couscous to the bowl and stir well. Season with salt and black pepper. Top the lettuce with the salad, and serve with blue corn chips (if using).

Serves 6

TIME-SAVER

Don't salt water until after it has come to a boil, if you salt it at all. Salted water has a higher boiling point and thus takes longer to bubble.

This salad goes together in less than 20 minutes, and there's just one trick to making it. Cook the macaroni until it's barely tender, about 9 minutes; it should be done just after you've finished slicing the tomatoes. Stop chopping and rinse the macaroni under cold running water for about 2 minutes to be sure it's at cool room temperature. Then set it aside to drain while you continue with chopping the celery. Before adding the macaroni, shake the colander vigorously to remove as much water as possible.

If you have leftovers, it may be necessary to stir in extra mayonnaise after the salad has been refrigerated for more than 24 hours, since the macaroni will absorb some.

> ✳ *If using lettuce, you may need to rinse, drain, and pat it dry. Do it while the macaroni drains.*

HAM-CHEESE PASTA SALAD

2 cups (8 ounces) elbow macaroni
⅓ cup reduced-fat mayonnaise, or more to taste
2 tablespoons Dijon mustard
½ teaspoon onion powder
¼ teaspoon black pepper, or more to taste
8 ounces deli ham, such as baked Virginia ham,
    sliced ¼ inch thick
1 pint cherry tomatoes
2 large ribs celery (for 1 cup chopped)
1 cup (4 ounces) already-shredded sharp Cheddar cheese
Ice cubes
6 lettuce leaves (optional)

1. Place the macaroni in 2½ quarts of already-boiling unsalted water and cook until tender, 9 minutes.

2. While the macaroni cooks, combine the mayonnaise, mustard, onion powder, and pepper in a 3-quart or larger serving bowl and beat, using a wire whisk or fork, to blend well. Cut the ham into bite-size cubes and add to the bowl. Cut the tomatoes in half and add to the bowl, then coarsely chop the celery and add. Add the cheese and stir gently but thoroughly to mix with the dressing.

3. When the macaroni is done, pour it into a colander to drain and throw in 2 handfuls of ice cubes. Rinse the macaroni under cold running water and toss with the ice cubes until it reaches cool room temperature, about 2 minutes. Drain well, removing any unmelted ice cubes.

4. Place a lettuce leaf (if using; see Box) on each serving plate. Add the drained macaroni to the bowl with the ham mixture and toss well to mix. Spoon onto plates or over lettuce to serve.

Serves 6

SEASHORE PASTA SALAD

1 package (16 ounces) medium shell pasta
1 pint cherry tomatoes
1 large or 2 medium cucumbers (for 2 cups chunks)
3 scallions (green onions; for ¼ cup chopped; optional)
¾ cup reduced-fat mayonnaise
2 teaspoons garlic powder
½ teaspoon salt, or to taste
¼ teaspoon black pepper, or to taste
1 container (6 ounces) lump crabmeat, drained
Ice cubes

1. Place the shells in 2½ quarts of already-boiling unsalted water and cook until firm-tender, 9 to 11 minutes.

2. Meanwhile, slice the tomatoes in half and place in a 3-quart or larger serving bowl. Peel the cucumbers and cut them into bite-size chunks. If using scallions, chop them, including enough of the tender green tops to make ¼ cup, and add to the bowl along with the mayonnaise, garlic powder, salt, and pepper. Stir well to mix. Set the bowl aside. Drain the crabmeat, pick through to remove any shell, and set aside.

3. When the pasta is tender, pour it into a colander to drain and throw in 2 handfuls of ice cubes. Rinse the shells under cold running water and toss with the ice cubes until the shells reach cool room temperature, about 2 minutes. Drain well, removing any unmelted ice cubes.

4. Add the cooled shells and reserved crabmeat to the bowl with the sauce, toss well to mix, and serve.

Serves 6

From Alicia:

Trapped at home by a child with the chicken pox, I was thrilled when my friend Melanie Abbott brought over some party leftovers. I had barely finished the first bite of this terrific salad before I was asking for the recipe. I didn't believe her when she told me how simple it is.

We've added crab to her original recipe, making it a wonderful splurge for the height of summer when crabmeat doesn't cost a fortune. If you don't want to spring for crab, substitute half a pound of peeled, steamed shrimp or leave the seafood out entirely. Either way, this recipe makes a fabulous summer dinner. It's also nice for a bridesmaid's lunch or late-summer baby shower. Leftovers refrigerate well for 3 days.

From Beverly:

One of my favorite childhood memories is of driving to the city with my mother to shop for back-to-school clothes. Afterward, we'd go to the hotel dining room across from the department store and order a "ladies' lunch plate" of rich shrimp salad garnished with watermelon pickles. It was a special treat then, and with the current price of shrimp, it still is today.

The ease of this recipe depends on being able to buy already-cooked-and-peeled shrimp from your supermarket seafood case. Otherwise, use frozen cooked medium to large shrimp. Tiny frozen salad shrimp and canned shrimp don't have enough flavor or texture for this salad.

We usually make this salad without raw onion to save time, but onion lovers will miss the flavor. (You know who you are, so add them if you prefer.)

LADIES' LUNCH SHRIMP SALAD

4 large lettuce leaves
3 hard-boiled eggs (see Box, facing page)
⅓ cup reduced-fat mayonnaise
⅓ cup reduced-fat Thousand Island salad dressing
1 teaspoon lemon juice from frozen concentrate
½ teaspoon Worcestershire sauce
½ teaspoon onion powder
¼ teaspoon black pepper
1 pound already-cooked-and-peeled shrimp
2 large ribs celery (for 1 cup diced)
½ small onion (for ¼ cup minced; optional)
Salt to taste

1. If the lettuce is not prewashed, rinse it, drain, and spin or pat dry. Place a lettuce leaf on each serving plate.

2. Peel the eggs, place them in a 2-quart or larger bowl, and chop them fine, using two sharp knives or a chopping utensil. Add the mayonnaise, Thousand Island dressing, lemon juice, Worcestershire, onion powder, and pepper. Stir well to mix.

3. Reserve 4 whole shrimp for garnish. If the remaining shrimp are large, use kitchen scissors or a sharp knife to cut them in half or into bite-size pieces. Add them to the bowl. Cut the celery into medium-size dice and add it to the bowl. Finely mince the onion (if using) and add. Stir well to mix with the dressing, seasoning with salt. Top each lettuce leaf with the salad, dividing evenly. Garnish each salad with a whole shrimp and serve.

Serves 4

A word about:
HARD-BOILED EGGS

From Beverly:

Anytime I make hard-boiled eggs, I always make extras. They last, in the shell, for 1 week in the refrigerator and a bag of boiled eggs can make a week's meals a lot easier. Not only can you make deviled eggs, egg salad sandwiches, or a chef's salad, boiled eggs are an essential flavor for our especially easy Ladies' Lunch Shrimp Salad (see facing page).

Making hard-boiled eggs is a snap. Place them in a saucepan that has a lid and add enough cold water to just cover the tops. Salt the water well to make peeling easier, and bring the water to a boil. At this point, two methods will work. You can continue to boil the eggs, uncovered, for 10 to 15 minutes, depending on their size. Since this method is not exact, I prefer the way my mother has always done it. When the water boils, continue to cook the eggs, uncovered, for 3 minutes. Then simply cover the pot, remove it from the heat, and let the pot sit for at least 20 minutes—or until you get around to remembering it. I've been cooking eggs this way for twenty years (and Mom has for forty), and we promise you'll get a perfect hard-cooked egg every time.

Now that you've got all of these eggs at your disposal, what if you get confused about which are cooked and which are not? Here's a hint: Mark the cooked ones with an X in pencil and you'll have no trouble recognizing them.

From Beverly:

This recipe is my answer to the July Fourth picnic dilemma. If I spend half the holiday frying chicken and stuffing eggs, I'll be pooped before the fireworks pop. But not if I take pasta in a sweet-and-sour sauce that's studded with succulent shrimp—one dish that's part salad, part entrée, and satisfying enough so nobody minds not having three side dishes.

I find this dish goes together even faster if I buy already-peeled shrimp and Kirby cucumbers, which don't need to be peeled. I can throw it together at the last minute, since transport time to the picnic in the ice chest cools it off and gives the flavors a chance to develop. (If you're making the salad for home consumption, stick it in the freezer for 10 minutes of hyper-chill.)

PICNIC PASTA WITH SHRIMP

BOIL THE H_2O

1 package (16 ounces) rotini (pasta twists)
4 to 5 small Kirby (pickling) cucumbers (for 2 cups sliced)
1 scallion (green onion)
Sweet-and-Sour Dressing (recipe follows)
1 pound fresh already-peeled raw shrimp
Ice cubes

1. Place the rotini in 2½ quarts of already-boiling unsalted water and cook until firm-tender, 8 minutes.

2. Meanwhile, cut the unpeeled cucumber lengthwise into quarters. Line up the quarters side by side on a cutting board and cut them all at once into ¼-inch-thick slices. (You should have about 2 cups.) Place the cucumber in a 3-quart or larger serving bowl. Cut the scallion into thin slices, including about an inch of the tender green top, and add it to the bowl. Set aside.

3. Make the Sweet-and-Sour Dressing. It should take about 3 minutes.

4. Add the peeled shrimp to the pasta (after it's cooked for 8 minutes) and cook until they just turn pink, 2 minutes more.

5. When the shrimp and rotini are done, pour them into a colander to drain and throw in 2 handfuls of ice cubes. Rinse the pasta and shrimp under cold running water and toss with the ice cubes until the rotini reaches cool room temperature, about 2 minutes. Drain well, removing any unmelted ice cubes.

6. Add the shrimp and rotini to the bowl with the vegetables. Pour on the dressing and toss well to mix. Serve at once or refrigerate, covered, until ready to eat.

Serves 6

SWEET-AND-SOUR DRESSING

3 tablespoons rice wine vinegar or distilled white vinegar

3 tablespoons reduced-sodium soy sauce

2 tablespoons vegetable oil

1 tablespoon ketchup

1 tablespoon sugar

½ teaspoon bottled chopped ginger

½ teaspoon bottled minced garlic

Combine all the ingredients in an 8-ounce or larger jar that has a lid. Cover and shake well to blend. Use right away or refrigerate. The dressing will stay fresh for several weeks.

Makes about ⅔ cup

This dressing goes well with any Asian-style salad. Doubled, the recipe also makes a wonderful marinade for chicken or fish.

CHAPTER FIVE

Pasta

asta saves our sanity on a weekly basis. When we're absolutely at a loss for what to cook, we put a pot of water on to boil and throw in some pasta and whatever vegetables we happen to have on hand. Ten minutes later, pile on the cheese and dinner is done. It works for us, and it works for a lot of other people we know. In fact, while we were working on this cookbook, the title would often come up in conversations with friends and new acquaintances. Many of them were eager to share their favorite quick-cooking ideas. Nine times out of ten, these recipes centered around pasta.

If so many people are already noodling around their desperation, we wondered whether we should be giving them still more pasta recipes. In sharing our dilemma with relatives, friends, and anyone else who would listen, the answer was a resounding yes. People told us they love pasta, but they often resort to the same old recipes over and over again. Urge us to branch out, they said, and make it quick.

So here goes. We've fiddled with a dozen old-favorite recipes (both ours and friends') to make them faster and easier without sacrificing flavor. Plus, we've added recipes that rely mainly on pantry ingredients you can easily keep on hand. To pry pasta lovers out of a rut, there are a few off-the-wall ideas we bet you'll love. And you're bound to be tempted by our simple quartet of cheese- and meat-filled pastas. Finally, we've concocted a whole section of Super Stress-Saving, No-Cook Sauces that'll get you out of the kitchen without working up a sweat.

"On nights when we're ready for a straightjacket, dinner often looks like this: Pasta."

From Alicia:

My sister-in-law, Lynn Clark-Brady, makes a wonderful vegetarian dish very similar to this, but being the true meat lover I am, ground beef found its way into the ingredients list.

The secrets to getting a dish this flavorful to the table so quickly are the pepper stir-fry mix and chili-style tomatoes. The frozen pepper mix saves the time of cutting a red, yellow, and green bell pepper without compromising the flavor. The chili-style tomatoes are lightly seasoned and chopped to the perfect size for this dish.

> ✳ *This dish is also good without beef if you're craving a vegetarian meal. Just add 1 tablespoon of oil to cook the pepper mix before adding the corn.*

RIGHT-AWAY BEEF PENNE

2 cups (8 ounces) penne
1 pound extra-lean ground beef, fresh or frozen (see Box)
2 cups frozen green, red, and yellow bell pepper stir-fry mix
2 cups frozen white or yellow corn kernels
1 tablespoon chili powder
1 teaspoon ground cumin, or to taste
½ teaspoon onion powder
1 can (16 ounces) red kidney beans
1 can (14½ ounces) chili-style diced tomatoes
½ cup already finely shredded sharp Cheddar cheese

1. Place the penne in 2½ quarts of already-boiling unsalted water and cook until tender, 11 to 13 minutes.

2. Meanwhile, if the beef is frozen, run hot water over it so you can remove any packaging. Place the meat on a microwave-safe plate and microwave it 3 minutes, uncovered, on high, to begin defrosting. Place the beef (fresh or partially defrosted) in an extra-deep 12-inch nonstick skillet and cook over high heat. Turn and break up the meat, stirring occasionally, until most of the meat is crumbled and browned, about 5 minutes.

3. Add the pepper stir-fry mix, the corn, chili powder, cumin, and onion powder to the meat, stirring well. Continue to cook until the meat is completely brown, 3 to 4 minutes more.

4. Drain the beans and add them to the skillet, along with the tomatoes with their juice. Reduce the heat to medium and cook for 5 minutes, stirring occasionally.

5. When the penne is tender, drain it and stir into the beef mixture. Sprinkle the cheese evenly on top, cover the skillet, and cook just until the cheese melts, about 1 minute, then serve.

Serves 6 generously

MEASURING PASTA

We always used to cook too much pasta, and the left-overs got pushed to the back of the fridge. Forgotten, they turned green—or even purple. So how much was enough to cook, but not too much? After months of guessing (and usually being wrong), we decided to nail down this mystery once and for all. We spent most of a morning weighing, measuring, and boiling. Here's what we found:

In practically every case, 2 ounces of dried pasta—regardless of shape—is a reasonable portion for most adults, provided it's served with a typical sauce of vegetables and meat. Vegetarian recipes such as macaroni and cheese may require a slightly larger amount of pasta per person. Also, if you have toddlers, teenagers, or "carbo-loaders," you'll need to decrease or increase accordingly.

Here are the exact measures we determined:

1. Orzo (rice-shaped pasta): Two ounces dried measures ⅓ cup and yields 1 cup of cooked orzo. To feed a family of four, cook 1⅓ cups dried orzo.

2. Elbow macaroni (and other short tubular or shaped pastas): Two ounces dried measures ½ cup and yields 1⅓ cups cooked. To feed four, cook 2 cups dried macaroni.

3. Ziti (and other medium-short tubular or shaped pastas): Two ounces dried measures ½ cup and yields 1½ cups cooked. To feed four, cook 2 cups dried ziti.

4. Spaghetti (and other long solid pastas): Two ounces dried yields 1 cup cooked spaghetti. To feed four, cook an 8-ounce box of dried spaghetti. Since you can't fit long pasta into a cup mea-sure, you'll need to go by dry weight or learn what 2 ounces looks like. To help you visualize, go get a U.S. penny. Place it on the counter. Grab enough long pasta tightly in your fist so that the tips exactly cover that penny. That's 2 ounces.

If you're like us, beef stroganoff is a dish you enjoyed years ago but let get sidetracked when you started worrying about fat and cholesterol. Now, with the wide availability of extra-lean ground beef, reduced-fat mushroom soup, yolk-free noodles, and "lite," or reduced-fat, sour cream (also called "sour half-and-half"), this is a recipe that deserves dusting off. If you buy a package of already-sliced mushrooms, you won't believe how easy stroganoff can be. Cooking the green beans in the same pot with the noodles saves both cooking and cleanup time.

HAMBURGER STROGANOFF IN A HURRY

BOIL THE H₂O

1 bag (12 ounces) yolk-free egg noodles
1 pound extra-lean ground beef, fresh or frozen
1 large onion (for 1 cup chopped)
1 teaspoon bottled minced garlic
2 cups already-sliced fresh mushrooms
1 package (9 ounces) frozen French-style green beans
   (see Box, facing page)
¼ cup dry sherry
1 tablespoon ketchup
2 teaspoons Dijon mustard
1½ teaspoons Worcestershire sauce
½ teaspoon paprika
1 can (10¾ ounces) reduced-fat cream of mushroom soup
⅔ cup reduced-fat sour cream
Salt and black pepper to taste

1. Place the noodles in 2½ quarts of already-boiling unsalted water and cook 5 minutes.

2. Meanwhile, if the beef is frozen, run it under hot water so you can remove any packaging. Place the meat on a microwave-safe plate and microwave 2 minutes, uncovered, on high, to begin defrosting. While the meat microwaves, peel the onion, then begin heating a 12-inch nonstick skillet over medium heat.

3. Add the beef (fresh or partially defrosted) to the skillet, raise the heat to medium-high, and cook, stirring often, turning and breaking up the meat as it begins to brown. Coarsely chop the onion, adding it to the skillet as you chop. Add the garlic and mushrooms. Continue to cook, stirring frequently, until the meat

is crumbled and browned, about 5 minutes. Add the green beans to the pasta pot, cover the pot to bring it back to a boil, then crack the lid, and cook until the noodles are tender and the beans heated through, 5 minutes more.

4. Meanwhile, add the sherry, ketchup, mustard, Worcestershire, paprika, and the mushroom soup to the skillet. Stir well until it is completely incorporated. Lower the heat to simmer the mixture, then add the sour cream and continue to cook, stirring constantly, until the sour cream is completely incorporated, 1 minute. Season with salt and pepper.

5. Drain the noodles and toss to evenly distribute the beans. Place some on each of the serving plates. Top with the sauce and serve.

Serves 6

✸ *Frozen French-style green beans also come in 16-ounce plastic bags. If you buy the beans in a bag, use half of it for this recipe.*

From Alicia:

Traditional two-hour lasagna just doesn't fit into my hectic schedule anymore. This recipe was the result of a six o'clock craving and a box of broken noodles. (The box fell from the top shelf of my pantry, and although the noodles shattered on impact, I didn't have the heart to throw them away.)

In testing this dish, we found its mild flavor to be particularly appealing to children. In my family, everyone thought it was leftover lasagna, since it didn't come out in neat little squares. Okay, so this lasagna won't win a beauty contest, but all of the great flavor is still here. When I'm desperate, spending two hours for beauty's sake just isn't worth it.

REAL-LIFE LASAGNA

8 ounces lasagna noodles (for 4 cups broken)
1 pound extra-lean ground beef, fresh or frozen
Olive oil cooking spray
1 large onion (for 1 cup chopped)
2 teaspoons bottled minced garlic
¼ cup fresh parsley (optional)
2 teaspoons dried Italian seasoning
2 cans (14½ ounces each) chopped or diced tomatoes
1 can (6 ounces) tomato paste
1 cup low-fat cottage cheese
2 cups (8 ounces) already-shredded mozzarella cheese

1. Firmly whack the noodle box on the counter 10 times to break the noodles into pieces. Place the broken noodles in 2½ quarts of already-boiling unsalted water and cook until the noodles are tender, 8 to 10 minutes.

2. Meanwhile, if the beef is frozen, run it under hot water so you can remove any packaging. Place the meat on a microwave-safe plate and microwave for 3 minutes, uncovered, on high, to begin defrosting.

3. Spray with olive oil cooking spray an extra-deep 12-inch non-stick skillet that has a lid, and heat it over medium heat while peeling and coarsely chopping the onion. Add the onion to the skillet as you chop, and cook to soften, stirring from time to time.

4. Add the beef (fresh or partially defrosted) to the skillet and raise the heat to high. Turn and break up the meat, stirring occasionally, until most of the meat is crumbled and browned. Add the garlic, parsley (if using), and the Italian seasoning, and continue to cook until the meat is completely brown, 2 minutes more.

5. Add the tomatoes with their juice and the tomato paste. Stir well, then cover the skillet and reduce the heat to low. Let the mixture cook while draining the noodles (if they are tender).

6. Add the cottage cheese, 1 cup of the mozzarella, and the noodles, stirring well. Smooth the mixture evenly in the skillet and sprinkle the remaining cup of mozzarella over the top. Cover, and simmer for 2 minutes more to melt the cheese and serve.

Serves 6

HOW TO BOIL WATER

The Italians cook their pasta in huge vats of water, and it takes a lot of time to bring an enormous pot to a raging boil. We've found that pasta cooks perfectly well—with less overall time—in a bit less liquid. Here's how we do it:

Pour 2½ quarts (10 cups) of unsalted water into a 4½-quart or larger Dutch oven or soup pot. Notice the water level in relation to the top of the pot and you won't need to measure again.

Next, put a tight-fitting lid on the pot and place it over the highest heat. It should boil in roughly 9 minutes, but always be careful when using very high heat. Be prepared to lower the heat once the water starts boiling; you don't want a big, bubbling pot of water overflowing on the stove, especially with kids around. Add the pasta and cover the pot just until the water returns to a boil. Then crack the lid a little so the water won't boil over and mess up your stove (once the water returns to boiling, you can uncover the pot entirely, as long as the water maintains a rolling boil). Stirring the pasta from time to time keeps it from sticking together. Time your cooking so you can drain the pasta just before serving to keep it from getting gummy.

We always think of meatballs as part of a wintry meal. Maybe it's because we have to heat the kitchen up to simmer them all day. Recently we've been thrilled to find several good brands of frozen meatballs that make it much easier to enjoy them—even when it's warm outside. With the Mediterranean-inspired combination of meatballs, squash, artichokes, and black olives—you can also use pitted, oil-cured, Greek-style olives, which have a more intense flavor—this is a good choice for a sunny day.

If you are only serving four initially, note that leftovers refrigerate well for several days.

SUMMER MEATBALLS AND YELLOW SQUASH

2 cups (12 ounces) orzo (rice-shaped pasta)
1 teaspoon olive oil
1 small onion (for ½ cup chopped)
1 bag frozen pre-cooked meatballs (about 40 meatballs;
 1¼ pounds)
1 tablespoon bottled minced garlic
2 cans (14½ ounces each) Italian-style stewed tomatoes
1 small can (8 ounces) Italian-style tomato sauce
1 tablespoon dried oregano
2 medium yellow squash (for 1½ cups sliced; see Box,
 facing page)
1 can (14 ounces) artichoke hearts packed in water
1 can (3.8 ounces) pitted sliced black olives
Black pepper to taste (optional)
¼ cup already-crumbled feta cheese (optional)

1. Bring 2½ quarts of unsalted water to a boil in a covered 4½-quart or larger Dutch oven or soup pot. When the water reaches a rapid boil, add the orzo and cook until tender, 7 to 8 minutes.

2. Meanwhile, heat the oil in a 4½-quart Dutch oven or soup pot over medium-low heat. Peel and coarsely chop the onion, adding it to the pot as you chop. Cook until soft, about 2 minutes.

3. While the onion cooks, place the meatballs on a microwave-safe plate and microwave 2 minutes, uncovered, on high, to begin defrosting.

4. Add the garlic to the pot and continue to cook, stirring, 1 minute more. Raise the heat to medium. Add the stewed tomatoes, tomato sauce, and oregano. Stir to mix and let cook while you slice the squash into ⅛-inch circles. Add the squash and partially defrosted meatballs to the pot and stir to coat with sauce. Raise the heat to high, cover the pot, and bring the mixture to a boil.

5. Meanwhile, drain the artichokes and coarsely chop them. Drain the olives and add them, along with the artichokes, to the pot. Let the mixture boil about 4 minutes to blend the flavors, stirring occasionally to keep it from sticking.

6. Drain the orzo, season to taste with black pepper (if using), and place some on each serving plate. Top with meatballs and sauce and serve, garnished with feta cheese (if using).

Serves 8

✳ *A 10-ounce package of frozen yellow squash can be substituted for the fresh squash. Microwave the frozen squash for 3 minutes, covered on high, and drain well before adding it to the sauce.*

BEEFY NOODLES WITH SOUR CREAM SAUCE

2 cups (8 ounces) ziti
1 pound extra-lean ground beef, fresh or frozen
1 teaspoon vegetable oil
1 large onion (for 1 cup chopped)
1 cup already-sliced fresh mushrooms
2 cups low-sodium vegetable juice, such as V-8
1 tablespoon ketchup
½ teaspoon garlic powder
½ teaspoon celery salt
¼ teaspoon dried oregano or dried Italian seasoning
1 cup reduced-fat sour cream (see Box, facing page)
Salt and black pepper to taste

1. Place the ziti in 2½ quarts of already-boiling unsalted water and cook until tender, 12 to 14 minutes.

2. Meanwhile, if the beef is frozen, run hot water over it so you can remove any packaging. Place the meat on a microwave-safe plate and microwave 3 minutes, uncovered, on high, to begin defrosting.

3. Heat the oil in a 12-inch nonstick skillet over medium heat. Peel and coarsely chop the onion, adding it to the pan as you chop. Add the beef (fresh or partially defrosted) to the skillet and raise the heat to high. Cook, turning and breaking up the meat, and when it begins to crumble and brown, add the mushrooms. Cook until their juice is released and the beef is completely browned, about 5 minutes, stirring frequently. Add the vegetable

This is one of those hamburger and pasta combinations that is always a hit with children. The ingenious thing about this recipe is the sauce. It's made with vegetable juice, which packs every bite with vegetable flavor. You'd never know the only thing you have to peel and chop is an onion.

juice, ketchup, garlic powder, celery salt, and oregano. Stir well to mix, then reduce the heat to medium-low.

4. Simmer the mixture while the ziti finishes cooking, stirring from time to time. Immediately drain the ziti, add it to the skillet, and stir well to mix. Stir in the sour cream, salt, and black pepper and cook for 1 minute more to heat through. Remove from the heat and serve.

Serves 4 generously

> ✳ *Depending on the brand you purchase, reduced-fat sour cream might be called everything from "lite" to "sour half-and-half." No matter the name, the carton will list a fat comparison to whole sour cream. This is how you can be sure it contains fewer fat grams than regular sour cream and is therefore "reduced-fat."*
>
> *If you prefer using whole sour cream, it will work fine as a substitute in all of our recipes. However, we do not recommend using completely fat-free sour cream in any of them.*

DON'T JUST STAND THERE—COOK!

You'll see one word over and over again in nearly all Desperation Dinners recipes, and that's "meanwhile." If you're going to put a quality meal on the table in 20 minutes, you won't have any time to waste. If the first recipe step calls for 3 minutes of microwave defrosting, you'll probably need to be peeling and chopping an onion during that time. So as soon as you complete one task, move on to the next step.

From Beverly:

Reta Ebanks, a Jamaican grandmother who now lives in Miami, spent many years living in London, where she was once employed as a cook in a pub. This recipe is based on hers for pasta sauce—Jamaican style. When my children were infants and Reta would come to baby-sit, sometimes she'd offer to make what she called "mince." On "mince" days, my husband could tell what was for dinner before he even walked through the front door. Reta's dish was so aromatic that it created envy in the neighborhood.

Reta's "mince" required simmering all afternoon until the vegetables disintegrated and the meat was incredibly tender. My adapted version of her recipe is chunkier, with more vegetables. The additional vegetables don't significantly change the flavor, and the shorter simmer puts this exotic recipe well within range for the desperate cook.

JAMAICAN MACARONI

BOIL THE H$_2$O

2 cups (8 ounces) elbow macaroni
1 pound extra-lean ground beef, fresh or frozen
20 already-peeled baby carrots (for about 1 cup sliced)
1 large green pepper (for 1½ cups chopped)
1 large onion (for 1 cup chopped)
1 can (14½ ounces) diced tomatoes
¼ cup Worcestershire sauce
2 teaspoons garlic powder
1½ teaspoons seasoning salt, such as Lawry's
½ teaspoon black pepper
¼ teaspoon hot pepper sauce (optional)

1. Place the macaroni in 2½ quarts of already-boiling unsalted water and cook until tender, 9 to 11 minutes.

2. Meanwhile, if the beef is frozen, run it under hot water so you can remove any packaging. Place the meat on a microwave-safe plate and microwave 3 minutes, uncovered, on high, to begin defrosting. Meanwhile, begin cutting the carrots in ¼-inch circles and seeding and chopping the bell pepper.

3. Place the meat (fresh or partially defrosted) in an extra-deep 12-inch nonstick skillet and cook over high heat. Turn and break up the meat, stirring occasionally. Meanwhile, finish slicing the carrots and chopping the bell pepper. When the meat is partially browned (and fully defrosted, if originally frozen), add the carrots and bell pepper to the skillet. Stir well. Peel and coarsely chop the onion, adding it to the skillet as you chop.

4. Add the tomatoes and their juice, the Worcestershire, garlic powder, seasoning salt, black pepper, and hot pepper sauce (if using). Stir well, then continue to cook, stirring frequently, to soften the vegetables and thicken the sauce, 7 minutes more.

5. As soon as the macaroni is tender, drain it and set aside until the sauce is thick. Then add it to the skillet, stir well to coat with sauce, and serve.

Serves 4

CHEESY HAM CASSEROLE

8 ounces angel hair pasta
2 teaspoons vegetable oil
1 small onion (for ½ cup chopped)
½ medium green bell pepper (for ½ cup chopped)
½ teaspoon bottled minced garlic
2 cups (8 ounces) diced baked ham (see Box, page 142)
1 can (14½ ounces) diced tomatoes
1 can (14½ ounces) stewed tomatoes
Black pepper to taste
1 cup (4 ounces) already-shredded sharp Cheddar cheese

1. Bring 2½ quarts of unsalted water to a boil in a covered 4½-quart or larger Dutch oven or soup pot. When the water reaches a rapid boil, add the angel hair pasta and cook until firm-tender, 4 minutes.

2. Meanwhile, heat the oil in an extra-deep 12-inch nonstick skillet that has a lid over medium-high heat. Peel and finely dice the onion, adding it to the skillet as you dice. While the onion is cooking, seed and chop the bell pepper, adding it as you chop.

3. Add the garlic and ham and cook until the ham starts to brown, 2 to 3 minutes. While the ham mixture cooks, drain both cans of tomatoes, adding them to the skillet when the ham has slightly browned. Stir well. Set the skillet off the heat.

Whenever we have to feed more than 10 people, we frequently invest in a store-bought, spiral-sliced ham. A special treat to most of us, these hams fit any menu, from picnic to sit-down dinner.

A big ham always means leftovers. Toward the butt end you no longer find those convenient slices, so one solution is to chop the remaining ham into small chunks, pop them into a zipper-top bag, and refrigerate to use later in the week. This recipe requires 2 cups of meat and will absorb most of the leftovers from an average-size ham, and since these hams are expensive, you'll get an extra meal for your money.

From Beverly:

The idea for this recipe originated with a side dish in a now-defunct mom-and-pop Italian restaurant in Chapel Hill, North Carolina. I tasted the sweet-and-sour pepperonata combination and fell in love. It took a year to get up the nerve to call the chef and beg for his secret. The payoff was that the recipe turned out to be as fast as it is delicious.

My eating habits have changed in the 15 years since I discovered this dish, so I've cut back on the oil and sugar and added pasta and sausage to turn it into an easy entrée.

It's especially pretty with the rainbow of bell peppers, but you can use all one color as well.

4. When the pasta is done, drain well and stir it into the skillet. Return the skillet to medium heat, and the black pepper, and continue to cook, uncovered, for 2 minutes.

5. Sprinkle the cheese over the pasta mixture and cover the skillet. Cook until the cheese melts, about 2 minutes. Then uncover the skillet and continue to cook until most of the liquid has evaporated, about another 2 minutes.

6. Remove the skillet from the heat and cut the pasta mixture into 4 sections, taking care not to scar the skillet bottom. Serve at once.

Serves 4 generously

PEPPERONATA WITH PENNE AND SAUSAGE

2 cups (8 ounces) penne
1 teaspoon olive oil
4 links Italian sausage (¾ to 1 pound total), sweet or hot
    (see Box, facing page)
1 large onion (for 1 cup slices)
1 medium green bell pepper (for 1 cup strips)
1 medium red bell pepper (for 1 cup strips)
1 medium yellow bell pepper (for 1 cup strips)
1 can (14½ ounces) diced or whole tomatoes
2 tablespoons light or dark brown sugar, lightly packed
1 tablespoon balsamic or red wine vinegar
4 bay leaves
½ teaspoon dried basil
Salt and black pepper to taste
Already-grated Parmesan cheese (optional)

1. Place the penne in 2½ quarts of already-boiling unsalted water and cook until tender, 11 to 13 minutes.

2. Meanwhile, heat the oil over medium heat in an extra-deep 12-inch nonstick skillet that has a lid. Pierce the sausages several times with a fork and add them to the skillet. Let brown, turning the links occasionally while peeling and thinly slicing the onion. Add the onion to the pan as you slice, separating it into rings.

3. Seed the peppers and cut into long strips about ½ inch wide. Add them to the skillet, stir, cover the skillet, and raise the heat to high. Keeping the skillet covered as much as possible, add the tomatoes with their juice, the brown sugar, vinegar, bay leaves, and basil. Stir well. Bring the mixture to a boil.

4. Lower the heat to medium-high and boil until the sausage is no longer pink in the middle and the vegetables are tender but not mushy, about 7 minutes, uncovering to stir occasionally.

5. Drain the penne and place some on each serving plate. Season the sausage mixture with salt and black pepper and top each pasta portion with some of the sauce, making sure to remove and discard the bay leaves. Garnish with Parmesan cheese (if using).

Serves 4

✳ *If you're concerned that there may be too much fat in regular (pork) Italian sausages, substitute Italian-style turkey sausage links. They work well in this recipe.*

From Alicia:

When I have leftover turkey, I always make tetrazzini. The blend of vegetables, pasta, cheese, and tender turkey makes me actually look forward to the day after Thanksgiving. But why should I have to wait for leftovers to enjoy this creamy casserole? In most recipes, turkey and chicken are interchangeable, so when I don't have turkey, I just substitute chicken breasts. And to make this a true Desperation Dinner, I transformed it into a speedy skillet meal. Elbow macaroni makes the dish easier to handle in the skillet than traditional spaghetti.

OH-SO-EASY TETRAZZINI

1½ cups (6 ounces) elbow macaroni
4 skinless, boneless chicken breast halves
     (about 1⅓ pounds total; see Box, facing page)
1 teaspoon vegetable oil
1 large onion (for 1 cup chopped)
1 cup already-sliced fresh mushrooms
1 cup already-shredded carrots
1 cup frozen green peas
1 teaspoon bottled minced garlic
1 teaspoon Worcestershire sauce
¼ teaspoon black pepper
1 can (10¾ ounces) reduced-fat cream of mushroom soup
1 can (10¾ ounces) reduced-fat cream of chicken soup
½ cup milk, skim, low-fat, or whole
½ cup already-shredded Parmesan cheese
1½ cups (6 ounces) already finely shredded sharp
     Cheddar cheese

1. Place the macaroni in 2½ quarts of already-boiling unsalted water and cook until tender, 9 to 11 minutes.

2. Meanwhile, if the chicken is frozen, run it under hot water so you can remove any packaging. Place the chicken on a microwave-safe plate and microwave 2 minutes, uncovered, on high, to begin defrosting.

3. While the chicken defrosts, heat the oil over medium heat in an extra-deep 12-inch nonstick skillet that has a lid. Peel and coarsely chop the onion, adding it to the skillet as you chop. Add the mushrooms and begin to cook, stirring occasionally.

4. Meanwhile, cut the chicken (fresh or partially defrosted) into bite-size chunks, adding them to the skillet as you cut. Raise the

heat to medium-high and cook for 2 minutes, stirring from time to time. Add the carrots, peas, garlic, Worcestershire, and pepper and continue to cook until the chicken is no longer pink, 4 to 5 minutes more.

5. While the mixture cooks, pour both cans of soup, the milk, and the Parmesan cheese into a 1-quart or larger bowl and stir well to combine. Drain the macaroni and set it aside.

6. When the chicken is no longer pink in the center, add the soup mixture, then gently stir in the macaroni to coat with sauce. Reduce the heat to low. Scatter the Cheddar cheese on top, cover, and cook just until it melts, about 3 minutes. Remove from the heat and serve.

Serves 6

> ✳ *To make Turkey Tetrazzini, use 2 cups of leftover cooked turkey or turkey from the deli and add it along with the peas and carrots in step 4. Proceed immediately to step 5.*

From Alicia:

This was my first Desperation Dinner. I discovered it long before I ever became a desperate cook when our friends, Alicia and Frank Casadonte, prepared it for a house full of people at the beach one summer.

I brought the recipe home, changed a few things, and it fast became a favorite standby. It's one of the few of my "old life" recipes that I still have time to make.

You'd think this dish would be too simple to serve company, but the flavor is surprisingly complex. Wine adds body and zest to the sauce, but if you don't have any, leave it out.

ALICIA'S CHICKEN WITH OLIVES

★★

8 ounces thin spaghetti (spaghettini)
4 skinless, boneless chicken breast halves,
    (about 1⅓ pounds total), fresh or frozen
1 tablespoon olive oil
Salt and black pepper to taste
1 teaspoon bottled minced garlic
1½ teaspoons Italian seasoning
1 can (14½ ounces) Italian-style stewed tomatoes
¼ cup red or white wine (optional)
1 can (2¼ ounces) sliced black olives

1. Bring 2½ quarts of unsalted water to a boil in a covered 4½-quart or larger Dutch oven or soup pot. When the water reaches a rapid boil, add the spaghetti and cook until tender, 9 minutes.

2. Meanwhile, if the chicken is frozen, run it under hot water so you can remove any packaging. Place the chicken on a microwave-safe plate and microwave 3 minutes, uncovered, on high, to begin defrosting.

3. Cut the chicken (fresh or partially defrosted) into 1½-inch chunks. Heat the oil in a 12-inch nonstick skillet over high heat. Add the chicken and salt and pepper lightly. Cook, stirring occasionally, until the chicken is lightly browned all over, about 6 minutes (see Note).

4. Add the garlic and Italian seasoning. Cook and stir for 30 seconds. Add the tomatoes with their juice and the wine (if using), then bring to a boil, uncovered, over high heat. Boil rapidly, stirring occasionally, until the sauce is thick, about 5 minutes. Drain the olives.

5. Meanwhile, when the pasta is tender, drain and set aside. Add the olives to the skillet and stir.

6. Remove the sauce from the heat, toss the sauce with the drained spaghetti and serve, arranging the chicken pieces on top.

Serves 4

Note: If you have an electric stove, you may need to reduce the heat.

TIME·SAVER

Put a pot of water on to boil as soon as you walk through the door from work (before changing clothes or reading the mail), and you'll be halfway to cooking pasta, steaming rice, or boiling potatoes when it's time to start dinner.

THE PASTA BOWL

From Alicia:

I've always wanted one of those Italian ceramic extra-large serving bowls that works for both pasta and salads. However, my thrifty side has always balked at paying $75 or more for a bowl. (Even if I did own one, I probably wouldn't use it for fear of its getting broken.) The good news is that the big pasta bowl look has become so popular, there are now lots of manufactured imitations that substitute nicely.

   Mass-produced bowls don't have the variations of hand-thrown pottery or the one-of-kind color combinations. But for less than half the price, you get an attractive, functional bowl that will serve you well. Even more accessible are the plastic versions sold practically everywhere—from discount stores to boutiques. These colorful beauties usually cost less than $20 and make any meal more festive.

From Alicia:

Chicken Parmesan is one of my favorite pasta entrées. Before I had children, this classic was one of my regular menu items. But I was never able to convince my daughters that it should be one of their favorites, too. Then I decided to serve the dish as chicken fingers instead of as one big piece. Who would have thought that cutting the chicken into strips would make such a difference to kids? My husband and I don't mind the change in appearance so long as the flavor is still spectacular.

My youngest likes the sauce as a dip and eats the noodles on the side.

CHICKEN FINGERS PARMESAN

8 ounces thin spaghetti (spaghettini)
4 skinless, boneless chicken breast halves
    (about 1⅓ pounds total), fresh or frozen
½ cup plain fine, dry bread crumbs
½ cup already-grated Parmesan cheese
1 teaspoon dried basil
1 tablespoon olive oil
1 can (14½ ounces) pasta-style chopped tomatoes
1 can (6 ounces) tomato paste
⅓ cup water
½ cup already-shredded mozzarella cheese

1. Bring 2½ quarts of unsalted water to a boil in a covered 4½-quart or larger Dutch oven or soup pot. When the water reaches a rapid boil, add the spaghetti and cook 9 minutes.

2. Meanwhile, if the chicken is frozen, run it under hot water so you can remove any packaging. Place the chicken on a microwave-safe plate and microwave 2 minutes, uncovered, on high, to begin defrosting. Cut the chicken (fresh or partially defrosted) into ½-inch strips. Combine the bread crumbs, Parmesan, and basil in a large zipper-top plastic bag.

3. Heat the olive oil over medium heat in a 12-inch nonstick skillet that has a lid. Place the chicken in the crumbs, shaking the bag to coat the pieces well, then place them in the hot oil. Raise the heat to high and cook until the chicken is cooked through, 4 to 5 minutes, turning to lightly brown on all sides.

4. Remove the chicken from the skillet to a plate and set aside. Add the tomatoes, tomato paste, and water to the skillet. Stir well.

5. Return the chicken strips to the skillet, covering them with sauce. (Reserve strips for anyone who prefers them plain.) Reduce the heat to low and sprinkle the mozzarella evenly over the contents of the skillet. Cover and continue to simmer until the cheese melts, 1 to 2 minutes.

6. Drain the spaghetti and place some on each serving plate. Top with the chicken and sauce and serve.

Serves 4

PRIMO CHICKEN-VEGETABLE PASTA

2 cups (8 ounces) rotini (pasta twists)
2 skinless, boneless chicken breast halves (about ⅔ pound total), fresh or frozen
1 teaspoon olive oil
1 large onion (for 1 cup chopped)
12 sun-dried tomato pieces, not packed in oil
2 teaspoons bottled minced garlic
2 cups (8 ounces) fresh broccoli florets (see Box, page 150)
1½ cups already-sliced fresh mushrooms
½ cup white wine
½ cup half-and-half
½ cup already-grated Parmesan cheese
Salt and black pepper to taste

*A*lla primavera literally means "spring style," a kind of Italian cooking in which fresh vegetables are served blanched to a crisp-tender stage. The most popular dish featuring these fabulous vegetables is the popular pasta primavera, which inspired this recipe. Our version uses the convenience of already-sliced mushrooms and broccoli florets to speed you through preparation. We've added chicken to the mix for a bit more substance, but it can easily be omitted. If you can find tricolored rotini, it makes for a festive dish.

1. Place the rotini in 2½ quarts of already-boiling unsalted water and cook until tender, 9 to 11 minutes.

2. Meanwhile, if the chicken is frozen, run it under hot water so you can remove any packaging. Place the chicken on a microwave-safe plate and microwave 2 to 3 minutes, uncovered, on high, to begin defrosting.

3. Heat the oil in a 12-inch nonstick skillet over medium heat. Peel and coarsely chop the onion, adding it to the skillet as you chop. Let the onion cook, stirring from time to time.

4. Meanwhile, coarsely chop the sun-dried tomato pieces and place in a 2-cup glass measure. Add 1 cup water and microwave 3 minutes, uncovered, on high. Remove the tomatoes from the microwave and let them stand in the water to soften, 5 minutes. Meanwhile, cut the chicken (fresh or partially defrosted) into bite-size pieces. Raise the heat under the skillet to high and add the chicken as you cut.

5. Immediately add the garlic, broccoli, and mushrooms. Stir-fry until the broccoli is brilliant green, 2 minutes. Add the wine and cook for 2 minutes more, stirring occasionally, to evaporate the alcohol. Meanwhile, drain the sun-dried tomatoes and add them to the skillet. Reduce the heat to medium and add the half-and-half and Parmesan cheese. Cook until the broccoli is crisp-tender, about 3 minutes more, stirring frequently. (The sauce will be very thin.)

6. Drain the rotini and place some on each serving plate. Season the sauce with salt and pepper, top each pasta portion with it, and serve.

Serves 4

A word about:
IQF CHICKEN BREASTS

Individually quick-frozen (IQF) skinless, boneless chicken breasts can be a desperate cook's best ally. It's the "individually quick-frozen" part that's key. Roughly 10 breasts come in a zipper-top plastic bag, and you can easily remove as many as you need, when you need them.

For the desperate cook, IQF breasts solve a big problem inherent with the boneless breasts purchased on foam trays at the meat counter. When you freeze those trays, all the chicken clumps together in a solid block that takes forever to defrost. For the recipes in this book, we zap the IQF breasts for a couple of minutes in the microwave, and then they're recipe-ready.

IQF chicken comes in a variety of forms. We use the skinless, boneless chicken breast "halves," and that's what the number of chicken pieces and the weight called for in our recipes are based on. Chicken breast "portions" are the closest substitute, but portions don't contain the breast fillet. This means they are smaller and weigh less. (The fillet is also called the "tender" portion, and you can purchase IQF bags of "tenders" only.) If you buy portions instead of breast halves, be sure to use enough pieces to equal the weight called for in our ingredients lists.

In our experience, the IQF chicken is found in different locations in different supermarkets. First check near the frozen turkeys and other frozen specialty birds. Then look along the general frozen foods aisles. If you don't find this thoroughly convenient chicken, ask your supermarket manager to begin stocking it immediately.

> "*Bags of IQF chicken breasts are a revolutionary concept for busy cooks. Just reach in the bag and grab exactly what you need.*"

TUXEDO CHICKEN

6 cups (12 ounces) bow tie pasta (farfalle)
4 skinless, boneless chicken breast halves
    (about 1⅓ pounds total), fresh or frozen
1 tablespoon butter
1 small onion (for ½ cup chopped)
2 cups frozen chopped broccoli
1 container (8 ounces) reduced-fat sour cream
1 cup half-and-half
1 tablespoon grainy Dijon mustard
2 teaspoons Worcestershire sauce
¼ teaspoon garlic powder

1. Bring 2½ quarts of unsalted water to a boil in a covered 4½-quart or larger Dutch oven or soup pot. When the water reaches a rapid boil, add the bow ties and cook until tender, 9 minutes.

2. Meanwhile, if the chicken breasts are frozen, run them under hot water so you can remove any packaging. Place the chicken on a microwave-safe plate and microwave 3 minutes, uncovered, on high, to begin defrosting. While the chicken defrosts, melt the butter on medium-low in a 12-inch nonstick skillet. Peel and chop the onion, adding it to the skillet as you chop. Cook until the onion is soft, about 3 minutes.

3. Slice the chicken (fresh or partially defrosted) into ½-inch strips. Raise the heat to medium-high and add the chicken. Cook until the chicken is no longer pink in the center, 3½ to 4 minutes, stirring often. Meanwhile, place the broccoli in a microwave-safe dish and microwave 3½ to 4½ minutes, covered, on high, until it is just warm.

Pasta shaped like bow ties is as fun to eat as it is to look at. This recipe features a lovely Dijon-flavored cream sauce that perfectly accents the chicken and broccoli. The little crevices in each bow tie capture the right amount of sauce for every bite.

4. Remove the chicken from the skillet with a slotted spoon and set aside. Reduce the heat to medium-low. Stir the sour cream and half-and-half into the chicken juices to blend well, then add the mustard, Worcestershire, and garlic powder. Stir well and continue to cook until the sauce is slightly thick, about 2 minutes. Do not boil.

5. Return the chicken to the skillet and add the broccoli, then raise the heat to medium-high and bring the sauce almost to a boil. Reduce the heat to low and simmer to blend the flavors, 1 to 2 minutes. Do not boil.

6. Meanwhile, drain the bow ties and place some on each serving plate. Top with the chicken mixture and serve.

Serves 6

TIME-SAVER

Boiling large quantities of water goes much faster if you start half of the water in the large pot and half of it on another burner in a smaller pot. Cover them both and when they are boiling, carefully combine all of the water into the larger pot.

A word about:
MILK FAT

In all of our recipes calling for dairy products, we have used the lowest possible fat level that will produce food we're still happy to eat. We do not advise using a lower fat level than what is specified. It would be fine, however, to increase the fat level of any dairy product according to what you have on hand and your personal dietary preference.

For example: If a recipe calls for half-and-half, do not substitute whole or low-fat milk. But, you may "go up" in fat content and substitute heavy cream. Following this same idea, if a recipe calls for skim milk, feel free to use any fat level of milk you have on hand.

We do not recommend using fat-free dairy products in our recipes. Fat-free products become temperamental when heated and so we stay away.

Our desperate version of the Italian classic, chicken cacciatore, contains some twists on tradition, so we decided to anglicize its name—"cacciatore" means hunter in Italian. Chicken cacciatore is usually made with bone-in chicken and takes about an hour to cook. Switching to boneless chicken and thickening the sauce with cornstarch cuts the time to 20 minutes. However, the full-bodied, savory flavor remains intact, so whatever you call it, you'll end up with a great, quick meal.

HUNTER'S CHICKEN

8 ounces thin spaghetti (spaghettini)
4 skinless, boneless chicken breast halves
    (about 1⅓ pounds total), fresh or frozen
1 teaspoon olive oil
1 medium onion (for ¾ cup chopped)
1 teaspoon bottled minced garlic
2 large carrots or 12 already-peeled baby carrots
    (for ⅔ cup sliced)
1 medium green bell pepper (for 1 cup sliced)
1 can (14½ ounces) Italian-style stewed tomatoes
⅔ cup dry white wine or chicken broth
2 teaspoons Worcestershire sauce
2 bay leaves
1 tablespoon cornstarch
3 tablespoons water
Black pepper to taste

1. Bring 2½ quarts of unsalted water to a boil in a covered 4½-quart or larger Dutch oven or soup pot. When the water reaches a rapid boil, add the spaghetti and cook until tender, 9 minutes.

2. Meanwhile, if the chicken is frozen, run it under hot water so you can remove any packaging. Place the chicken on a microwave-safe plate and microwave 2 minutes, uncovered, on high, to begin defrosting.

3. Heat the oil over medium-high heat in a 12-inch nonstick skillet that has a lid. Peel and coarsely chop the onion, adding it to the skillet as you chop. Add the garlic. Peel the carrots, slice into ¼-inch circles, and add them to the pan. Seed the bell pepper, slice into ¼-inch strips, and add them to the pan. Cover and cook to soften the vegetables, 3 minutes.

4. Meanwhile, slice the chicken (fresh or partially defrosted) into ½-inch strips and add to the skillet, along with the tomatoes with their juice, the wine, Worcestershire, and bay leaves. Raise the heat to high and cook, covered, until the chicken is no longer pink in the center, about 9 minutes, uncovering occasionally to stir.

5. When the spaghetti is tender, drain and cover to keep warm.

6. Combine the cornstarch and water in a small container that has a lid. Shake well until the lumps disappear, then set aside. When the chicken is done, lower the heat to medium. Give the cornstarch mixture another shake and add it, a little at a time, stirring constantly until the sauce reaches the desired thickness. Season with black pepper to taste. Place some of the spaghetti on each serving plate. Top with the sauce, making sure to remove and discard the bay leaves, and serve.

Serves 4

> ### TIME-SAVER
> Buy a sharp vegetable peeler. If you have a peeler and don't think it makes peeling carrots and potatoes easier, chances are it's dull and you need a new one.

I first sampled this dish at a locally owned restaurant in Raleigh, North Carolina, called Crowley's. I was so impressed with it I asked the owner, John Ray, if he would share the recipe with me, and when he agreed, I was thrilled to find that I can prepare this impressive classic in less than 20 minutes.

Italy's famous Marsala wine is what makes the recipe so special. It is available in dry and sweet varieties, but the dry works best here.

MIND-THE-CLOCK CHICKEN MARSALA

BOIL THE H2O

8 ounces linguine
3 skinless, boneless chicken breast halves (about
    1 pound total), fresh or frozen
1 package (1.4 ounces) powdered demi-glaze
    (see Box, facing page)
½ cup all-purpose flour
½ teaspoon salt
¼ teaspoon black pepper
2 teaspoons extra-virgin olive oil
1 medium onion (for ¾ cup chopped)
2 cups already-sliced fresh mushrooms
⅔ cup dry Marsala wine

1. Place the linguine in 2½ quarts of already-boiling unsalted water and cook until tender, 9 to 11 minutes.

2. Meanwhile, if the chicken is frozen, run it under hot water so you can remove any packaging. Place the chicken on a microwave-safe plate and microwave 2 minutes, uncovered, on high, to begin defrosting. While the chicken microwaves, prepare the demi-glaze according to the package directions and set aside.

3. Combine the flour, salt, and pepper in a zipper-top plastic bag and shake to mix. Cut the chicken (fresh or partially defrosted) into bite-size pieces, drop them into the bag, and shake to coat.

4. Heat the oil in a 12-inch nonstick skillet over medium heat. Add the chicken and cook for 2 minutes, stirring from time to time. Peel and thinly slice the onion. Add them to the skillet along with the mushrooms and cook until the vegetables are softened and the chicken is no longer pink, 3 to 4 minutes.

5. When the linguine is tender, drain and cover to keep warm.

6. Add the wine to the skillet and heat, stirring and scraping to loosen any bits stuck to the pan bottom. Add the reserved demi-glaze and stir to coat the chicken pieces well. While the sauce heats through, place some linguine on each serving plate. Top with the sauce and serve.

Serves 4

OIL AND VINEGAR

Our recipes call for different varieties of oil and vinegar. Here's how you'll know which is best for each recipe.
 • If a recipe specifies extra-virgin olive oil, do not substitute unless you absolutely must. The recipe depends on the fruity, bold flavor present only in a good-quality, extra-virgin oil. We most typically use extra-virgin olive oil in salad dressings and some pasta dishes.

• If a recipe simply calls for olive oil, use any type of olive oil you have on hand: extra-virgin to pure to light.

• We call for peanut oil mainly in Asian stir-fry recipes. It adds a subtle flavor and holds up well at high temperatures. If you do not have any, substitute one of the vegetable oils below.

• If a recipe specifies vegetable oil, use any oil you have on hand *except* olive oil. Canola oil, safflower oil, soybean oil, corn oil, or a blend will all be acceptable.

• If a recipe calls for red wine vinegar, rice wine vinegar, or balsamic vinegar, the recipe depends on the distinct, fruity taste inherent in the individual vinegar specified. Try not to substitute unless you absolutely must.

• If a recipe calls for the cider vinegar or distilled white vinegar, you may use them interchangeably.

✳ *Demi-glaze (also spelled "demi-glace") is made by reducing a mixture of beef stock and sherry until it forms a thick sauce. The resulting glaze is intensely flavored and used to strengthen the flavor of other sauces. Demi-glaze is available dried, packaged in an envelope. Look for it near the pasta sauces or soups in your supermarket. We use the Mayacama brand.*

From Beverly:

My mother, Dorothy Mills, calls this her Friday night salvation supper. That's when she and my father make the forty-five-minute drive to their house at Topsail Beach in North Carolina. "I walk into that empty kitchen and I immediately start craving seafood," she told me. "Your father is always glad I don't have anything else to fix, because this is one of his favorite meals."

First choice for this dish is already-peeled raw shrimp; second is already-cooked, peeled shrimp.

TOPSAIL SPAGHETTI

8 ounces thin spaghetti (spaghettini)
1 teaspoon olive oil
1 medium onion (for ¾ cup chopped)
1 tablespoon bottled minced garlic
1 can (14½ ounces) Italian-style stewed tomatoes
1 small can (8 ounces) tomato sauce
1 teaspoon dried Italian seasoning
¼ teaspoon black pepper
¼ teaspoon crushed hot red pepper (optional)
Salt to taste
8 ounces already-peeled raw or cooked shrimp
¼ cup already-grated Parmesan cheese

1. Bring 2½ quarts of unsalted water to a boil in a covered 4½-quart or larger Dutch oven or soup pot. When the water reaches a rapid boil, add the spaghetti and cook until tender, 9 minutes.

2. Meanwhile, heat the oil in a 12-inch nonstick skillet over medium heat. Peel and coarsely chop the onion, adding it to the skillet as you chop. Add the garlic and cook, stirring from time to time, until the onion is soft, about 3 minutes.

3. Add the tomatoes and their juice, tomato sauce, Italian seasoning, black pepper, crushed hot red pepper (if using), and salt. Raise the heat to high, bring the mixture to a boil, reduce the heat to medium-low and simmer to blend the flavors and thicken slightly, 5 to 8 minutes. Stir from time to time.

4. Just before the spaghetti is done, add the shrimp to the sauce, raise the heat to high and cook until they are just pink, 3 to 4 minutes for raw. If shrimp are precooked, reduce time to 2 to 3 minutes to heat through. Stir frequently.

5. When the shrimp are cooked, drain the spaghetti and place some on each serving plate. Top with sauce and 1 tablespoon Parmesan cheese. Serve at once.

Serves 4

NO-STRESS SPAGHETTI

8 ounces thin spaghetti (spaghettini)
1 teaspoon olive oil
1 cup frozen chopped onions
½ teaspoon bottled minced garlic
½ teaspoon dried Italian seasoning
½ teaspoon Worcestershire sauce
1 jar (28 ounces) spaghetti sauce
2 cans (6½ ounces each) chopped clams

1. Bring 2½ quarts of unsalted water to a boil in a covered 4½-quart or larger Dutch oven or soup pot. When the water reaches a rapid boil, add the spaghetti and cook until tender, 9 minutes.

2. Meanwhile, heat the oil in a 12-inch nonstick skillet or 2-quart saucepan over medium heat. Add the onions, garlic, Italian seasoning, and Worcestershire. Cook, stirring often, 30 seconds. Add the spaghetti sauce.

3. Drain 1 can of clams and add them to the skillet (reserve the juice for another use). Add the other can of clams, undrained, to the skillet. Stir well to blend the sauce, about 1 minute. Bring to a slow boil, then reduce the heat to low and simmer while waiting for the pasta to finish cooking. When the spaghetti is tender, drain it and place some on each serving plate. Top with the sauce and serve.

Serves 4 generously

From Beverly:

This was one of the first Desperation Dinners I ever made, and it continues to be a meal I rely on year after year. As long as I keep some pasta, a jar of red sauce, and a couple of cans of clams in my cupboard, I feel safe. No matter how mean life gets, I know that in just 10 minutes, I can fight back with food that feeds the spirit as well as the body.

Up until about a year ago, I was satisfied making this dish with only one can of clams. But lately it seems there's a lot more juice in the can and a lot less clams. That's why the recipe calls for one can of drained clams and one can undrained. If you don't mind fewer clams, one can will do. Feel free to use your favorite bottled spaghetti sauce.

From Alicia:

As soon as I bought Clifford Wright's book, *Cucina Rapida,* I was dying to try a recipe. But I found myself with virtually none of the fresh ingredients he called for in any of the recipes. So I adapted a shrimp, spinach, and tomato dish of his to use frozen and pantry items I keep on hand. When I shared the adapted recipe with Beverly, she was so impressed she served it to dinner guests. No one knew that just 20 minutes before dinner, all of the ingredients were either in the freezer or cupboard.

FANCY SHRIMP FETTUCCINE

BOIL THE H₂O

12 ounces fettuccine
1 pound already-peeled-and-cooked shrimp
½ cup water
1 package (10 ounces) frozen chopped spinach
2 tablespoons plus 1 teaspoon olive oil
¼ cup lemon juice from frozen concentrate
2 teaspoons bottled minced garlic
1 teaspoon dried basil
¼ teaspoon black pepper
1 can (14½ ounces) diced tomatoes
Already-grated Parmesan cheese (optional)

1. Place the fettuccine in 2½ quarts of already-boiling unsalted water and cook until tender, 10 to 12 minutes. Meanwhile, finely chop 2 shrimp. Place the chopped shrimp and the ½ cup water in a 2-cup glass measure and microwave, uncovered, on high for 1 minute to make a broth. Set aside.

2. Place the block of frozen spinach in a microwave-safe dish, cover, and microwave, on high, for 3 minutes to defrost. Meanwhile, combine the remaining shrimp, the 2 tablespoons oil, the lemon juice, garlic, basil, and pepper in a 1-quart or larger bowl. Set aside.

3. Heat the 1 teaspoon oil in a 12-inch nonstick skillet over medium heat. Drain the tomatoes and add, along with the shrimp broth mixture and spinach. Raise the heat to high and cook, stirring to break up any frozen spinach, 5 minutes.

4. Drain the fettuccine and cover to keep warm. Add the reserved shrimp mixture to the skillet and cook until heated through, 2 minutes more. Place some fettuccine on each serving plate. Top with the heated sauce and Parmesan cheese (if using), and serve.

Serves 6

CREAMY CLAMS

8 ounces angel hair pasta
3 strips bacon (turkey, regular, or low-sodium)
1 large onion (for 1 cup chopped)
2 teaspoons olive oil
2 teaspoons bottled minced garlic
¼ teaspoon dried oregano or dried Italian seasoning
2 cans (6½ ounces each) chopped clams
½ cup frozen green peas (optional)
½ cup half-and-half
¼ cup already-grated or -shredded Parmesan cheese
Black pepper to taste

1. Bring 2½ quarts of unsalted water to a boil in a covered 4½-quart or larger Dutch oven or soup pot. When the water reaches a rapid boil, add the pasta and cook until tender, 3 to 5 minutes.

2. Meanwhile, cook the bacon in a 12-inch nonstick skillet over medium-low heat until browned, about 4 minutes. While the bacon cooks, peel and coarsely chop the onion. Set aside.

3. Remove the bacon to a plate lined with paper towels. (If not using turkey bacon, drain off any fat.) Heat the oil in the same skillet and add the onion, garlic, and oregano. Raise the heat to medium and cook to soften the onion, 3 minutes. Meanwhile, crumble or chop the bacon and set aside.

4. Add the clams with their juice and the peas (if using). Raise the heat to high and boil for 2 minutes. Add the half-and-half and reduce the heat to low. Cook 2 minutes to heat the liquid, then stir in the Parmesan cheese and bacon and cook to melt the cheese, 2 minutes more. Season with black pepper.

5. Meanwhile, drain the pasta and place some on each serving plate. Top with the sauce and serve.

Serves 4

From Beverly:

A huge thank-you goes to my sister-in-law, Liza Bennett, for sharing this wonderful 15-minute recipe for creamy clam sauce. With her blessing, I substituted turkey bacon for the pancetta (Italian bacon) she's able to buy easily in New York City. Turkey bacon still gives a bold, smoky flavor, and I don't have to make a trip to a specialty butcher. Parmesan cheese, sprinkled in at the end of cooking, thickens the sauce and makes it adhere nicely to the pasta. I find myself craving this meal at least once a week.

PASTA WITH SALMON CREAM

A package of smoked Nova Scotia salmon will store in the refrigerator for months unopened, making it a wonderful resource for unexpected emergencies. The package is about the size of a business envelope, so it doesn't take up much precious refrigerator room. Only 3 ounces of the smoky fish (the kind typically used on bagels) is needed to flavor a sauce for four. This mild, creamy sauce lets the smoked fish take center stage.

8 ounces fettuccine
1 teaspoon olive oil
1 medium onion (for ¾ cup chopped)
1 cup frozen green peas (optional)
½ cup grated Parmesan cheese, plus additional for serving
½ cup half-and-half
2 teaspoons lemon juice from frozen concentrate
1½ teaspoons bottled minced garlic
¼ teaspoon crushed hot red pepper (optional)
¼ teaspoon dried dill
1 package (3 ounces) smoked Nova Scotia salmon
⅔ cup fat-free plain yogurt or reduced-fat sour cream

1. Place the fettuccine in 2½ quarts of already-boiling unsalted water and cook 10 to 12 minutes. Meanwhile, heat the oil in a 12-inch nonstick skillet over medium heat. Peel and coarsely chop the onion, adding it to the skillet as you chop. Cook until soft, about 2 minutes.

2. Add the peas (if using), ½ cup Parmesan cheese, half-and-half, lemon juice, garlic, hot red pepper (if using), and dill. Cook, stirring occasionally, to thicken the sauce slightly, 5 minutes. Do not boil. While the sauce thickens, cut the salmon into bite-size pieces.

3. When the sauce has thickened slightly, stir in the salmon and cook just to warm through, 2 minutes. Remove from the heat and stir in the yogurt.

4. When the fettuccine is tender, drain and place it in a 3-quart or larger serving bowl. Add the sauce and toss well to mix. Serve at once, passing additional Parmesan cheese at the table.

Serves 4

GREEK PASTA

8 ounces vermicelli

8 sun-dried tomato pieces, not packed in oil

2 tablespoons olive oil

3 to 4 bunches scallions (green onions; for 1¾ cups chopped)

1 teaspoon bottled minced garlic

2 teaspoons dried Italian seasoning

1 pound sea scallops

1 can (2¼ ounces) sliced black olives

2 tablespoons white wine

½ cup already-crumbled feta cheese

We always say, if a recipe has feta cheese in it, what's not to like? Even better, if the recipe takes only minutes to zap together, it's a winner. This combination of Greek-inspired seasonings and seafood would be a favorite even if it took an hour to prepare. But since it doesn't, we get to enjoy it a lot more often.

1. Bring 2½ quarts of unsalted water to a boil in a covered 4½-quart or larger Dutch oven or soup pot. When the water reaches a rapid boil, add the vermicelli and cook until tender, 4 to 5 minutes.

2. Meanwhile, coarsely chop the sun-dried tomato pieces and place in a 2-cup glass measure. Add 1 cup water and microwave 3 minutes, uncovered, on high. Remove the tomatoes from the microwave and let them stand in the water to soften, 5 minutes.

3. Meanwhile, heat the oil in a 12-inch nonstick skillet over medium heat. Cut the scallions into ¼-inch slices, using enough of the tender green tops to make 1¾ cups and adding them to the skillet as you cut. Add the garlic and Italian seasoning, and cook until the scallions are softened, 1 minute. Add the scallops and cook, stirring frequently, until they are just opaque, 3 minutes.

4. Drain the sun-dried tomatoes and olives and add them to the skillet along with the wine and feta cheese. Cook for 1 minute to blend the flavors, then remove from the heat.

5. Drain the vermicelli well and place it in a 3-quart or larger serving bowl. Add the scallop mixture, toss, and serve.

Serves 4

From Beverly:

From Beverly:

S andra Burnett, a chef and former restaurant owner, graciously shared this recipe. Her "Granny Deaton" lived across the street from my "Grandma Hood," and Sandra has been a role model from the earliest days of my culinary career. I have both admired her ambition and savored her incredible food. These days, Sandra is one of the most sought-after caterers in Raleigh, North Carolina. When she gets home from a grueling day in the kitchen and doesn't know what to eat, this is the recipe she makes. Sandra relies on homemade pesto that she freezes in the summer, but the refrigerated variety from the supermarket makes a perfectly fine substitute.

SANDRA'S PENNE WITH SUMMER SAUCE

3 cups (12 ounces) penne or other short tubular
    pasta
2 teaspoons olive oil
1 extra-large Vidalia or other sweet onion (for
    1½ cups chopped)
2 cloves garlic
1 package (8 ounces) already-sliced fresh mushrooms
½ cup white wine
4 fresh, ripe medium Roma (plum) tomatoes
    (about 12 ounces)
½ cup commercially prepared pesto
1 cup half-and-half
½ cup already-grated Parmesan cheese, plus additional
    for serving
Salt and black pepper to taste

1. Place the penne in 2½ quarts of already-boiling unsalted water and cook until tender, 11 to 13 minutes.

2. Meanwhile, heat the oil in a 12-inch nonstick skillet over medium heat. Peel and chop the onion and garlic, adding them to the pan as you chop. Add the mushrooms and wine, stir, and raise the heat to medium-high. Cook, stirring occasionally, for 5 minutes.

3. While the vegetables cook, slice off the stem end of the unpeeled tomatoes. Cut them in half lengthwise and scoop out the seeds with a small spoon or your finger. Discard the seeds; then slice the tomatoes thinly lengthwise. (You should have about

1½ cups.) Place the tomato strips in a 3-quart or larger serving bowl and set aside.

4. When the onion is soft and the mushrooms have released their juices, remove the skillet from the heat. Using a slotted spoon to leave behind as much juice as possible, remove the vegetables to the bowl with the tomatoes and set aside.

5. Discard any juice remaining in the skillet, then, taking care not to burn yourself, wipe out the skillet with several paper towels. Place the skillet over medium-low heat and add the pesto and half-and-half. Stir well and heat the mixture to just before the boiling point. Reduce the heat to a simmer and cook until the sauce gets slightly thicker, about 4 minutes.

6. Meanwhile, when the penne is tender, drain it and add to the serving bowl with the reserved vegetables.

7. Stir the ½ cup Parmesan cheese into the skillet with the half-and-half mixture and continue to cook to melt the cheese, 2 minutes. Pour the sauce over the penne and vegetables. Season with salt and pepper to taste, toss well, and serve at once, passing extra cheese at the table.

Serves 6 generously

> *"What do good movies and reliable recipes have in common? The ones you're bound to like best are those friends recommend."*

We all have family members with special dietary needs or peculiarities of the palate. As much as we love them, family members who can't eat this and won't eat that can be frustrating—and challenging—for the already-too-busy cook.

My sister-in-law is a vegetarian. Her husband, my brother, is a marathon runner who counts every gram he eats when training for a race. My joy in having them to dinner is always tempered by the apprehension involved in finding a meal that suits everyone's special needs. Although they are happy eating a salad and bread or plain pasta, it always seems inhospitable if my guests don't get to enjoy what the rest of us are eating.

Since "carbo-loading" is part of being a long-distance runner, a vegetarian version of my quickie pasta sauce always makes an appropriate meal.

My typical vegetable choices are onions, carrots, and yellow squash, but you can easily substitute your own favorites.

VEGETABLE MARINARA

3 cups (12 ounces) ziti
1 teaspoon olive oil
1 medium onion (for ¾ cup chopped)
2 teaspoons bottled minced garlic
2 large carrots or 12 already-peeled baby carrots
*   (for ⅔ cup sliced)*
2 medium yellow squash (for 1½ cups sliced)
1 cup already-sliced fresh mushrooms
1 can (14½ ounces) pasta-style chopped tomatoes
1 can (14½ ounces) diced tomatoes
1 can (6 ounces) tomato paste
1 teaspoon dried basil

1. Place the ziti in 2½ quarts of already-boiling unsalted water and cook until tender, 12 to 14 minutes. Meanwhile, heat the oil in a 4½-quart Dutch oven or soup pot over medium-high heat. Peel and coarsely chop the onion, adding it to the pot as you chop. Add the garlic and continue to cook, stirring occasionally.

2. While the onion softens, peel the carrots (if necessary) and slice them into ¼-inch circles, adding them to the pot as you slice. Slice the squash into ¼-inch circles and add them to the pot. Add the mushrooms, cover the pot, and continue to cook until the carrots are tender, about 6 minutes.

3. While the vegetables cook, open the cans. When the carrots are tender, add both of the tomatoes with their juice, the tomato paste, and basil. Stir well. Cover the pot and cook over medium heat until bubbly, about 4 minutes.

4. When the ziti is tender, drain it and place some on each serving plate. Top with the sauce and serve.

Serves 6

FETTUCCINE ALFREDO (ALMOST)

8 ounces fettuccine
1½ teaspoons butter
½ cup reduced-fat cream cheese (see Note)
1⅓ cups skim milk
⅛ teaspoon white pepper
⅛ teaspoon ground nutmeg
¾ cup (3 ounces) already-grated or -shredded Parmesan cheese,
plus additional for serving

1. Place the fettuccine in 2½ quarts of already-boiling unsalted water and cook until tender, 10 to 12 minutes.

2. Meanwhile, melt the butter over medium heat in a 2½-quart or larger saucepan. Add the cream cheese and milk, stirring constantly with a wire whisk until well blended and smooth, 3 minutes.

3. Add the pepper and nutmeg. Gradually add the ¾ cup Parmesan cheese, stirring constantly with the whisk. Stir briskly until the cheese is melted and incorporated, about 3 minutes. (The sauce will be thin.) Remove from the heat and let stand, covered, until the fettuccine is tender.

4. Drain the fettuccine and place in a 3-quart or larger serving bowl. Give the sauce another brisk stir, then pour it over the fettuccine, tossing well to mix. Serve at once, passing additional Parmesan cheese at the table.

Serves 4

Note: Some brands of reduced-fat cream cheese call the product "light" cream cheese and some call it "Neufchatel" cheese. We do not recommend fat-free cream cheese for this recipe.

From Alicia:

The first time I tasted fettuccine Alfredo, I fell instantly in love. The creamy texture and hint of nutmeg were heavenly. Then I saw an article that called Alfredo sauce "heart attack on a plate," and I was devastated. Traditional fettuccine Alfredo can have as many as 60 grams of fat in a one-cup serving.

I knew I couldn't continue to indulge, so I started to experiment. Thanks to reduced-fat cream cheese, I now have a lighter version I can do at home in 20 minutes. This sauce, with less than 15 grams of fat per serving, is thinner than the traditional version, but the great flavor is still there—and gone is the threat of cardiac arrest.

✳ *Good-quality Parmesan cheese is essential to great Alfredo sauce. Many supermarkets stock freshly shredded Parmesan in the deli. If you can't find that, look for the fancy shredded Parmesan with the other shredded cheeses in the dairy case.*

From Alicia:

Here's a great recipe for made-from-scratch tomato sauce. No, I haven't lost my mind. With two jobs and two kids, I don't have time to compete with Martha Stewart. And yet, I *am* talking homemade—a sauce complete with the unmistakable taste of summer's best.

This recipe makes 6 cups of sauce, so you'll have about half the batch left over. But since it's no more trouble to go ahead and cook the extra sauce and it's so flexible, you get a jump start on dinner later on. Store the leftover sauce for up to 5 days refrigerated or 3 months frozen. Dress it up by adding ground meat or Italian sausage. It also makes a great starting point for lasagna.

Our recipe specifies rotini, but this all-purpose sauce is wonderful with any pasta you have on hand.

ROTINI WITH FRESH TOMATO SAUCE

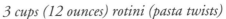

3 cups (12 ounces) rotini (pasta twists)
2 tablespoons extra-virgin olive oil
3 pounds (4 to 6 large) fresh, ripe tomatoes
    (for about 8 cups sliced)
1 can (6 ounces) reduced-sodium tomato paste
2 teaspoons bottled minced garlic
2 teaspoons sugar, or to taste
2 tablespoons chopped fresh parsley (optional)
1 tablespoon chopped fresh oregano, or 1 teaspoon dried
1 tablespoon chopped fresh basil, or 1 teaspoon dried
Salt and black pepper to taste

1. Place the rotini in 2½ quarts of already-boiling unsalted water and cook until tender, 9 to 11 minutes.

2. Meanwhile, heat the oil in a 4½-quart Dutch oven or soup pot over low heat. Core and dice the tomatoes (but do not peel or seed), adding them to the oil as you dice. After the first tomato is added, raise the heat to medium. When all the tomatoes are added, cover the pot and raise the heat to high. Add the remaining ingredients, keeping the pot covered as much as possible. Cook over high heat for 5 minutes, uncovering occasionally to stir.

3. Uncover the pot, reduce the heat to medium-low, and cook for 5 minutes more to blend the flavors, stirring occasionally.

4. Drain the rotini and place some on each serving plate. Top with the sauce and serve.

Serves 6, with 3 cups of sauce left over for another recipe

PANTRY PASTA

⅔ bag (8 ounces of a 12-ounce bag) yolk-free wide egg noodles
1 teaspoon vegetable oil
⅓ cup frozen chopped onions
1 teaspoon bottled minced garlic
⅓ cup fat-free canned chicken broth
⅓ cup peanut butter
2 tablespoons reduced-sodium soy sauce
2 tablespoons distilled white vinegar
1 tablespoon lemon juice from frozen concentrate (optional)
1 tablespoon sugar
1 teaspoon bottled chopped ginger (optional)
3 scallions (green onions; for ¼ cup chopped; optional)
1 large can (10 ounces) white-meat chicken (optional)
½ cup unsalted dry-roasted peanuts (optional)

1. Place the noodles in 2½ quarts of already-boiling unsalted water and cook until tender, 10 to 12 minutes. Meanwhile, heat the oil in an 8-inch or larger nonstick skillet over medium heat. Add the onions and garlic and cook to soften, 1 minute, stirring often.

2. Stir in the chicken broth, peanut butter, soy sauce, vinegar, lemon juice (if using), sugar, and ginger (if using). Reduce the heat to low and simmer 5 minutes, stirring often. Meanwhile, finely chop the scallions (if using), including enough of the tender green tops to make ¼ cup.

3. When the noodles are tender, drain and place them in a 3-quart or larger serving bowl. Drain the chicken (if using), and add it to the bowl, along with the green onions. Pour the sauce over the noodles. Toss well to mix. Garnish with chopped peanuts (if using), and serve.

Serves 4

The simplicity and versatility of this recipe makes it perfect for when you want to delay that trip to the supermarket just one more day. The sauce goes well with any kind of pasta, any type of oil, any sort of onion, all types of sweeteners, any kind of peanut butter, and—well, you get the idea. For added flavor and nutrition, we like to throw a couple handfuls of frozen green peas into the noodle pot in the last 2 minutes of cooking.

All of the optional ingredients intensify the flavor, but the sauce is still yummy without them.

TIME-SAVER

Get creative with the names of new foods to spark young children's interest. Example: When we serve our kids Rotini with Fresh Tomato Sauce, we call it Saucy Twists. Pantry Pasta becomes Nutty Noodles. By using names they find fun, we get no arguments from our kids, and that surely saves us time.

TWO-FOR-ONE NOODLES

This is the first of two intertwined recipes that start the same and end up differently. Our friend Betsy Devine says her husband and daughters especially love the first recipe—the ricotta noodles. Then the next night she takes the leftover noodles and builds her favorite dish—Mock Spinach and Ricotta Lasagna.

Betsy calls this the sanity-saving dish of the year. She fixes a favorite for her family one night and is rewarded with her own favorite dish the next night. That means two nights of stress-free dinners that please the whole family. Leftovers store in the refrigerator for 4 days.

> ✳ *If you have fresh basil substitute 1 tablespoon chopped for the dried. Chop it when you chop the parsley, if using, in step 2.*

4 cups (16 ounces) penne
2 tablespoons olive oil
1 small onion (for ½ cup diced)
3 slices bacon (turkey, regular, or low-sodium)
1 tablespoon fresh parsley leaves (optional)
1 large container (15 ounces) reduced-fat ricotta cheese
¼ cup already-grated Parmesan cheese, plus additional for serving
½ teaspoon dried basil (see Box)
3 tablespoons hot water from the pasta pot
Salt and black pepper to taste

1. Place the penne in 3 quarts of already-boiling unsalted water and cook until tender, 11 to 13 minutes.

2. Meanwhile, heat the oil in an 8-inch or larger nonstick skillet, over low heat. Peel and dice the onion and add it to the skillet. Coarsely chop the bacon, add it to the skillet and cook until the onion is tender and the bacon is not quite crisp, about 3 minutes. While the onion and bacon cook, chop the parsley (if using).

3. Using a slotted spoon, remove the bacon and onion to a 3-quart or larger serving bowl. To the bowl add the ricotta, the ¼ cup Parmesan cheese, parsley, basil, and hot cooking water from the pasta pot. Stir well and set aside.

4. Drain the penne well and pour half immediately into the bowl with the ricotta mixture. Stir well to mix, then add the remaining penne and stir well again. Season with salt and pepper and serve, passing extra Parmesan at the table.

Serves 8 or 4 with leftovers to make the lasagna on page 172

A word about:
DAIRY PRODUCTS

From Beverly:

Long live dairy products! And live long they do—from one month to four—unopened in your fridge. At the moment, there's a month to go before my nonfat yogurt is kaput, two months left to rely on my "lite" sour cream, and nearly four months before I must decide the fate of my reduced-fat ricotta and shredded Cheddar cheese.

Thanks to the war on cholesterol, I had all but forgotten this luxury of ultra-pasteurized shelf life. Now, with all of the fat-trimmed dairy products on the market, I am once again happily checking expiration dates and "sell-by" dates at my local supermarket refrigerator case.

Dairy products normally are safe to use for one week after their sell-by dates. An expiration date, on the other hand, is the last day the manufacturer believes the food should be consumed. However, expiration dates usually apply to sealed packages. After opening the product at home, the food scientist we consulted at North Carolina State University recommended the old take-a-whiff test: If it smells funny, throw it out. To help these still-sealed products last longest, food-science researchers advise turning your refrigerator to its coldest setting.

I'm a firm believer in scrutinizing package dates at the supermarket. In my experience, the cartons toward the back of the shelf usually have a more distant expiration or sell-by date. I want the most time I can get, because what all of this time really buys is bailout potential. When I'm convinced there's nothing in the house to eat, I'll remember that container of unopened cheese or yogurt. In a matter of minutes, I can whip up a sauce for pasta, turn leftover vegetables into a brand-new side dish, or jazz up plain old chicken breasts. On desperate nights, I figure a little cholesterol is better than starvation.

Use the leftovers from the Two-for-One Noodles as the base for this quick lasagna. Any favorite jarred spaghetti sauce, with or without vegetables or meat, will do.

The leftover Two-for-Ones can be held for 4 days in the refrigerator, which gives your family plenty of time between the two meals.

MOCK SPINACH AND RICOTTA LASAGNA

PRE HEAT OVEN

1 package (10 ounces) frozen chopped spinach
4 cups leftover Two-for-One Noodles (half of recipe, page 170)
1 jar (26 ounces) spaghetti sauce
1 cup (4 ounces) already-shredded mozzarella cheese

1. The oven should be already heated to 425°F.

2. Place the block of frozen spinach in a microwave-safe dish, cover, and microwave on high for 5 minutes to defrost.

3. Meanwhile, place the Two-for-One Noodles in a 13 × 9-inch glass baking dish, separating any that may be stuck together. When the spinach is defrosted, drain well and scatter over the noodles. Top with the spaghetti sauce and sprinkle with the cheese.

4. Bake until bubbly hot, 12 minutes. Serve at once.

Serves 4

BALSAM MOUNTAIN INN'S FANCY FETTUCCINE

8 ounces fettuccine
1 can (14 ounces) artichoke hearts packed in water
1 tablespoon butter
1½ cups already-sliced fresh mushrooms
⅓ cup (½ package) Knorr Fine Herb Soup and Recipe Mix
½ teaspoon dried basil
1½ cups low-fat or skim milk
½ cup already-shredded Cheddar cheese
½ cup already-shredded Parmesan cheese
1 tablespoon all-purpose flour

1. Place the fettuccine in 2½ quarts of already-boiling unsalted water and cook until tender, 10 to 12 minutes.

2. Meanwhile, drain and coarsely chop the artichoke hearts. Melt the butter in a 3-quart saucepan, over medium heat. Add the artichokes and mushrooms and cook, stirring occasionally, until tender, about 2 minutes. Add the soup mix and basil and stir well. Add the milk and the Cheddar and Parmesan cheeses and stir until the cheeses are melted.

3. Sprinkle in the flour and stir until the sauce is the consistency of warm pudding. Reduce the heat to the lowest setting and simmer, stirring occasionally, while the fettuccine finishes cooking.

4. Drain the fettuccine and place some on each serving plate. Top with sauce and serve.

Serves 4

We just love recipes with secret ingredients. You'd never guess that the cryptic component in this sauce is nothing more complicated than a packet of Knorr Fine Herb Soup and Recipe Mix.

This recipe comes from chef Noell Teasley of the Balsam Mountain Inn in Balsam, North Carolina. We sized it for home use and were thrilled to find that the sauce takes just minutes to prepare.

You'll only use half the envelope of soup mix, and since the sauce for this dish does not store well, pop the extra mix into a zipper-top bag and save it for another batch. The dish is so simple and satisfying, you'll probably find yourself reaching for the remaining soup mix sooner than you'd expect.

This is a wonderful cold-weather meal— rich and fortifying. Bits of sun-dried tomatoes add a burst of flavor in every bite and contrast nicely with the fennel seeds in the Italian sausage. If pine nuts aren't available, you can substitute walnut pieces or just omit nuts altogether.

ITALIAN-STYLE TORTELLINI

1 bag (14 ounces) frozen cheese tortellini
½ pound Italian sausage links, sweet or hot
12 sun-dried tomato pieces, not packed in oil
1 large onion (for 1 cup chopped)
2 teaspoons bottled minced garlic
¼ cup pine nuts (optional)
¼ cup already-grated Parmesan cheese

1. Bring 2½ quarts of unsalted water to a boil in a covered 4½-quart or larger Dutch oven or soup pot. When the water reaches a rapid boil, add the tortellini and cook until tender, 7 to 9 minutes.

2. Meanwhile, remove and discard the casings from the sausage and fry the meat in a 12-inch nonstick skillet over medium heat. Stir occasionally to prevent sticking and to break up the pieces.

3. While the sausage cooks, coarsely chop the sun-dried tomato pieces and place in a 2-cup glass measure. Add 1 cup water and microwave 3 minutes, uncovered, on high. Remove the tomatoes from the microwave and let them stand in the water to soften, 5 minutes. While they soften, peel and coarsely chop the onion, adding it to the skillet with the sausage as you chop. Cook until soft, 3 minutes, stirring occasionally. Add the garlic and stir.

4. Remove the sun-dried tomatoes from the liquid with a slotted spoon, reserving the liquid. Add the tomatoes and pine nuts (if using) to the skillet, and stir. Cook until the sausage is no longer pink. If dry add ¼ to ½ cup of the reserved soaking liquid.

5. Drain the tortellini and pour them into a 3-quart or larger serving bowl. Add the meat mixture and the Parmesan cheese, tossing well to mix and melt the cheese. Serve at once.

Serves 4

A word about:
STUFFED PASTA

It's getting easier to be a desperate cook. Now most supermarkets sell ravioli and tortellini—wonderful pillows filled with meat, vegetables, or cheese that add a whole new dimension to the quick pasta dinner.

For starters, these filled pastas cook in just 5 to 10 minutes. That's an obvious benefit. Second, they're appearing in lots of flavor combinations, which cuts the boredom quotient.

Finally, they're foolproof. Tortellini and ravioli taste great plain, and that means your contribution to dinner can range from something as simple as a little olive oil and Parmesan cheese to a homemade cream sauce. We tend to stick somewhere in the middle, adding a little Italian sausage, a bit of broccoli, or an assertive pantry ingredient like roasted red peppers.

There are several options for buying filled pastas. Cheese or meat-filled ravioli and tortellini from the supermarket freezer case are probably the most widely available and most reasonably priced. These work well in all of our recipes. Several national brands have also started to offer "fresh" filled refrigerated pastas. Look for these near the refrigerated pasta sauces in the dairy section of the supermarket. The refrigerated ravioli and tortellini often come in gourmet flavors and cost a little more. If you happen to live in a city where the grocery offers a good-quality dried tortellini or ravioli (or makes its own), these can also be substituted.

Our home freezer pantries wouldn't be complete without a bag of filled pasta. They're fast, filling, and served plain or tossed with a bit of butter, they even appeal to toddlers. What more could we ask?

For our friend Julie Realon, this meal eliminated the ho-hum of yet another night of pasta. "I would have never thought to put raisins in this dish, but it's wonderful," said Julie, a preschool director and mother of three who helped test many of the recipes for this book in her own kitchen. "I love pasta, and this is so different from what I usually fix," she said.

It *is* different, and the contrast between the savory meat filling of the tortellini and the sweet raisins is what makes it so unique. We tested this recipe with a brand of tortellini found in the refrigerated section of the supermarket. We've noticed that the kinds of meat fillings available in tortellini are not always the same from week to week. The type of meat doesn't matter, but we've found that the stronger flavor of meat does work better than cheese for this dish. If you go with a frozen meat tortellini, check the package directions for cooking time. You may have to cook it a bit longer in step 1.

Tortellini with Raisin Butter

2 packages (7 ounces each) refrigerated meat-filled tortellini
4 tablespoons (½ stick) butter
2 teaspoons vegetable oil
1 package (8 ounces) already-sliced fresh mushrooms
¼ cup pine nuts
¼ cup raisins

1. Bring 2½ quarts of unsalted water to a boil in a covered 4½-quart or larger Dutch oven or soup pot. When the water reaches a rapid boil, add the tortellini and cook until tender, 5 to 7 minutes.

2. Meanwhile, put the butter in a 1- or 2-cup glass measure and cover with a paper towel to prevent splatters. Microwave on high until the butter melts completely, about 45 seconds. Set aside.

3. Heat the oil in a 12-inch nonstick skillet over medium heat. Add the mushrooms and cook until they release their juices, 5 to 6 minutes. Drain the mushrooms in a colander and set aside.

4. Off the heat and taking care not to burn yourself, wipe the skillet bottom with paper towels to remove any remaining juice, then return the pot to medium-low heat and prepare to pour the butter. Notice that the white milk solids will have sunk to the bottom of the measuring cup. Very slowly pour the top, yellow butter only into the pot. Discard the remaining milk solids. Cook the butter to bring it to a golden brown, 5 minutes, stirring frequently. Watch carefully; you don't want to overbrown the butter.

5. Add the pine nuts and cook, stirring until the nuts are lightly toasted, 1 minute more. Stir in the reserved mushrooms and the

raisins and cook another 30 seconds to heat through. Remove from the heat.

6. When the tortellini are tender, drain and return to the pot. Pour in the butter sauce. Stir gently to coat the pasta and serve.

Serves 4

CREAMY RAVIOLI AND BROCCOLI

1 bunch fresh broccoli or 3 cups already-cut florets
½ cup already-grated Parmesan cheese
½ cup whole-milk ricotta cheese
2 tablespoons olive oil
1 tablespoon reduced-fat real bacon bits (not imitation)
½ teaspoon crushed hot red pepper (optional)
1 large package (25 ounces) frozen ravioli, preferably beef

1. Bring 2½ quarts of unsalted water to a boil in a covered 4½-quart or larger Dutch oven or soup pot. Meanwhile, cut the florets from the broccoli stalk and set aside. Combine the Parmesan, ricotta, oil, bacon bits, and hot red pepper (if using) in a 3-quart or larger serving bowl. Stir well to mix and set aside.

2. When the water reaches a rapid boil, add the broccoli and ravioli. Cover and bring the water back to a boil. Crack the lid and cook at a medium boil until the pasta is tender, about 5 minutes.

3. When the pasta is done, drain it and the broccoli in a colander, shaking to remove as much water as possible, and add to the serving bowl. Toss well to coat with the sauce and serve.

Serves 4

The ingenious thing about this recipe is that you cook the broccoli with the ravioli. (We like anything that saves on cleanup.) The Parmesan sauce goes together in a snap.

TIME-SAVER

Just as we do in the recipe for Creamy Ravioli and Broccoli, when you cook pasta and vegetables for the same meal, throw sturdier ones, such as asparagus, cauliflower, or carrot chunks right in with the pasta. Separate before serving with a slotted spoon.

From Beverly:

A two-dollar jar of roasted red peppers can turn a plain old pasta meal into an elegant feast. When my husband asked on the spur of the moment to bring a West Coast colleague home for some southern hospitality, this is the meal I served. Since this sauce whips together in about 12 minutes, I still had time to make a salad, hide the dirty laundry, and move a zoo's worth of stuffed animals off the living room sofa.

If you boiled the cream a little longer in step 4 until reduced by half to make a very thick sauce, it would be delicious spooned over chicken, beef, or fish.

RAVIOLI WITH ROASTED RED PEPPER CREAM

1 large package (25 ounces) frozen cheese ravioli
1 jar (7 ounces) roasted sweet red peppers, drained
½ cup white wine
1 cup heavy (or whipping) cream
¾ cup (3 ounces) already-grated Parmesan cheese

1. Bring 2½ quarts of unsalted water to a boil in a covered 4½-quart or larger Dutch oven or soup pot. When the water reaches a rapid boil, add the ravioli and cook until tender, about 5 minutes.

2. Meanwhile, using a strainer or colander, drain and rinse the red peppers to remove the seeds. Blot them on paper towels to remove any excess moisture. Put the peppers in a 2-quart saucepan off the heat. Using two blunt-edged knives (like dinner knives), cut the peppers into bite-size pieces.

3. Add the wine to the pan, and place over high heat. Bring to a boil and continue to cook until only about 2 tablespoons of liquid remain, 4 to 5 minutes. (Watch carefully in the last minute of boiling. The liquid will evaporate quickly.)

4. Add the cream, bring to a boil, and boil to thicken slightly, 3 to 4 minutes, stirring from time to time. Remove from the heat, add the Parmesan, and stir until melted, about 2 minutes.

5. When the ravioli is done, drain well and divide it among 4 shallow pasta bowls or soup bowls. Top each serving with ½ cup sauce and serve.

Serves 4

A word about:
NO-COOK SAUCES

From Beverly:

When I'm on vacation, I love to cook. Finally, life slows down. Mornings I sit on the beach and sift through recipes I've collected throughout the year, while afternoons find me stirring pots and turning fresh peaches into pie. At least that's how it goes for the first few days. By Friday I'll have hit vacation nirvana, a state identified by the ability to stare at scenery for hours and the inability to move. That's when I switch to the Desperation Vacation Mode. The objective is a fabulous meal that demands no more than 15 minutes, and one that won't turn the kitchen into a summer Hades.

It can be done. In our recipes for Spaghettini with Smoked Oyster Sauce, Pizza Pasta, or Summer's Best Pasta (all on the next few pages), the only thing you have to cook is the pasta. In these recipes, everything gets thrown into a gigantic bowl, and the hot pasta melts the cheese as you toss it all together.

The key to our no-cook sauces is to focus on just a few intense ingredients. While Desperation Dinners usually call for dried herbs, we do prefer fresh in most of our no-cook sauces because the bright, raw flavor really stands out. My favorite no-cook sauce is nothing more than vine-ripened tomatoes, garlic, extra-virgin olive oil, a bit each of mozzarella and best-quality Parmesan cheese, and some fresh basil leaves. We call this our Basic No-Cook Sauce, and even though you have to chop a few herbs and dice a tomato, that's all there is to it.

No matter which no-cook sauce you choose, you'll love the way they go together quickly without steaming up the kitchen. This method is so easy, it hardly feels like cooking. After all, why would you want to stress a spirit that's finally reached the state of absolute relaxation?

"'Keep it simple. Keep it simple. Keep it simple.' How many times do we need to remind ourselves?"

This dish allows for lots of substitutions. Use Canadian bacon, bottled real bacon bits, or hard salami in place of the pepperoni. If you have fresh tomatoes, use two (chopped but not peeled) as an alternative to the dried ones. We like the corkscrew shape of rotini, but any substantial short pasta will do.

PIZZA PASTA ⬛ 😊

2 cups (8 ounces) rotini (pasta twists)
10 sun-dried tomato pieces, not packed in oil
1 cup water
1 ounce sliced pepperoni (about 10 to 12 slices)
2 cloves garlic
1 can (2¼ ounces) sliced black olives
2 tablespoons extra-virgin olive oil
1½ teaspoons Italian seasoning
½ teaspoon balsamic vinegar
¼ cup fresh parsley leaves (optional)
¾ cup (3 ounces) already-shredded Parmesan cheese
½ cup already-shredded mozzarella cheese
Black pepper to taste

1. Bring 2½ quarts of unsalted water to a boil in a covered 4½-quart Dutch oven or larger soup pot. When the water reaches a rapid boil, add the rotini and cook until tender, 9 to 11 minutes.

2. Meanwhile, coarsely chop the sun-dried tomato pieces and place in a 2-cup glass measure. Add the water and microwave 3 minutes, uncovered, on high.

3. While the tomatoes microwave, line a microwave-safe plate with paper towels and place the pepperoni in a single layer on the plate. When the tomatoes are done, remove them from the microwave and let stand to soften, 5 minutes. Then, microwave the pepperoni on high until the slices release some of their oil but are still tender, about 30 to 45 seconds. Set aside.

4. Peel and finely mince the garlic and place it in a 3-quart or larger serving bowl. Drain the black olives and add them to the bowl along with the oil, Italian seasoning, and vinegar. Stir well and set aside. Drain the sun-dried tomatoes and add them to the bowl. Chop the pepperoni slices roughly into quarters and add them to the bowl. Chop the parsley (if using) and add.

5. Drain the rotini, add it to the bowl with the sauce, and stir to mix. Sprinkle with both of the cheeses, tossing as you sprinkle until the cheeses melt. Season with black pepper and serve.

Serves 6

ZITI WITH BASIC NO-COOK SAUCE ★★☺

2 cups (8 ounces) ziti
4 large or 6 medium fresh, ripe Roma (plum) tomatoes
   (about 1¼ pounds)
3 cloves garlic
¼ cup extra-virgin olive oil
¼ cup fresh basil leaves, tightly packed
1 cup (4 ounces) already-shredded mozzarella cheese
⅓ cup already-grated Parmesan cheese

1. Bring 2½ quarts of unsalted water to a boil in a covered 4½-quart or larger Dutch oven or soup pot. When the water reaches a rapid boil, add the ziti and cook until tender, 9 minutes.

2. Meanwhile, cut off and discard the core ends of the tomatoes but leave the skin on. Chop the tomatoes into bite-size pieces and add them to a 3-quart or larger serving bowl. Peel and chop the garlic, and add it to the bowl. Pour in the oil. Chop the basil and stir it into the tomato mixture, then set the bowl aside.

3. Drain the ziti and add it to the bowl with the sauce. Stir to mix. Sprinkle with both of the cheeses, tossing as you sprinkle until the cheeses melt. When all the cheese is melted, serve.

Serves 4

This is a simple combination, but we have found that the fresh flavors are addictive. This recipe is adapted from one of our favorite cookbooks, *Cucina Fresca* by Viana La Place and Evan Kleiman. In the summer, when tomatoes are dripping with juice, you can substitute any variety for the Roma.

S moked oysters make this dish rich and exotic with no more work than opening a can. Since smoked oysters will keep indefinitely in the pantry, it's a nice way to make a seafood dish when fresh isn't available. (We even take them on camping trips.)

> ✳ *Can't find smoked oysters? This dish is equally impressive with smoked mussels or smoked clams.*

SPAGHETTINI WITH SMOKED OYSTER SAUCE ★★

12 ounces thin spaghetti (spaghettini)
1 large fresh, ripe tomato or 3 large fresh, ripe Roma (plum) tomatoes (for about 1 cup chopped)
2 cloves garlic
10 fresh basil leaves
1 tin (3.7 ounces) smoked oysters (see Box)
2 tablespoons extra-virgin olive oil
⅓ cup already-grated Parmesan cheese
⅓ cup already-shredded mozzarella cheese

1. Bring 2½ quarts of unsalted water to a boil in a covered 4½-quart or larger Dutch oven or soup pot. When the water reaches a rapid boil, add the spaghetti and cook until tender, 9 minutes.

2. Meanwhile, use a serrated knife to core and dice the unpeeled tomato into a 3-quart or larger serving bowl, working directly over the bowl to catch the juices.

3. Peel and mince the garlic and add it to the bowl. Chop the basil and add it to the bowl. Drain the oysters well, then blot them with paper towels to remove as much oil as possible. Chop and add them to the bowl. Add the olive oil, stir well, and set aside.

4. Drain the spaghetti and add it to the bowl with the sauce. Stir to mix. Sprinkle with the cheeses, tossing as you sprinkle until the cheeses melt. When the cheese is melted, serve.

Serves 6

SUMMER'S BEST PASTA

2 cups (8 ounces) ziti
¼ cup extra-virgin olive oil
4 to 5 large fresh, ripe Roma (plum) tomatoes
*   (for 1½ cups chopped)*
1 cup already-shredded carrots
1 medium yellow squash (for ¾ cup coarsely chopped)
5 scallions (green onions; for ½ cup sliced)
2 cloves garlic
¼ cup fresh basil leaves, tightly packed
Salt and black pepper to taste
¾ cup (3 ounces) already-shredded mozzarella cheese

1. Bring 2½ quarts of unsalted water to a boil in a covered 4½-quart or larger Dutch oven or soup pot. When the water reaches a rapid boil, add the ziti and cook until tender, 9 minutes.

2. Meanwhile, pour the oil into a 3 quart or larger bowl. Cut the unpeeled tomatoes into bite-size pieces, then add to the bowl along with the carrots. Chop the squash into ¼-inch chunks and add them to the bowl. Cut the scallions into ¼-inch slices, including enough of the tender green tops to make ½ cup, and add them to the bowl. Peel and finely chop the garlic, and shred the basil, and add both to the bowl. Stir well to mix and set aside.

3. Drain the ziti and add it to the bowl with the sauce. Season with salt and pepper and stir to mix. Sprinkle on the cheese, tossing as you sprinkle until the cheese melts. When all the cheese is melted, serve.

Serves 4

This is summer eating at its best. It's a great way to use those last few vegetables in the bin before the next trip to the market. Fresh basil adds a nice zip. The smaller you chop the vegetables, the softer they will be when it's time to eat. We like them in chunks so we can really taste sunshine freshness in every bite.

You won't believe what this recipe does for a humble can of tuna. This is our idea of perfect beach food, but it gives a jolt of summer even in winter. This pasta sauce also makes a wonderful salad if you omit the cheese and pasta and serve it on lettuce. Garnish either variation with lemon wedges for extra flavor.

TUNA AND FUSILLI ALFRESCO

2 cups (8 ounces) short fusilli
¼ cup extra-virgin olive oil
3 medium or 2 large fresh, ripe Roma (plum) tomatoes
    (for 1½ cups strips)
½ cup fresh parsley leaves, tightly packed (see Box)
2 cloves garlic
1 small can (2¼ ounces) sliced black olives
2 tablespoons capers, drained
1 large can (12 ounces) white tuna packed in water
Salt and black pepper to taste
¾ cup (3 ounces) already-shredded Parmesan cheese

1. Place the fusilli in 2½ quarts of already-boiling unsalted water and cook until tender, 12 minutes.

2. Meanwhile, pour the oil into a 3-quart or larger serving bowl. Cut the unpeeled tomatoes into bite-size strips (you should have about 1½ cups). Add the strips to the bowl.

3. Chop the parsley and add it to the bowl. Peel and chop the garlic and add it to the bowl. Drain the olives and add, along with the capers. Drain the tuna, flake it with your fingers into bite-size chunks, and add it to the bowl. Stir well to mix and set aside.

4. Drain the fusilli and add it to the bowl with the sauce. Season with salt and pepper and stir to mix. Sprinkle with the cheese, tossing as you sprinkle until the cheese melts. When the cheese is melted, serve.

Serves 4

> ✳ *Normally we don't specify fresh herbs in our recipes, but parsley is the exception; available all year, it will keep for up to 5 days if you treat it like you would fresh flowers. Just trim the stem ends and stick them in a glass of water, then pop it in the refrigerator.*

APOLLO'S PASTA

3 cups (12 ounces) rotini (pasta twists)
1 can (14 ounces) artichoke hearts packed in water
4 teaspoons anchovy paste or 2 anchovy fillets (optional)
1 large fresh, ripe tomato or 3 large fresh, ripe Roma (plum)
*   tomatoes (for about 1 cup chopped)*
¼ cup fresh parsley, tightly packed (optional)
1 small can (2¼ ounces) sliced black olives
1 package (4 ounces) already-crumbled feta cheese
⅓ cup extra-virgin olive oil
2 tablespoons red wine vinegar
½ teaspoon dried Italian seasoning, or more to taste
Black pepper to taste

1. Place the rotini in 2½ quarts of already-boiling unsalted water and cook until tender, 9 to 11 minutes.

2. Meanwhile, drain the artichokes and place in a 3-quart or larger bowl. Using 2 sharp knives or a chopping utensil, cut the artichokes in the bowl into bite-size pieces. If using the anchovies, press them between several paper towels to remove most of the oil, then mince finely and add them to the bowl.

3. Coarsely chop the unpeeled tomato and add it to the bowl. Chop the parsley (if using) and add. Drain the olives and add, along with the cheese, oil, vinegar, and Italian seasoning. Stir well to mix and set aside.

4. Drain the rotini and add it to the bowl with the sauce. Season with black pepper, toss well, and serve.

Serves 6

This ultra-quick pasta dish is basically a Greek salad on rotini—a sunny end to a busy day any time of the year. The anchovy paste is optional, but it does add the classic salty flavor we love in our Greek salads.

WINTER PESTO PASTA

1 package (16 ounces) thin spaghetti (spaghettini)
8 sun-dried tomato pieces, not packed in oil
½ cup water
2 cloves garlic
1 package (10 ounces) frozen chopped spinach
½ cup shelled walnut pieces
½ cup already-grated Parmesan cheese
1 teaspoon dried basil
½ teaspoon salt
¼ cup sliced black olives
⅓ cup extra-virgin olive oil

This rich pesto was inspired by a recipe we found on the back of a box of spaghetti. Our friend, Susan Cannon, tested the recipe, and passed the results around to the kids who happened to be playing on her deck that day. "I couldn't believe it, but every one of them ate it," Susan said. "Maybe that's because I didn't tell them it was spinach."

This recipe makes enough pesto to serve a dozen people, but the left-overs freeze well for another meal (defrost it in the refrigerator). If you do want to serve 12 people, cook 2 packages (16 ounces each) of thin spaghetti and use all of the sauce.

1. Bring 2½ quarts of unsalted water to a boil in a covered 4½-quart or larger Dutch oven or soup pot. When the water reaches a rapid boil, add the spaghetti and cook 9 minutes.

2. Meanwhile, place the sun-dried tomatoes in a 2-cup glass measure and add the water. Microwave 1½ minutes, covered on high, or until the water boils. Remove the tomatoes from the microwave and let them stand in the water to soften, 5 minutes.

3. While the tomatoes microwave, peel the garlic. Turn on the motor of your food processor and drop the garlic through the feed tube onto the moving blade. Process until minced, about 30 seconds.

4. As soon as the sun-dried tomatoes finish microwaving, place the block of frozen spinach in a microwave-safe dish and microwave, covered, on high, for 5 minutes to defrost.

5. Meanwhile, add the walnuts to the processor with the garlic and pulse until the nuts are finely chopped, about 1 minute. Measure the Parmesan cheese, basil, and salt into the processor.

Drain the tomatoes and add them, along with the thawed spinach and its juice, and the olives. Process until finely chopped, stopping once midway to scrape down the sides of the bowl.

6. Scrape down the sides of the bowl again. With the motor running, slowly add the oil (in a thin stream) through the feed tube. Continue to process until thoroughly combined, about 30 seconds (see Box).

7. Drain the spaghetti and place it in a 4-quart or larger serving bowl. Add half of the pesto (1 cup plus 2 tablespoons) and toss until evenly distributed. Serve at once.

Serves 6 with half the sauce left over for another meal

✳ *Winter pesto is thick, but if you like a thinner sauce, add water, a tablespoon at a time, at this point to reach the desired consistency.*

CHAPTER SIX

Food on

L ife would be a lot easier if we never ate anything except sandwiches. But on a frosty night after a twelve-hour day, there's just something about cold bread and cold meat that doesn't cut it at the dinner table. All of that changes if you warm the bread and pour a steamy, rich, fragrant filling on top.

Open-face sandwiches are a welcome change from rice and noodles night after night. The French have long appreciated the crouton—not those tidbits sprinkled in salad, but a substantial slab of toasted crusty bread with a savory stew or soup ladled on top. If you've ever experienced the pleasure of scooping up the last bits of wonderful gravy with your dinner roll, you know what we mean.

Most of the meals in this chapter are designed with this indulgence in mind, yet not a single recipe is time consuming. About half of them, like Hungarian Goulash on Rye Toasts, Empanadas with Chili Cheese Sauce, and Creamy Chicken on Croissants, revolve around a thick, rich gravy, and plenty of it. Several of the recipes are surprisingly elegant. We wouldn't hesitate an instant to serve Seafood on the Half Shell or Spanikopita in Pastry Cups to dinner guests.

Finally, we've included recipes that will remind you of the comforting open-faced sandwiches of childhood. Sloppy Janes (even better than Sloppy Joes), Pizza in a Panic, and our Creamy

bread

Tuna Melt are stress-saving standbys that will sustain the family without sapping your sanity.

Of course, in a pinch, most of these meals would be perfectly suitable with rice or noodles. But when you're in the mood for something slightly unexpected, treat yourself to the ease of a sandwich while spoiling your family with the sensual experience of food on bread.

"With some interesting bread, suddenly the whole meal seems a lot more special."

These turnovers are a quick and easy version of Latin empanadas—flaky pastries filled with savory ground meat or fruit. In many Spanish-speaking countries, empanadas are eaten as a snack. We've added a meaty cheese sauce to beef up the meal and make it hearty enough for dinner. We found these turnovers to be so substantial that just one will do, unless you know someone with a bigger-than-average appetite. It's a rich dish, so we suggest serving a plain steamed vegetable, such as broccoli, on the side.

Make sure that your meat is either fresh or already defrosted if frozen before you start the recipe.

✳ *If you happen to have any of the sauce left over, it's wonderful as a snack with corn chips.*

EMPANADAS WITH CHILI-CHEESE SAUCE

1 pound extra-lean ground beef
6 reduced-fat refrigerated biscuits, such as Pillsbury Grands!
(see Note, facing page)
1 envelope (1¼ ounces) taco seasoning mix
¼ cup water
1 can (14½ ounces) diced tomatoes
1 cup store-bought salsa-cheese sauce, such as Pace or
Old El Paso

1. The oven should be already heated to 450°F.

2. Place the beef in a 12-inch nonstick skillet over high heat. Cook, turning and breaking up the meat, until it is crumbled and browned.

3. Meanwhile, use a rolling pin or straight-sided glass to flatten each biscuit until it measures about 4½ inches across and is about ¼ inch thick. (If the biscuits stick, flour the rolling pin.) Place the flattened biscuits on an ungreased baking sheet.

4. When the meat is browned, stir in the taco seasoning mix and water. Remove the skillet from the heat. Place 2 tablespoons of the meat in the center of each biscuit; leave the meat you have left over in the skillet. Fold the dough over the meat to form a turnover, stretching it as necessary (don't worry if the dough tears a little), then press down on the edges with the tines of a fork to seal. Bake the turnovers until golden brown, about 8 minutes.

5. Meanwhile, add the tomatoes with their juice and the salsa-cheese sauce to the skillet with the leftover meat and place over

low heat, stirring well. Cook until heated through, continuing to simmer until the turnovers are done, stirring from time to time.

6. To serve, place the turnovers on individual serving plates and top with about ⅓ cup of the chili-cheese sauce.

Serves 6

Note: Since refrigerated biscuits come in cans of eight, you'll have two biscuits left over. While your oven is hot, go ahead and bake the extras, following package directions. Once they cool, pop them in a plastic bag. To reheat, microwave each biscuit for 20 seconds on 30 percent power.

> ✳ *If you need to turn this recipe into a Super Stress Saver, forget about making turnovers and bake the biscuits according to package directions. Stir the cheese and tomatoes in with all of the meat in step 4. When the biscuits are done, split them in half and top with lots of sauce.*

A word about:
BREAD

Nearly all of the recipes in this chapter would be perfectly fine served over any type of bread. We've featured a variety to give examples of what works, but feel free to substitute whatever you have on hand—bagels to baguettes, whole wheat rolls to toasted sandwich white.

Similarly, if your bread situation is desperately lacking, steam a pot of rice or boil some pasta. They make a fine bed, too. Don't let a shortage of the exact kind of bread keep you from enjoying these comforting, flavorful recipes.

SLOPPY JANES ☺

1¼ to 1½ pounds extra-lean ground beef, fresh or frozen
1 teaspoon vegetable oil
1 large onion (for 1 cup chopped)
½ medium green or red bell pepper (for ½ cup chopped)
1 tablespoon dark or light brown sugar, firmly packed
2 teaspoons red wine vinegar or cider vinegar
2 teaspoons Worcestershire sauce
1½ teaspoons bottled minced garlic
1 large can (15 ounces) tomato sauce
1 can (6 ounces) tomato paste
Salt and black pepper to taste
12 slices (about 1 inch thick) French bread

Sloppy Joes were a favorite childhood treat for both of us, and since we thought they'd be an effortless meal, we started sampling the major brands of commercially prepared mixes. We were sadly disappointed. They're quick, but we're spoiled. The reality of those cans and packages just wasn't as wonderful as we remembered. So, we decided to create our own perfect sauce—slightly sweet offset by just the right vinegar pucker; thick and rich with tomatoes, with a hint of garlic and onion. The result was so flavorful, we thought our sandwiches deserved something to set them apart. Hence the name: Sloppy Janes.

French bread elevates these sandwiches to a slightly more sophisticated level, but if you're a traditionalist, go ahead and pour our sauce over a hamburger bun. Or, for fun for the kids, spoon it into hot dog buns. However you eat them, we're betting you won't believe the bold taste, especially considering how quickly they go together.

1. Turn on the broiler.

2. If the beef is frozen, run it under hot water so you can remove any packaging. Place the beef on a microwave-safe plate and microwave 3 minutes, uncovered, on high, to begin defrosting.

3. Meanwhile, heat the oil in a 12-inch nonstick skillet over medium heat. Peel and coarsely chop the onion, adding it to the skillet as you chop.

4. Add the beef (fresh or partially defrosted) to the skillet and raise the heat to high. Cook, turning and breaking up the meat occasionally, until it is crumbled and browned, 5 minutes. Meanwhile, seed and chop the bell pepper, and add it to the skillet.

5. Add the brown sugar, vinegar, Worcestershire, and garlic, then stir in the tomato sauce and tomato paste. Lower the heat to a simmer and cook 5 minutes more, stirring until all of the tomato paste is thoroughly incorporated. Season with salt and pepper.

6. While the meat mixture simmers, place the bread slices on a large baking sheet and toast in the broiler on both sides until crisp, about 2 minutes per side.

7. Place two pieces of toast on each serving plate, spoon the meat mixture on top, and serve.

Serves 6

BEEF BBQ ON CORN MUFFINS

1 teaspoon vegetable oil
1 medium onion (for ¾ cup strips)
2 tablespoons Worcestershire sauce
1 tablespoon lemon juice from frozen concentrate
1 tablespoon honey
1 teaspoon Dijon mustard
¼ teaspoon black pepper
½ teaspoon salt (optional)
1 pound leftover or deli roast beef
4 large store-bought corn muffins

This is a great way to use that leftover roast from Sunday's dinner. Or you can prepare the recipe with a good-quality roast beef from the deli. Either way, you'll love the simplicity of stirring together the sauce, adding the cooked meat, and spooning it over purchased muffins. What could be easier? Add a little deli slaw plus your favorite canned baked beans, and dinner is on the table in less than 15 minutes.

1. Heat the oil in a 12-inch nonstick skillet over medium heat. Meanwhile, peel and halve the onion, and cut each half into thin slices, adding them to the pan as you slice. Cook the onion until soft, 2 minutes. Add the Worcestershire, lemon juice, honey, mustard, pepper, and salt (if using). Stir well, then reduce the heat to a simmer and cook until the sauce is slightly thickened, 5 minutes.

2. While the sauce simmers, cut the beef into bite-size pieces and add to the skillet. Stir well to coat the beef with sauce and just heat through. Remove from the heat.

3. Warm the muffins in the microwave on high for 45 seconds to 1 minute. Quarter the muffins and arrange on individual serving plates. Spoon the beef mixture over the muffins and serve.

Serves 4

Hungarian goulash, also called "shepherd's stew," is the national dish of Hungary. Traditional goulash has a potent caraway flavor. We've found that we don't care for such a strong taste, and don't usually have caraway seeds on our spice shelf. So, to us, the hint of caraway from the rye bread in our rendition is subtle and more pleasing.

HUNGARIAN GOULASH ON RYE TOASTS

2 tablespoons vegetable oil
1¼ pounds boneless tender veal roast such as loin,
    already cut into ½ inch cubes (see Box, facing page)
Salt and black pepper, to taste
1 large onion (for 1 cup chopped)
20 already-peeled baby carrots (for about 1 cup sliced)
1 medium green or red bell pepper (for 1 cup chopped)
3 tablespoons tomato paste or ketchup
1 can (15 ounces) sliced white potatoes
½ teaspoon concentrated beef broth, such as Knorr, or
    beef bouillon crystals, or ½ beef bouillon cube
¼ cup water
1 tablespoon paprika
1 teaspoon bottled minced garlic
4 slices caraway-seed rye bread
¾ cup reduced-fat sour cream

1. Heat the oil in a 4½-quart Dutch oven or soup pot over medium heat. Season the meat with salt and black pepper and add it to the pot. Begin to cook, stirring frequently. Meanwhile, peel and chop the onion, adding it to the pot as you chop. Stir occasionally.

2. Slice the carrots into ¼-inch circles and add them to the pot. Seed the bell pepper, coarsely chop, and add it to the pot. Add the tomato paste and drain and add the potatoes. Raise the heat to high. Add the beef broth concentrate, water, paprika, and garlic, stirring well. Cover and continue to boil for 4 minutes.

3. Reduce the heat to low and continue to simmer until the meat is tender and just cooked through, about 3 minutes more.

4. Meanwhile, toast the bread in a toaster or toaster oven. Just before serving, remove the pot from the heat and stir in the sour cream. Season with salt and black pepper, if desired.

5. Place a piece of toast on each serving plate, top with the stew, and serve.

Serves 4

✳ *Don't only think of veal for this recipe. An exceptionally tender cut of beef or pork, such as tenderloin, cut into small cubes, also works well in this stew.*

GETTING SOME HELP FROM THE BUTCHER

Desperate cooks usually know when a veal or lamb steak is going to end up cut into smaller pieces for soup or stew. That's why they ask the butcher to cut the meat for them.

Although tender cuts of beef are often found sliced for stir-fries and cubed for stews, you don't often see veal or lamb packaged that way. But most butchers are more than willing to cut any large piece of meat to your specifications. It's quick work for them while you continue to shop. Then you just swing back by the meat counter to pick it up before heading to the cash register.

When you get home, throw it in the freezer or fridge and when you need the meat you don't have to worry about cutting up a large piece. Don't feel limited by what's already wrapped for you in the meat case. When you're desperate, you need all the assistance you can get.

This Indian-inspired dish is really cross-cultural, the result of a wild day of culinary experimentation. A little of this and a little of that, and before we knew it, we ended up with this beautiful stew the color of goldenrod. The exotic blend of spices depends on a good-quality curry powder. On your next trip to the market, splurge on a tin of imported curry powder—the difference in flavor is worth spending a little more.

CURRIED LAMB IN PITA BOWLS

1 pound extra-lean ground lamb or beef, fresh or frozen
1 teaspoon vegetable oil
1 large onion (for 1 cup chopped)
2 teaspoons bottled minced garlic
2 teaspoons bottled chopped ginger
1½ teaspoons curry powder
1 teaspoon ground cumin
½ teaspoon paprika
½ teaspoon ground turmeric
½ teaspoon salt
1 package (8 ounces) already-shredded carrots
¼ cup mango chutney, such as Major Grey's
1 can (13¾ ounces) artichoke hearts packed in water
1 small can (7¾ ounces) chickpeas
2 large pita breads (6 or 9 inches each)
3 tablespoons cornstarch
¼ cup water
2 cups low-fat plain yogurt (see Box, facing page)

1. Turn on the toaster oven or oven to 400°F.

2. If the meat is frozen, run it under hot water so you can remove any packaging. Place the meat on a microwave-safe plate and microwave 3 minutes, uncovered, on high, to begin defrosting.

3. Meanwhile, heat the oil in a 12-inch nonstick skillet over medium heat. Peel and coarsely chop the onion, adding it to the skillet as you chop.

4. Add the meat (fresh or partially defrosted) to the skillet and raise the heat to high. Cook, turning and breaking up the meat

occasionally. While it cooks, add the garlic, ginger, curry powder, cumin, paprika, turmeric, and salt, stirring well to coat. Stir in the carrots and chutney.

5. Drain the artichoke hearts and rinse and drain the chickpeas, and add both to the skillet. Reduce the heat to medium-high and continue to cook until the meat is crumbled and browned, about 8 minutes.

6. Meanwhile, wrap the pita breads in aluminum foil and place in the toaster oven until warmed through, 6 to 8 minutes. Combine the cornstarch and water in a small container that has a lid. Shake well until the lumps disappear, then set aside.

7. When the meat is cooked through, reduce the heat to medium and gently stir in the yogurt. Shake the cornstarch mixture again and drizzle it evenly over the stew. Stir gently but thoroughly, then simmer until the yogurt is heated through and the sauce is thick, 2 to 3 minutes more.

8. To serve, cut the pitas in half, place each half in an individual serving bowl, and open to form a pocket. Ladle 1½ cups stew into each pocket and serve.

Serves 4

❋ *We don't recommend using fat-free yogurt in this dish. Although they both flavor the curry equally well, low-fat gives it a creamier texture and prettier color.*

From Beverly:

This is a dinner you deserve after a hard day at the office. It's not cheap to make, and there are more than just a few calories. But when you need to feel pampered on the spur of the moment, this is the meal.

The idea for this recipe resulted from watching my sister-in-law Liza Bennett cook scallops on vacation at the beach. She'd stir for a miraculously few minutes and marvelous things would happen. When I asked if she thought a similar recipe would work over croissants, she quipped, "Seafood on the half shell." The recipe she came up with is even more inspired than the name. Buy already-cooked shrimp, and you can throw it together before that unexpected guest—or anyone else—is famished.

SEAFOOD ON THE HALF SHELL

4 frozen croissants
2 tablespoons butter
2 tablespoons vegetable oil
2 cloves garlic
1 cup already-sliced fresh mushrooms
¼ cup all-purpose flour
½ teaspoon black pepper
½ teaspoon onion powder
½ pound bay scallops
1 cup white wine
1 bottle (8 ounces) clam juice
¼ cup fresh parsley leaves (optional)
½ pound already-cooked-and-peeled shrimp

1. The oven should be already heated to 350°F.

2. Slice the croissants lengthwise and bake according to package directions, or until slightly crisp.

3. Meanwhile, heat 1 tablespoon each of the butter and oil in a 4½-quart Dutch oven or soup pot over low heat. While the oil heats, peel and mince the garlic. Add to the pot along with the mushrooms and cook until soft, about 5 minutes. (While the mushrooms cook, begin step 4.)

4. Combine the flour, pepper, and onion powder in a zipper-top plastic bag and shake to mix. Add the scallops and toss in the flour to lightly coat. Remove the scallops from the bag and shake off as much excess flour as possible. Reserve the flour in the bag.

5. With a slotted spoon, remove the mushrooms and garlic from

the pot to a 1-quart or larger bowl. Set aside. Raise the heat under the pot to medium and add the remaining 1 tablespoon each butter and oil. Cook the scallops until lightly browned, about 2 minutes, stirring from time to time. With a slotted spoon, remove the scallops to the bowl with the mushrooms and garlic.

6. Add the wine and ¾ cup of the clam juice to the skillet. Cook to blend the flavors, about 7 minutes, stirring occasionally. While the broth cooks, chop the parsley (if using). Combine 2 tablespoons of the reserved flour and the remaining ¼ cup clam juice in a small container that has a lid. Shake well until the lumps disappear, then drizzle the mixture evenly over the broth, stirring constantly until it is the desired gravylike thickness, 2 to 3 minutes. Return the reserved mushrooms and scallops to the pot along with the shrimp and parsley, stirring gently to mix. Heat just until the shrimp are warm, about 2 minutes.

7. Arrange 2 croissant halves on each plate. Remove the seafood mixture from the heat, spoon it over the croissants, and serve.

Serves 4

TIME-SAVER

Growing your favorite fresh herb is not really a time-saver, just a good idea. Most herbs will thrive in a pot on a sunny deck or porch. Home-grown parsley and basil will add tremendous flavor to your cooking without requiring a trip to the supermarket.

From Beverly:

More than a decade ago, my friend Sandy Furr shared a recipe for an amazingly simple tuna dip. All you have to do is stir together a can of drained tuna, a small carton of cottage cheese, and mayonnaise. Served on a sturdy wheat cracker, this dip is testimony to the fact that sometimes the whole really is more than the sum of its parts. Back in those days I was a single newspaper reporter on the run. When I'd hit my apartment late and exhausted after covering a warehouse fire or some other catastrophe, I used to whip up this dip and call it dinner. This "dip" was so satisfying that I decided to expand the recipe, serve it on English muffins, and turn it into a real dinner.

> ✸ *If you like a little crunch in your muffins, toast them while the tuna mixture is warming in step 3.*

CREAMY TUNA MELT

2 large ribs celery (for 1 cup diced)
1 small onion (for ½ cup chopped)
Cooking oil spray
1 large can (12 ounces) white tuna packed in water
1½ cups low-fat cottage cheese
½ cup reduced-fat mayonnaise
1 tablespoon lemon juice from frozen concentrate
¼ teaspoon garlic powder, or more to taste
3 English muffins (see Box)
1 cup (4 ounces) already-shredded sharp Cheddar cheese

1. Place the broiler rack in the position nearest the heating element and turn on the broiler.

2. Dice the celery, and peel and finely chop the onion. Spray a 12-inch nonstick skillet with cooking oil spray and place it over medium heat. Add the celery and onion and cook until the onion is tender, about 2 minutes.

3. Drain the tuna and add it to the skillet along with the cottage cheese, mayonnaise, lemon juice, and garlic powder. Stir well to combine and break up the tuna chunks. Cook just long enough to warm the ingredients, 2 to 3 minutes, stirring frequently. Remove the pan from the heat and set aside.

4. Spray a 13 × 9-inch glass baking dish with cooking oil spray. Split the English muffins in half and place the halves, split side up, side by side in the baking dish. Spread the tuna mixture evenly over the muffins and sprinkle with the cheese. Broil until the cheese melts, 2 to 3 minutes. Serve at once.

Serves 6

CORNY CHICKEN CASSEROLE

2 cups frozen green, red, and yellow bell pepper stir-fry mix
2 cups frozen chopped broccoli
1 can (15¼ ounces) whole-kernel corn
1 large can (10 ounces) white-meat chicken
1 can (10¾ ounces) reduced-fat cream of chicken soup
1 small can (8½ ounces) cream-style corn
Black pepper to taste
4 extra-large (or 6 regular) store-bought corn muffins
2 cups (one 8-ounce package) already finely shredded sharp
    Cheddar cheese

1. The oven should be already heated to 475°F (see Box).

2. Combine the bell pepper mix and broccoli in a 1½-quart microwave-safe bowl and microwave, uncovered, on high, for 3 minutes or until almost completely defrosted.

3. Meanwhile, drain the whole-kernel corn and the chicken and combine in a 13 × 9-inch glass baking dish. Add the soup, cream-style corn, and bell pepper–broccoli mixture. Season with black pepper. Stir well to mix, spread evenly in the dish, and bake, uncovered, for 10 minutes.

4. Meanwhile, cut each muffin into 4 wedges. After the casserole has baked for 10 minutes, remove it from the oven and sprinkle evenly with the cheese. Place the muffin wedges on top of the dish at evenly spaced intervals. Continue to bake, uncovered, until the cheese is melted and the casserole is bubbly around the edges, about 5 minutes more. Remove from the oven and serve.

Serves 6

This casserole is the ultimate in comfort food. It's not fancy, just simple and satisfying. On particularly busy nights, you'll appreciate how quickly it goes together. A bit of defrosting and then dump and bake. What could be easier?

✳ *If your oven tends toward the hotter side, reduce the baking temperature to 450°F. Or, if the casserole starts to brown too quickly, reduce the oven temperature accordingly.*

From Alicia:

This recipe is based on a meal my husband and I enjoyed at a wedding lunch several years ago. The surprising balance between the elegant puff-pastry shell and the homey blend of vegetables and chicken in a cream sauce made a lasting impression.

Our version uses the convenience of already-shredded and frozen vegetables and a cream base made from reduced-fat soup and sour cream, and we also use flaky croissants to accommodate a dinner-size portion. Even with the shortcuts, the dish is better than I remember—fancy enough to serve guests but simple enough to satisfy children.

CREAMY CHICKEN ON CROISSANTS

3 skinless, boneless chicken breast halves (about 1 pound total), fresh or frozen
4 frozen croissants
1 cup already-shredded carrots
1 cup frozen green peas
1 cup frozen small whole onions (pearl onions)
1 teaspoon olive oil
1 can (10¾ ounces) reduced-fat cream of mushroom soup
¾ cup low-fat milk
1 teaspoon Worcestershire sauce
1 teaspoon low-sodium chicken bouillon crystals (optional)
¼ cup reduced-fat sour cream
1 cup (4 ounces) already finely shredded sharp Cheddar cheese
¼ teaspoon black pepper

1. The oven should be already heated to 325°F.

2. If the chicken is frozen, run it under hot water so you can remove any packaging. Place the chicken on a microwave-safe plate and microwave 3 minutes, uncovered, on high, to begin defrosting. Meanwhile, slice the croissants lengthwise and bake them according to package directions, or until slightly crispy.

3. While the croissants bake, layer the carrots, peas, and onions in a 2-quart microwave-safe dish. Remove the chicken from the microwave after its 3 minutes, then microwave the vegetables 5 minutes, covered, on high. Stir once after 2½ minutes.

4. While the vegetables cook, heat the oil in a 4½-quart Dutch oven or soup pot over medium heat. Cut the chicken into bite-size pieces adding them to the pot as you cut. When all of the chicken is added, raise the heat to medium-high. Cook the chicken until no longer pink all over, about 4 minutes, stirring from time to time.

5. Lower the heat to medium and add the soup and milk, stirring well to dissolve any lumps. Remove the vegetables from the microwave and drain, then add to the pot and stir well. (Do not let the mixture boil. Reduce the heat if necessary.) Meanwhile, add the Worcestershire, chicken bouillon (if using), sour cream, cheese, and pepper. Stir well and cook to melt the cheese, about 1 minute more.

6. Meanwhile, place 2 croissant halves on each serving plate. Top with the chicken mixture and serve.

Serves 4

Note: No pearl onions? Don't let that stop you from enjoying this festive dish. Use frozen chopped onions instead.

"The main ingredient of America's first Desperation Dinner was, no doubt, a can of cream of mushroom soup."

This is a brilliant recipe born of complete confusion. First it was going to be chimichangas. Next it was supposed to be tacos. Then it ended up as tostadas. And, the Avocado Salsa was intended to be used with a different meal altogether.

Sometimes that's what happens when you're desperate. You can't think straight, much less cook straight. Our first reaction was to groan—a morning's work wasted. Then we took a bite. Never mind whatever the salsa was designed for— this combination was truly inspired. We're just not sure by what—or whom.

> ✳ *Frozen chicken is not convenient for this particular recipe, but if that's all you have, defrost the meat completely in the microwave before beginning to cook.*

CHICKEN TOSTADAS

3 skinless, boneless chicken breast halves
*   (about 1 pound total; see Box, this page)*
2 teaspoons bottled minced garlic
1 can (4.5 ounces) chopped green chilies
6 tostada shells (half 4.5-ounce package; see Box, facing page)
1 can (16 ounces) refried black beans, regular or fat-free
¾ cup (3 ounces) already-shredded Mexican-blend cheese
Avocado Salsa (see recipe, facing page)
6 lettuce leaves (optional)

1. The oven should be already heated to 425°F.

2. Place the chicken, garlic, and chilies with their juice in a 2-quart microwave-safe dish. Cover and microwave on high for 6 minutes, then let the breasts rest in the microwave for 5 minutes more.

3. Meanwhile, place the tostada shells on an ungreased baking sheet. Spread each with about ¼ cup refried beans, then sprinkle with 2 tablespoons cheese. Bake the shells in the preheated oven until the beans are heated through and the cheese melts, about 5 minutes.

4. While the shells bake, make the Avocado Salsa and set aside. Rinse and drain the lettuce (if using), pat it dry, then shred the leaves. When the chicken is done, shred the meat by using 2 forks to pull it apart. Stir well to mix in the garlic and chilies.

5. Place a tostada shell on each serving plate. Top each with about ⅓ cup chicken, shredded lettuce, and a heaping ¼ cup salsa and serve.

Serves 6

AVOCADO SALSA

1 can (14.5 ounces) salsa-style chopped tomatoes
3 scallions (green onions; for ¼ cup chopped)
1 ripe California avocado

1. Pour the tomatoes with their juice into a 2-quart or larger bowl. Slice the scallions with enough of the tender green tops to make ¼ cup and add them to the bowl.

2. Cut the unpeeled avocado in half lengthwise and in half again through the width to make quarters. Remove the pit, slide off the peel, and cut the avocado into ¼-inch dice, adding it to the bowl as you cut. Stir to mix and serve at once.

Makes about 2¼ cups

This salsa makes a remarkable party dip or a topping for most any Mexican entrée. If you slice the avocado into quarters before peeling and lift the meat away from the seed, it takes just seconds to prepare.

✳ *Tostadas are flat, crisp corn tortilla shells, like a taco only not folded. If you can't find tostada shells, just stuff the filling inside a taco shell. (The chicken mixture will make 12 tacos.)*

These dainty puff-pastry cups are pretty enough to serve at a party, but there's only one trick. The pastry shells are supposed to be baked in their frozen state, which takes longer than we like to spend in the kitchen. To speed things up, we just pop the box into the refrigerator the day or night before. Thawed puff pastry will sometimes bake at a slightly crooked angle, but with the spinach-cheese sauce spilling over the sides, you can't tell the difference. Any brand of puff-pastry shells will do. Just omit the turkey to turn this recipe into a very satisfying vegetarian entrée for four people (defrost only four pastry shells).

SPANAKOPITA IN PASTRY CUPS

1 box (10 ounces) puff-pastry shells, thawed
2 boxes (10 ounces each) frozen chopped spinach
3 tablespoons margarine or butter
1 small onion (for ½ cup chopped)
2½ cups low-fat milk
3 tablespoons flour
2 packages (4 ounces each) already-crumbled feta cheese
¼ teaspoon dried dill
1 tablespoon lemon juice from frozen concentrate
¼ teaspoon black pepper
Salt to taste (optional)
1½ cups already-cooked cubed turkey or chicken breast meat (optional)

1. The oven should be already heated to 400°F.

2. Bake the thawed pastry shells on an ungreased baking sheet until golden brown, 16 to 18 minutes.

3. Meanwhile, place the spinach in a microwave-safe bowl and microwave 15 minutes, covered, on high, until defrosted and hot. Melt the margarine in a 12-inch nonstick skillet over medium-high heat. While the margarine melts, peel and coarsely chop the onion, adding it to the skillet as you chop. Cook until soft, about 3 minutes, stirring occasionally. While the onion cooks, measure out the milk and set it aside.

4. When the onion is soft and translucent, reduce the heat to medium. Sprinkle the flour over the onion and cook for 1 minute, stirring constantly, to remove the raw taste from the

flour. Add the milk, a little at a time, stirring constantly. Cook, stirring frequently, until the sauce thickens, 3 to 5 minutes.

5. Reduce the heat to low. Add the feta cheese, dill, lemon juice, pepper, and salt (if desired). Stir to melt the cheese, about 1 minute. Remove from the heat and set aside while you check on the puff pastry and spinach; they both should be done by now. Remove them from the oven and microwave respectively.

6. Drain the spinach well. Return the skillet to the heat and stir in the spinach and turkey (if using). Stir well to mix.

7. Remove the tops from the puff-pastry shells and set them aside. Remove the uncooked dough circles from the shells and discard. Place the shells on individual serving plates and fill each with ¾ cup of the spinach mixture. Replace the reserved pastry tops and serve.

Serves 6

"When you're in a flavor pinch, frozen concentrated lemon juice becomes addictively simple."

Now that supermarkets carry such great already-prepared pizza crusts, there's really no excuse not to whip up pizza at home. That's what I decided after scrutinizing my checkbook in hopes of paying off the credit card bill. You see, at my house, pizza is the ultimate panic food. Pick up the phone, and dinner appears. This bailout system was working extremely well for me—to the tune of $80 a month.

No way was I giving up the one food everyone in the family craves. But in less time than it takes for delivery and at a fraction of the cost, I've found I can make perfectly wonderful pizza in my very own oven. The secret is these partially baked pizza crusts, but in a real panic any bread will do, from bagels to leftover hamburger buns.

> ✹ *Microwaving the mushrooms before assembling the pizza helps to keep them moist during baking.*

PIZZA IN A PANIC

2 cups already-sliced fresh mushrooms
1 can (6 ounces) tomato paste
½ cup water
½ teaspoon garlic powder
½ teaspoon onion powder
½ teaspoon dried Italian seasoning
1 large (12-inch) partially baked pizza crust, such as Boboli
1 cup (4 ounces) already-shredded mozzarella cheese
1½ ounces pepperoni (about 26 slices)

1. The oven should be already heated to 450°F.

2. Microwave the mushrooms in a covered 1-quart microwave-safe dish for 2 minutes on high (see Box).

3. Meanwhile, combine the tomato paste, water, garlic powder, onion powder, and Italian seasoning in a small bowl and stir well to blend. Spread the sauce on the partially baked crust and sprinkle with the cheese.

4. Drain the liquid from the mushrooms and scatter them over the cheese. Top with the pepperoni slices. Bake until the cheese is bubbly and begins to brown at the edges, 10 to 12 minutes. Serve at once.

Serves 4

PICANTE PIZZA

1 large (12-inch) partially baked pizza crust, such as Boboli
1 can (16 ounces) refried beans, regular or fat-free
1 cup bottled salsa
1 cup (4 ounces) already-shredded Colby-Jack cheese
½ cup frozen corn kernels
5 scallions (green onions; for ½ cup chopped)
1 can (2¼ ounces) sliced black olives, drained

1. The oven should be already heated to 450°F.

2. Place the partially baked crust on a pizza pan or baking sheet and spread the beans over it with the back of a spoon. Pour the salsa over the beans and spread it evenly with the back of the spoon. Sprinkle the cheese on top of the salsa.

3. Rinse the corn in a colander under cold running water to defrost. Let it drain while you wash and coarsely chop the scallions with enough tender green tops to make about ½ cup. Sprinkle the scallions over the pizza. Drain the olives and sprinkle them on top.

4. Give the corn in the colander a firm shake to remove as much water as possible, then sprinkle it over the olives. Bake the pizza for 12 minutes until the cheese is melted and the edges of the crust are browned. Cut into wedges to serve.

Serves 4

In Spanish, *picante* means hot or spicy and often it is used in English as an adjective referring to spicy food. You determine whether this pizza will be mild or picante by the spice level of salsa you choose. For a super-hot kick, add sliced jalapeño peppers. We like the combination of Colby and Monterey Jack, but Cheddar or any Mexican-style cheese will do.

From Beverly:

Cooking eggplant at home always seemed like too much trouble. I'd read that eggplant needed to be salted and left sitting to remove any bitter flavor. And then the task of peeling such a huge vegetable seemed like so much work. Finally, when the deep purple orbs were on sale at the supermarket, I forged ahead. Of course I had no intention of following the soaking and sitting regimen, and in this highly seasoned stew, it didn't matter. I left the eggplant peel on, and it added a chewy texture without being tough. If you want easy eggplant, this recipe is a good place to start.

MIDDLE EASTERN EGGPLANT AND PITA POINTS

PRE HEAT OVEN

1 tablespoon olive oil
1 large onion (for 1 cup chopped)
1 large eggplant (1 to 1½ pounds; for 4 cups chunks)
½ cup white wine or water
4 cloves garlic
1 large red or green bell pepper (for 1 cup strips)
2 cans (14½ ounces each) stewed tomatoes
1½ teaspoons ground cumin
½ teaspoon paprika
½ teaspoon black pepper
¼ teaspoon ground turmeric (optional)
3 pita breads (4 or 6 inches each)
1 cup low-fat cottage cheese
¼ cup already-crumbled feta cheese

1. A toaster oven or oven should be already heated to 400°F (see Box, facing page).

2. Heat the oil in a 4½-quart Dutch oven or soup pot over medium-low heat. Meanwhile, peel and coarsely chop the onion, adding it to the pot as you chop. Stir from time to time. While the onion cooks, cut the eggplant into 1-inch slices, leaving on the peel. Cut each eggplant slice into pieces that measure roughly an inch square, adding them to the pot as you cut. Add ¼ cup of the wine, raise the heat to medium and let cook, stirring from time to time.

3. While the eggplant cooks, peel and coarsely chop the garlic and stir it into the mixture in the pot. Seed and coarsely chop the bell pepper, then add, continuing to stir from time to time.

4. Add the remaining ¼ cup wine, the tomatoes, cumin, paprika, black pepper, and turmeric (if using). Raise the heat to medium-high, cover, and cook until the eggplant is soft, about 5 minutes. Meanwhile, wrap the pita breads in aluminum foil and begin to warm them in the toaster oven.

5. Stir the cottage and feta cheeses into the eggplant mixture. Reduce the heat to low and continue to cook, uncovered, for 1 minute.

6. Slice the warmed pitas into 4 wedges. Place 3 wedges, point ends to the outside, in each soup bowl. Spoon the eggplant mixture over the pita points and serve.

Serves 4 generously

✳ *No need to heat up your big oven for this recipe. A toaster oven—if you have one—will warm up the pita breads in a flash.*

CHAPTER SEVEN

Breakf

FOR DINNER

From Alicia:

One Saturday morning, my then four-year-old daughter wandered into the kitchen and asked, "Do I smell bacon?" It nearly broke my heart to face her expectant gaze and break the news: Breakfast would be cold cereal—again.

The truth was we hadn't had a weekend feast of pancakes, eggs, bacon, and all the trimmings in months. My family used to spend Saturday mornings sleeping late, cooking, and lingering at the table. These days we find ourselves dashing off to soccer games, seminars, and school fund-raisers.

But my daughter's question got me to thinking. I decided our favorite feast shouldn't be shelved just because Saturday mornings had veered out of control.

Who says breakfast can't wait until dinner?

Most breakfast foods are quick and require minimal preparation, perfect for Desperation dining. The meal can be as stress-saving as fried eggs with cheese served with toast and microwaved bacon. Or if you have 20 minutes, try something a little more interesting, but equally easy, like homemade "pancake" crepes filled with sausage and vegetables or French Toast à l'Orange, a citrus-laced twist on the classic dish.

ast

"Who says breakfast can't wait until dinner?"

Although I welcome warm maple syrup anytime, Beverly says she just can't eat sweet foods past five o'clock unless they're intended to be dessert. If you, too, fall into the savory-only dinner camp, try Beverly's exceptionally easy Short-Order Tortilla or Seaside Eggs Benedict.

Of course, you could serve any of these recipes for breakfast or brunch. We find they're particularly nice to have on hand for overnight guests. While the coffee is brewing, you can whip up a fabulous breakfast worthy of lingering over with friends and family. Or wait and serve any of the meals in this chapter as a calming and comforting dinner after a grueling day. Our favorite breakfast foods are too good to miss. "Breakfast for dinner" is a welcome compromise.

In Spain, *tortilla* means "omelet," only with potatoes thrown in. You'll find one sitting on the bar in all but the fanciest of restaurants, and the Spanish are just as likely to make it a snack as a light meal. With the help of sliced canned potatoes, our *tortilla* goes together in no time—the hardest thing is cracking the eggs. Part of the beauty of the dish is its simplicity. You won't believe how good it tastes.

SHORT-ORDER TORTILLA

Cooking oil spray
3 strips bacon (regular, reduced-sodium, or turkey)
1 large onion (for 1 cup chopped)
½ large green or red bell pepper (for ¾ cup chopped)
1 can (14½ ounces) sliced new potatoes (for 1½ cups)
1 teaspoon bottled minced garlic
Black pepper to taste
6 large eggs

1. Place the broiler rack on the second level away from the heating element and turn on the broiler.

2. Coat a heavy 12-inch cast-iron skillet with cooking oil spray. Preheat it over medium heat while cutting the bacon into bite-size pieces. Begin to fry the bacon, stirring occasionally to prevent sticking.

3. While the bacon cooks, peel and coarsely chop the onion. Immediately add it to the skillet and cook until soft, about 3 minutes, stirring occasionally. Meanwhile, seed and chop the bell pepper, adding it to the skillet as you chop. Stir occasionally. Add the drained potatoes, garlic, and black pepper and continue to cook, stirring occasionally, while breaking the eggs into a 1-quart or larger bowl. Whisk the eggs until foamy and set aside.

4. When the bacon is nearly crisp, add the eggs and cook, without stirring, until the edges and bottom begin to get dry, 2½ to 3 minutes.

5. Place the skillet under the broiler and cook until the top of the tortilla is light gold, 2½ to 3 minutes. Run a knife around the edge to loosen, then cut it into wedges and serve.

Serves 4

EASY OMELET

Cooking oil spray
1 teaspoon olive oil
3 large eggs
1 tablespoon water
1 Roma (plum) tomato or ½ fresh, ripe globe tomato
¼ cup already finely shredded sharp Cheddar cheese
¼ cup already-grated or -shredded Parmesan cheese
2 tablespoons reduced-fat sour cream
2 teaspoons Dijon mustard
½ teaspoon bottled minced garlic
½ teaspoon dried Italian seasoning (optional)
Salt and black pepper to taste

1. Spray with cooking oil spray the sides of a 12-inch nonstick skillet that has a lid. Add the olive oil and set the skillet over medium-low heat. Break the eggs into a 1-quart or larger bowl, add the water, and beat with a whisk or fork until the eggs are foamy. Pour the eggs into the skillet and cook, without stirring, until the edges are set and the middle is only slightly runny, 3 to 4 minutes.

2. While the omelet cooks, core the tomato and cut it into 4 crosswise slices and measure out the cheeses. Combine the sour cream, mustard, and garlic in a bowl and stir to blend. Set aside.

3. Pour the sour cream mixture into the center of the still runny omelet and spread it over the surface. Turn the heat to low to prevent overbrowning, then sprinkle the Italian seasoning (if using) over one half of the omelet. Lay the tomato slices on top of the seasoning, overlapping them if necessary. Sprinkle both cheeses over the tomatoes and season with salt and pepper to taste.

4. Using a wide metal spatula, fold the plain half of the omelet over the filled half, then cover and continue to cook until the cheese melts, 1 to 2 minutes. Cut the omelet in half and serve.

Serves 2

From Beverly:

One night, staring at refrigerator shelves bare except for eggs, a smattering of cheese, a half-eaten summer tomato, and the last bit of sour cream, I grudgingly made what I expected would be a poor omelet indeed, only to learn that sometimes the very best ideas—and omelets—are born of sheer desperation.

This is a good meal for a couple to whip together after the kids are in bed, since it only serves two. Or, if you need a quick meal just for the kids, make this omelet to taste, leaving out the mustard and any other ingredients your kids won't eat.

FRANTIC FRITTATA

1 tablespoon plus 2 teaspoons olive oil
1 large onion (for 1 cup chopped)
6 large eggs
2 packages (8 ounces each) already-sliced mushrooms
  (about 5⅓ cups)
8 ounces deli ham, sliced about ⅛ inch thick
1 cup good-quality already-shredded Parmesan cheese
Salt and black pepper, to taste

E very great culinary tradition seems to have its own version of an omelet, complete with a special name and a slightly different twist. The Italians call theirs *fritta-ta*. The differences are that the omelet is open-faced rather than folded and the filling ingredients are mixed throughout.

Our Desperation version is quite simple and relies on quality ingredients for flavor. We like it best with a honey-cured or smoked deli ham, and we always make sure we choose a good-quality shred-ded Parmesan cheese rather than the grated cheese from the can.

This dish is about as easy as scrambling eggs, except that scrambling is the last thing you want to do. That said, we have one tiny word of caution: When you pour the egg, ham, and mushroom mixture into the hot skillet, you'll have to find a way of distributing the ham and mushrooms evenly without stirring. Since the pan is too full to jiggle, we have found that a few gentle pushes with the back of a spoon do the job nicely.

1. Turn on the broiler.

2. Heat the 1 tablespoon of the oil in a heavy 12-inch cast-iron skillet over medium heat. Peel and coarsely chop the onion, adding it to the skillet as you chop. Cook for 1 minute to soften slightly. While the onion cooks, break the eggs into a 1-quart or larger bowl and set aside.

3. Immediately add the mushrooms to the skillet and continue to cook until they release their liquid, 4 to 5 minutes, stirring from time to time.

4. Meanwhile, beat the eggs with a whisk until foamy. Chop the ham into ½-inch pieces and add to the eggs, along with the cheese and a sprinkling of salt and pepper.

5. When the mushrooms have released their liquid, use a slotted spoon to transfer the vegetables to the bowl with the egg mixture. Discard all of the juices from the skillet, then immediately put it back on the burner, over medium heat. Add the 2 teaspoons olive oil and heat, rotating the pan to distribute the oil evenly. Stir the egg mixture thoroughly and pour it into the skillet. With the back of a spoon, push (do not stir) the ham and mushrooms through-out the egg to distribute them evenly.

6. Cook, without stirring, until only the surface is runny, about 7 minutes. Immediately put the skillet under the broiler and cook until the surface is just set but not brown, about 2 minutes.

7. Before serving, run a knife around the edge of the frittata to loosen. Serve at once by slicing into 4 wedges.

Serves 4

COMPANY EGGS

2 tablespoons butter
½ medium onion (for ⅓ cup chopped)
½ medium green bell pepper (for ½ cup chopped)
6 ounces reduced-fat cream cheese
12 large eggs
¾ cup low-fat milk
1½ teaspoons salt
¼ teaspoon black pepper

1. Heat 1 tablespoon of butter in a 12-inch nonstick skillet over medium heat. Meanwhile, peel and coarsely chop the onion, adding it to the pan as you chop. Seed and chop the bell pepper and add to the skillet. Cook until the onion is tender and the water from the vegetables has evaporated, 2 to 3 minutes.

2. Meanwhile, cut the cream cheese into small chunks and set aside. Break the eggs into a 2-quart or larger bowl and add the milk, salt, and black pepper. Using a whisk, beat until foamy. Add the egg mixture to the skillet and reduce the heat to medium-low. Cook for 1 minute. Add the cream cheese and slowly scramble until the eggs are just done, 5 minutes. Serve at once.

Serves 6

From Beverly:

I discovered this dish at the William Thomas House, a bed-and-breakfast inn in downtown Raleigh, North Carolina, where my husband and I celebrated our eighth wedding anniversary. Granted, the atmosphere was romantic, but I don't think that's why I thought these were just about the best eggs I had ever tasted. Owner and chef Sarah Lofton graciously shared the recipe, and I have since seen similar versions in several community cookbooks. We've substituted light cream cheese and significantly cut back on the butter, but this is still a sinful concoction best saved for special occasions.

Looking forward to meat for dinner, but there's none in the house? If you have a carton of eggs and some Mexican staples, you can still make a delicious dinner that will make you forget about meat altogether. (You will use up your egg quotient for the next few days, but this dish is worth it.) The splash of salsa on top adds the heat to this recipe, so if you like it spicy, choose the hottest you can find.

DINNER HUEVOS IN A HURRY

1 teaspoon olive oil
2 cups frozen green, red, and yellow bell pepper
  stir-fry mix
10 large eggs
½ cup reduced-fat sour cream
4 large (10-inch) flour tortillas
Cooking oil spray
1 can (14½ ounces) Mexican-style stewed
  tomatoes
¾ cup bottled salsa
1 cup (4 ounces) already-shredded cheese, such as
  Monterey Jack, Cheddar, Colby, or a combination

1. Turn on the broiler.

2. Heat ½ teaspoon of the oil in a 12-inch nonstick skillet over medium-high heat. Add the pepper stir-fry mix and cook until defrosted and soft, about 2 minutes, stirring once or twice. Meanwhile, break the eggs into a 2-quart or larger bowl and beat with a whisk until light and frothy.

3. Remove the vegetables to a small bowl with a slotted spoon. Discard any juice left in the pan then taking care not to burn yourself, wipe out the skillet using several layers of paper towels.

4. Heat the remaining ½ teaspoon oil in the same skillet over medium heat. Add the eggs and stir until soft- or medium-scrambled, about 5 minutes. Drain any accumulated juice from the reserved peppers and add them to the eggs. Add the sour cream and stir lightly to incorporate. Remove the skillet from the heat.

5. Stack the tortillas and microwave, uncovered, on high, until warmed through, about 45 seconds to 1 minute. Meanwhile, coat a 13 × 9-inch baking dish with cooking oil spray. Lay the tortillas out flat and spread one quarter of the egg mixture in the middle of each, then roll it up, tucking in the ends, burrito style. As each tortilla is rolled, carefully place it in the baking dish. Spoon the tomatoes and the salsa evenly over all and sprinkle with the cheese.

6. Broil the casserole until the cheese melts and bubbles, 2 to 3 minutes. Serve at once.

Serves 4

BACON AND TOMATO PIE

Cooking oil spray
1 cup Italian-style fine dry bread crumbs
1 cup (4 ounces) already finely shredded sharp
  Cheddar cheese
3 large fresh, ripe tomatoes (about 1½ pounds total; see Box,
  page 220)
3 large eggs
½ cup skim or low-fat milk
1 tablespoon red wine vinegar (see Box, page 220)
¼ teaspoon salt (optional)
¼ teaspoon black pepper
2 slices bacon (regular, reduced-sodium, or
  turkey)
1 teaspoon olive oil (if using turkey bacon)
1 medium onion (for ¾ cup chopped)

From Alicia:

Every summer I seem to have the fortunate problem of too many tomatoes. This recipe is one of the ways I put my bountiful crop to use.

Instead of a traditional pastry crust, this pie makes its own delicious variation when the juice from the tomatoes blends with Italian-style bread crumbs. With a spinach salad (pre-washed baby spinach leaves from a bag, tossed with bottled dressing and store-bought croutons) and mint iced tea, this pie makes the perfect summer supper.

> ✹ *If you make this dish with any other than fully vine-ripe, juicy tomatoes, reduce the amount of vinegar to 1 teaspoon.*

1. The oven should be already heated to 450°F.

2. Spray the bottom and sides of a 10-inch square casserole dish with cooking oil spray. Sprinkle ½ cup of the bread crumbs evenly over the bottom of the dish, then sprinkle with the cheese. Working quickly with a serrated knife, core the tomatoes and cut into ¼-inch-thick slices. Layer the slices over the crumbs and cheese.

3. Combine the eggs and milk in a 1-quart or larger bowl. Using a whisk or fork, beat until foamy. Stir in the vinegar, salt (if using), and pepper. Pour the mixture over the tomatoes in the casserole and put the dish into the oven. Set a timer for 12 minutes.

4. While the pie bakes, set a 10-inch or larger nonstick skillet over medium-high heat. Cut the bacon into bite-size pieces and add them to the skillet as you cut. Fry until some of the fat is released and the edges start to brown, about 2 minutes. If using turkey bacon, add the olive oil. Meanwhile, peel and coarsely chop the onion, adding it to the skillet as you chop. Cook until almost all of the bacon is crisp and the onions are soft, about 4 minutes, stirring from time to time.

5. When the bacon is crisp, add the remaining ½ cup bread crumbs to the skillet and stir well to mix. Stir and cook for 1 minute to lightly toast the crumb mixture then remove from the heat.

6. When the timer goes off, remove the dish from the oven and tilt it to distribute any juices to the sides of the dish. Return it to the oven and continue to cook until the pie has begun to brown at the edges, 3 to 4 minutes. Remove from the oven. Don't worry if there is a small amount of juice on top; this is from the tomatoes. Sprinkle the reserved bacon-crumb mixture evenly over the pie. Cut into four wedges and serve.

Serves 4

BRUNCH RICE BURRITOS

1 teaspoon olive oil

1 large onion (for 1 cup chopped)

½ large green bell pepper (for ¾ cup chopped)

6 large eggs

½ cup skim milk

Salt and black pepper to taste

1 can (4½ ounces) chopped green chilies

1 large can (3.8 ounces) sliced black olives

1 teaspoon chili powder

½ teaspoon ground cumin

3 cups leftover cooked rice

*1 cup (4 ounces) already-shredded Mexican blend
    or taco-style cheese*

12 corn or flour tortillas, any size

1. Heat the oil in a 12-inch nonstick skillet over medium heat. Peel and coarsely chop the onion, adding it to the skillet as you chop. Cook for 1 minute to soften slightly. Meanwhile, seed and chop the bell pepper and add it to the skillet. Cook, stirring from time to time and lowering the heat slightly if the onion starts to brown.

2. While the vegetables cook, break the eggs into a 2-quart or larger bowl. Add the milk and a sprinkling of salt and black pepper and beat with a whisk until foamy. Drain the chiles and olives and add to the bowl along with the chili powder and cumin. Stir well to mix.

3. Pour the egg mixture into the skillet with the vegetables and let cook, without stirring, until the eggs just begin to set, 3 to 4 minutes. Add the rice and cheese and stir gently to separate the grains. Continue to cook, stirring from time to time, until the eggs are no longer runny, 2 to 3 minutes.

This is the recipe you pull out on the night when you walk in the house at six-thirty, the family's starving, and you have nothing more in the fridge than half a dozen eggs and some leftover rice and cheese. This flexible dish is as easy to make as scrambled eggs, yet the outcome tastes like you've been slaving for hours.

4. Meanwhile, heat the tortillas in the microwave according to package directions.

5. Remove the egg mixture from the heat. Spoon it into the warm tortillas, wrap burrito style, and serve at once.

Serves 6

We liked our Brunch Rice Burritos (page 221) so much we decided to do another take on it from a different part of the world. Homey and satisfying, this version is highlighted by olives, artichoke hearts, and flavor-packed feta cheese. It's so easy to put together, you'll find yourself steaming extra rice just to have enough to enjoy this flexible entrée later in the week.

GREEK-STYLE BRUNCH RICE

1 teaspoon olive oil
1 large onion (for 1 cup chopped)
½ large green bell pepper (for ¾ cup chopped)
6 large eggs
½ cup skim or low-fat milk
1½ teaspoons dried Italian seasoning
Salt and black pepper, to taste
3 large (6-inch) pita breads
1 can (3.8 ounces) sliced black olives
1 can (14 ounces) artichoke hearts packed in water
3 cups leftover cooked rice
1 package (4 ounces) already-crumbled feta cheese
1 cup frozen green peas (optional)

1. Turn on the oven or toaster oven to 350°F.

2. Heat the oil in a 12-inch nonstick skillet over medium heat. Peel and coarsely chop the onion, adding it to the skillet as you chop. Cook for 1 minute to soften slightly. Meanwhile, seed and chop the bell pepper and add it to the skillet. Cook, stirring from time to time and lowering the heat if the onion starts to brown.

3. While the vegetables cook, break the eggs into a 2-quart or larger bowl. Add the milk, Italian seasoning, and a sprinkling of salt and black pepper and beat with a whisk until foamy.

4. Wrap the pita breads in aluminum foil and heat in the oven while finishing the dish. Pour the egg mixture into the skillet with the vegetables and let cook, without stirring.

5. Meanwhile, drain the olives and artichokes, coarsely chopping the artichokes. When the eggs start to set around the edges, add the artichokes and olives along with the rice, feta cheese, and green peas (if using). Stir gently to separate the rice grains and mix in the vegetables. Continue to cook, stirring occasionally, until the eggs are no longer runny and all the ingredients are heated through, 3 to 5 minutes.

6. Cut each warmed pita into 6 wedges. Place 3 on each serving plate. Spoon the egg mixture to the side of the pita points and serve at once.

Serves 6

"Leftover rice is a wonderful tool, if you have enough and know what to do with it."

A word about:
LEFTOVER RICE

Whenever you have leftover rice, freeze it for future use. Measure the rice by 1-cup increments into a zipper-top plastic freezer bag, writing the amount on the outside of the bag. Before sealing, fluff the rice with a fork to prevent clumping.

To use frozen leftover rice, remove it from the bag, place it in a microwave-safe bowl, and microwave it, covered, on high for 1 minute per cup. Fluff it with a fork and continue with the recipe.

This method defrosts the rice, but will not heat it through. To use the rice plain, heat it for 2 to 3 minutes per cup.

From Beverly:

To my mind, eggs Benedict is just an excuse to eat hollandaise sauce, but making the sauce from scratch is a pain, and I prefer not to use the stuff in the packets. This microwave version was revolutionary for me. When I saw it in a community cookbook called *Market to Market,* by the Service League of Hickory, North Carolina, I have to admit I was skeptical. We changed the type of mustard used, but the sauce still goes together in 2 minutes and is so amazing, you'll be tempted to make it every day. However, it is quite fattening, so save this dish for special occasions.

Traditional eggs benedict is made with Canadian bacon, but once I tasted it with imitation crab in a café in Fort Lauderdale, Florida, this is the way I've always made it. You can substitute Canadian bacon if you prefer.

SEASIDE EGGS BENEDICT

6 cups water
1 tablespoon vinegar (any kind except balsamic)
Microwave Hollandaise Sauce (recipe follows)
4 large eggs
2 English muffins
8 ounces (1 package) flake-style imitation crabmeat (surimi)

1. Combine the water and vinegar in a nonreactive 12-inch skillet that has a lid. Bring to a boil over high heat.

2. Meanwhile, make the Microwave Hollandaise Sauce.

3. Carefully break the eggs, one at a time, directly into the boiling water. Cover the skillet and turn down the heat to a simmer. Time the eggs for exactly 2 minutes, and then remove the pan from the heat, leaving the eggs in the water.

4. While the eggs poach, split the muffins and toast them. Place the crabmeat in a microwave-safe dish and microwave, uncovered, on high, for 45 seconds to 1 minute.

5. Place one muffin half, face up, on each serving plate. Sprinkle a thin layer of crab over the muffins, using up about half of the crab. (If the crab is in large chunks, flake it with your fingers.) Remove the eggs from the water with a slotted spoon, taking care to drain off all the water, and place one on each muffin half. Top with another layer of crab and ¼ cup of sauce. Serve at once.

Serves 4

MICROWAVE HOLLANDAISE SAUCE

This sauce also tastes great made with half-and-half, but the texture will be much thinner than a traditional hollandaise.

4 tablespoons (½ stick) butter
2 large eggs
1 tablespoon lemon juice from frozen concentrate
¼ cup heavy (or whipping) cream
½ teaspoon Dijon mustard

1. Place the butter in a 2-cup glass measure and microwave, uncovered, on high for 30 seconds. Remove the butter from the microwave and stir until completely melted.

2. Separate the eggs (see page 237), placing the yolks in a small bowl and setting the whites aside for another purpose. Beat the yolks well with a whisk or fork, then add, along with the lemon juice and cream, to the butter and stir well. Microwave the mixture, uncovered, on high, for 1 minute, stirring every 15 seconds with a fork. When ready, the sauce will be just slightly thick.

3. Remove the sauce from the microwave and stir in the mustard. Cover with plastic wrap and set aside until ready to serve.

Makes about 1 cup

From Beverly:

Regardless of what the package says, it takes at least half an hour of simmering, copious amounts of water, and patient pot-tending to produce creamy, soft, southern-style grits. The process is similar to making an Italian risotto. My regular life almost never allows time for that, and there are times I really miss my grits. Quick-cooking couscous—which is a grain-like pasta you could almost consider a first cousin to grits, but in the wheat family—makes a wonderful substitute that's ready to eat in just a few minutes. With cheese added, it's really hard to tell the difference.

This is a typical southern breakfast, and a fine dinner, too, especially if it's served with buttermilk biscuits and sliced ripe tomatoes.

> ❋ *If you don't have country ham, you can use baked Virginia ham from the deli, which you should have sliced no thinner than ¼ inch. The cooking time in step 2 will not be as long as for the country ham.*

IMPOSTOR GRITS AND HAM

1¾ cups water
1 tablespoon butter
2 teaspoons dried onion flakes
½ teaspoon bottled minced garlic
1 cup quick-cooking couscous
2 center-cut slices (¾ pound total) country ham (see Box)
1 can (10¾ ounces) Cheddar cheese soup
½ cup already-shredded sharp Cheddar cheese
¾ cup low-fat milk

1. Combine 1½ cups of the water, the butter, onion flakes, and garlic in a 2-quart or larger saucepan that has a lid and bring to a boil, covered, over high heat. Add the couscous and remove the pan from the heat. Let stand, covered, for 5 minutes.

2. While the water comes to a boil, heat a 12-inch cast-iron or nonstick skillet over medium-high heat. Cut each ham slice into 4 pieces. Add the ham to the hot skillet (the pieces may overlap at first) and fry until the slices begin to brown, about 5 minutes. Jiggle the pan from time to time to keep the slices from sticking. Turn the slices over, add the remaining ¼ cup water, and continue to fry until the second sides begin to brown, about 5 minutes, turning the slices over as necessary to brown evenly on both sides.

3. After the couscous is done, fluff it with a fork to separate the grains. Place the saucepan over medium-low heat and gently stir in the soup, cheese, and milk. Cook, stirring gently, until the cheese melts and the mixture is heated through.

4. Place two slices of ham on each serving plate, spoon the couscous alongside, and serve.

Serves 4

HASH BROWN CASSEROLE

1 package (12 ounces) light breakfast-style bulk sausage
1 medium onion (for ¾ cup chopped)
1 medium green bell pepper (for 1 cup chopped)
1 cup already-sliced fresh mushrooms
4 cups frozen southern-style cubed hash brown potatoes
½ cup water
Salt and black pepper, to taste
1½ cups (6 ounces) already finely shredded sharp
   Cheddar cheese

1. Set an extra-deep 12-inch nonstick skillet that has a lid over medium heat. Add the sausage to the hot skillet and stir frequently to break it into pieces. While the sausage releases its fat, peel and chop the onion, adding it to the skillet as you chop. Seed and chop the bell pepper, and add it to the skillet. Coarsely chop the sliced mushrooms and add them. After all the vegetables are added, cook until they are softened and the sausage is almost completely cooked, 2 minutes more.

2. If the hash browns are frozen in big clumps, bang the bag on the counter to loosen; or, after measuring out the amount you're using, rinse under running water in a colander and drain. Scatter the hash browns over the sausage and vegetables and add the water. Cover and cook for 4 minutes. Uncover and raise the heat to medium-high. Cook, stirring often, until the potatoes start to brown, 7 to 8 minutes more, reducing the heat if the potatoes begin to overbrown. Season with salt and black pepper.

3. Sprinkle the cheese evenly over the mixture, cover, and cook until the cheese melts, about 1 minute, then serve.

Serves 4

From Alicia:

Once, while traveling home from the South Carolina coast, my husband and I stopped for lunch at a truck stop on Interstate 26. Two clues told us that this was indeed an authentic establishment: The building was tiny compared to the mammoth parking lot, and the restaurant served breakfast around the clock.

That day's special was a sausage and hash brown casserole. I couldn't resist. My husband settled on the blueberry pancakes. As our waitress shouted our requests to the cook, I was amazed at what sounded like a foreign language.

"Scattered, smothered, and covered, all the way, and a short stack made blue," she yelled.

"Scattered, smothered, and covered" stuck in our family vocabulary for years and actually became a catch-phrase for any dish that did not serve up as expected. This recipe is a 20-minute version of the original and tastes great any time of day. Be sure to put the ketchup bottle on the table, and enjoy.

From Beverly:

When I was growing up in the rural South, my mother would fix an enormous Sunday lunch, which was usually called dinner by southerners in those days. The eating would continue until about two o'clock in the afternoon and the dishwashing could easily last until three. When suppertime rolled around at seven, this was the only point in her week that Mom truly had no patience for the kitchen. But since the closest restaurant was 30 miles away and she had three hungry children, Mom would trudge to the stove and whip up some creamed chipped beef on toast. It was my first encounter with "breakfast for dinner."

I had all but forgotten this simple, comforting dish until one day I noticed Stouffer's rendition in my supermarket freezer case. Since I can always use an easy Sunday supper, I decided to try it. It tasted as good as I remembered, but I like a little more texture. That's why I add celery and green pepper.

CREAMY CHIPPED BEEF

*2 packages (11 ounces each) frozen creamed chipped beef,
    such as Stouffer's*
1 small onion (for ½ cup diced)
2 large ribs celery (for 1 cup diced)
¾ cup white wine or sherry
½ large green bell pepper (for ¾ cup chopped)
1½ teaspoons bottled minced garlic
2 teaspoons Worcestershire sauce
¼ teaspoon dried thyme
¼ teaspoon white pepper (optional)
¼ cup already-grated or -shredded Parmesan cheese
4 slices pumpernickel or other hearty bread

1. Pierce both pouches of beef to vent, place in a microwave-safe dish and microwave 10 minutes on high. Meanwhile, peel and dice the onion and dice the celery. Combine in a 12-inch non-stick skillet, add the wine, and set over high heat. Bring the wine to a boil while seeding and chopping the bell pepper.

2. Add the bell pepper to the skillet and boil until the vegetables are crisp-tender, about 3 minutes. Stir from time to time. While the vegetables boil, add the garlic, Worcestershire, thyme, and white pepper (if using). Most of the wine will evaporate.

3. At this point, the beef should be microwaved. Cut the tops off the pouches and add the beef and all of the sauce to the skillet. Reduce the heat to a simmer and add the Parmesan cheese. Stir the mixture well and simmer to let the cheese melt and flavors blend, 2 to 3 minutes. Meanwhile, toast the bread.

4. Place a toast slice on each individual serving plate, spoon the chipped beef and vegetables over, and serve.

Serves 4

FRENCH TOAST À L'ORANGE

2 large eggs
⅔ cup half-and-half
⅓ cup orange juice
1 teaspoon ground cinnamon
1 tablespoon margarine
8 slices day-old French bread, each 1 inch thick
Confectioners' sugar, for garnish (optional)
Warm maple syrup, for serving

1. Turn on the oven to the lowest setting.

2. Combine the eggs, half-and-half, orange juice, and cinnamon in a shallow bowl, and beat with a wire whisk until the eggs are frothy and all ingredients are mixed.

3. Heat an extra-deep 12-inch nonstick skillet or a griddle over medium-high heat. Add half of the margarine, and melt, tilting the skillet to coat the entire pan bottom. Dip 4 slices of the bread, one at a time, in the egg mixture to cover completely, letting excess egg drip back into the bowl, then place in the skillet. Cook until golden brown and crisp on the bottom, 1½ to 2 minutes. Turn the slices and cook for an additional 1½ to 2 minutes. Remove to a heatproof serving platter and keep warm in the oven. Melt the remaining margarine in the skillet and repeat with the remaining bread and egg mixture.

4. When all of the toast is cooked, sprinkle with confectioners' sugar (if using) and serve immediately with warm maple syrup.

Serves 4

French toast is an age-old method for reviving stale bread—just dip it into a mixture of eggs and milk and fry to a golden brown. Of course practically any bread will do, but thick-sliced French bread is still our favorite.

We got the idea for adding orange juice to the milk and egg mixture from a recipe in *The Silver Palate Good Times Cookbook*, in which the authors make French toast from a scrumptious concoction of heavy cream, eggs, orange liqueur, and croissants. Our combination of half-and-half and orange juice gives a similar flavor without being quite so fattening.

Use margarine instead of butter to grease the griddle because it won't burn at the higher temperature you need to prepare the dish. The higher heat gives a more even browning and better texture to the toast.

We like to serve French Toast à l'Orange with sausages and fresh orange slices, in addition to lots of the warm maple syrup.

From Alicia:

When I visited England, it was not until we got out of London that I got a real taste of English country food. After a walking tour of the city of Coventry, we headed into a small pub for a late breakfast. Even though it was May, the weather felt more like February to my southern bones. Cold, a little lonely for home, and famished, we sat down to exactly what I had been craving—an English home-cooked meal.

"Pub pie" was the house special—a flaky crust filled with whatever Cook Lonnie happened to fancy. On this particular day, chunks of English bacon and apples were smothered in a creamy sauce with a hint of Dijon mustard. It was pure heaven.

I had forgotten this lovely meal until, more than a decade later, Beverly made a Canadian bacon and apple mixture that she served over English muffins. I was instantly transported to that classically dreary day in Coventry when English home cooking took on a new meaning for me.

ENGLISH MUFFIN "PUB PIE"

4 English muffins
Cooking oil spray
8 slices (about 4 ounces) Canadian bacon
1 large onion
1 tablespoon butter
3 tart cooking apples, such as Granny Smith
2 teaspoons granulated sugar
1 cup half-and-half
1 tablespoon light or dark brown sugar, firmly packed
1 tablespoon Dijon mustard

1. Turn on the oven to the lowest setting.

2. Split the muffins and toast them. Meanwhile, spray a 12-inch nonstick skillet with cooking oil spray and set it over high heat. Place the bacon in the pan and fry it until it just begins to brown, about 1 minute on each side. While the bacon cooks, peel the onion, slice it thin, and set aside.

3. When the bacon is lightly browned, remove the skillet from the heat and place the bacon slices on paper towels to drain briefly. Arrange the toasted muffin halves on a baking sheet or large ovenproof serving platter and place a bacon slice on each half. Place in the oven to keep warm.

4. Taking care not to burn yourself, wipe out the skillet using several layers of paper towels. Set the skillet over low heat, add the butter, and melt it. Add the onion slices and begin to cook.

5. Meanwhile, cut the apples in half and remove the cores. Place the apples, cut side down, on a cutting board and cut into

¼-inch-thick slices, leaving the peel on. Add them to the skillet as you cut. Sprinkle with the granulated sugar and raise the heat to medium-high. Cook until the apples and onion slices are tender, about 5 minutes.

6. Meanwhile, combine the half-and-half, brown sugar, and mustard in a 2-cup measure or small bowl and whisk to blend.

7. When the apples and onion slices are tender, remove the baking sheet from the oven, leaving the oven on, and scatter the apples and onions evenly over the bacon-topped muffins. Return the baking sheet to the oven.

8. Pour the half-and-half mixture into the same skillet and bring it almost to a boil over medium heat, whisking constantly. Cook, whisking, for 1 minute more (do not let the sauce boil), then remove the pan from the heat.

9. Transfer two muffin halves to each individual serving plate, making sure each has enough apple and onion mixture, top with sauce, and serve.

Serves 4

"Deep desperation always hits when you least expect it. For sanity's sake, you're best off heading back to basics."

CHAPTER EIGHT

Easy

When desperate times call for uncomplicated food, we head back to the basics—all-purpose entrées like Lemony Chicken Piccata, Pork au Poivre, and Flash-in-the-Pan Fish Fillets that are practically mindless and that often can be cooked in even less than 20 minutes. There's a reason our mothers used to depend on plain chicken, fish, and pork chops. They endured disaster days, too, and these were no-stress meals they could rely on. We soon found ourselves craving some of our mothers' other standby recipes. Meals like meat loaf and stuffed bell peppers are comfort foods for sure, but too time consuming. We've streamlined these recipes to make them suit our 20-minute time frame, yet they still taste like memories of home. In short, these are recipes that any of our moms could appreciate.

Many other recipes, such as our Apple-Glazed Burger Steaks, Ham Strips with Orange Marmalade Glaze, and Mahi Mahi with Curry-Yogurt Mayonnaise, take a basic approach and add a shot of extra flavor. Even so, the recipes are still quick and easy.

Other recipes in this chapter focus on easy cooking techniques that have stood the test of time across several cultures. Again, we've simplified cooking methods and classic recipes, even when fancy names would have you convinced otherwise. For example, we've found that a lovely béarnaise can be made in less than 10 minutes with a little push from the microwave. While the sauce cooks, you can

fry a steak and sit down to a meal worthy of a French bistro in less than 20 minutes.

We generally like to assume that desperate cooks may have no options other than blocks of frozen meat in the freezer. However, in this one chapter, some of the meat is pounded and pan-fried. For these recipes you must start with fully defrosted meat. If you don't have any, check our microwave defrosting tips on page 243.

A dozen recipes in this chapter call for preheating the oven. To our mind, these are best reserved for wintry weather when you welcome the idea of a toasty kitchen. A typical gas oven takes about 10 minutes to preheat to 350°F, and about 3 minutes more to shoot up to 450°F. If you decide it's an oven-dinner day, plan on preheating it as soon as convenient, for example the minute you walk in the door from work. It's the same idea as putting a pot of water on to boil. By the time you change your clothes, assemble yourself back in the kitchen, and do the quick preparation necessary for our oven entrées, the oven heat level should be up to speed.

Finally, this chapter contains eight recipes for cooking on a gas grill. Grilling makes just about any food seem special, and there are those days when cooking outside is just the sanity-saver you need. In the past, our problem with grilling has been the fact that we usually can't get our act together ahead of time to marinate or we don't have the time to wait for charcoals to smolder. These recipes are designed to overcome just such obstacles. You'll find all the details you need for Desperation grilling on page 294.

"We've simplified cooking methods and classic recipes, even when fancy names would have you convinced otherwise."

From Beverly:

The first time my friend cooked this steak for me, I was horrified. Forget the fact that his grandfather had made it this way for decades, perfectly fine meat was clearly being ruined.

Of course I was wrong. The light, crisp crust outside is the perfect complement to the juiciness inside. And my friend accomplished it all without ever having to struggle with a charcoal grill.

A tender cut is best for this recipe, but it doesn't have to be the finest tenderloin. I prefer sirloin or loin strip.

POP'S PAN-FRIED STEAK AND POTATOES

¼ cup all-purpose flour
½ teaspoon garlic powder
½ teaspoon salt, plus additional to taste
¼ teaspoon black pepper, plus additional to taste
3 tablespoons olive oil
1¼ to 1½ pounds boneless beefsteak, cut from the loin (about ¾ inch thick), defrosted if frozen
4 cups (about ½ bag) frozen southern-style (cubed) hash brown potatoes

1. Turn on the oven to its lowest setting. Combine the flour, garlic powder, ½ teaspoon salt, and ¼ teaspoon pepper in a large zipper-top plastic bag, and set aside.

2. Heat 2 tablespoons of the oil in an extra-deep 12-inch non-stick skillet over medium-high heat.

3. Meanwhile, cut the meat into 4 equal portions and add them to the bag with the flour mixture. Shake well to coat.

4. Add the steak pieces to the skillet and cook 5 minutes on each side for medium rare or until desired doneness. (If the oil starts to smoke, lower the heat to medium.)

5. While the meat cooks, place the hash browns in a shallow 2-quart microwave-safe casserole dish and microwave, uncovered, on high, for 3 minutes or until defrosted. When the steak is done, remove the pieces to a serving platter, leaving room in the center for the potatoes, and keep warm in the oven.

6. Raise the heat under the skillet to high, add the potatoes, and shake the skillet to distribute them evenly. Drizzle the remaining

1 tablespoon oil over the potatoes and cook until golden brown, 6 to 8 minutes, stirring from time to time by using a tossing motion. Season with salt and pepper. In the final 2 minutes of cooking, pour any steak juices that have accumulated on the platter back into the skillet and stir until absorbed.

7. Remove the potatoes from the heat, mound in the middle of the platter, and serve.

Serves 4

"About half of our friends complain they make the same five meals over and over again."

A word about:
HIGH HEAT

Speed is a basic concept behind Desperation recipes; that usually requires browning and boiling over medium-high to high heat. Of course, when using high heat, you sometimes walk that thin timeline between perfectly cooked and burned.

Obviously, it is never our intention that you burn your food. It is true, however, that stoves, cookware, and ingredients vary. If you're cooking away and the food starts to burn or brown too quickly, immediately lift the pan off the heat. Then adjust the burner temperature. An advantage to gas burners is immediate heat reduction. But if you're cooking on an electric stovetop, you'll need to wait half a minute or so before returning the pan to the burner.

Remember, when cooking over high heat, it is always best to keep a constant eye on the stove.

Why wait until you go out to a fancy restaurant to feast on fabulously prepared beef with a classic French sauce? Even desperate folks need to treat themselves every now and again. And what you might have believed too difficult for a hurried evening becomes so simple with the microwave technique for preparing the sauce.

Traditional béarnaise sauce is made with shallots and whole cream. If you happen to have either of them on hand, you may substitute equal quantities for the onion and the half-and-half.

PAN-SEARED TENDERLOIN WITH BÉARNAISE

1 tablespoon olive oil
4 beef tenderloin steaks (filets mignons; each 1½ inches thick
*   and about 4 ounces), defrosted if frozen*
1 small onion (for ½ cup chopped)
2 tablespoons distilled white vinegar
2 tablespoons white wine
¼ teaspoon dried tarragon
2 large eggs
4 tablespoons (½ stick) butter
¼ cup half-and-half
1 teaspoon lemon juice from frozen concentrate

1. Turn on the oven to its lowest setting.

2. Heat the oil in a 12-inch nonstick skillet over medium-high heat. Add the steaks and cook to desired doneness, 5 to 6 minutes per side for medium rare. If the steaks finish cooking before the sauce is completed, remove to a platter and keep warm in the oven.

3. While the steaks cook, prepare the béarnaise. Peel and finely chop the onion, then combine it in a small (1-quart) saucepan with the vinegar, wine, and tarragon. Bring to a boil over high heat and continue to boil until only about 1 teaspoon of liquid is left in the pan with the onion (see Note), about 2 minutes. Remove from the heat and set aside.

4. Separate the eggs, placing the yolks in a small bowl and setting the whites aside for another purpose. Beat the yolks well with a

fork. Place the butter in a 2-cup glass measure and microwave, uncovered, on high, until almost melted, about 45 seconds. Remove the butter from the microwave and stir until completely melted, then stir in the half-and-half, lemon juice, and egg yolks. Microwave the mixture, uncovered, on high, for 1 minute, stirring every 15 seconds with the fork. When done, the sauce will be just slightly thick. Remove from the microwave and stir in the reserved onion mixture.

5. Place each steak on a serving plate, top with ¼ cup béarnaise and serve.

Serves 4

Note: Be sure to let enough liquid evaporate, watching it carefully during the final minute. At that point, it will evaporate quickly.

"If you put your spice jars in alphabetical order, you'll know exactly where the tarragon is."

A word about:
SEPARATING EGGS

You don't have to be nimble-fingered to separate eggs, but it's best to handle the task with a little delicacy. Since you want to keep the yolk intact, rap the middle of the shell on a sharp counter edge with only moderate enthusiasm. You should get a crack that's big enough to split the egg without it cascading all over your workspace. Once cracked, split the eggs gently—we've broken many a yolk by trying to force open a stubborn shell. Working over a bowl to catch the white, transfer the yolk back and forth between shell halves until it is white-free. Then place the yolk in a small bowl, and move on to the next egg. If you won't be using the whites in a recipe, cover the bowl with plastic wrap and refrigerate for up to 4 days. Frozen they will keep for up to 1 year. Thaw them overnight in the refrigerator.

Roast beef and cheese both perform best in this recipe if they're sliced about ⅛ inch thick. Since the beef slice will be large, you'll need a large deli slice of cheese, as well.

ROAST BEEF ROLL-UPS WITH HORSERADISH CREAM

Cooking oil spray

1⅓ cups store-bought refrigerated mashed potatoes, such as Simply Potatoes (see Box, facing page), or leftover mashed potatoes

4 slices (about 1 pound total) deli roast beef (sliced ⅛ inch thick)

4 large slices (about ¼ pound total) deli sharp Cheddar cheese (sliced ⅛ inch thick)

Horseradish Cream (optional; recipe follows)

1. The oven should be already heated to 450°F. Spray a shallow 10-inch square casserole dish with cooking oil spray.

2. Place the mashed potatoes in a microwave-safe bowl and microwave, covered, on high, for 2 minutes.

3. Meanwhile, top each slice of beef with a slice of cheese. Carefully spoon ⅓ cup of the potatoes along one short end of each cheese and beef stack and mold into a log shape. Roll the beef and cheese around the potatoes. Place the roll-ups, seam side down, in the prepared casserole dish. Cover with aluminum foil and bake for 6 minutes.

4. While the roll-ups bake, make the Horseradish Cream (if using).

5. Place each roll-up on a serving plate, top each with some of the cream sauce, and serve.

Serves 4

HORSERADISH CREAM

4 tablespoons (½ stick) butter
2 eggs
¼ cup half-and-half
2 teaspoons prepared horseradish
Dash of garlic powder (optional)

1. Put the butter in a 2-cup glass measure and microwave, uncovered, on high, for 30 seconds. Remove the butter from the microwave and stir until completely melted. Separate the eggs (see page 237), placing them in a small dish and setting the whites aside for another purpose. Beat the yolks well with a fork. Add the yolks and half-and-half to the butter and stir well.

2. Microwave the mixture on high, uncovered, for 1 minute, stirring well every 15 seconds with the fork. Remove from the microwave and stir in the horseradish and garlic powder (if using). Cover the cup with plastic wrap and set aside until ready to serve.

Makes ¾ cup

> ✳ *Commercially prepared refrigerated mashed potatoes are especially convenient if you don't have any leftover potatoes on hand. We tested this recipe using the Simply Potatoes brand. Many supermarkets stock these near the eggs.*

ROLL-UPS

When there's nothing left in the refrigerator except sliced deli meat, cheese, and a sprinkling of vegetables, don't settle for another cold sandwich. You can fix our beef (facing page), corned beef (page 240), ham (page 256), or turkey (page 272) roll-ups.

Practically a whole meal, each of the four roll-up dishes is featured with a different scrumptious sauce that is microwave quick. These roll-ups are so impressive, we've even served them for fancy brunches and luncheons as well as dinner. The timing is different for each, so follow the instructions carefully.

This unique roll-up plays off the flavors of a Reuben sandwich. Most people have strong feelings about sauerkraut. If you have a favorite brand, by all means use it. We prefer the kind in a jar that's found alongside the packaged deli meats and hot dogs in the refrigerator case, but there are also good-quality bagged brands.

REUBEN ROLL-UPS WITH ISLAND CREAM SAUCE

PRE HEAT OVEN

Cooking oil spray
1⅓ cups sauerkraut
8 slices (about ¾ pound total) deli corned beef
    (sliced ⅛ inch thick)
4 slices (about ¼ pound total) deli Swiss cheese
    (sliced ⅛ inch thick)
Island Cream Sauce (optional; recipe follows)

1. The oven should be already heated to 450°F. Spray a shallow, 10-inch square casserole dish with cooking oil spray.

2. Place the sauerkraut in a microwave-safe bowl and microwave, covered, on high, for 1 minute. Meanwhile, slightly overlap 2 slices of corned beef, forming 1 wide slice. Top the beef with a slice of cheese. Carefully spoon ⅓ cup of the kraut along one short end of each cheese and beef stack. Roll the beef and cheese around the kraut. Place the roll-ups, seam side down, in the prepared casserole dish. Cover with aluminum foil and bake until the cheese is melted, about 10 minutes.

3. While the roll-ups bake, make the Island Cream Sauce (if using).

4. Place each roll-up on a serving plate, top with some of the sauce, and serve.

Serves 4

ISLAND CREAM SAUCE

4 tablespoons (½ stick) butter
2 large eggs
¼ cup half-and-half
2 tablespoons bottled Thousand Island salad dressing

1. Place the butter in a 2-cup glass measure and microwave, uncovered, on high, for 30 seconds. Remove the butter from the microwave and stir until completely melted.

2. Separate the eggs (see page 237), placing the yolks in a small dish and setting the whites aside for another purpose. Beat the yolks well with a fork, then add, along with the half-and-half, to the butter and stir well.

3. Microwave the mixture, uncovered, on high, for 1 minute, stirring well every 15 seconds with the fork. Remove from the microwave and stir in the Thousand Island dressing. The sauce will be thin. Cover with plastic wrap and set aside until ready to serve.

Makes about ¾ cup

Serve this sauce with Reuben Roll-Ups to give them that signature taste, or with plain baked, poached, grilled, or pan-seared fish.

From Alicia:

My mom makes the best meat loaf I've ever tasted. Back when my husband and I were dating, mentioning that it was meat loaf night was a sure way to get him over for dinner. Naturally, I set to perfecting it so I could fix it for him myself.

After we were married, Mom's meat loaf remained a favorite. Then children came into our lives. No longer did I have time to use fresh bread for bread crumbs, measure out what seemed like hundreds of ingredients, and then bake the concoction for well over an hour.

Missing the homey, satisfying meal as much as my husband did, I decided to see if there was an easier way. I played around with the original recipe and came up with this recipe for delicious mini meat loaves. They go together in a blink and then cook right on the stovetop.

Now everyone, especially my husband, is happy to see meat loaf back on the menu. It's not precisely Mom's recipe, but it's so close I bet she'd have a hard time telling the difference.

MOM'S MINI MEAT LOAVES

1 pound extra-lean ground beef, defrosted if frozen
1 small onion (for ½ cup chopped)
1 large egg
½ cup fine dry bread crumbs, plain or Italian-style
¼ cup low-fat milk
½ cup already-grated Parmesan cheese
1 tablespoon fresh parsley leaves (optional)
1 tablespoon Worcestershire sauce
1 tablespoon Dijon mustard
½ teaspoon salt
¼ teaspoon black pepper
1 cup ketchup or 1 can (8 ounces) tomato sauce

1. Crumble the meat into a large bowl. Peel and finely chop the onion and add it to the bowl. Add the egg, beat it slightly, then add the bread crumbs, milk, and Parmesan cheese and mix all together with your hands. Tear the parsley (if using) into smaller pieces with your fingers, then add them and the remaining ingredients, except for the ketchup, and mix again with your hands.

2. Heat a 12-inch nonstick skillet that has a lid over medium-high heat.

3. Meanwhile, form the meat mixture into 6 patties no more than 1 inch thick. Place in the hot skillet and cook until the meat is browned and cooked through, 4 to 6 minutes on each side.

4. Pour the ketchup evenly over the patties and cover the skillet, reducing the heat to medium-low. Continue to cook for 1 minute to heat the ketchup through. Remove from the heat and serve.

Serves 6

A word about:
MICROWAVE DEFROSTING

From Alicia:

For years, I used my microwave for heating leftovers and melting butter, but I never touched the defrost setting. Visions of the rubbery chicken breasts my mother used to pull from her first microwave oven still haunted me. The breasts she tried to defrost would come out fully cooked on the edges and still completely frozen in the middle.

But today's microwaves are smarter. The defrost setting on mine alternately zaps the meat with full power and then lets it rest. Some other microwaves use partial power (50 to 70 percent) to defrost. Whatever oven model you have, if it was purchased after 1990, it probably has a defrost setting. Though the times may vary from oven to oven, our experiments show that it takes about 10 minutes to defrost four boneless chicken breasts. Four thin-sliced boneless pork chops take about 7 minutes. A pound of ground beef defrosts in 8 to 9 minutes. This timing is for thawing meat completely. It is different from the partial defrosting we call for in many of our recipes. There, a quick zap in the microwave is intended to yield meat that is still mostly frozen.

In this chapter only, the times for fully defrosting meat are not included in the 20 minutes we typically allow for our recipes. If you do not have the extra time to defrost, we suggest choosing a recipe in which frozen meat is an option and partial defrosting is included as part of the instructions.

But if you need to begin your recipe with fully defrosted meat, our advice is to get to know your microwave. The defrost setting can speed you on to dinner in a matter of minutes.

"Speed is a basic concept behind Desperation recipes."

Tacos are an easy, child-friendly meal. But I never used to make them because I could never remember to buy the seasoning packets at the supermarket. One night I decided to experiment and found that all it takes to come up with well-seasoned taco meat is just a few dry spices and a bit of ketchup. It's easy, cheaper, and tastes great, too.

Finish off these tacos with your favorite cheese and any other toppings you like, such as shredded lettuce and sour cream. But by all means whip up Alicia's So-Simple Salsa. It easily goes together in less than 5 minutes.

BEEF TACOS WITH SO-SIMPLE SALSA

12 taco shells
1 teaspoon chili powder
½ teaspoon ground cumin
½ teaspoon onion powder
½ teaspoon garlic powder
1 pound extra-lean ground beef, defrosted if frozen
2 tablespoons ketchup
¼ cup water
So-Simple Salsa (recipe follows)
Already-shredded cheese of choice such as Mexican blend,
*   taco style, Monterey Jack, or Cheddar*
Additional toppings of choice, such as shredded lettuce, or
*   reduced-fat sour cream*

1. Turn on the oven to 350°F. Place the taco shells on a large baking sheet and measure out the chili powder, cumin, and onion and garlic powders into a small bowl.

2. Place the beef in a 12-inch nonstick skillet over high heat. Cook, turning and breaking up the meat until it's almost completely crumbled and browned. Then stir in the spices. Add the ketchup and water, reduce the heat to medium, and cook for 5 minutes, stirring occasionally.

3. Meanwhile, place the taco shells in the oven until crisp, 5 to 7 minutes. Make the So-Simple Salsa.

4. To assemble the tacos, place 2 tablespoons of beef in each shell. Add the desired toppings, ending with the salsa. Serve at once.

Serves 6

SO-SIMPLE SALSA

1 clove garlic
¼ cup fresh cilantro, loosely packed
½ lime
1 can (14½ ounces) Mexican-style stewed tomatoes

Peel the garlic. Turn on a blender or food processor and drop the garlic onto the moving blade. Process until finely chopped. Add the cilantro and pulse to chop fine. Squeeze the juice from the lime half into the blender. Add the tomatoes and pulse 2 or 3 times for chunky salsa or blend until smooth, about 15 seconds. Serve at once or refrigerate until ready to serve.

Makes about 2 cups

FREEZE YOUR CHEESE

Desperate cooks freeze their cheese. We started freezing cheese when we got tired of throwing away huge hunks because of mold. Mold seems to lurk in the refrigerator and wait for an expensive block of cheese to appear so it can attack. But frozen, the cheese stays fresh for months. The relatively new already-shredded cheeses that come in resealable plastic bags work equally well in our recipes frozen or thawed.

If you don't know what you're going to fix for dinner, having an array of frozen cheeses increases your options. To keep the bags handy, store them all together in a gallon-size, zipper-top bag.

There are two kinds of cheese we keep both in the refrigerator and freezer—sharp Cheddar (because we use so much of it) and Parmesan (because thawed is preferable for garnishing pasta at the table).

To use frozen cheese, give the bag a couple of whacks on the counter to loosen the shreds and proceed with the recipe.

From Alicia:

This salsa was born, like so many other recipes in this book, out of true desperation. But for once it was not my desperation, but my husband's.

When he hits the bag of chips, he's one of those people who insists they be smothered with salsa. I try to keep a hefty supply in the cupboard, waiting on his cravings.

One evening there was not a drop of salsa in the house. So, I grabbed a can of Mexican-style stewed tomatoes and threw them in the blender. What happened was truly amazing—the chopped up tomatoes tasted like salsa. Then I added some garlic, cilantro, and a squirt of lime, and, like magic, it became authentic-tasting, restaurant-quality salsa.

We still turn to the bottled salsas that fill the supermarket shelves, but now they're the last resort. My "homemade" salsa has become our new favorite.

Don't use any more than a pound of meat for this recipe. Bigger burgers won't cook fast enough.

HAMBURGER STEAK WITH MUSHROOM GRAVY

1 pound extra-lean ground beef, defrosted if frozen
½ cup plain fine dry bread crumbs
1¾ cups low-fat milk
1 teaspoon onion powder
1 teaspoon seasoning salt, such as Lawry's
2 teaspoons vegetable oil
1 package (8 ounces) already-sliced mushrooms
2 tablespoons all-purpose flour
Salt and black pepper to taste

1. Combine the beef, bread crumbs, ¼ cup of the milk, the onion powder, and seasoning salt in a 2-quart or larger bowl and mix thoroughly with your hands.

2. Heat the oil over medium heat in a 12-inch nonstick skillet that has a lid. Meanwhile, shape the meat into four 3½-inch patties about ½ inch thick, adding them to the skillet as you make them, and grouping them toward the center. Sprinkle the mushrooms around the patties, on the outside part of the skillet, then cover the skillet and cook for 5 minutes.

3. Meanwhile, combine the remaining 1½ cups milk and the flour in a 2-cup container that has a lid and shake well until any lumps disappear. Set aside.

4. Uncover the skillet after 5 minutes; the juices should have risen to the surface of the patties. Push the mushrooms out of the way, if necessary, and carefully turn the patties over. Continue to cook, stirring the mushrooms often, until the meat is cooked

through to personal preference, 4 to 7 minutes. Lower the heat if the meat begins to brown too quickly. Place each patty on a serving plate.

5. Shake the flour-milk mixture again and pour it into the skillet with the mushrooms to make a gravy. Reduce the heat to low and cook, stirring constantly and scraping any brown bits from the bottom of the skillet, until the gravy is heated through and reaches the desired thickness, 1½ to 2 minutes. Season with salt and black pepper, spoon the gravy over the patties, and serve.

Serves 4

BURGERS WITH GRAVY

From Beverly:

What could be easier than frying up hamburgers? Not only is it convenient, it's a meal everyone in my family is sure to eat. However, I can never remember to buy hamburger buns. Even when I do, they always mold before we can use them all. I tried sticking the leftovers in the freezer only to find them months later, crumbled and dry.

One night when I really wasn't in the mood to cook, I reached for the ground beef and got a brain flash. What if I spiced up the hamburgers a bit and served them with gravy? The idea reminded me of the country-style steak my mom used to make, only this would be a lot easier and a lot faster. The result was a delicious way to fix hamburgers any time I like without making me feel bad about the buns. We've developed three variations on this theme, including an Italian-style one (page 248) and one using ground turkey (page 274).

"The only thing we want to know about time is how to save it."

A tomato-based gravy gives these Italian-inspired burgers a different twist. Our friend Marietta Wynands, who tested the recipe, likes to serve these burgers over leftover rice.

ITALIAN-STYLE HAMBURGER STEAKS

1 pound extra-lean ground beef, defrosted if frozen
½ cup Italian-style fine dry bread crumbs
1 can (15 ounces) Italian-style tomato sauce or 1¾ cups
*   bottled spaghetti sauce*
2 teaspoons Worcestershire sauce
1 teaspoon onion powder
1 teaspoon garlic powder
1 teaspoon dried Italian seasoning
2 teaspoons olive oil
¼ cup water, or as needed
2 tablespoons already-grated Parmesan cheese
Black pepper to taste

1. Combine the beef, bread crumbs, ¼ cup of the tomato sauce, the Worcestershire, onion powder, garlic powder, and Italian seasoning to a 2½-quart or larger bowl and mix thoroughly with your hands.

2. Heat the oil over medium heat in a 12-inch nonstick skillet that has a lid. Meanwhile, shape the meat into four 3½-inch patties, about ½ inch thick, adding them to the skillet as you make them. Cook the patties for 5 minutes on the first side.

3. While the patties cook, pour the remaining tomato sauce into a 2-cup measure. Add enough water (about ¼ cup) to make 1¾ cups sauce. Stir to blend and set aside.

4. After 5 minutes, when the juices have risen to the surface of the patties, carefully turn the patties over. Cover and continue to cook until the meat is cooked through to personal preference, 4 to 7 minutes. Place each patty on a serving plate.

5. Pour the tomato sauce into the skillet. Add the Parmesan cheese and cook until the sauce is heated through, 1 to 2 minutes, stirring constantly and scraping any brown bits from the bottom of the skillet. Season with black pepper, spoon the gravy over the patties, and serve.

Serves 4

Confetti Stuffed Peppers

4 medium green bell peppers
1 pound extra-lean ground beef, defrosted if frozen
1 large onion (for about 1 cup chopped)
1 cup frozen corn kernels
1 cup leftover cooked rice
1 can (14½ ounces) stewed tomatoes
1 teaspoon Worcestershire sauce
1 teaspoon dried basil
½ to 1 teaspoon garlic powder, to taste
Black pepper to taste
1 cup (4 ounces) already-shredded sharp Cheddar cheese

1. Slice the top off each bell pepper and use a spoon to scoop out the seeds and membranes. Place the peppers, open side up, in an 8-inch square microwave-safe casserole dish that has a lid. Pour 2 cups of water into the casserole, taking care not to get any water inside the pepper cavities. Microwave the peppers, covered, on high, until the peppers are just crisp-tender, 5 minutes.

We decided there had to be a way to enjoy the lovely flavors of baked stuffed peppers without turning the pepper into an army-green blob. Cooking the peppers in the microwave while you prepare the stuffing is the answer. These peppers are crisp-tender and retain the fresh flavor and brilliant green of the raw vegetable.

If you don't have a covered casserole, use a microwave-safe dish and cover with microwave-safe plastic wrap.

2. Meanwhile, heat a 12-inch nonstick skillet over high heat. Add the beef and cook, stirring and breaking it up occasionally. Peel and finely chop the onion, adding it to the skillet as you chop. When the meat is almost completely crumbled and browned, after about 3 minutes, stir in the corn, rice, and tomatoes. Add the Worcestershire, basil, garlic powder, and black pepper. Stir well and cook until the corn and rice have heated through, about 2 minutes. Stir in ⅔ cup of the Cheddar cheese and remove from the heat.

3. Remove the peppers from the dish with a slotted spoon, draining off any water. Pour all the water out of the dish. Fill the peppers with as much stuffing as will fit and return them to the casserole. Spoon any remaining stuffing around the peppers. Sprinkle the remaining ⅓ cup cheese over all.

4. Microwave the peppers, uncovered, on high, until the cheese melts, about 1 minute. Serve each pepper accompanied by extra stuffing.

Serves 4

VEAL SOFRITO WITH FRESH GARLIC

2½ cups "instant" (5-minute) rice
2 teaspoons olive oil
1 large onion (for 1 cup chopped)
1 medium green or red bell pepper (for 1 cup chopped)
3 cloves garlic
1 tablespoon lemon juice from frozen concentrate
2 teaspoons Worcestershire sauce
Salt and black pepper to taste
12 ounces veal scallops, defrosted if frozen (see Box)
¼ cup white wine, apple juice, or water

1. Bring 2½ cups water to a boil in a 2-quart saucepan. Meanwhile begin steps 2 and 3. When the water boils, add the rice, cover the pan, and remove from the heat until ready to serve.

2. Heat the oil in a 12-inch nonstick skillet over low heat. Peel and chop the onion. Raise the heat to medium-high and add the onion.

3. Seed and chop the bell pepper and peel and chop the garlic, adding them to the skillet as you chop. Add the lemon juice and Worcestershire and continue cooking for about 5 minutes, stirring often. Season with salt and black pepper.

4. When the vegetables are just tender, remove them from the skillet and arrange them in a circle on the outer edge of a serving platter. Pour any juice from the skillet over the vegetables.

5. Return the skillet to high heat. Add the veal and cook until it just begins to brown, 1 minute on each side, or until desired doneness. Arrange the meat on the serving platter with the

From Beverly:

When you have no idea what to cook, fry an onion. I do this a lot, and without fail, family members sniff their way into the kitchen clamoring to know what's for dinner. The aroma of browning onion is a powerful appetite stimulant and makes everybody think dinner is more sophisticated than it usually is. This recipe takes the browning onion a step further, and it's my own version of a Latin American *sofrito criollo.* In many Spanish-speaking cultures, sofrito is the spicy base for numerous popular dishes, like beans and rice or sautéed beef.

✳ *We chose very thin veal slices, usually called scallops, for this dish because they are more tender when cooked very quickly. When you don't feel like splurging or if you don't eat veal, substitute the thinnest beefsteaks, such as minute steaks.*

vegetables, leaving space in the center for the rice. Add the wine to the skillet and cook 1 minute, scraping up any brown bits stuck to the bottom. Add the cooked rice to the skillet and stir 1 minute, to absorb the pan juices.

6. Spoon the rice into the center of the serving platter. Pass the platter and let everyone serve themselves.

Serves 4

This recipe is so easy, we almost didn't include it in this cookbook. But after we mentioned honey mustard pork chops in our newspaper column and failed to give a recipe, readers wrote us asking for it. It really does produce flavorful chops with almost no effort at all. If you want a stronger mustard taste, just add more.

MIRACLE BAKED PORK CHOPS

2 teaspoons honey mustard
4 boneless center-cut pork loin chops (each ½ inch thick,
about 1 pound total), defrosted if frozen
Cooking oil spray

1. The oven should be already heated to 425°F.

2. Smear ½ teaspoon mustard over one side of each chop. Spray a 13 × 9-inch or larger baking pan with cooking oil spray. Place the chops in the pan, mustard side up, and cover with aluminum foil.

3. Bake just until the chops are no longer pink, 15 to 16 minutes; do not overcook. Serve immediately.

Serves 4

PORK CHOPS, RICE, AND AUTOMATIC GRAVY

4 boneless pork loin chops, (each ½ inch thick; about 1½ pounds total), defrosted if frozen
1 tablespoon vegetable oil
Salt and black pepper to taste
3 cups leftover or already-cooked rice, preferably converted (20-minute) rice
⅓ cup water
2 teaspoons Worcestershire sauce

1. Place the chops, one at a time, between 2 sheets of wax paper or plastic wrap. Pound the meat with several whacks of a meat mallet or rolling pin until it is about ⅓ inch thick. Peel off the paper while you heat the oil in a 12-inch nonstick skillet over medium heat. Sprinkle the chops on both sides with salt and pepper and add to the skillet. Cook until the chops are golden brown outside and just cooked through, 3 to 4 minutes on each side. (Do not overcook.) When the chops are done, remove them to a serving platter, leaving room in the center for the rice, and cover to keep warm.

2. Add the rice, water, and Worcestershire to the skillet. Cook until the rice is golden brown, 3 to 4 minutes, stirring often by using a tossing motion. Season with salt and black pepper. In the final 2 minutes of cooking, pour any juices that have accumulated on the platter back into the skillet and stir until absorbed into the rice. Spoon into the center of the serving platter, and serve.

Serves 4

Pan-frying is about as easy as it gets, and this recipe adds an unexpected bonus. By tossing leftover rice into the pan after the chops are cooked, you'll make an automatic "gravy" of sorts. The leftover brown bits from the bottom of the pan give the rice a slightly brown, warm burnish, similar to the effect you achieve with rice pilaf cooked in beef broth. It's a light flavor that blends particularly well with the richness of the pork. While the chops cook, you'll have plenty of time to make a simple salad or one of the bread fix-ups in Quick Sides, Chapter Nine to turn this into a complete meal.

When the temperatures turn bitter, fortify yourself with some inner heat. Hot sauces made with cayenne, jalapeño, or habanero peppers are climbing the trend charts with boutique names like Trappey's Bull Louisiana Hot Sauce, Yucatan Sunshine, and Frank's Original Redhot. If you're in a hurry and forgot to plan ahead, marinated meat is usually out of the question. The intense flavors of hot pepper sauces don't depend on time to gather strength. Shake and sauté.

Hot sauces vary quite a bit in heat levels, and that makes it challenging to create an all-purpose recipe. In an unscientific evaluation, we dabbed a variety of sauces directly on the tongue and found that some make you blow smoke while others don't. But any hot pepper sauce can be used in this recipe—in any amount, depending on personal tolerance. We were looking for a vague burn that would warm you up without wearing you out. This, by the way, is not a dish to serve to children.

WINTER'S WARMEST PORK LOIN

2 teaspoons vegetable oil
1 pound pork tenderloin
1 large onion (for 1 cup sliced)
¼ cup distilled white vinegar or cider vinegar
1 tablespoon hot pepper sauce, or to taste
1 tablespoon light or dark brown sugar, tightly packed, or
    granulated sugar
2 tablespoons water, if necessary
Salt to taste (optional)

1. Heat the oil in a 12-inch nonstick skillet over medium-high heat. Meanwhile, cut the pork into ¼-inch-thick slices (some pieces may look more like strips), adding the meat to the skillet as you slice. Cook for about 5 minutes on the first side.

2. While the meat cooks, peel and cut the onion into ¼-inch slices. Separate the slices into rings and scatter them over the pork. Let cook while you prepare the sauce.

3. Combine the vinegar, hot pepper sauce, and sugar in a 1-cup glass measure. Microwave for 30 seconds on high, then stir to dissolve the sugar. Immediately pour the sauce over the meat and onion rings.

4. Turn the pork slices over and cook just until the pork is cooked through, about 5 minutes more. If the pan becomes dry, lower the heat and add 2 tablespoons water. Season with salt (if using), and serve the meat topped with the onion rings.

Serves 4

PORK AU POIVRE

1¼ pounds pork tenderloin
3 tablespoons butter
1 tablespoon vegetable oil
1 tablespoon coarsely ground black pepper (see Box)
2 tablespoons Cognac, brandy, or whiskey

1. Cut the pork into ¾-inch-thick slices to make about 16 slices. Heat 1 tablespoon of the butter and the oil in a 12-inch nonstick skillet over medium-high heat. Take a pinch of pepper and rub it into one side only of each pork slice to coat well.

2. When the butter has melted, lower the heat under the skillet to medium. (Use medium-low for an electric stove.) Add the meat to the skillet, pepper side down first, and cook turning once until just cooked through, about 5 minutes on each side.

3. Remove the pork to a serving platter. Turn the heat to low and add the Cognac to the juices in the skillet. Raise the heat to medium-high and bring the liquid to a boil. Boil 30 seconds just to evaporate the alcohol.

4. For electric stoves, remove the skillet from the heat. For gas, turn the heat to the lowest setting. Add 1 tablespoon of the butter to the skillet. Pressing it with a spoon and using a swirling motion, rub the butter around the bottom of the pan until it just dissolves. Repeat with the remaining tablespoon of butter. Pour immediately over the pork, and serve.

Serves 4

*P*oivre means "pepper" in French, and this is a variation on the classic dish steak au poivre. Most recipes we researched used enough pepper to put quite a burn in your throat. We decided to tone it down a bit, but feel free to adjust the seasonings to personal preference. This is a simple dish that's made slightly sophisticated by the flavor of the Cognac and butter and the heat from the pepper. Timing and heat adjustments in our recipes usually work for both gas and electric burners. For this recipe they are slightly different, so both are noted.

> ✳ *Coarsely ground black pepper is available in the spice section of the supermarket. Finely ground tastes fine, too, it just won't look as pretty. If you have a pepper mill and the time, grind your own for the freshest taste.*

This terrific combination is springtime rolled up into dinner. Fresh spinach, ham, and mild mozzarella cheese can be paired, if you wish, with the creamy orange-flavored glaze that follows.

HAM ROLL-UPS WITH ORANGE CREAM

PRE HEAT OVEN

Cooking oil spray
4 ounces fresh spinach leaves
4 slices (about ½ pound total) honey-cured deli ham
    (sliced ⅛ inch thick)
4 slices (about ¼ pound total) deli mozzarella cheese
    (sliced ⅛ inch thick)
Orange Cream (optional; recipe follows)

1. The oven should be already heated to 450°F. Spray a shallow 8- to 10-inch square casserole dish with cooking oil spray.

2. Rinse the spinach thoroughly and remove and discard any tough stems. Spin the leaves in a salad spinner, or pat dry with paper towels.

3. Top each slice of ham with a slice of cheese, then with a layer of spinach leaves (about 6 per roll-up). Staring at a short end, roll up each stack and secure with a toothpick. Place the roll-ups, seam side down, in the prepared casserole dish.

4. Wet your hand under running water and flick the excess water over the ham; the effect you want is as if you misted the ham with a spray bottle. Cover with aluminum foil and bake until the spinach is fork-tender and the ham begins to brown around the edges, about 10 minutes.

5. While the roll-ups bake, make the Orange Cream (if using).

6. Place each roll-up on a serving plate, top with some of the orange sauce, and serve.

Serves 4

ORANGE CREAM

4 tablespoons (½ stick) butter
2 large eggs
¼ cup half-and-half
2 tablespoons plus 1 teaspoon orange juice
Pinch of ground cloves or nutmeg

1. Place the butter in a 2-cup glass measure and microwave, uncovered, on high, for 30 seconds. Remove the butter from the microwave and stir until completely melted. Set aside.

2. Separate the eggs (see page 237), placing the yolks in a small dish and setting the whites aside for another purpose. Beat the yolks well with a fork, then add, along with the half-and-half, to the butter and stir well.

3. Microwave the mixture, uncovered, on high, for 1 minute 15 seconds, stirring well every 15 seconds with the fork. Remove from the microwave and stir in the orange juice and the cloves or nutmeg. The glaze will be thin. Cover with plastic wrap and set aside until ready to serve.

Makes about ¾ cup

A microwaved cousin to the traditional hollandaise, this sauce is terrific over any steamed vegetable.

A word about:
QUICK SIDE DISHES

Most of the recipes in this book work up into complete meals and for obvious reason. Entrée recipes, on the other hand, usually require side dishes to fill out the menu, and on a 20-minutes-from-start-to-dinner schedule, who has the time? The answer: You do. Surprised? You won't be once you click into our Desperation solutions mode.

One of our most successful tricks for dealing with hectic nights is to anticipate them in advance. On days when we're not so pressed for time, we steam extra vegetables and make giant batches of rice pilaf or pasta salad. (Rice pilaf and pasta salad recipes found in the Quick Sides chapter can easily be doubled.) These convenient leftovers can be refrigerated for days, so all you need to add is the meat or fish.

Then there are the days when we aren't so lucky as to have a ready stash of leftovers. We've developed a list of favorite bailout side dishes that can be put together in a matter of minutes. Some of them take advantage of convenience items from the supermarket, such as our stir-ins for refrigerated mashed potatoes, and "fresh-packed" fruit found in jars in the produce section.

The following list contains some of our standby side dishes for basic meat, poultry, and fish entrées. This is set up as a pick-and-choose list to give you maximum flexibility. What sides you serve with any given entrée really depends on what you have on hand.

We divide sides into three categories, Vegetables Plus, Fruits, and Starches, and all are dishes you can fix with one eye closed and a hand tied behind your back. Well, not really, but almost. Even on a typical desperate night, you'll find something here to best complement your meal—so relax.

VEGETABLES PLUS
Sliced tomatoes
Sliced cucumbers
Carrot sticks
Iceberg lettuce wedges with bottled dressing
Bell pepper strips
Frozen corn, prepared in the microwave
Pre-mixed (packaged) lettuce blends
Pitted whole black olives
Canned beans, such as black-eyed peas, pork and beans,
    baked beans, red kidney beans, Great Northern beans,
    and refried beans
Jarred three-bean salad
Chopped tomatoes over shredded lettuce
Quartered tomatoes and sliced cucumbers with
    red wine vinegar
Deli coleslaw
Deli carrot and raisin salad

FRUITS
Canned pineapple rings
Fresh blueberries, raspberries, or strawberries
Fresh apple slices
Fresh pear slices
Canned peach slices
Jarred applesauce
"Fresh-packed" (bottled) mango slices,
    orange segments, or papaya strips
Fresh cantaloupe slices
Fresh watermelon wedges
Fresh honeydew melon chunks

"On those rare nights when the main dish takes care of itself, wouldn't it be nice if the rest of the meal required only 3 minutes of actual work?"

(continued)

(continued)

STARCHES

Deli potato salad

Deli pasta salad with vegetables

2 cups refrigerated mashed potatoes, such as Simply Potatoes brand
  Stir in halfway through microwaving:
  - *2 tablespoons butter and ½ teaspoon dried dill*
  - *2 tablespoons sour cream*
  - *already-shredded sharp Cheddar cheese to taste*
  - *2 tablespoons already-crumbled feta cheese*
  - *2 tablespoons crumbled blue cheese*
  - *2 tablespoons butter and 1 teaspoon bottled minced garlic*
  - *2 tablespoons commercial pesto*
  - *2 tablespoons real bacon bits*
  - *2 tablespoons fresh chopped herbs of choice*

2 cups leftover rice. See box on reheating rice on page 223.
  Stir in halfway through microwaving:
  - *2 tablespoons real bacon bits and 2 tablespoons sour cream*
  - *2 tablespoons raisins and 2 tablespoons chopped pecans*
  - *2 tablespoons crushed pineapple and 1 tablespoon sliced or slivered almonds*
  - *½ cup frozen peas and 1 tablespoon butter*
  - *½ cup frozen chopped broccoli and 2 tablespoons reduced-sodium soy sauce*
  - *1 small can sliced water chestnuts, drained and chopped, and 1 tablespoon sesame oil*

Flour or corn tortillas sprinkled with cheese and zapped in the microwave just until the cheese melts

Assorted bakery breads, plain or toasted, with butter, cream cheese, or pesto

Assorted crackers with cheese

"Long live dairy products!"

BUTTERED RUM-GLAZED HAM

Cooking oil spray
½ cup light or dark brown sugar, firmly packed
4 tablespoons (½ stick) butter, cut in pieces
1½ teaspoons rum (see Note)
¼ teaspoon ground cinnamon
⅛ teaspoon ground cloves
2 baked Virginia or honey-cured ham steaks from the deli
(each ⅜ inch thick and about 6 ounces)
¼ cup raisins (optional)

1. Turn on the broiler. Spray an 8- or 9-inch square baking dish with cooking oil spray.

2. Combine the brown sugar, butter, rum, cinnamon, and cloves in a 2-cup glass measure. Microwave, uncovered, on high, for 1 to 2 minutes or just until the sugar dissolves. Meanwhile, cut the ham into strips about 3 inches long and ½ inch wide. Remove the glaze from the microwave and stir.

3. Arrange the ham strips in the baking dish in a single layer. Brush or spoon half of the glaze over the ham, coating well. Broil 4 minutes.

4. Remove the baking dish from the broiler and turn the ham strips over. Brush with the remaining glaze and sprinkle with the raisins (if using). Broil until the edges start to brown, about 3 minutes more, and serve.

Serves 4

Note: For a nonalcoholic version of this recipe, use 1 teaspoon rum flavoring mixed with 1 teaspoon water.

From Alicia:

My affection for ham is such that my husband dubbed me the Pork Queen early on in our relationship. (Being young and in love, I took that as a compliment). Naturally, I hate waiting on an occasion to purchase a large ham to enjoy my favorite variety of pork.

This recipe plus Ham with Balsamic Maple Glaze (page 262) and Ham Strips with Orange Marmalade Glaze (page 263) make use of ham steaks, baked Virginia or honey-cured, from the supermarket deli. Have each steak sliced ⅜ inch thick and weigh about 6 ounces.

There's nothing ordinary about any one of these glazes. Ho-hum ham suddenly becomes an exciting midweek dinner entrée. This first one is a classic, whether you include the raisins or not.

Tart dried cherries are the stars of this lovely sweet-and-sour combination. Dried cherries are becoming more widely available in supermarkets, especially those that make use of the bulk-bin buying concept. You can also check gourmet shops and health food stores.

Dried cranberries, also widely available, make a particularly delicious substitute for the cherries during the holidays.

HAM WITH BALSAMIC MAPLE GLAZE

Cooking oil spray
2 baked Virginia or honey-cured ham steaks from the deli
*   (each ⅜ inch thick and about 6 ounces)*
¼ cup maple syrup
1 tablespoon balsamic vinegar
¼ cup dried cherries

1. Turn on the broiler. Spray an 8- or 9-inch square baking dish with cooking oil spray.

2. Cut the ham into strips about 3 inches long and ½ inch wide. Arrange the strips in the baking dish in a single layer.

3. Combine the syrup and vinegar in a 1-cup glass measure and stir to blend. Pour half the glaze over the strips. Broil the ham 3 minutes. Remove the baking dish from the broiler and turn the strips over. Broil until the edges start to brown, 1½ to 2 minutes more.

4. Remove the baking dish from the broiler and set aside. Add the cherries to the remaining syrup in the glass measure and microwave, uncovered, on high, for 1½ minutes or until the cherries absorb most of the syrup. Pour the cherries over the ham and serve.

Serves 4

HAM STRIPS WITH ORANGE MARMALADE GLAZE

Bottled orange marmalade makes the glaze for these ham strips especially easy and attractive. It's not overly sweet, though, thanks to the spicy Dijon mustard and fresh garlic.

Cooking oil spray
1 clove garlic
½ cup orange marmalade
2 teaspoons Dijon mustard
2 baked Virginia or honey-cured ham steaks from the deli
    (each ⅜ inch thick and about 6 ounces)

1. Turn on the broiler. Spray an 8- or 9-inch square baking dish with cooking oil spray.

2. Peel and finely mince the garlic (or use a garlic press) and place it in a 2-cup glass measure. Stir in the marmalade and mustard. Microwave, uncovered, on high, for 1 minute or just until the jam liquefies. Meanwhile, cut the ham into strips about 3 inches long and ½ inch wide. Remove the glaze from the microwave and stir.

3. Arrange the ham strips in the baking dish in a single layer. Brush or spoon half of the glaze over the ham, coating well. Broil 3 minutes.

4. Remove the baking dish from the broiler and turn the ham strips over. Brush with the remaining glaze and broil until the edges start to brown, 1½ to 2 minutes more. Serve at once.

Serves 4

From Alicia:

I'd always thought blackened meats were too difficult to cook at home, so I kept ordering them when dining out.

Finally, I decided to give the method a try, and discovered that it can easily be duplicated, not only outdoors on the grill, but also on the kitchen stovetop.

You really only need two things to successfully prepare delicious blackened chicken: a cast-iron skillet (it will crust the chicken better than a nonstick skillet) and great spices. (Check out our Super Seasonings Mix following this recipe.) In the Desperation version, you add the butter to the pan while it's hot and then immediately add the chicken. This way less butter is needed and there's less smoke. However, we do suggest that an outside-vented exhaust fan over your stove be running on high during the preparation of this recipe to take care of the fumes.

SMOKIN' CAJUN CHICKEN

¼ cup Super Seasoning Mix (recipe follows)
4 skinless, boneless chicken breast halves
(about 1⅓ pounds total) defrosted if frozen
2 tablespoons butter

1. Heat a large cast-iron skillet over high heat.

2. While the skillet is heating, add the seasoning mix to a gallon-size zipper-top plastic bag. Place each chicken breast half in the bag and shake to coat with the seasoning mix. (There will be seasoning mix left in the bag. Add more to each breast by rubbing it in with your fingers if you want a more intense flavor.) Set the chicken aside. Discard any leftover spices.

3. When the skillet is very hot, add the butter to the pan and swirl it around to evenly melt and coat the bottom of the pan. Immediately place the chicken breasts in the skillet. Cook to sear the spices on the meat, 2 to 3 minutes. Turn, and cook on the second side, 1 to 2 minutes more.

4. Once the spices have seared on both sides, reduce the heat to medium-high, and turn and cook the chicken on each side until it is cooked through, about 3 minutes on each side. Remove from the skillet and serve immediately.

Serves 4

SUPER SEASONING MIX

1½ tablespoons paprika
1 tablespoon garlic powder
1 tablespoon onion powder
1 tablespoon dried thyme
1 teaspoon black pepper
1 teaspoon cayenne pepper
1 teaspoon dried basil
1 teaspoon dried oregano

Combine all the ingredients in a small bowl and stir well to mix. Store in an airtight container; an empty spice jar works well.

Makes about ½ cup

You'll find lots of commercial spice mixes on the market now, with Prud-homme's Magic brand of seasonings among the most widely distributed. But it's unbelievably easy to whip up your own. Salt is the primary ingredient in most commercial mixes, but our seasoning mix contains no salt, relying on the herbs and seasonings to carry the flavor.

This flash-baked recipe takes the convenience of roasting and combines it with the flavors of fried chicken. By pounding the meat to less than ½ inch thick, you ensure a tender, evenly baked piece of meat, and in under 20 minutes.

FLAKE BAKED CHICKEN

4 skinless, boneless chicken breast halves
    (about 1⅓ pounds total), defrosted if frozen
4 tablespoons reduced-fat mayonnaise
2 cups plain cereal flakes (see Note)
½ teaspoon garlic powder
½ teaspoon onion powder
¼ teaspoon salt
¼ teaspoon black pepper

1. The oven should be already heated to 475°F.

2. Place the chicken breasts, one at a time, between 2 sheets of wax paper or plastic wrap. Pound the breasts with several whacks of a meat mallet or rolling pin so they are an even ½ inch thick. Peel off the paper and arrange the breast halves in a single layer in a 13 × 9-inch glass baking dish. (To fit in one layer, the outside of the chicken may stretch up the sides of the baking dish. This is fine, because the chicken will shrink as it cooks.) Spread 1 tablespoon of the mayonnaise on the top of each breast, coating well. Set aside.

3. Combine the cereal, garlic powder, onion powder, salt, and pepper in a large zipper-top plastic bag. Using a rolling pin, crush the cereal, then shake the bag to mix well. Sprinkle the crumbs evenly over the chicken and bake until the chicken is cooked through and the crumbs start to brown, about 15 minutes. Serve at once.

Serves 4

Note: Any rice flake or corn flake cereal will do, but be sure to choose one that isn't high in sugar content or the chicken will be too sweet.

LIME-GARLIC CHICKEN SAUTÉ

4 skinless, boneless chicken breast halves
(about 1⅓ pounds total), defrosted if frozen
2 tablespoons olive oil
1 large onion (for 1 cup chopped)
4 cloves garlic
1 lime
Salt and black pepper to taste

1. Place the chicken breasts, one at a time, between 2 sheets of wax paper or plastic wrap. Pound the breasts with several whacks of a meat mallet or rolling pin so they are an even ½ inch thick. Peel off the paper and set the breasts aside.

2. Heat the oil in an extra-deep 12-inch nonstick skillet over medium heat. Meanwhile, peel and chop the onion, adding the chicken to the skillet, then the onion around it. Cook until the chicken is golden brown on the bottom, about 4 minutes. Stir the onion from time to time.

3. While the chicken and onion cook, peel and finely chop the garlic. Cut the lime in half and cut one half into 4 wedges. Set aside. Reserve the remaining half.

4. Sprinkle the chicken breasts evenly with the garlic, then turn them. Squeeze the juice from the remaining lime half evenly over the contents of the skillet. Continue to cook until the chicken is cooked through, 4 to 5 minutes. Stir the onions frequently to brown them evenly and prevent burning. Season with salt and pepper. Serve, garnished with the lime wedges.

Serves 4

From Beverly:

When we lived in Miami, my husband and I occasionally ate at Islas de Canarias, a widely popular restaurant in Miami's Little Havana neighborhood. They served an irresistible chicken dish that was simple, yet superb, elevated by a splash of fresh citrus juice. That dish inspired this one.

From Alicia:

Although it seems as if most of us don't fry meat like we used to, chicken schnitzel is one of those dishes I hate to see go out of style. Use a nonstick pan and only 2 tablespoons of oil, and this classic German favorite comes back into the realm of today's possibilities. This schnitzel would be perfect with mashed potatoes and sauerkraut.

SIZZLED CHICKEN SCHNITZEL

¼ cup all-purpose flour
½ teaspoon dried basil
¼ teaspoon salt
¼ teaspoon black pepper
4 skinless, boneless chicken breast halves
　　(about 1⅓ pounds total) defrosted if frozen
2 tablespoons olive oil
½ cup plain dry bread crumbs
1 large egg

1. Combine the flour, basil, salt, and pepper in a large zipper-top plastic bag. Place the chicken breasts, one at a time, between 2 sheets of wax paper or plastic wrap. Pound the breasts with several whacks of a meat mallet or rolling pin to thin them evenly to a thickness of about ½ inch. Peel off the paper and add the breasts to the bag with the flour mixture. Shake well to coat.

2. Heat the oil in a 12-inch nonstick skillet over medium-high heat. Meanwhile, spread the bread crumbs on a plate and beat the egg in a small bowl, using a whisk or fork. Dip the chicken breasts, one at a time, first into the egg and then into the bread crumbs to coat on both sides, shaking off excess crumbs. Add the breasts to the skillet as you coat them.

3. Cook the breasts until the chicken is cooked through with a golden brown crust, 3 to 4 minutes on each side. If the crumb coating begins to overbrown, reduce the heat to medium.

4. Place each breast on a serving plate and serve.

Serves 4

EASY CHICKEN ENCHILADAS

PRE HEAT OVEN

Cooking oil spray
1 large can (10 ounces) white meat chicken
⅓ cup bottled green taco sauce with tomatillos
⅔ cup reduced-fat sour cream
4 large (10-inch) flour tortillas
1 can (16 ounces) refried beans
½ cup left over cooked rice (optional)
1 cup (4 ounces) already-shredded taco-style cheese
1 jar (16 ounces) mild or medium salsa
2 tablespoons reduced-fat mayonnaise

1. The oven should be already heated to 450°F. Spray a 13 × 9-inch glass baking dish with cooking oil spray.

2. Drain the chicken and combine in a small bowl with the green taco sauce and ⅓ cup of the sour cream.

3. Assemble the enchiladas by placing one fourth of the chicken mixture on each tortilla. Top the chicken with one fourth of the beans, then one fourth of the rice (if using). Sprinkle on about 2 tablespoons cheese. Roll up the filled tortillas, tucking in both ends enchilada style, and place them seam side down in the baking dish.

4. In the same bowl you used to mix the chicken, stir together the salsa, remaining ⅓ cup sour cream, and the mayonnaise and pour evenly over the enchiladas. Cover with aluminum foil and bake until the sauce bubbles, 8 to 10 minutes.

5. Remove the baking dish from the oven and sprinkle the remaining 2 tablespoons shredded cheese over the enchiladas. Continue to bake, uncovered, until the cheese melts, about 3 minutes, then serve.

Serves 4

It's easy to whip up Mexican food that tastes tons better than the ho-hum tacos at the local fast-food outlet. If you want to go a step farther and compete with your favorite Mexican sit-down restaurant, all you need to do is delve a bit more deeply into the ethnic section of the grocery store. There we discovered green taco sauce and realized what had been keeping many of our homemade Mexican dishes from tasting authentic. It was the flavor of the tomatillo. Also called Mexican green tomatoes, tomatillos have a complex flavor with hints of lemon, apples, and herbs.

It doesn't matter what brand of green sauce you buy, or whether it's specifically called taco sauce. All you need is a sauce that includes tomatillos. (Other typical ingredients mixed in would be green tomatoes, onions, and peppers.) Once we sampled our homemade creations with tomatillos added, it was as if our taste buds did a double take: "Ah, yes—tastes like restaurant food!"

LEMONY CHICKEN PICCATA

½ cup all-purpose flour
½ teaspoon salt
¼ teaspoon black pepper
¼ teaspoon garlic powder
4 skinless, boneless chicken breast halves (about
　　1⅓ pounds total), defrosted if frozen
1 tablespoon vegetable oil
1 lemon
1 tablespoon butter
½ teaspoon honey

You'll want to use a fresh lemon when preparing this classic Italian dish. Often prepared using veal scallops, the fresh zippy flavor of the lemons complements chicken as well.

1. Combine the flour, salt, pepper, and garlic powder in a shallow dish and set aside.

2. Place the chicken breasts, one at a time, between 2 sheets of wax paper or plastic wrap. Pound the breasts with several whacks of a meat mallet or rolling pin so they are an even ½ inch thick. Peel off the paper and cut the breasts in half lengthwise.

3. Heat the oil in an extra-deep 12-inch nonstick skillet over high heat. Meanwhile, dip the chicken pieces into the flour mixture to coat on both sides, shaking off any excess. Add the pieces to the skillet and cook until lightly browned, about 2 minutes.

4. While the chicken cooks, cut the lemon in half. Cut one half into thin slices, and set aside. Squeeze the juice from the other half into a small bowl (picking out any seeds that fall in) and set aside.

5. Turn the chicken and sauté until lightly browned and cooked through, another 2 minutes. Remove the chicken to a platter.

6. Add the butter to the skillet and reduce the heat to low. When the butter is melted, remove from the heat and stir in the lemon juice and honey. Immediately drizzle the lemon mixture over the chicken. Garnish with the reserved lemon slices and serve.

Serves 4

CHICKEN CHILI QUESADILLAS

2 large cans (10 ounces each) white meat chicken (see Box)
2 tablespoons chili powder
2 teaspoons bottled minced garlic
Cooking oil spray
12 large (10-inch) flour tortillas
2 cups (one 8-ounce package) already-shredded Mexican-blend cheese
Reduced-fat sour cream, for serving (optional)
Bottled mild salsa, for serving (optional)

1. The oven should be already heated to 450°F.

2. Place the chicken, undrained, with the chili powder and garlic in a microwave-safe casserole that has a lid, and microwave, covered, on high, for 5 minutes.

3. Meanwhile, spray 2 baking sheets with cooking oil spray and arrange 3 of the flour tortillas on each sheet. When the chicken mixture is ready, spread it over the tortillas, dividing evenly. Sprinkle with the cheese. Top with the remaining tortillas and press lightly with your hands so they adhere. Bake until the tortillas are crisp and the cheese is melted, 5 to 7 minutes.

4. Cut each carefully into quarters, using a sharp serrated knife. Serve accompanied by sour cream and salsa, if desired.

Serves 6

From Alicia:

My kids call this party food—their way of saying it's fun. And these quesadillas really are a blast to make and to eat.

Usually I'm in such a hurry just to get dinner on the table that I ban everyone under four feet tall from the kitchen until it's time to eat. But these quesadillas cry out for an assembly line, and my children are thrilled to "help fix" dinner.

❋ *We like the shredded texture of canned chicken in this recipe, but feel free to substitute leftover poached or plain grilled chicken. Add ½ cup water to the casserole dish in Step 2 if you are using leftover chicken.*

Once we became desperate cooks, we avoided including asparagus in our dishes because we still harbored the notion they had to be peeled. Wrong! In fact, if we peeled the pencil-thin stalks we use here, they'd fall apart. Just snap off the tough ends and proceed with the recipe. It's that easy.

Although the roll-ups are great plain, we've topped them with an unusual version of hollandaise sauce, made in less than 3 minutes in the microwave.

TIME-SAVER

Asparagus stems will break off at the appropriate point if you hold the stalk with both hands and bend. There's no need to trim tender stalks, just snap off the tough ends and proceed.

SMOKED TURKEY ROLL-UPS

½ cup white wine or water
8 ounces fresh pencil-thin asparagus
4 slices (about ¾ pound total) deli smoked turkey
*   (sliced ⅛ inch thick)*
4 slices (about ¼ pound total) deli Swiss cheese
*   (sliced ⅛ inch thick)*
Microwave Holland-Glaze Sauce (optional; recipe follows)

1. The oven should be already heated to 450°F.

2. Place the wine in a 2-cup glass measure and microwave, uncovered, on high, for 3 minutes.

3. Meanwhile, snap off the tough ends of the asparagus where they break naturally. Rinse the asparagus and drain. Top each slice of turkey with a slice of cheese. Divide the asparagus into 4 equal portions and place each portion along one short end of a cheese and turkey stack. Roll the turkey and cheese around them. Place the roll-ups, seam side down, in a shallow 8- to 10-inch square casserole dish. Pour the hot wine into the dish, cover with aluminum foil, and bake for 5 minutes.

4. If using the Microwave Holland-Glaze Sauce, prepare it while the roll-ups bake.

5. Remove the roll-ups from the oven, uncover, and bake until the asparagus are fork-tender and the turkey begins to brown, about 10 minutes more. Place each roll-up on a serving plate, top with some of the sauce, and serve.

Serves 4

MICROWAVE HOLLAND-GLAZE SAUCE

4 tablespoons (½ stick) butter
2 large eggs
¼ cup half-and-half
1 teaspoon lemon juice from frozen concentrate (optional)
2 tablespoons frozen cranberry juice cocktail concentrate
*   (see Note)*

1. Place the butter in a 2-cup glass measure and microwave, uncovered, on high, for 30 seconds. Remove the butter from the microwave and stir until completely melted. Set aside.

2. Separate the eggs (see page 237), placing the yolks in a small dish and setting the whites aside for another purpose. Beat the yolks well with a fork, then add, along with the half-and-half and lemon juice (if using) to the butter and stir well.

3. Microwave the mixture, uncovered, on high, for 1 minute, stirring well every 15 seconds with the fork. The sauce will be cooked through but thin. Remove from the microwave and stir in the cranberry juice concentrate. Cover with plastic wrap and set aside until ready to serve.

Makes about ¾ cup

Note: To make cranberry juice from the remaining concentrate, just add the full amount of water called for—no adjustment is necessary.

This thin glaze-style sauce adds a great finishing touch to the classic flavors of the smoked turkey and asparagus in the preceding recipe, and is also a good way to turn green beans or plain steamed asparagus into a special treat.

APPLE-GLAZED BURGER STEAKS

Poultry seasoning is an easy-to-find spice blend and gives these burgers a flavor reminiscent of southern-style breakfast sausage. The sugar from the applesauce rises to the top of the patties as they cook and caramelizes, giving them a slightly sweet crust.

1 large egg
1 pound lean ground turkey, defrosted if frozen
2 tablespoons applesauce
1 teaspoon onion powder
1 teaspoon garlic powder
1 teaspoon seasoning salt, such as Lawry's
½ teaspoon poultry seasoning
2 teaspoons vegetable oil
1 cup warm water
2 tablespoons all-purpose flour
Salt and black pepper to taste

1. Separate the egg (see page 237), setting the yolk aside for another purpose. Combine the ground turkey, egg white, applesauce, onion powder, garlic powder, seasoning salt, and poultry seasoning in a 2-quart or larger bowl and mix thoroughly with your hands.

2. Heat the oil over medium heat in a 12-inch nonstick skillet that has a lid. Meanwhile, shape the meat into four 3½ inch patties about ½ inch thick, adding them to the skillet as you make them. Cook the patties for 5 minutes on the first side. The meat will be very tender, so do not move the patties while they cook.

3. While the patties cook, combine the water and flour in a 1½ cup or larger container that has a lid and shake well until any lumps disappear. Set aside.

4. After 5 minutes, when the juices have risen to the surface of the patties, carefully turn the patties over. Cover and continue to cook until the meat is cooked through, about 7 minutes. Place each patty on a serving plate.

5. Shake the flour-water mixture again and pour it into the skillet. Reduce the heat to low and cook, stirring constantly and scraping any brown bits from the bottom of the skillet, until the gravy reaches the desired thickness, 1½ to 2 minutes. Season with salt and pepper, spoon the gravy over the patties, and serve.

Serves 4

GOLDEN FRIED FILLETS

1 cup plain cereal flakes (for ¼ cup crumbs)
2 tablespoons all-purpose flour
1 tablespoon Old Bay seasoning
1 tablespoon butter
4 thin fish fillets (about 6 ounces each), such as flounder, trout, or tilapia

1. Pour the cereal flakes into a large zipper-top plastic bag, and crush them with a rolling pin to make fine crumbs. Add the flour and Old Bay seasoning, and shake to mix well.

2. Melt the butter in an extra-deep 12-inch nonstick skillet over medium heat. Meanwhile, add the fillets to the bag, one at a time, close the bag, and shake to coat with the crumb mixture. Shake off the excess crumbs into the bag. Add each fillet to the skillet as it is coated. When all the fish is in the pan, raise the heat to medium-high.

3. Cook the fillets until they are golden brown on one side, 4 to 5 minutes. Turn the fillets over and cook until they are browned on the second side, about 4 minutes. They should be opaque throughout and flake easily with a fork.

4. Carefully place a fillet on each serving plate and serve at once.

Serves 4

Corn flake crumbs—or crumbs from other plain types of cereal flakes—give this fish a lovely golden burnish, and the Old Bay seasoning reminds us of a Maryland crab boil.

A word about:
BUYING
FRESH FISH

Fresh fish cooks so quickly and needs so little extra attention to make it scrumptious. It's the perfect desperate solution—almost. When it comes to fish, the emphasis is on "fresh." The ideal time to eat it is right after you catch it, or right after you bring it home from the store.

We've dealt with this dilemma by declaring that supermarket day is also fish day. We often buy some coleslaw from the deli along with some corn muffins from the bakery to complete a speedy feast. Our baked fish dishes are perfect to pop in the oven while you're putting away the groceries, and the pan-fried fillets need little attention except a quick flip midway through cooking.

Depending on where you live, buying good-quality fish may or may not be challenging. The experts used to recommend choosing fish with clear eyes, bright red gills, and shiny, slick skin. In many supermarkets today, even specialty ones, these clues are simply not available. The fish have been headed, scaled, filleted, and in many cases, skinned. There is precious little to go on.

Finding a reliable fish store becomes your best alternative. Whether fish fillets are sold at the meat counter of the supermarket or in a specialty section of the store, plan to have a conversation with the seafood manager. Find out whether the fish sold is previously frozen (much of it is frozen at sea) or fresh, and on what days of the week shipments arrive. If you're lucky enough to have access to a store that sells fish that has not been frozen, this is a store that cares. Prices are likely to be higher, but the quality will be higher, too. Freezing the fish at sea immediately after it is caught is a relatively new technique that yields good quality if handled properly by the store. Chances for quality improve if the fish is defrosted carefully and is displayed whole on crushed ice or in pieces on trays set on the ice (as opposed to packaged on foam trays in the meat case).

Beyond trusting the advice of a reliable seafood manager as to how fresh the fish is, the other best clues are smell and texture. All fish has a fishy odor, but the fresher the fish, the milder the odor. If the fillets reek, don't buy them. As for texture, the meat should be firm and have a bit of a sheen. The flesh should not be sticky, separating into flakes or otherwise starting to crumble.

BUYING SHRIMP

Shrimp are expensive, but they are so full of flavor and quick to cook that we go ahead and splurge from time to time. What kind of shrimp to buy depends a lot on what's available. Our first priority is to buy shrimp that are already peeled, because peeling shrimp is an added annoyance best avoided when we're you-know-what. As for size, we generally prefer medium shrimp so you'll get one in practically every bite without having to cut them.

We also prefer to buy shrimp raw so that any juices that may be released in cooking will end up in the dish. Sometimes the only already-peeled shrimp you can buy are already cooked, too. But that's okay. All but one recipe in this book can be made with already-cooked shrimp with wonderful results. (The exception is Grilled Shrimp Dijon, page 303, which, because of the grilling, needs to start with raw shrimp.)

It's best to buy shrimp fresh, but sometimes the only shrimp available are frozen. Again, choose already-peeled, raw, medium-size shrimp if you can find them. A minute or two of rinsing frozen shrimp under cool tap water will begin to defrost them sufficiently. Then it will only take an extra minute or two to cook a partially frozen shrimp to the desired pink outside and white inside. If the frozen shrimp are already cooked, just toss them into the sauce to thaw. Again, it will only take an extra minute or two.

"The fresher the fish, the milder the odor."

B ay leaves, lemon, and white wine perfume these fish fillets with a light essence that complements the delicate sweetness of the fish. Here's one aroma of cooking fish that you won't mind wafting through your kitchen.

LEMON-STEAMED FILLETS

¼ *cup all-purpose flour*
½ *teaspoon salt*
¼ *teaspoon black pepper*
1 *tablespoon butter*
4 *thin fish fillets (about 6 ounces each), such as red snapper,*
   flounder, or trout
½ *cup white wine or water*
1 *lemon*
8 *bay leaves*

1. Combine the flour, salt, and pepper in a large zipper-top plastic bag. Shake to mix well.

2. Melt the butter over medium heat in an extra-deep 12-inch non-stick skillet that has a lid. Add the fillets to the bag one at a time, close the bag, and shake to coat with flour. Shake off the excess flour into the bag. Add each fillet to the skillet as it is floured. When all the fillets are in the pan, raise the heat to medium-high.

3. Cook the fillets until they are lightly browned on one side, about 2 minutes. Meanwhile, measure the wine into a 1-cup glass measure. Cut the lemon in half and squeeze the juice from one half into the measuring cup with the wine (picking out any seeds that fall in). Reserve the remaining lemon half.

4. Turn the fillets and cook until they are lightly browned on the second side, about 2 minutes more. Reduce the heat to medium. Add the wine mixture and cover the skillet.

5. Slice the remaining lemon half into 4 slices, uncover the skillet, and place 1 slice over each fillet. Place a bay leaf on either side

of each lemon slice. Re-cover the pan. Cook until the fillets are opaque throughout and flake easily with a fork, 4 to 5 minutes.

6. Carefully remove the bay leaves and place a fillet on each serving plate and serve.

Serves 4

BOB'S FAMOUS FISH

2 tablespoons butter
1 lime
½ orange
½ lemon
1 teaspoon Worcestershire sauce
4 mild white fish fillets (about 6 ounces each), such as red snapper, cod, or flounder
¼ cup Italian-style fine dry bread crumbs

1. The oven should be already heated to 400°F.

2. Melt the butter in a 1-quart saucepan over low heat. Squeeze the juice from the lime, orange, and lemon directly into the pan (picking out any seeds that fall in). Add the Worcestershire, raise the heat to medium, and cook the mixture until it sizzles. Swirl the pan to mix the sauce and remove from the heat.

3. Arrange the fillets skin side down (if the fillets are not skinned) in one layer in a 13 × 9-inch baking dish. Pour the sauce over the fish and sprinkle with the bread crumbs. Bake, uncovered, until the fish is opaque throughout and flakes easily with a fork, 8 to 12 minutes. Carefully place a fillet on each serving plate and serve at once.

Serves 4

This recipe comes with a strong endorsement from Felicia Gressette, a former food editor of the *Miami Herald.* It's her husband's invention.

"Bob mastered this when he lived in Sarasota and used to fish for his supper," she said. "It's easy, and the moisture helps keep the fish from getting dried out."

This is an easy dish to prepare and very pretty to serve. It's a Super Stress Saver that's fancy enough for company.

FISH FLORENTINE

¼ cup all-purpose flour

2 teaspoons seasoning salt, such as Lawry's

½ teaspoon garlic powder

1 tablespoon olive oil

4 thin fish fillets (about 6 ounces each), such as cod, flounder, or trout

2 packages (9 ounces each) creamed spinach, preferably Stouffer's

1. Combine the flour, seasoning salt, and garlic powder in a large zipper-top plastic bag. Shake to mix well.

2. Heat the oil in an extra-deep 12-inch nonstick skillet over medium heat. Meanwhile, add the fillets to the bag, one at a time, close the bag, and shake to coat with flour. Shake off the excess flour into the bag. Add each fillet to the skillet as it is floured.

3. Meanwhile, microwave the spinach according to package directions until hot.

4. Cook the fillets until they are golden brown on one side, 7 to 8 minutes. Turn the fillets over and cook until browned on the second side, about 4 minutes more. They should be opaque throughout and flake easily with a fork.

5. When the fish is done, carefully place a fillet on each serving plate. Spoon ½ cup creamed spinach across the center of each one and serve.

Serves 4

FLASH-IN-THE-PAN FISH FILLETS

1 tablespoon butter
1 small onion (for ½ cup chopped)
¼ cup all-purpose flour
½ teaspoon dried thyme (optional)
½ teaspoon salt
¼ teaspoon black pepper
4 thin fish fillets, (about 6 ounces each) such as sole,
    flounder, or trout
1 lemon (optional)

1. Melt the butter in an extra-deep 12-inch nonstick skillet over medium heat. Meanwhile, peel and finely chop the onion, adding it to the skillet as you chop. Stir from time to time.

2. Combine the flour, thyme (if using), salt, and pepper in a large zipper-top plastic bag. Shake to mix well. Add the fillets to the bag, one at a time, close the bag, and shake to coat with flour. Shake off the excess flour into the bag. Push the onions to the side of the pan, and add each fillet to the pan as it is floured.

3. Cook the fillets until they are golden brown on one side, 4 to 5 minutes. Turn the fillets over. Scatter the onions over the top of the fish. Cook until the fillets are browned on the second side, about 4 minutes. They should be opaque throughout and flake easily with a fork.

4. Meanwhile, halve the lemon (if using), setting 1 half aside for another purpose. Cut the remaining half into 4 wedges. Carefully place a fillet and lemon wedge on each serving plate and serve.

Serves 4

This basic recipe provides a practically mindless approach to fish on the stovetop. Its extremely mild flavor appeals to children. For the **adults, we** like to serve it with our Fish Camp Tartar Sauce on page 285.

Our friend Debi Williams, who tested this recipe, was impressed with how attractive it is.

"My husband commented on how this looked like something you'd order at a pricey restaurant," she said. "We served it with a green salad and the color combination was striking."

Most everyone has heard the famous 10-minute fish rule, which says to cook fish for 10 minutes per inch of thickness. The truth, however, is that the cooking times vary from oven to oven and from fish to fish. Check these salmon steaks after 9 minutes of roasting, then at 3-minute intervals. Fully cooked salmon will be light pink throughout at the thickest part and still moist. Our steaks were done at 12 to 13 minutes.

GARLIC-ROASTED SALMON

Cooking oil spray
4 salmon steaks (each 1 inch thick and about 8 ounces)
1 teaspoon vegetable oil
4 cloves garlic
1 teaspoon bottled minced ginger

1. The oven should be already heated to 500°F.

2. Spray your oven broiler pan, and its rack, with cooking oil spray. Place the salmon steaks on the rack and drizzle them with the oil.

3. Peel and finely mince the garlic. Sprinkle each steak with one fourth of the garlic and ¼ teaspoon of the ginger, patting them lightly and evenly over the surface of the fish. Bake the steaks, uncovered, until the fish flakes easily with a fork, 9 to 13 minutes.

4. Transfer the fish steaks to individual serving plates and serve at once.

Serves 4

MAHI MAHI WITH CURRY-YOGURT MAYONNAISE

PRE HEAT OVEN

Mahi mahi is sometimes called dolphin or dolphinfish, but don't worry, this is not Flipper's cousin. This is a mildly flavored, medium-firm fish that pairs well with our mild sauce. Just a hint of curry adds an exotic touch without overpowering the fish. Be sure not to use fat-free yogurt in this recipe because it won't tolerate the high baking temperature.

¼ cup plain low-fat yogurt
2 tablespoons reduced-fat mayonnaise
¼ teaspoon curry powder
Salt and black pepper to taste
Cooking oil spray
1 mahi mahi fillet (1¼ to 1½ pounds)

1. The oven should be already heated to 500°F.

2. Stir together the yogurt, mayonnaise, and curry powder in a small bowl.

3. Spray a baking dish, large enough to fit the fish, with cooking oil spray. Place the fillet, skin side down if the fillet is not skinned, in the dish and sprinkle lightly with salt and pepper. Spread the yogurt mixture evenly over the fish and bake, uncovered, until the fish flakes easily with a fork, 13 to 15 minutes.

4. Cut the fillet into four portions, carefully place one on each serving plate, and serve.

Serves 4

From Alicia:

Nearly every Friday night when I was growing up, we went out to eat fish. Around Mint Hill, the favorite gathering place was called simply The Fish Camp. Fried seafood, Calabash style, was what we craved.

My dad, the adventurous one in the family, loved to order "Hot Cats." These were not the meaty farm-raised catfish fillets of today. They were small, whole catfish, battered, peppered, and then fried to a crisp.

Between wiping the perspiration from his brow and gulping iced tea, Dad would order plate after plate of the fiery little fish. Watching him enjoy his "Hot Cats" was almost as much fun as picking out a treat at the twelve-foot-long candy counter on our way out.

This recipe is a lighter version of Dad's favorite fish, with less oil and pepper to suit today's tastes.

HOT CATS WITH FISH CAMP TARTAR SAUCE

¼ cup vegetable oil
½ cup all-purpose flour
1 tablespoon black pepper
4 catfish fillets (about 1 pound total)
Salt to taste
Fish Camp Tartar Sauce (optional; recipe follows)

1. Heat the oil in an extra-deep 12-inch nonstick skillet over medium-high heat.

2. Meanwhile, spread the flour on a plate. Rub pepper into both sides of each fillet and sprinkle with salt. Press each fillet into the flour to coat on both sides, shaking off any excess.

3. When the oil is hot, add the fillets to the skillet and cook until they are golden brown on both sides and flake easily with a fork, about 4 minutes per side.

4. While the fillets cook, make Fish Camp Tartar Sauce (if using).

5. Remove the fillets to a plate lined with paper towels to drain. Serve at once with the tartar sauce.

Serves 4

FISH CAMP TARTAR SAUCE

¼ cup reduced-fat mayonnaise
1 tablespoon sweet pickle relish
1 teaspoon lemon juice from frozen concentrate
¼ teaspoon celery seed

Combine all the ingredients in a small bowl and stir well to blend. Serve at once or cover and refrigerate until ready to serve.

Makes about ⅓ cup

Spend less than 5 minutes to stir up this tartar sauce and the payoff will be great flavor and a little less fat than store-bought.

A word about: LEMON JUICE

If you have fresh lemons on hand, then by all means squeeze away. Using fresh isn't much trouble, even on desperate nights, especially if you invest in a cone-shaped manual juicer (from 99¢ to $4 at kitchen and variety stores). Adding to their convenience, lemons store well for up to a month in the vegetable bin of your refrigerator.

But when you're desperate, frozen concentrated lemon juice makes a good substitute. We prefer the frozen concentrate because it tastes much better than the juice found in bottles or lemon-shaped plastic containers. Frozen concentrate comes in a solid block from the frozen foods section of the supermarket. At home, just toss the plastic container into the refrigerator. Thawed, it stays fresh for several weeks.

GINGERED SALMON CROQUETTES

48 small square soda crackers with unsalted tops
1 can (6 ounces) skinless, boneless salmon
1 small onion
¼ cup reduced-fat sour cream
3 tablespoons reduced-fat mayonnaise
1 tablespoon lemon juice from frozen concentrate
1 teaspoon bottled chopped ginger
1 teaspoon bottled minced garlic
1 teaspoon Worcestershire sauce
2 tablespoons vegetable oil
1 tablespoon plus 1 teaspoon mango chutney, such as
  Major Grey's

1. Place the soda crackers in a 2-quart or larger bowl and crush with your hands to make medium-fine crumbs (see Box, facing page). You should have roughly 2 cups of crumbs. Pour 1 cup of the crumbs onto a plate and reserve.

2. Add the salmon and its liquid to the bowl with the remaining crumbs. Peel the onion and grate enough on a handheld grater to make 1 tablespoon with juice. Add the grated onion to the salmon, setting the remaining onion aside for another use. Stir in the sour cream, 1 tablespoon of the mayonnaise, the lemon juice, ginger, garlic, and Worcestershire.

3. Heat the oil in a 12-inch nonstick skillet over medium heat. Shape the salmon mixture into four 3-inch patties about ½ inch thick. Press both sides of each patty into the reserved cracker crumbs to coat, adding each patty to the hot oil as it is coated. Cook until golden brown, about 3 minutes on each side.

"I have to admit I was skeptical about the chutney mayonnaise, but my whole family really liked it," said Terry Sullivan, who tested several recipes for this book. "This is my favorite Desperation recipe so far."

Bottled chopped ginger adds an unusual twist to ordinary salmon croquettes. The ginger tastes remarkably like fresh, and it will keep refrigerated for several months. Some brands offer a bottled chopped garlic-ginger combination, which will nicely substitute for the bottled ginger and garlic here. Use 2 teaspoons.

4. Meanwhile, combine the remaining 2 tablespoons mayonnaise and the chutney in a small bowl and stir to blend well.

5. Place the patties on serving plates and top each with a dollop of chutney mayonnaise to serve.

Serves 4

> ✳ *Crushing the crackers is quick to do by hand, but a food processor also works well.*

A word about: BOTTLED CHOPPED GINGER

When was the last time you spent 15 minutes trying to peel and grate a gnarled "root" of fresh ginger? If you're like us, it's not an ordeal you want to tackle in a time crunch. That's why we were thrilled to discover a relatively new product—bottled chopped ginger—sold in the produce section of the supermarket.

Compared with the dried ground ginger we used to substitute for fresh, bottled chopped ginger is revolutionary. With the bottled, you get a burst of fresh ginger flavor, although not the same level of "hot" spiciness—with absolutely no hassle.

Since there simply isn't enough time to peel and grate fresh ginger for a 20-minute Desperation recipe—and we figure it isn't a staple of the average kitchen anyway—we happily stick to the bottled.

For those times when you're planning to spend all afternoon cooking the evening meal, by all means invest in fresh ginger, and feel free to substitute equal amounts of fresh ginger for the bottled in any of our recipes. Otherwise, indulge in the convenience of the already-chopped, bottled kind.

SHRIMP-FILLED SOFT TACOS ⭐ ⭐

This dish takes just 10 minutes to put together, since the super-market has already cooked the shrimp. It's especially flexible because you can use any combination of typical taco toppings you happen to have on hand. Our favorites include shredded lettuce, chopped tomato, shredded cheese, bottled salsa, sour cream, and commercial guacamole.

1 teaspoon olive oil
1 teaspoon bottled minced garlic
1 package (16 ounces) frozen green, red, and yellow bell pepper
  stir-fry mix
½ teaspoon ground cumin
½ teaspoon chili powder
1 pound already-cooked-and-peeled shrimp
8 small (8-inch) flour tortillas
Salt and black pepper to taste
Toppings of choice (see suggestions in Sidebar)

1. Heat the oil in a 12-inch nonstick skillet over medium heat. Add the garlic and cook 30 seconds. Add the frozen pepper stir-fry mix and raise the heat to high. Add the cumin and chili powder and stir well. Cook until the vegetables have thawed, 3 to 3½ minutes, stirring frequently.

2. Stir in the shrimp and cook until they are just heated through, about 2 minutes.

3. While the shrimp mixture simmers, wrap the tortillas in microwave-safe plastic wrap and microwave on high until warmed through, 1 to 2 minutes.

4. Remove the shrimp mixture from the heat and season with salt and pepper. Place the tortillas on each individual serving plate and spoon the shrimp mixture into the center of each, dividing evenly and using a slotted spoon to drain off excess juices. Fold the tortillas over taco style and place two on each serving plate. Serve with the toppings of your choice.

Serves 4

GET-CRAZY CLAM FRITTERS

1 large egg
1 can (6½ ounces) chopped or minced clams
1 small onion
3 tablespoons vegetable oil
¾ cup reduced-fat buttermilk biscuit mix
½ teaspoon crushed hot red pepper, or to taste (see Box)
1 tablespoon fresh parsley leaves (optional)
¼ teaspoon garlic powder
¼ teaspoon black pepper

1. In a 2-quart or larger bowl, beat the egg well with a whisk or fork. Stir in the clams with their juice. Peel the onion and grate enough on a handheld grater to make 1 tablespoon, with juice. Add the grated onion to the clam mixture, setting the remaining onion aside for another use.

2. Heat the oil in an extra-deep 12-inch nonstick skillet over medium-high heat. Line a platter with paper towels. Meanwhile, add the biscuit mix, crushed hot red pepper, parsley (if using), garlic powder, and black pepper to the clam mixture, stirring well to mix.

3. Pour the batter by scant ¼-cupfuls into the hot oil. Fry only 3 to 4 fritters at a time, turning them when the edges have set and the batter bubbles in the middle, 1½ to 2 minutes. (If the fritters cook too quickly, lower the heat.) Cook until golden brown on the second side, 1 to 2 minutes.

4. Remove the fritters to the platter and set aside to drain while you fry the remaining batter. You should have a total of 8 fritters.

Makes about 8 fritters; serves 4

From Beverly:

With just a few pantry ingredients, you can transport yourself to Key West. Okay, I know they make fritters with conch at Florida's southern-most point. But when you need a little taste of Marga-ritaville to add some spice to the end of a humdrum day, crack open the canned clams, put a little Jimmy Buffet on the CD player, and dance your way through this incredibly simple recipe. (Tequila helps, too, but that's another story.)

> ✳ *There's enough crushed red pepper here to really wake you up, so if you're feeding kids, fry up the first batch without red pepper and then stir ¼ tea-spoon or so into the remaining batter for the adults.*

From Beverly:

As the editor of *Coastwatch Magazine* and co-author of *Coastal Carolina Cooking,* my good friend Kathy Hart knows practically everything there is to know about seafood. Most of the crabcake recipes in her cookbook call for a full pound of crabmeat. Getting the meat at a reasonable price is easier if you live on the coast, but most cooks don't have that luxury. Nevertheless, since crabcakes cook up in just minutes for a simple, yet elegant meal, I asked Kathy to devise a recipe that would stretch a moderate amount of meat without sacrificing the signature flavor. This recipe yields four rich, meaty crabcakes bursting with the taste of Carolina blue crab.

CAROLINA CRABCAKES WITH CREAMY HORSERADISH

1 can (6 ounces) pasteurized crab claw meat
1 small onion (for ½ cup chopped)
½ large green bell pepper (for ¾ cup chopped)
2 large eggs
½ cup plain dry bread crumbs
¼ cup reduced-fat mayonnaise
2 teaspoons Worcestershire sauce
¼ teaspoon black pepper
⅛ teaspoon salt
4 tablespoons (½ stick) margarine
Creamy Horseradish (optional; recipe follows)

1. Place the crabmeat in a 2-quart or larger bowl. Sift through the meat with your fingers to remove any shell or cartilage.

2. Peel and finely chop the onion and add it to the bowl as you chop. Seed and finely chop the bell pepper, and add it to the bowl as you chop. Separate one of the eggs (see page 237), setting the white aside for another purpose. Add the egg yolk, whole egg, bread crumbs, mayonnaise, Worcestershire sauce, black pepper, and salt. Stir with a spoon to combine.

3. Melt the margarine in an extra-deep 12-inch nonstick skillet over medium-high heat. Meanwhile, using your hands, shape the mixture into four 3-inch patties about ½ inch thick, adding the patties to the skillet as you shape them.

4. Fry the patties until golden on one side, 3 to 4 minutes. Turn and fry until golden on the second side, 3 to 4 minutes more. While the patties cook, make the Creamy Horseradish (if using). Place each patty on a serving plate and serve at once with the horseradish.

Serves 4

❋ *A can of pasteurized claw meat costs about $8 to $10, depending on the season of the year. The cans will keep, unopened in the refrigerator, for a full year. Look for the cans packed on ice in the seafood section of the supermarket.*

CREAMY HORSERADISH

The horseradish and Dijon mustard create a tempting sauce to serve with the sweet Carolina Crabcakes.

¼ cup reduced-fat sour cream
1½ teaspoons drained prepared horseradish
1 teaspoon Dijon mustard

Combine all the ingredients in a small bowl and stir to blend well.

Makes about ¼ cup

These spicy black beans are a perfect foil to the mild northern Italian staple polenta. Adding flavor and a subtle depth to the cornmeal base are Parmesan cheese and canned vegetable broth. Top this dish off with bottled salsa and sour cream and enjoy.

SPICY BLACK BEANS AND POLENTA

1 tablespoon olive oil
1 medium onion (for ¾ cup coarsely chopped)
1 small jarred pimiento
¼ cup white wine (optional)
1 teaspoon bottled minced garlic
1 teaspoon dried oregano
2 cans (15 ounces each) black beans
2 cans (14½ ounces each) vegetable broth
½ teaspoon dried rosemary
1 cup yellow cornmeal
½ cup already-grated Parmesan cheese
1 tablespoon butter

1. Heat the oil over medium heat in a 2-quart saucepan that has a lid. Peel and coarsely chop the onion, adding it to the pan as you chop. Raise the heat to high and cook until the onion is tender, about 3 minutes. Drain, dice, and add the pimiento, the wine (if using), garlic, and oregano, and cook for 1 minute more.

2. Drain one can of the beans and add them to the saucepan along with the undrained can. Stir well, cover, and reduce the heat to medium. Let the mixture cook, uncovering occasionally to stir, while preparing the polenta.

3. Combine the vegetable broth and rosemary in a 4½-quart Dutch oven or soup pot and bring to a boil, covered, over high heat, about 4 minutes. Uncover and lower the heat to medium, but maintain a moderate boil. Whisking constantly, slowly add the cornmeal to the boiling broth. Continue to whisk until the mixture reaches a porridgelike consistency, 2 to 3 minutes.

4. Remove the polenta from the heat and stir in the grated Parmesan and butter. Place some polenta in each serving bowl. Top with the beans and serve.

Serves 4

BLACK BEAN BURRITOS

2 teaspoons vegetable oil
1 small onion (for ½ cup coarsely chopped)
2 cans (15 ounces each) black beans
1 can (4.5 ounces) chopped mild green chilies
1 jar (16 ounces) mild salsa
6 large (10-inch) flour tortillas
1½ cups (6 ounces) already-shredded Monterey Jack cheese
Reduced-fat sour cream, for serving (optional)

1. Heat the oil in a 12-inch nonstick skillet over medium heat. Meanwhile, peel and coarsely chop the onion, adding it to the skillet as you chop. Cook for 2 minutes.

2. While the onion cooks, rinse and drain the beans and drain the chilies well in a colander. When the onion is softened, add the beans, chilies, and salsa. Stir well and cook until the mixture thickens, about 5 minutes.

3. While the bean mixture simmers, wrap the tortillas in microwave-safe plastic wrap and microwave on high until warmed through, 1 to 2 minutes.

4. Place one tortilla on each individual serving plate. Spoon some of the bean mixture in the center of each tortilla and top with ¼ cup cheese. Fold the tortillas, tucking in one end burrito style, and serve, accompanied by sour cream (if using).

Serves 6

From Alicia:

I always keep the ingredients for burritos on hand, and in less than 15 minutes we're eating dinner. These burritos give you an extra bonus—they're healthy, too. You can adjust the spice level by substituting a hotter salsa, but for those who like mild food, this version is perfect.

This recipe makes six big burritos. Serve them with Speedy Spanish Rice (see 328), shredded lettuce, and extra salsa for a hearty, quick dinner.

A word about:
GRILLING

"Part of pulling off a quick, healthy meal is having the right equipment."

From Beverly:

Don't tell my husband, but the real reason I like grilling outdoors is because it's the only time he'll actually cook. Okay, so I still make the sauces and whip up the marinades. But my devoted spouse actually carries raw food out of the kitchen and brings it back ready to serve. And he enjoys doing it. That leaves me with one less dirty pan and time to make a rice pilaf or a quick dessert.

For obvious reasons, I encourage grilling on a regular basis. But on weeknights, and even on hectic weekends, we often find ourselves unprepared. We forgot to marinate anything or we don't have hours to slave over the coals. When you haven't planned ahead, the grilling options shrink dramatically. That's where the Desperation version of "Out on the Grill" comes in. Each of the eight main dishes here, as well as the Great Grilled Vegetable Kebabs (see page 321) can be prepared, start to finish, in 20 minutes or less.

For Desperation grilling, we recommend investing in a gas grill, even if you're a diehard charcoal devotee. Lighting a grill with the push of a button simply means you're able to cook outside even when it's crazy inside. Gas grills are ready for cooking almost instantly. Double-check your instructions, but in general, gas grills don't need more than a couple of minutes of preheating. One other advantage is that you can often control the heat setting with a dial much like that of your oven. If you don't already own a gas grill, consider investing about $20 in one of the tabletop gas models that run on mini propane tanks. We've used one for years on beach picnics, and they work surprisingly well.

RIO GRANDE RIB-EYES

1 teaspoon garlic powder
1 teaspoon onion powder
1 teaspoon chili powder
½ teaspoon ground cumin
Salt to taste
4 boneless rib-eye beefsteaks (each ½ inch thick and about
*   5 ounces), defrosted if frozen*

1. Turn on a gas grill to high.

2. Combine the garlic, onion, and chili powders and cumin in a small bowl. Sprinkle salt to taste on both sides of each steak, then rub just one side of each with 1 scant teaspoon of the seasoning mix.

3. Start the steaks on the grill spiced side down. For medium steaks, grill, covered, 3 minutes on the first side and 2 minutes on the second. For medium-rare, cook 2 minutes on each side.

4. Place each steak on a serving plate and serve.

Serves 4

This robust southwestern-inspired meat rub is a good way to get a marinated flavor when you don't have time to marinate. Buy rib-eye beefsteaks ½ inch thick and they'll grill in 5 minutes or less. We like to serve this steak with our So-Simple Salsa on page 245.

This recipe comes from Mary Goodwin, a reader of our Desperation Dinners newspaper column and mother of three who lives in Westlake, Ohio. She cuts boneless steak into slices before marinating. By slicing it, you allow the steak to absorb sufficient flavor in about 10 minutes, and because the slices are only ½ inch thick, they grill perfectly in just 5 minutes.

There's one caveat: You need to use tender, good-quality meat, since 10 minutes isn't quite long enough for the tenderizing you typically expect from a marinade.

Mary says this recipe is a favorite at her house. It's a hit at ours, too.

CHINESE STEAK ON THE SPOT

1 tablespoon vegetable oil
1 tablespoon reduced-sodium soy sauce
3 tablespoons maple syrup or honey
3 tablespoons bottled chopped ginger
2 cloves garlic
1 pound tender boneless beefsteak, such as sirloin or rib-eye, defrosted if frozen

1. Turn on a gas grill to high.

2. In a glass dish large enough to hold the steak, combine the vegetable oil, soy sauce, maple syrup, and ginger and beat with a fork to blend well. Peel and mince the garlic and add it to the dish. Mix well.

3. Cut the beef crosswise into slices about ½ inch thick. Place the slices in the marinade and toss well to coat. Let stand at room temperature for at least 10 minutes (see Note).

4. For medium-rare steak grill the slices 5 minutes, turning once during grilling, and brushing with marinade several times. Serve at once.

Serves 4

Note: The sliced meat can also be marinated, covered, in the refrigerator for up to 8 hours; the flavor will get even better.

BROWN MUSTARD BEEF KEBABS

¼ cup spicy brown mustard
1 tablespoon light or dark brown sugar, firmly packed
½ teaspoon garlic powder
1¼ pounds beef sirloin already cut into cubes for kebabs,
*   defrosted if frozen*

1. Turn on a gas grill to high.

2. Combine the mustard, brown sugar, and garlic powder in a small bowl and stir to blend well. Secure the meat on metal skewers at least 12 inches long. Don't overload any one skewer.

3. Place the skewers on the grill and brush the meat with some of the sauce. Cook, uncovered, turning periodically and brushing with the remaining sauce, 6 minutes for medium-rare.

4. Remove the beef from the skewers and serve.

Serves 4

The basting sauce here is similar to a mustard-based marinade, and it gives you the same sweet-and-sour flavor even when you do not have several hours to wait for the meat to soak. If you buy pre-cut kebab meat, this recipe goes together in a snap. Our supermarket cuts kebabs in 1½ × 1-inch rectangles, so the cooking times here are based on this size.

✳ *We prefer metal skewers for kebabs because they are reusable and do not require the extra step of soaking in water like bamboo skewers do. Many supermarkets now sell the inexpensive metal skewers in the cooking equipment section.*

These chops are perfectly wonderful plain on the grill, but when you're in the mood for something a little different, pair them with Pretty Pineapple Salsa. You could even make your salsa first and then grill the chops, and still be ready to eat in 20 minutes.

GRILLED PORK WITH PRETTY PINEAPPLE SALSA

4 boneless center-cut loin pork chops (each ¾ inch thick and about 4 ounces), defrosted if frozen
Vegetable oil
Salt and black pepper to taste
Pretty Pineapple Salsa (recipe follows)

1. Turn on a gas grill to high.

2. Brush the pork chops lightly on both sides with vegetable oil and season with salt and pepper. Grill, covered, 6 minutes on the first side, then turn the chops and continue to grill, with the lid open, until cooked through, about 5 minutes. Do not overcook.

3. While the chops cook, make the Pretty Pineapple Salsa.

4. Place each chop on a serving plate, top with some of the salsa, and serve, if desired, with the remaining salsa.

Serves 4

PRETTY PINEAPPLE SALSA

*1 small can (8 ounces) pineapple tidbits packed in juice
    (see Box)*
1 medium very ripe tomato (for ½ cup chopped)
1 small onion
2 or 3 sprigs fresh cilantro or parsley
1 tablespoon bottled unsweetened lime juice
⅛ teaspoon salt
⅛ teaspoon crushed hot red pepper

1. Drain the juice from the pineapple and reserve it for another use. Place the pineapple in a 2-quart or larger bowl. Core the unpeeled tomato, then dice it into bite-size pieces, cutting it over the bowl with the pineapple to capture the juice. Add it to the bowl.

2. Peel the onion and grate enough on a handheld grater to make 2 tablespoons with juice. Add the grated onion to the bowl, setting the remaining onion aside for another use. Chop the cilantro and add it to the bowl. Add the lime juice, salt, and crushed red pepper and stir. Serve at once.

Makes about 1⅓ cups

This is pretty indeed, enough so you could serve it for entertaining. It tastes yummy with chicken and with fish, too. Be sure to use tidbit pineapple, which is smaller than chunks.

✴ *The salsa can also be made with fresh pineapple. To save time, choose pineapple already cut into cubes, which is found in the supermarket produce section, and cut them into bite-size pieces. For this recipe, use half of a 12-ounce bag.*

Grilling frozen chicken is a mindless adventure, provided you start with individually quick-frozen chicken breast halves. Glazed with a thin coating of ice that helps them hold their shape and keeps them from sticking together, the breasts move easily from freezer to grill. While the process takes a bit longer than starting with fully thawed chicken, you can still be ready to eat in roughly 15 minutes. Our method yields moist, plump chicken, and it's especially nice for nights when you don't want to heat up the kitchen.

GRILLED CHICKEN WITH MANGO SALSA

*4 skinless, boneless chicken breast halves
 (about 1⅓ pounds total), frozen
4 teaspoons olive oil
Salt and black pepper to taste
Mango Salsa (recipe follows)*

1. Turn on a gas grill to medium-high (about 400°F).

2. Rub each side of each breast half with ½ teaspoon oil. Season with salt and pepper.

3. Grill, covered, 5 minutes on the first side to partially defrost, then turn and grill 7 to 8 minutes on the second side. Turn back to the first side and continue to cook until the breasts are cooked through, about 3 minutes more.

4. While the chicken cooks, make the Mango Salsa.

5. Place each breast on a serving plate, top with some of the salsa, and serve, if desired, with any remaining salsa.

Serves 4

MANGO SALSA

10 to 12 strips fresh-packed mango
1 clove garlic
2 tablespoons fresh cilantro leaves
2 limes
½ teaspoon crushed hot red pepper, or to taste
Salt and black pepper to taste

1. Cut the mango into bite-size pieces and place in a 2-quart or larger bowl. Peel and mince the garlic and add it to the bowl. Coarsely chop the cilantro and add it as well.

2. Halve and juice the limes and stir in the juice, along with the crushed red pepper. Season with salt and black pepper and blend with a whisk or fork. Serve immediately or refrigerate until ready, up to 1 week in a container with a tight-fitting lid.

Makes about 1½ cups

Fruit-based salsas are the new gourmet trend for dressing up simple grilled and poached meats. But peeling, seeding, and chopping enough mangoes for a whole batch of salsa just doesn't fit our daily routine. So, no fruit salsa for us. Then we discovered "fresh-packed" fruit—already peeled, seeded, packed in containers, and recipe-ready. Located in supermarket produce departments, the most widely available brand is SunFresh. Pre-packaged fruit can be a bit more expensive, but for labor-intensive fruits like mangoes and oranges, we'll pay a little more for convenience. And, we get to enjoy this salsa.

My husband came up with this foolproof method for grilling fish when he grew tired of watching his fillets disintegrate and fall between the cracks of the grill. Making an aluminum foil boat for the fish keeps it moist, yet still allows it to get that distinct grilled flavor. The boats keep the grill clean, too, a bonus my husband appreciates.

❋ *Purchase fillets no more than an inch thick for this "boat" recipe and the one on page 304. Put one large fillet or two small ones in each boat. You will need 1 boat for every 2 fillets.*

FISH IN A BOAT, ITALIAN STYLE

4 thin fish fillets (6 ounces each), such as tilapia, red snapper, or flounder
1 small onion (for ½ cup sliced)
¼ cup olive oil
¼ cup red wine vinegar
1 teaspoon bottled minced garlic
1 tablespoon Worcestershire sauce
½ teaspoon dried basil
Salt and black pepper to taste

1. Turn on a gas grill to medium-high (about 400°F).

2. For 4 fillets, you will need 2 boats. For each, tear off a sheet of heavy-duty, freezer-weight aluminum foil roughly 20 inches long (or use 2 sheets of regular foil, stacking them on top of each other). Place 2 fish fillets in the center of the foil and fold up the edges, crimping to form a 1-inch-high lip all the way around the fish. Form the boat tight to the fish, working carefully to avoid puncturing or tearing the foil. Move the boat to a baking sheet for easier transport to the grill. Repeat the procedure for the remaining fillets.

3. Peel the onion and cut into ¼-inch slices. Separate the slices into rings and scatter them over the fish. Combine the oil, vinegar, garlic, Worcestershire sauce, and basil in a small bowl and beat with a wire whisk or fork to mix well. Pour half the mixture over the fish in each boat. Season with salt and pepper.

4. Carefully slide the boats off the baking sheet onto the grill and cook, with the grill uncovered, until the fish is opaque throughout and flakes easily with a fork, 10 to 12 minutes.

5. Use a wide metal spatula to slide the boats back onto the baking sheet. Carefully transfer each fillet from the foil to a serving plate, top with onions and a spoonful or two of the juices, and serve.

Serves 4

GRILLED SHRIMP DIJON

1 pound already-peeled jumbo shrimp
3 tablespoons butter or margarine
2 tablespoons Dijon mustard
Hot, cooked rice (optional)

1. Turn on a gas grill to medium-high, about 400°F.

2. Devein the shrimp. Secure the shrimp on metal skewers at least 12 inches long by piercing them twice, first through the body and then through the tail section, forming a C shape. Don't overload any one skewer.

3. Place the butter in a 2-cup glass measure and microwave, uncovered, on high, until almost melted, about 30 seconds. Whisk in the mustard until well blended. Brush both sides of the skewered shrimp with the sauce and grill, uncovered, until just pink on the first side, about 2 minutes. Turn and continue to grill just until the shrimp turn pink on the second side, about 2 minutes more. Do not overcook.

4. Remove the shrimp from the skewers and serve, over a bed of hot, cooked rice (if using).

Serves 4

From Beverly:

When some unexpected guests dropped by one evening right at dinnertime, I only had enough shrimp for two. Since my friends weren't anticipating dinner anyway, my thoughts turned to appetizers. Dijon mustard and a bit of butter were the only suitable sauce ingredients in my refrigerator, so I took a chance and decided to grill. The way my guests gobbled up the delectable morsels, you'd have though I had slaved for days. We all agreed that a tiny taste wasn't enough, that this recipe deserved to be a main course. This recipe is so quick to prepare, that there's plenty of time to devein the shrimp, something we do with jumbos.

Fresh fish was abundant when we lived in Miami Beach, so we cooked it often. We began to experiment with different marinades for "tin-foil fish," as we came to refer to my husband's special grilling method. Here's a version that's particularly popular at our house. Though the marinade ingredients are intense, this method produces a tasty, tender fish.

FISH IN A BOAT, ASIAN STYLE

4 thin fish fillets (6 ounces each), such as tilapia, red snapper,
or flounder (see Box, page 302)
1 small onion (for ½ cup sliced)
¼ cup peanut oil
¼ cup rice wine vinegar or distilled white vinegar
1 tablespoon dark sesame oil
1 tablespoon reduced-sodium soy sauce
1 teaspoon bottled minced garlic
1 teaspoon bottled chopped ginger
¼ teaspoon crushed hot red pepper (optional; see Box, facing
page)

1. Turn on a gas grill to medium-high (about 400°F).

2. For 4 fillets, you will need 2 boats. For each, tear off a sheet of heavy-duty, freezer-weight aluminum foil roughly 20 inches long (or use 2 sheets of regular foil, stacking them on top of each other). Place 2 fish fillets in the center of the foil and fold up the edges, crimping to form a 1-inch-high lip all the way around the fish. Form the boat tight to the fish, working carefully to avoid puncturing or tearing the foil. Move the boat to a baking sheet for easier transport to the grill. Repeat the procedure for the remaining fillets.

3. Peel the onion and cut into ¼-inch slices. Separate the slices into rings and scatter them over the fish. Combine the peanut oil, vinegar, sesame oil, soy sauce, garlic, ginger, and crushed red pepper (if using) in a small bowl and beat with a wire whisk or fork to mix well. Pour half the mixture over the fish in each boat.

4. Carefully slide the boats off the baking sheet onto the grill and cook, with the grill uncovered, until the fish is opaque and flakes easily with a fork, 10 to 12 minutes.

5. Use a wide metal spatula to slide the boat or boats back onto the baking sheet. Carefully transfer each fillet from the foil to a serving plate, top with onions and a spoonful or two of the juices, and serve.

Serves 4

※ *We like the heat the hot pepper gives the fish, but it's best to eliminate it if serving children.*

CHAPTER NINE

Quick

W hat do you serve with a store-bought cooked chicken, or with that leftover roast from Sunday supper, or even alongside a simple baked fish from our Easy Entrées chapter? On those fortunate nights when the main dish practically takes care of itself, wouldn't it be nice if the rest of the meal did, too? That's the idea behind Quick Sides—breads, salads, and vegetables that round out a meal without a lot of effort, take little time, and taste far better than something you can dump straight from a can or box. It's true you can buy boxed rice pilaf blends from the supermarket, but our versions contain far less sodium. And because we use 5- or 10-minute rice, they're twice as fast, too.

As for vegetables, we've included a selection of our fastest favorites—one for the grill, one for a high-temperature oven, and several that you can throw together on the stovetop without heating up the whole kitchen.

Our starch and vegetable sides are mainly intended to pair up with straightforward meats, such as baked chicken, pan-fried pork chops, or leftover meat loaf. When you're serving a skillet meal or pasta, all you'll need is a simple salad and some bread. Our made-from-scratch salad dressings mean that you can serve that simple salad night after night, add a different dressing, and nobody gets tired of the same old thing. Like the salad dressings, our bread fix-ups are perfect for rounding out a one-pot soup

Sides

"It's amazing the creative heights you can reach when faced with the prospects of a 6 o'clock check-out line."

meal or skillet casserole. If you serve our rich Pepper-Jack Corn Twirls with a bowl of leftover White Bean and Chicken Chili, you probably won't even need a salad. When the main dish is self-contained, a fabulous fast bread or speedy salad dressing can add a special, homey touch in literally minutes.

Go ahead—treat yourself to a store-bought chicken or pull out those leftovers. With some quick side dish ideas, your options for Desperation nights suddenly multiply. You'll find yourself with a real meal that's practically home-cooked, completely guilt-free, and with no stress.

A word about:
TOSSED SALAD

From Beverly:

Everyone in my family loves leafy greens. That means we can eat salad, in some form, three or four nights a week and no one is bored. Tossed salad sounds simple, but making it can get out of hand. Start washing, peeling, chopping, dicing, and pretty soon you've invested half an hour.

Stop. Make a Desperation Tossed Salad. Here's how:

1. Make sure the salad contains no more than five ingredients (not including dressing); often four will do. (I was sure I'd get protests when I first cut down, but not a soul in my family even noticed!)

2. Use only one ingredient that requires intensive washing. (A ten-dollar salad spinner for drying greens pays for itself with the time you'll save.)

3. Limit your salad to one ingredient that needs peeling and/or chopping.

4. Throw in two ingredients that come ready-to-eat out of a can, bag, or box. Some of my mainstay ingredients are produce items you can buy already washed, peeled, and sliced or shredded, such as baby carrots, fresh mushrooms, red and green cabbage, sprouts, and broccoli coleslaw mix. Reliable canned items include chickpeas, sliced black olives, pineapple tidbits, and marinated artichoke hearts. Other pantry items include sunflower seeds and nuts, french-fried onion rings, and commercially prepared croutons. From the freezer, try thawed but uncooked green peas or corn kernels.

5. Finally, you'll never feel deprived if you top the salad off with a dressing you love. About once a week, I make a big jar of vinaigrette. Every now and then I'll pull out one of our more intriguing dressings, such as Parmesan or Honeyed French (recipes, pages 309 to 311).

DESPERATION TOSSED SALAD ☺

Green leaf or romaine lettuce leaves (for 4 cups torn)
16 already-peeled baby carrots
16 cherry tomatoes
1 small can (2¼ ounces) sliced black olives
2 tablespoons already-toasted sunflower seeds
½ cup salad dressing of choice (below to page 311)

1. If the lettuce is not prewashed, rinse it, drain, and spin or pat dry. Tear enough leaves to make about 4 cups and place into a 2-quart or larger serving bowl.

2. Slice the carrots into thin circles and add. Halve the tomatoes and add to the bowl. Drain and add the olives. Add the sunflower seeds. Toss with your favorite dressing and serve at once.

Serves 4

MY VINAIGRETTE

⅔ cup extra-virgin olive oil
⅓ cup balsamic vinegar
1 teaspoon sugar
1 teaspoon garlic powder
1 teaspoon dried basil
½ teaspoon salt
½ teaspoon black pepper

Combine all the ingredients in a small jar that has a lid. Screw the lid on tightly, and shake vigorously until blended. Serve at once or refrigerate up to 2 weeks. Shake again just before serving.

Makes about 1 cup

Here's a typical, simple salad that goes together in about 5 minutes. It stays within the Desperation guidelines, yet the variations are endless.

From Alicia:

I've been making this quick oil-and-vinegar dressing for years without a written recipe. And I've probably been asked to jot it down a hundred times. So here it is, simple, satisfying, and—above all—the fastest dressing I can make.

Although it's sufficient to shake the ingredients in a jar or stir briskly, sometimes I blend it in the food processor or blender to emulsify the oil for a smoother texture.

From Alicia:

My sister-in-law, Lynn Clark-Brady, first perfected this dressing and then shared it with me. It has become my husband's favorite topper for everything from simple fresh spinach leaves to chef's salad.

SWEET AND SAVORY DIJON DRESSING

¾ cup reduced-fat mayonnaise
3 tablespoons honey
3 tablespoons Dijon mustard
1 tablespoon lemon juice from frozen concentrate

Combine all the ingredients in a 1-quart or larger bowl and beat with a whisk or fork to blend well. Serve at once or refrigerate up to 2 weeks.

Makes about 1 cup

As vinaigrettes go, this one is light, with only 10 calories per tablespoon. Its tangy flavor makes it a good choice when you're ready for something different. It's especially nice on young greens.

HARVEST VINAIGRETTE

1 small onion
⅓ cup reduced-sodium vegetable juice, such as V-8
1 tablespoon extra-virgin olive oil
½ teaspoon salt
2 tablespoons red wine vinegar
1 teaspoon Dijon mustard

Peel the onion and grate enough on a handheld grater to make 1 teaspoon with juice. Add the grated onion to an 8-ounce jar that has a lid, setting the remaining onion aside for another use. Add the rest of the ingredients to the jar, screw the lid on tight, and shake vigorously until thoroughly blended. Serve at once or refrigerate up to 2 weeks.

Makes about ½ cup

HONEYED FRENCH

1 clove garlic
¼ cup ketchup
2 tablespoons honey
2 tablespoons red wine vinegar
2 teaspoons Dijon mustard
½ cup vegetable oil

1. Peel the garlic and drop it through the feed tube of a food processor or lid opening of a blender onto a moving blade to chop. With the motor off, add the ketchup, honey, vinegar, and mustard. Pulse the motor to blend.

2. With the motor of the processor or blender on low, pour the oil slowly through the feed tube or lid opening. Process until the oil is completely incorporated. Serve at once or refrigerate up to 2 weeks.

Makes about 1 cup

From Alicia:

I'm a fan of sweet French dressings and have fixed dozens of different versions. This one is my favorite since it relies on honey for its sweet touch. Various types of honey will produce subtle flavor differences. We recommend a lightly colored variety such as clover or orange blossom for the best results.

PARMESAN DRESSING

⅔ cup reduced-fat mayonnaise
⅓ cup skim or low-fat milk
⅓ cup already-grated Parmesan cheese
1 tablespoon lemon juice from frozen concentrate
½ teaspoon garlic powder
½ teaspoon coarsely ground black pepper

Combine all the ingredients in a 1-quart or larger bowl and beat with a whisk or fork to blend well. Serve at once or refrigerate up to 1 week.

Makes about 1⅓ cups

This dressing can also double as a dip for fresh vegetables. Be sure to choose a good-quality grated Parmesan cheese, such as the brands that are typically sold in the deli department of the supermarket.

RED CABBAGE SALAD

½ cup fat-free plain yogurt
2 tablespoons frozen apple juice concentrate,
  preferably Granny Smith flavor
1 package (8 ounces) already-shredded red cabbage
⅓ cup already-chopped walnuts or other nut of choice,
  unsalted
⅓ cup raisins

Combine the yogurt and apple juice concentrate in a 2-quart or larger bowl and stir well to blend. Add the cabbage, nuts, and raisins and toss to coat with the dressing.

Serves 6

Thanks to packages of already-shredded red cabbage, available in the supermarket produce section, this salad goes together in less than 4 minutes. Dressed, it doesn't store for longer than a day, so if you don't think it's going to be eaten right away, halve the recipe or make the dressing in a separate container. Store any leftover, undressed salad in a plastic bag and add the dressing as needed. Make a pitcher of apple juice using the remaining concentrate and the full amount of water called for on the can.

CARROT SALAD

1 small can (8 ounces) pineapple tidbits packed in juice
¼ cup reduced-fat mayonnaise
1 package (8 ounces) already-shredded carrots
⅓ cup raisins
¼ cup already-chopped walnuts

Drain off ¼ cup of the juice from the pineapple into a 2-quart or larger serving bowl. Drain off any remaining juice and reserve for another use. Stir in the mayonnaise to blend well, then add the drained pineapple, carrots, raisins, and walnuts. Toss gently but thoroughly to coat with the dressing and serve at once or cover and refrigerate until ready to use.

Serves 6

Packages of already-shredded carrots banish the drudgery we used to dread when making one of our favorite kid-friendly salads, and the addition of pineapple juice to the mayonnaise makes a little go a long way. Although the dressing here is not as thick as that for traditional carrot salads, it's less fattening and still bursting with flavor.

SWEET-AND-SOUR BROCCOLI SLAW

1 package (3 ounces) chicken-flavored ramen soup
⅓ cup balsamic vinegar
¼ cup sugar
¼ cup vegetable oil
1 package (8 ounces) broccoli coleslaw mix
½ cup sliced almonds or unsalted sunflower seeds, or some of each

1. Combine the flavor packet from the soup mix with the vinegar, sugar, and oil in a 2-quart or larger serving bowl. Using a whisk, beat until well blended.

2. Add the broccoli slaw and ramen noodles, breaking the noodles into small pieces. Toss well to coat with dressing, then garnish with nuts and seeds as desired. Refrigerate for at least 10 minutes before serving.

Serves 6

The secret ingredient in this fast side salad is ramen noodles soup mix and the enclosed seasoning packet. These noodles can be found alongside the canned soups in the supermarket, or else in the Asian food section. The dry noodles absorb some of the dressing but retain their crunch, which adds a pleasing texture to the salad. Broccoli coleslaw mix is made from shredded broccoli stems and is available in the produce department. This slaw is wonderful both immediately and up to four days, if stored tightly covered in the refrigerator. Garnish with either almonds or sunflower seeds, or for an especially nutty flavor, use some of both.

TUTTI-FRUTTI SALAD

1 medium cantaloupe
2 Red Delicious apples
1 cup seedless grapes
1 pint blueberries
1 can (16 ounces) sliced peaches packed in light syrup
Orange Yogurt Fruit Dressing (recipe follows)

1. Halve, seed, and peel the cantaloupe, then cut into bite-size chunks and place in a 2-quart or larger serving bowl. Core the apples, cut each into 8 wedges, and add to the bowl; pick over the grapes and berries, then rinse, drain, and add to the bowl. Add the peaches, with their syrup, and toss gently but thoroughly to mix.

2. Spoon the salad into individual serving bowls and top with the Orange Yogurt Fruit Dressing to serve.

Serves 6

Here's our standard mixed fruit salad. Feel free to substitute your favorite fruits or other seasonal picks. When serving children, cut all of the fruit into bite-size chunks. This is wonderful topped with Orange Yogurt Fruit Dressing.

ORANGE YOGURT FRUIT DRESSING

½ cup plain low-fat yogurt
2 tablespoons orange juice
1 tablespoon honey

Combine all the ingredients in a 1-quart or larger bowl and beat with a whisk to blend well. Serve at once or cover and refrigerate up to 1 week.

Makes about ⅔ cup

Whether you use commercially prepared orange juice or squeeze fresh, this is a refreshing, quick topper for fruit salad.

A word about:
FRUIT SALAD

Fabulous fruit salad makes a snappy side dish, snack, or even breakfast. But ordinary fruit salads can be too time-consuming with all of the peeling, seeding, and chopping. Much like our Desperation Tossed Salad, you can make a Desperation Fruit Salad in less than 20 minutes. Here's how:

1. Limit your salad to no more than five fruits (not including dressing).

2. Try to use only one ingredient that requires peeling and seeding.

3. Use one fruit that doesn't need peeling and that is easy to seed, such as apples or pears of any variety.

4. Splurge and add a specialty fruit like fresh blackberries, blueberries, seedless grapes, or already-peeled and chunked fresh pineapple. All you have to do is rinse and throw them in.

5. End with a canned fruit. Granted it's not fresh, but with the twist of a can opener, you've got lots of added flavor and color. Plus, the juice from the canned fruit will help keep all of the fresh fruits from turning dark. If you don't have canned fruit on hand, a hearty splash of good-quality refrigerated orange juice moistens the fruit and keeps it from turning.

Bananas, cantaloupe, and honeydew melons are among our favorite choices for the peel-and-seed category because of the large fruit yield for the minimal work required. When it comes to specialty fruits, stick with what's in season and you'll pay less.

As for canned fruits, we like sliced peaches, pears, and pineapple chunks packed in light syrup. Mandarin orange segments are a bit more expensive but add nice flavor. If money is no object, check out the "fresh-packed" fruit sold in glass jars, in the supermarket produce section under the brand name SunFresh. The options include mango and papaya slices and orange and grapefruit sections.

Anytime you're putting the oven into over-drive, take full advantage of that high heat with this effortless side dish that complements most any meal. Because the asparagus don't boil in water, they retain their valuable nutrients and a brilliant color. Our friend Julie Realon, who shared this recipe, notes that it almost looks *too* simple. "But this is the best asparagus I've ever eaten," she says.

JULIE'S BEST-EVER BAKED ASPARAGUS

1 pound fresh asparagus (see Note)
2 tablespoons butter
Salt and black pepper to taste

1. The oven should be already heated to 450°F.

2. Rinse and drain the asparagus, then snap off the tough ends where they break naturally. Arrange the spear in a 13 × 9-inch baking dish in one or two layers.

3. Place the butter in a 1-cup glass measure and microwave, uncovered, on high, until melted, about 30 seconds. Drizzle over the asparagus and season with a sprinkle of salt and pepper. Cover the dish snugly with aluminum foil. Bake 15 minutes until crisp-tender, or longer to desired doneness. Serve at once.

Serves 4

Note: Choose pencil-thin asparagus, if possible, to avoid any urge you may have to peel them.

BACK-TO-BURGAW BUTTER BEANS

2 tablespoons butter
2 tablespoons all-purpose flour
2 cans (15¼ ounces each) baby lima beans
⅓ cup reduced-fat real bacon bits (not imitation)
2 tablespoons light or dark brown sugar
1 tablespoon plus 1 teaspoon Dijon mustard
*1 tablespoon plus 1 teaspoon lemon juice from frozen
   concentrate*
Black pepper to taste
½ cup already finely shredded sharp Cheddar cheese

1. Melt the butter over medium-low heat in a 12-inch nonstick skillet that has a lid. Add the flour a little at a time, stirring constantly with a wire whisk. When all of the flour has been added, cook, stirring, until the flour is a light golden color, about 1 minute.

2. Drain off the liquid from the cans of beans and add 1 cup to the flour mixture, stirring constantly with a wire whisk; discard any remaining liquid. Stir until smooth and slightly thick, 2 to 3 minutes.

3. Reduce the heat to low and add the bacon bits, brown sugar, mustard, lemon juice, and pepper. Stir to mix well.

4. Raise the heat to medium-low. Add the drained lima beans, stirring gently to coat with sauce. Sprinkle the top with cheese, cover, and simmer until the cheese melts, 2 to 3 minutes.

5. Remove from the heat and serve from the skillet.

Serves 6

From Beverly:

Butter beans are a mystery to most people who don't live in the South. They're cousins of lima beans, only smaller and sweeter. They're hard to grow, time-consuming to pick, and a pain to shell. At the insistence of my mother and grandmother, my youthful summers in Burgaw, North Carolina, were largely spent in this three-step production. While I never enjoyed servitude along the garden rows or thumbs blistered from shelling, I would have resented it more were it not for the sweet, succulent daily reward. Nothing compares to the flavor of home-grown butter beans.

Hooray—and alas—my butter bean days are over. This recipe brings back memories, yet doesn't spoil them. With a little brown sugar and a tad of mustard, ordinary canned "baby lima" beans become downright dignified.

From Beverly:

From Beverly:

When I could barely make ends meet on my first salary as a cub reporter, Margaret Barringer-Willis of Raleigh, North Carolina, used to let me wash dishes at her cooking school in exchange for a gourmet meal at the end of the evening. One of my favorite dishes was Margaret's green beans, which she sautéed with lots of garlic and butter. This is my variation on her original dish. Margaret always garnished her beans with toasted almonds, but we find them equally yummy without. This dish serves four—unless my daughter and I are at the table, in which case we have to force ourselves to share.

GARLICKY GREEN BEANS

1 pound fresh green beans
1 tablespoon extra-virgin olive oil
1 tablespoon butter
2 cloves fresh garlic
¼ cup white wine
1 teaspoon low-sodium chicken bouillon crystals
Black pepper to taste

1. Rinse the beans and drain well. Snap or trim off the tough ends, leaving the tender ends intact.

2. Heat the oil and butter in a 12-inch nonstick skillet over medium-high heat. Add the beans and stir to coat with the butter mixture.

3. Let the beans cook while you peel and mince the garlic. Add it to the skillet. Lower the heat to medium and cook until the beans turn bright green throughout, 4 to 5 minutes, stirring often.

4. Add the wine and bouillon crystals, raise the heat to high, and bring the liquid to a sizzle. Lower the heat to medium and cook, stirring frequently, until the beans are crisp-tender, about 5 minutes; or cook longer, to desired doneness. Season the beans with pepper and serve at once.

Serves 4

CHEDDAR CORN CAKES

1 large egg
½ cup frozen corn kernels
¼ cup plus 2 tablespoons buttermilk cornbread mix
¼ cup already-shredded sharp Cheddar cheese
¼ cup cottage cheese
2 tablespoons skim or low-fat milk
Cooking oil spray
Bottled salsa (optional)

1. Break the egg into a 2-quart or larger bowl and beat it lightly with a fork to break it up. Add the corn kernels, cornbread mix, Cheddar and cottage cheeses, and milk and stir well to mix.

2. Spray a 12-inch nonstick skillet with cooking oil spray and heat over medium heat. Drop the batter, one fourth at a time, into the skillet, to make 4 fritters. Flatten the mounds of batter lightly with the back of a spoon.

3. Fry the fritters until lightly browned, 2½ minutes per side. Serve at once, with salsa (if using) on the side.

Serves 4

There's cornbread mix, and then there's cornmeal mix. The difference is that cornbread mixes typically have sugar added. You can use either mix for this recipe, but if you use the cornbread mix, the fritters will be slightly sweet.

From Beverly:

In my family, this has been a longtime favorite way to use the abundance of squash from my Grandmama Hood's two-acre summer vegetable garden. My aunt Florence Strickland, who tested many recipes for this book, had always used fresh tomatoes before trying my quick version of the recipe. "The canned Italian tomatoes were just as good," she said. "I always serve this in small bowls with the juice."

SUMMER SQUASH MEDLEY

1 teaspoon olive oil
1 medium onion (for ¾ cup sliced)
2 medium zucchini (about 6 ounces each)
2 medium yellow squash (about 6 ounces each)
1 can (14½ ounces) Italian-style stewed tomatoes
2 teaspoons dried Italian seasoning
Salt and black pepper to taste

1. Heat the oil over medium heat in a 2-quart saucepan that has a lid. Meanwhile, peel and thinly slice the onion, adding it to the pan as you slice. Stir occasionally.

2. While the onion cooks, slice the zucchini and yellow squash into ¼-inch or thinner circles. Add them to the pan as you slice.

3. Raise the heat to medium-high and add the tomatoes and Italian seasoning. Stir gently, cover, and bring the mixture to a boil. Immediately reduce the heat to medium-low and cook 10 minutes, or until the squash and onions reach the desired tenderness.

4. Remove from the heat and season with salt and pepper. Spoon the vegetables, with some of the juice, into small bowls to serve.

Serves 6

GREAT GRILLED VEGETABLE KEBABS

1 large sweet onion (about 8 ounces)
1 large green or red bell pepper (about 8 ounces)
1 large zucchini (about 8 ounces)
8 large fresh mushrooms
⅓ cup bottled Italian vinaigrette

1. Turn on a gas grill to high.

2. Peel the onion and quarter it. Place the onion quarters in a microwave-safe casserole dish and microwave, covered, on high, for 1 minute to cook slightly. Meanwhile, begin seeding the bell pepper and cut it into quarters. Slice the zucchini into 1-inch-thick circles. Lightly rinse the mushrooms with water and drain well.

3. Build the skewers: Pierce 1 onion wedge with a metal skewer at least 12 inches long, starting at the inside center of each wedge so as to pierce each onion layer. Next, add a zucchini circle, piercing it through the skin. Follow with a mushroom, another zucchini circle, another mushroom, and end with the bell pepper, piercing it at the inside center.

4. Place the kebabs on the grill and brush with vinaigrette. Cook until all of the vegetables are crisp-tender, 8 to 10 minutes, turning as needed and brushing frequently with the vinaigrette. Serve at once.

Serves 4

Nothing is prettier than mixed vegetable kebabs, but we've always hated the way the onions never cook as fast as the rest of the vegetables. You're forced to choose between eating raw onions or charred green peppers. Microwaving the onions ahead of time to cook them just slightly solves the problem. If you quarter the onions and skewer them through the center of the point as we describe, you won't have to worry about the onions falling into the fire. They'll still be slightly crunchy, but without a raw taste.

We like to brush the kebabs liberally with a zesty Italian vinaigrette made with olive oil, such as the Newman's Own brand. This keeps them moist and produces a subtle hint of vinegar without overpowering the fresh vegetable flavor.

GENOA ORZO SALAD

1½ cups orzo pasta
Ice cubes
1 large can (3.8 ounces) sliced black olives
⅓ cup refrigerated pesto (see Note)
⅓ cup good-quality already-grated Parmesan cheese
Salt and black pepper to taste

1. Bring 2½ quarts of unsalted water to a boil in a covered 4½-quart or larger pot over high heat. When the water reaches a rapid boil, add the orzo and cook, covered, just until tender, 7 to 8 minutes.

2. Pour the orzo into a colander to drain and throw in 2 handfuls of ice cubes. Rinse the orzo under cold running water and toss with the ice cubes until the pasta is cool, about 2 minutes. Drain well, shaking to remove as much water as possible. Remove any unmelted ice cubes.

3. Transfer the orzo to a 2-quart or larger serving bowl. Drain the olives and add, then stir in the pesto and grated Parmesan. Season with salt and pepper and serve at once, or refrigerate until ready to serve, up to 4 days.

Serves 6

Note: Buy commercially prepared pesto in the refrigerator section of the supermarket. It's usually located with the refrigerated pastas near the cheese section.

W hat's this stuff that looks like rice but isn't rice? That's the question we always get whenever we serve orzo. Orzo is actually pasta, and it is indeed shaped like rice and even makes a handy substitute for it in many dishes. Some stores are now stocking tricolored orzo, which is especially pretty in this salad.

ORZO WITH MUSHROOMS AND SUN-DRIED TOMATOES

Serve this speedy pasta dish with a simple grilled chicken breast, a green salad, and crusty bread for a complete, easy dinner.

1 cup orzo pasta
1 cup already-sliced fresh mushrooms
8 sun-dried tomato pieces
½ cup good-quality already-grated Parmesan cheese

1. Bring 2 quarts of unsalted water to a boil in a covered 4-quart or larger pot over high heat. Add the orzo and cook, covered, just until tender, 7 to 8 minutes.

2. Meanwhile, chop the mushrooms and place in a microwave-safe casserole dish that has a lid. Using kitchen scissors, snip each sun-dried tomato into 5 or 6 pieces, adding them to the dish as you snip. Pour ½ cup water over the mushrooms and tomatoes, pressing the tomato pieces down into the water. Microwave, covered, on high, for 4 minutes.

3. Let the dish stand in the microwave, covered, 5 minutes to rehydrate the tomatoes, then drain the mushrooms and tomatoes in a colander and return to the casserole.

4. When the orzo is done, drain it well and add to the casserole with the vegetables. Stir in the grated Parmesan and serve.

Serves 6

You can't beat real, homemade mashed potatoes. But what you can beat is all the peeling, chopping, and boiling required for that homemade taste. Refrigerated mashed potatoes are a new convenience food that brings mashed potatoes to your table without the fuss. Fresh sweet onion and basil make these potatoes really special.

MASHED POTATOES WITH ONION AND BASIL

1 package (20 ounces) refrigerated mashed potatoes, such as Simply Potatoes
1 small sweet onion, such as Vidalia
1 tablespoon butter
1 tablespoon chopped fresh basil (see Note)

1. Peel back the plastic cover on the potatoes, leaving one side attached. Peel the onion and grate on a handheld grater and sprinkle over the potatoes. Chop the butter into small pieces and distribute it evenly over the onion. Sprinkle the basil over the butter. Replace the plastic covering over the potatoes and microwave on high for 2 minutes.

2. Stir the potatoes well and microwave for 1 minute more. Serve at once.

Serves 4

Note: If you don't have fresh basil, stir in 1 tablespoon of commercial pesto instead.

FRAGRANT RICE PILAF

1 tablespoon butter

1 medium onion (for ¾ cup chopped)

½ cup frozen green peas

1 can (14½ ounces) fat-free chicken broth (see Box)

¾ cup water

½ teaspoon garlic powder

½ teaspoon ground cumin

1 cinnamon stick or ¼ teaspoon ground cinnamon

2 whole cloves or ¼ teaspoon ground cloves (optional)

⅛ teaspoon ground turmeric

2½ cups "instant" (5-minute) rice

1. Melt the butter over medium heat in a 2-quart saucepan that has a lid. Meanwhile, peel and coarsely chop the onion, adding it to the pan as you chop. Cook for 1 minute to soften the onion slightly, then add the frozen peas and cook for 2 minutes to partially defrost them.

2. Add the broth, water, garlic powder, cumin, cinnamon, cloves (if using), and turmeric. Cover the pan, raise the heat to high, and bring the broth to a boil. Uncover, stir in the rice, and remove from the heat. Re-cover and let stand for 5 minutes.

3. Fluff the rice with a fork, remove and discard the cinnamon stick and cloves, and serve.

Serves 4

Quick-cooking rice allows you to make this exotic side dish from start to finish in 10 minutes flat. If time is not an issue, substitute 1¼ cups imported basmati rice (the liquid measurement is the same) and this recipe suddenly becomes company food.

✹ *To make this a vegetarian side dish, or for a stronger vegetable presence, substitute a can of vegetable broth for the chicken broth.*

This makes a lot of pilaf because it's really two recipes in one. If you serve half of the pilaf one night and throw the leftovers in the refrigerator, you can make our Two-for-One Rice Salad in just minutes for an easy side dish later in the week. If you don't feel like serving salad, the leftovers also reheat nicely in the microwave. Or you can just cut the recipe in half. Note that you don't have to thaw the peas before adding them to the rice. The heat from the rice will do the trick without turning the peas an awful khaki color.

ASIAN RICE PILAF

2 cans (14½ ounces each) fat-free chicken broth
1 package (14 ounces) "instant" (5-minute) rice
1 cup frozen green peas
1 tablespoon dark sesame oil
1 tablespoon reduced-sodium soy sauce
¼ teaspoon bottled chopped ginger

1. Bring the broth to a boil in a covered 4½-quart Dutch oven or soup pot. Add the rice, remove the pot from the heat, re-cover, and let stand 5 minutes.

2. When the rice has absorbed all of the liquid, stir in the frozen peas, sesame oil, soy sauce, and ginger.

3. Serve half of the mixture hot (six ½-cup servings) and store the other half in the refrigerator to make rice salad later in the week, using the Two-for-One Rice Salad recipe on the facing page.

Makes about 6 cups; 6 servings pilaf plus 6 servings salad

TWO-FOR-ONE RICE SALAD

3 tablespoons vegetable oil
1 tablespoon rice wine vinegar or red wine vinegar
½ teaspoon sugar
½ teaspoon bottled chopped ginger
2 cloves garlic
3 scallions (green onions; for ¼ cup sliced; optional)
3 cups leftover Asian Rice Pilaf (facing page)
1 medium carrot (for ¼ cup sliced)
1 medium rib celery (for ¼ cup sliced)
1 can (8 ounces) sliced water chestnuts
2 tablespoons unsalted roasted peanuts

Whenever we make our Asian Rice Pilaf, we always save the leftovers for this rice salad. It's like getting a free side dish later in the week.

> ✳ *To transform this rice salad into a main dish that serves four, stir in a 5-ounce can of well-drained white-meat-only chicken and serve atop lettuce leaves.*

1. Combine the oil, vinegar, sugar, and ginger in a 2-quart or larger serving bowl and beat with a whisk to mix well. Peel and mince the garlic and add it to the bowl. If using scallions, slice them thinly, including enough of the tender green tops to make ¼ cup. Add them to the bowl along with the cold rice pilaf.

2. Peel the carrot and trim the celery, then cut them into thin slices and add to the bowl. Drain the water chestnuts, coarsely chop, and add; coarsely chop the peanuts and add. Toss well to coat the rice and vegetables with dressing. Serve at once or refrigerate until ready to serve.

Serves 6

From Alicia:

I've always relied on packaged mixes for my Mexican and Spanish rices. But one evening when I couldn't spare 20 minutes to cook rice, I threw together this super-fast version of Spanish rice using 10-minute brown rice. Not only was it finished in half the time, we loved the zippy salsa and nutty rice flavors.

SPEEDY SPANISH RICE

1 can (14½ ounces) fat-free chicken broth
½ cup bottled salsa
3 cups quick-cooking (10-minute) brown rice

1. Combine the broth and salsa in a 2-quart or larger saucepan that has a lid and bring to a boil, covered, over high heat. Add the rice and reduce the heat to low. Cover and simmer for 5 minutes.

2. Remove the pan from the heat and uncover to fluff the rice with a fork. Re-cover and let the rice steam off the heat for 5 minutes longer. Serve at once.

Serves 6

Herbed cream cheese lends its robust flavor to the soft, flaky texture of refrigerated biscuits. The result is a bakery-quality bread that takes just minutes to put together. We like to use the oversize Pillsbury Grands! biscuits, which are big enough to fold over the filling.

BISCUIT TURNOVERS

1 large can (1 pound, 1.3 ounces) reduced-fat refrigerated
  biscuits (8 biscuits)
8 teaspoons chive-and-onion-flavored soft cream cheese

1. The oven should be already heated to 375°F.

2. Arrange the biscuits on an ungreased baking sheet and spoon 1 teaspoon of cream cheese in the center of each. Stretch the dough of each biscuit gently with your hands and fold it over to form a crescent shape. Crimp the edges with a fork to seal.

3. Bake until the tops are golden brown, 13 minutes. (The biscuits will pop open to reveal their cream cheese centers.) Serve warm.

Serves 8

A word about:
QUICK BREADS

Super, one-pot suppers are the backbone of our desperate way of life, and bread is the perfect side. When dinner is simple, interesting bread can elevate the entire meal.

We have several helpful tips for dealing with bread. The easiest is to make a habit of picking up several loaves whenever we're in the vicinity of a good bakery. We stick the extras in heavy-duty zipper-top plastic bags and pop them in the freezer. They'll store and reheat suitably for a couple of weeks.

When we have the energy to go a step beyond heat-and-serve, we reach for the box of corn muffin mix or a biscuit/baking mix like Bisquick. A biscuit mix—with about 5 minutes worth of stirring in just the right ingredients and 10 or so minutes of unattended oven time—can fill your home with that incredible fresh baked smell. The same goes for corn muffin mix.

And then there's what our grandmothers used to call "whop biscuits"—refrigerated tubes of dough that burst open when you whop them against the kitchen counter. Though our southern, biscuit-making grandmothers wouldn't be caught dead buying them, we slip a few tubes in our grocery carts on a regular basis. Spend a minute or two doctoring up refrigerator biscuit and bread stick dough and they taste—not like Grandma's—but surprisingly good. A bit of cheese, a dab of pesto, or a dusting of dried herbs is all it takes to give ordinary dough a home-baked touch. These same tricks work wonderfully with the flat Italian bread called *focaccia* (foh-CAH-chah), which is more or less a partially baked pizza crust now widely available in supermarkets.

Try our collection of favorite bread mix-ups and fix-ups and watch your table rise a notch or two in the esteem of family and friends.

A little garlic and cheese is all it takes to transform plain biscuits into a special event. These biscuits go a long way toward making leftover beef stew or a simple salad seem like just the dinner worth slowing down for.

GARLIC CHEESE DROP BISCUITS

Cooking oil spray
2 cups reduced-fat biscuit or baking mix, such as Bisquick
¼ cup already-shredded Parmesan cheese
½ cup already-shredded sharp Cheddar cheese
⅔ cup skim or low-fat milk
1 teaspoon bottled minced garlic

1. The oven should be already heated to 450°F. Spray a baking sheet with cooking oil spray.

2. Combine the remaining ingredients in a 2-quart or larger bowl and stir to mix. The dough will be stiff. Drop the dough onto the prepared baking sheet by heaping tablespoonfuls (or use a cookie-dough scoop) to make 12 biscuits.

3. Bake until the biscuits are golden brown, 10 to 12 minutes. Serve warm.

Makes about 12 biscuits

SOUR CREAM BISCUITS

2 cups reduced-fat biscuit or baking mix, such as Bisquick
½ cup skim or low-fat milk
⅓ cup reduced-fat sour cream
1 teaspoon freeze-dried chives (optional)

1. The oven should be already heated to 450°F.

2. Place the baking mix in a 2-quart or larger bowl. Add the milk, sour cream, and chives (if using) and stir well to blend. Drop the dough onto an ungreased baking sheet by rounded tablespoonfuls (or use a cookie-dough scoop) to make 16 biscuits.

3. Bake just until the bottoms are golden brown and the tops barely begin to brown, 7 to 9 minutes. Serve warm.

Makes 16 biscuits

Sour cream adds a lot more to the texture than it does to the flavor in this recipe, producing very fluffy, tender biscuits. Chives add a bit of sharpness, but if you decide to leave the herbs out, the biscuits would be perfect with a smear of strawberry jam or molasses.

"**F**antastic! Delicious! We couldn't stop eating them!" These were the comments from our recipe tester, who served these twirls with steaming bowls of chili.

> ✳ *Monterey Jack with jalapeños—or "pepper Jack," as it is called—isn't sold pre-grated, so you'll have to grate it yourself. If you hate to grate cheese, substitute already-shredded plain Monterey Jack or taco-blend cheese.*

PEPPER-JACK CORN TWIRLS

Cooking oil spray
1 package (11.5 ounces) refrigerated cornbread twists
4 ounces Monterey Jack cheese with jalapeño peppers (see Box)

1. The oven should be already heated to 375°F. Spray a baking sheet lightly with cooking oil spray.

2. Unroll the dough and separate it into two 5-inch sheets at the horizontal (long) perforation (each sheet of dough will have 8 short perforations). Lay the dough sheets out flat on your work surface.

3. Grate the cheese, using the largest holes of a handheld grater. You should have about 1 cup, lightly packed, of grated cheese. Sprinkle the cheese evenly over the dough sheets, then roll each sheet up into a log, starting on one long side. Cut through the dotted perforations on each log to make a total of 16 slices. Arrange the slices, cut side down, on the prepared baking sheet and bake until the twirls are just beginning to brown at the edges, 12 to 14 minutes. Serve warm.

Makes 16 twirls

MEXICAN MINI-MUFFINS PREHEAT OVEN

Cooking oil spray
1 large egg
⅓ cup skim or low-fat milk
1 small can (7 ounces) Mexicorn (corn with
red and green peppers)
1 package (8½ ounces) corn muffin mix
½ cup already-shredded taco-blend or Cheddar cheese
1 to 2 bottled pickled jalapeño peppers
(for 1 tablespoon chopped; optional)

1. The oven should be already heated to 400°F. Spray two 12-cup mini-muffin tins with cooking oil spray.

2. Break the egg into a 2-quart bowl and beat with a whisk or fork to break it up. Add the milk and beat well to blend. Drain the corn and add, along with the muffin mix and cheese. If using jalapeños, chop them fine and add. Stir just until the dry ingredients are moistened.

3. Using a tablespoon measure or a cookie-dough scoop, fill the prepared muffin cups about two-thirds full with batter. When the batter is used up, fill the unused cups halfway with water, to prevent burning.

4. Bake in the middle of the oven until the muffins just begin to brown around the edges and spring back when touched, 12 to 14 minutes. Serve warm.

Makes about 18 mini-muffins

Mexicorn, a canned blend of corn kernels and red and green bell peppers, gives these muffins color and a flavor boost. If you want to use the jalapeños but can't find bottled pickled ones, regular canned jalapeños will do.

Everywhere we go, it seems people are raving about broccoli bread. Broccoli bread is an innovative way to dress up cornbread mix, but it's usually made in a loaf and takes an hour start to finish. Here's a way to get the same flavor in 20 minutes. If there are any leftovers, wrap them in plastic wrap or aluminum foil and refrigerate for up to 3 days.

BROCCOLI-CHEESE MINI-MUFFINS

Cooking oil spray
1½ cups frozen broccoli cuts (pieces)
1 large egg
⅓ cup skim or low-fat milk
½ cup already finely shredded sharp Cheddar cheese
1 package (8½ ounces) corn muffin mix

1. The oven should be already heated to 400°F. Spray two 12-cup mini-muffin tins well with cooking oil spray.

2. Place the broccoli in a 2-cup glass measure and microwave, uncovered, on high, for 2 minutes.

3. Meanwhile, break the egg into a 2-quart bowl and beat with a whisk or fork to break it up. Add the milk and beat well to blend. Stir in the cheese. Stir in the muffin mix just until the dry ingredients are moistened.

4. Remove the broccoli from the microwave and press out any excess water. Finely chop the broccoli and add it to the batter. Using a tablespoon measure or a cookie-dough scoop, fill the prepared muffin cups about two-thirds full. When the batter is used up, fill the unused cups halfway with water, to prevent burning.

5. Bake in the middle of the oven until the muffins just begin to brown around the edges and spring back when touched, 12 to 14 minutes. Serve warm.

Makes about 20 mini-muffins

COWBOY MINI-CORN MUFFINS
PRE HEAT OVEN

Cooking oil spray
1 large egg
⅓ cup skim or low-fat milk
1 small can (2¼ ounces) sliced black olives
1 small can (8½ ounces) cream-style corn
1 teaspoon dried minced onion
1 package (8½ ounces) corn muffin mix

1. The oven should be already heated to 400°F. Spray two 12-cup mini-muffin tins well with cooking oil spray.

2. Break the egg into a 2-quart bowl and beat with a whisk or fork to break it up. Add the milk and beat well to blend. Rinse and drain the black olives, and add them to the bowl. Stir in the corn and minced onion. Stir in the muffin mix just until the dry ingredients are moistened.

3. Using a tablespoon measure or a cookie-dough scoop, fill the prepared muffin cups to the top. When the batter is used up, fill unused cups, if any, halfway with water, to prevent burning.

4. Bake in the middle of the oven until the muffins just begin to brown around the edges and spring back when touched, 12 to 14 minutes. Serve warm.

Makes 24 mini-muffins

These very moist muffins are both slightly sweet and slightly savory, and the addition of the creamed corn means that the batter is not as stiff as that of most muffins. If you have any leftovers, wrap them in plastic wrap or aluminum foil and refrigerate for up to 3 days.

With or without the sun-dried tomatoes this is the perfect bread for any Italian-style meal. We find ourselves making it for snacking, and it's terrific as a quickie appetizer when company comes.

FANTASTIC FOCACCIA

1 large (12-inch) partially baked pizza crust, such as Boboli
2 cloves garlic
2 teaspoons extra-virgin olive oil
1 tablespoon already-grated Parmesan cheese
3 oil-packed sun-dried tomato pieces (optional)
½ teaspoon dried basil or oregano

1. The oven should be already heated to 450°F.

2. Place the pizza crust on an ungreased baking sheet. Peel and finely mince the garlic. Combine the garlic and oil in a small bowl. Drizzle the mixture over the crust, then use the back of a spoon to spread the mixture over the surface of the bread. (You won't be able to cover it entirely.)

3. Sprinkle the surface with the grated Parmesan. If using the sun-dried tomatoes, mince them and sprinkle over the cheese. Sprinkle the basil over all.

4. Bake until the bread begins to brown and crisp slightly, about 8 minutes. Cut it into wedges and serve at once.

Serves 6

FETA FOCACCIA

This hearty bread is almost a meal in itself. Pair it with a tossed salad for a light summer supper for two.

1 large (12-inch) partially baked pizza crust, such as Boboli
2 tablespoons extra-virgin olive oil
3 large or 4 medium Roma (plum) tomatoes
1 small can (2¼ ounces) sliced black olives
⅓ cup already-crumbled feta cheese, or more to taste
1 teaspoon dried oregano

1. The oven should be already heated to 450°F.

2. Place the pizza crust on an ungreased baking sheet. Drizzle the oil over the crust, then use the back of a spoon to spread it over the entire surface.

3. Cut the tomatoes into ¼-inch crosswise slices and arrange them evenly over the crust. Drain the olives and sprinkle them on, then sprinkle on the feta and oregano.

4. Bake until the bread begins to brown and crisp slightly, about 8 minutes. Cut it into wedges and serve at once.

Serves 6

With its rainbow of peppers, this bread can do double duty as a vegetable side dish.

MIXED PEPPER FOCACCIA

PRE HEAT OVEN

2 cups frozen green, red, and yellow pepper stir-fry mix
1 large (12-inch) partially baked pizza crust, such as Boboli
2 tablespoons extra-virgin olive oil
2 teaspoons bottled minced garlic, or more to taste
½ cup already-shredded mozzarella cheese, or more to taste

1. The oven should be already heated to 450°F.

2. Microwave the pepper stir-fry mix, uncovered, on high, for 2 minutes to defrost.

3. Meanwhile, place the pizza crust on an ungreased baking sheet. Drizzle the oil, then the garlic over the crust. Use the back of a spoon to spread it over the entire surface.

4. Remove the peppers from the microwave and place them on four layers of paper towels. Fold the peppers up in the towels and press to squeeze out excess moisture. Sprinkle the peppers and cheese evenly over the crust.

5. Bake until the bread begins to brown and crisp slightly, about 8 minutes. Cut it into wedges and serve at once.

Serves 6

FABULOUS FRENCH BREAD

6 tablespoons refrigerated pesto
6 slices (each 1 inch thick) French bread
1 large fresh, ripe tomato
½ cup already-shredded mozzarella cheese

1. Turn on the broiler.

2. Spread 1 tablespoon of the pesto over each slice of bread. Cut the tomato into 6 equal slices and place a slice on each piece of bread. Sprinkle each slice evenly with the cheese. Arrange the bread slices on an ungreased baking sheet.

3. Broil until the cheese is bubbly, about 4 minutes. Serve at once.

Serves 6

Pesto, a sauce made from ground fresh basil, olive oil, pine nuts, and Parmesan cheese, gives these robust slabs of bread a gourmet touch. Look for plastic containers of pesto in the supermarket refrigerator case, near the cheese and fresh pasta.

PESTO CRESCENTS

1 package (8 ounces) refrigerated crescent dinner rolls
4 teaspoons refrigerated pesto

1. The oven should be already heated to 375°F.

2. Unroll the dough and separate it into triangles along the perforations. Spread ½ teaspoon pesto over each triangle, then roll them up into crescents according to package directions. Arrange on an ungreased baking sheet.

3. Bake until golden brown, 11 to 13 minutes.

Serves 4

A quick spread of commercial pesto creates an elegant swirl through each crescent roll. The bonus is that it tastes as good as it looks.

ITALIAN HERB BREADSTICKS

1 can (11 ounces) refrigerated breadstick dough
3 tablespoons extra-virgin olive oil
¼ teaspoon dried Italian seasoning

1. The oven should be already heated to 350°F.

2. Remove the dough from the package and follow the directions for twisting and placing the breadsticks on an ungreased baking sheet.

3. Brush each breadstick with olive oil and sprinkle with the Italian seasoning.

4. Bake until golden brown, about 15 minutes. Serve warm.

Serves 4

B e sure to use a good, fruity olive oil, and you'll have breadsticks that taste as wonderful as they look.

CHAPTER TEN

Desserts

From Beverly:

I f we're going to eat dessert, it ought to be worth the calories. This is what I have come to call the Dessert Rule. In my thinner days, if a recipe involved chocolate, I would somehow squeeze it into the schedule. Midnight. Whenever. We all have priorities. But along with climbing cholesterol counts, priorities began to shift, and my husband and I stopped eating dessert on a daily basis. Two immediate changes resulted. First, forsaking dessert made the dinner grind a lot easier. It was simply one less thing to fuss over. Second, on those occasions when I did indulge, I became exceedingly picky. Cherished dessert calories can't be wasted on cardboard cakes.

But it's a sad fact that most exquisite desserts take time, and that's where the Dessert Rule and my life as a desperate cook comes to blows. Delectable desserts that'll be ready to serve in just 20 minutes are precious few. Even though I'm trying to behave, every now and then one of those rotten days will come along when I really deserve cheering up. On those days, give me something sweet and sinful, something homemade, and give it to me *now.*

I call these Regular Dessert Days. These are the days when I usually crave something reminiscent of childhood, like Practically Perfect Peach Crisp or rich brownies still warm from the oven, as found in our Magic version made in the microwave.

Then there are life's little emergencies, those times when you need to create a dessert for unexpected guests or times when you'd like to bring dessert to an impromptu potluck dinner or picnic. That's when our Amazing Apple Tart or Angel Biscuits with Blueberries can pull you out of a pinch.

Finally, there are those days when desperate parents are faced with children who are desperate for dessert. Maybe they've been extra good or braved an extra-big boo-boo, and what the whole family needs is a big batch of Presto Praline Cookies, So-Sweet Sopaipilla Chips, or Orange Butter Balls.

Some of our recipes are what we call Power-Assisted Desserts. This is dessert in overdrive—a sweet concoction that practically makes itself on days when you don't have time to measure flour or deal with the mixer. With a few pantry staples, some good-quality specialty items, and 15 minutes or less, you can throw together a treat as fancy as our Heavenly Cream Cake or Individual Lemon-Ginger Trifles. There are all sorts of ways to serve quick and flavorful desserts using common ingredients easily kept on hand. Plop a scoop of vanilla ice cream into a pretty dish and drizzle on one of our instant sauces made with cocoa or fruit preserves. Add a little squirt-can whipped cream, and suddenly a scoop of ice cream is a scrumptious sundae.

Whatever your own daily dessert emergencies may be, you can pull from this collection of our favorite, and most reliable, spur-of-the-moment confections that are definitely worth every calorie.

"When I really deserve cheering up, give me something sweet and sinful . . ."

From Alicia:

Don't get me wrong—you can't beat homemade pound cake. And I have had some of the best ever made, both from my grandmother and Beverly's (who happens to be known across several counties for her famous recipe). But when a dessert is needed, I often turn to dear old Sara Lee. Topped with an incredible sauce like this coulis, frozen store-bought pound cake (or cheesecake) makes a respectable base for a dessert that's ready to eat in 5 minutes.

Slicing the cake while it is still frozen and placing on the dessert plates allows the cake to defrost while you make the sauce.

✳ *A coulis is a thick purée made from fruit or vegetables. The beautiful garnet-colored coulis here is fancy enough for last-minute guests or perfect for a spontaneous celebration. Be sure to buy quick-frozen whole fruit, found in plastic bags in the supermarket freezer case.*

PAPAYA AND STRAWBERRY COULIS OVER POUND CAKE

1 frozen all-butter pound cake (10¾ ounces)
1 cup (8 ounces) individually frozen strawberries
¼ cup light or dark rum or unsweetened apple juice
7 fresh-packed papaya strips (for ¾ cup chopped; see Note)
Real whipped light cream in an aerosol can (optional)

1. Remove the cake from its packaging, cut it into 6 slices, and place them on individual serving plates.

2. Combine the strawberries and rum in a blender. Cover and pulse on and off until the mixture becomes a coarse purée. Chop the papaya strips into bite-size pieces, add them to the blender, and pulse until the mixture is smooth.

3. Pour ¼ cup purée over each cake slice and top with an attractive dollop of whipped cream (if using). Serve at once.

Serves 6

Note: You'll find glass jars of fresh-packed papaya strips, sold under the SunFresh name, in the produce section of the supermarket.

ANGEL BISCUITS WITH BLUEBERRIES

2 cups reduced-fat buttermilk biscuit or baking mix, such as Bisquick

½ cup skim or low-fat milk

⅓ cup reduced-fat sour cream

3 tablespoons sugar

1⅔ cups fresh blueberries

1 teaspoon almond extract

1½ cups nondairy whipped topping, such as Cool Whip

1. The oven should be already heated to 450°F.

2. Place the biscuit mix in a 2-quart or larger bowl. Add the milk, sour cream, and sugar and stir. The dough will be sticky.

3. Drop the dough onto an ungreased baking sheet by heaping ¼-cupfuls for 6 large biscuits. Bake in the middle of the oven just until the bottoms of the biscuits are golden brown but the tops have barely begun to brown, 9 to 11 minutes.

4. While the biscuits bake, rinse and drain the blueberries. Set aside. Stir the almond extract into the whipped topping and set aside.

5. When the biscuits are done, remove them from the oven and slice in half (see Box). Spoon roughly 3 tablespoons of whipped topping on each bottom biscuit half and top with ¼ cup blueberries. Replace the biscuit tops over the berries, and dollop with roughly 1 tablespoon whipped topping per biscuit. Garnish the toppings with the remaining blueberries and serve.

Serves 6

Here's a way to dress up some very ordinary ingredients that you're likely to have on hand. Any type of fresh berries, or even sliced peaches or nectarines, will produce heavenly shortcakes. The sour cream makes the biscuits light as clouds and keeps them an angelic white. They're sure to impress unexpected guests or lift your family's spirits on an ordinary night.

Although yummy straight out of the oven, we sometimes like to slice the biscuits and let them cool while we eat our evening meal. The assembly takes about 5 minutes.

❋ *Time permitting, the biscuits may be set aside to cool in step 5 and the assembly of the shortcakes completed later.*

This sweet, yet tart dessert is refreshing—not only for its flavor but for the minimal effort required in making it. This is a half-brainer. If you can stir, you can turn out these beautiful individual trifles.

Lemon curd is a sweet, creamy concoction that is sold in most large super-markets. (Check the jam shelves or the specialty items shelves.) The trifle assembly will be easier if you use wide-mouthed dessert dishes; the presentation is especially elegant in stemmed or footed glasses, such as red wine goblets or dessert compotes.

> ❋ *The lemon curd must be at room tem-perature so it will blend properly with the yogurt. If the lemon curd has been refriger-ated, microwave it, uncovered, on the defrost setting (or 50 percent power), for 1 minute to bring it to room temperature.*

INDIVIDUAL LEMON-GINGER TRIFLES

20 gingersnap cookies (for 1 cup crushed)
2 containers (8 ounces each) low-fat lemon yogurt
½ cup lemon curd, at room temperature (see Box)
½ cup already-chopped pecans
Real whipped light cream in an aerosol can
4 lemon slices, for garnish (optional)

1. Place the cookies in a food processor and process to make fine crumbs. (Or put the cookies in a freezer-weight plastic bag and pulverize them with a rolling pin.) Set aside.

2. Combine the yogurt and lemon curd in a 2-quart or larger bowl and whisk or stir to blend well.

3. Assemble the trifles: Place 2 tablespoons of the cookie crumbs in the bottom of each of 4 wide-mouthed dessert dishes. Top the crumbs with ¼ cup of the yogurt mixture. Sprinkle another 2 tablespoons cookie crumbs evenly over the yogurt and sprinkle on a heaping tablespoon of the pecans. Spoon another ¼ cup yogurt mixture over the pecans. Squirt an attractive dollop of whipped cream on top. Garnish each trifle with some of the remaining pecans and a lemon slice (if using).

4. Place the trifles in the freezer to chill for at least 10 minutes before serving; if not serving immediately, store in the freezer for up to 20 minutes and then move the dishes to the refrigerator.

Serves 4

PRACTICALLY PERFECT PEACH CRISP

⅓ cup honey
4 tablespoons (½ stick) butter
1 cup quick-cooking rolled oats
½ cup already-chopped walnuts or pecans
1½ teaspoons ground cinnamon
2 cans (16 ounces each) peaches packed in light syrup

1. Turn on the broiler.

2. Combine the honey and 2 tablespoons of the butter in a 2-cup glass measure and microwave, uncovered, on high, 1 minute.

3. Meanwhile, combine the oats, nuts, and cinnamon in a 2-quart or larger bowl. Remove the honey mixture from the microwave and stir until the butter melts completely. Add to the oat mixture and stir to mix well.

4. Drain the peaches, discarding the syrup, and arrange them in a shallow glass baking dish, such as an 8- or 9-inch pie plate. Microwave, uncovered, on high, 1 minute. Remove from the microwave and top the fruit with the oat mixture. Place the crisp under the broiler until the oats are golden brown, 3 to 4 minutes. Meanwhile, place the remaining 2 tablespoons butter in a 1-cup glass measure and microwave, uncovered, on high, for 25 seconds or until melted, then drizzle it over the browned oats. Serve at once or place in a slightly warm oven until ready to serve.

Serves 4

From Alicia:

At my house when I was growing up, freshly picked blackberries always bubbled into a fabulous cobbler. Fall's best apples and cranberries would magically turn into a warm crisp topped with a combination of oats and honey. But let's face it, peeling all that fruit and making homemade pastry for cobbler takes time. Sometimes I crave one of these childhood treats when I don't have two hours to make and bake it. That's when I turn to this speedy version of the fruit crisp from my childhood.

Using canned peaches not only enables you to prepare this quickly, it allows you to make it any time of the year.

From Beverly:

There are times when my desperation is downright depressing. There I was in New York City, one of a group being wined and dined by the Big Apple's best chefs. They fed us exquisite creations like Coconut-Glazed Sugarcane-Skewered Tuna Loin with Malanga Purée. Meanwhile, back in North Carolina, my family was subsisting on a vat of vegetable soup.

These gracious chefs sent us away from the annual food journalists' conference with enough complicated recipes to wallpaper the average kitchen—which, back home is about all they're good for. At my house, it's a choice: four hours in the kitchen vs. clean underwear, my son's soccer game, and bargain-hunting for back-to-school clothes.

In these moments when my culinary trade-offs make me sad, I reach for this recipe. In 20 minutes flat, I can produce a rich dessert I'd gladly serve to a New York chef. Suddenly, desperation doesn't seem so bad.

AMAZING APPLE TART

1 refrigerated pie crust dough, such as Pillsbury
1 can (20 ounces) sliced apples packed in water (see Note)
1 snack-size cup or can (3.5 ounces) fat-free vanilla pudding
½ cup caramel-flavored ice cream topping sauce

1. The oven should be already heated to 425°F.

2. Place the crust on an ungreased baking sheet. Fold ¼ inch of the crust edge inward and press it with your fingers to make a thicker edge. With the tines of a fork, prick the crust all over inside the rim. Bake until the crust barely begins to brown, about 8 minutes.

3. Meanwhile, drain the apples and set aside.

4. Remove the crust from the oven. Working carefully because the crust and baking sheet are hot, spread the pudding evenly over the crust. Arrange the drained apple slices over the pudding, overlapping them slightly in a spiral pattern until the surface is covered. Refrigerate any leftover slices for another use.

5. Place the caramel sauce in a 1-cup glass measure and microwave, uncovered, on high, for 15 seconds or until it reaches a pourable consistency. Drizzle the sauce over the apples in a thin stream. Return the tart to the oven and bake until the crust is golden brown, about 8 minutes. Serve slightly warm, cut into wedges.

Serves 8

Note: If you can't find sliced apples packed in water, substitute apple pie filling, only rinse the apples very gently under cool running water to remove the syrup, draining thoroughly.

MAGIC BROWNIES

½ cup (1 stick) butter
4 squares (1 ounce each) unsweetened baking chocolate
2 large eggs
1 cup sugar
2 teaspoons vanilla extract
½ teaspoon salt
½ cup all-purpose flour
½ cup already-chopped nuts of choice (optional)
Cooking oil spray
½ cup semisweet chocolate chips

1. Combine the butter and chocolate squares in a 2-cup glass measure and microwave, uncovered, on high, until the butter is almost completely melted, about 2 minutes.

2. Meanwhile, beat the eggs in a 2-quart or larger bowl with a whisk until foamy. Whisk in the sugar, vanilla, and salt.

3. Stir the chocolate and butter mixture until the chocolate is completely melted and the mixture is blended, then add it to the egg mixture and stir well to blend. Stir in the flour and then the nuts (if using). Spray an 8-inch square or 9-inch round microwave-safe baking dish with cooking oil spray and pour in the batter. Sprinkle the chocolate chips evenly on top.

4. Microwave, uncovered, on high, until the batter is just set and a toothpick inserted in the middle comes out clean, 4½ to 5 minutes, rotating the dish a quarter turn after every 60 seconds (see Note). Do not overbake. Cool until barely warm and serve.

Makes sixteen 2-inch squares

Note: The timing is based on a 700-watt oven. Adjust the time according to your oven power.

From Beverly:

My friend Denise Deen has three young children, yet still volunteers her living room for baby showers, impromptu sing-alongs, and countless church meetings. And, there are always homemade muffins or cookies on her coffee table to welcome guests. But it was the still-warm brownies that really impressed me.

"How do you do it?" I demanded.

"I just microwave them," she said in her what's-the-big-deal voice.

I couldn't believe it. Any cookies I'd ever tried to microwave tasted like Frisbees. So I took her recipe, played around with it, and came up with a version that even I can do.

The secrets to these moist, fudgy brownies are the small amount of flour used and being careful not to overbake. When done, they will still be shiny and moist on the very top but will continue to cook as they cool. Let the brownies cool while you eat dinner, and by the time dessert rolls around, you'll have sinful, still-warm brownies, too.

These addictive chips are awesome enough to eat straight out of the oven, but drizzled with a little warm honey or chocolate syrup to taste, they are simply heavenly.

So-sweet Sopaipilla Chips

2 large (10-inch) flour tortillas
3 tablespoons butter
2 tablespoons sugar
1 teaspoon ground cinnamon
¼ cup honey or chocolate syrup, or to taste

1. Turn on the oven to 375°F.

2. Stack the tortillas on top of each other and cut into 8 equal triangles with a pizza cutter or knife. Place the butter in a shallow microwave-safe dish and microwave, uncovered, on high, until melted, about 25 seconds. Meanwhile, combine the sugar and cinnamon in a small bowl and set aside.

3. Drag one side of each triangle through the butter, then over the edge of the bowl to remove the excess. Place the triangles, butter side up, on an ungreased 15 × 10-inch baking sheet. Sprinkle with the cinnamon-sugar.

4. Bake for 8 minutes or until the tortillas barely begin to crisp. Remove to a serving plate and let them rest 2 minutes to cool and crisp further.

5. Meanwhile, warm the honey or chocolate syrup in the microwave. Drizzle over the sopaipilla chips to serve.

Makes 16 chips

No-Fail French Crêpes

1 large egg
1¼ cups skim or low-fat milk
¾ cup plus 1 tablespoon reduced-fat biscuit or baking mix,
    such as Bisquick
2 tablespoons butter, as needed
⅔ cup seedless, fruit-only raspberry jam
Real whipped light cream in an aerosol can

1. Turn on an electric griddle to 350°F. Or begin heating a 12-inch nonstick skillet over medium-high heat.

2. Whisk the egg in a 2-quart or larger bowl. Whisk in the milk. Add the biscuit mix and whisk until there are few lumps. The batter will be thin. Butter the griddle, using about 1½ teaspoons of the butter.

3. Cook 2 crêpes at once by pouring the batter by scant ¼-cupfuls onto the hot griddle. Cook on the first side until the crêpes begin to set and tiny bubbles appear on the surface, about 1 minute. Turn and cook for another 30 seconds. Remove the crêpes to a plate. Repeat, buttering the griddle as needed, until all the batter is used.

4. While the crêpes cook, measure out the jam into a small bowl and whisk until smooth. Set aside.

5. Assemble the crêpes: Spread 1 tablespoon jam over one side of each crêpe. Squirt a generous amount of whipped cream over the jam. Starting at that edge, gently roll up the crêpe. Garnish each with about 1 teaspoon of the remaining jam and a dollop of cream. Serve at once.

Makes about 8 crêpes; serves 4

From Alicia:

In high school and college, in every French class I ever took, we always cooked crêpes on "culture day." They sound elegant, and they are, but elegant doesn't have to mean difficult to do. After all, high-school students can do it. (The trick to these no-fail crêpes is the baking mix, which produces a smooth, even batter that is more forgiving than a classic recipe.)

For weeks after this indulgent lesson, I would satisfy my craving by making dozens of crêpes with every conceivable filling. You can get as complicated as stewing your own fruits, or keep things quick and simple (as we have here) with jam and whipped cream. Be sure to buy seedless, all-fruit jam, of any flavor that suits, and a squirt can with real (not nondairy) cream. Beverly likes to finish her crêpes off with a drizzle of chocolate syrup.

PRESTO PRALINE COOKIES

½ cup (1 stick) each butter and margarine, or 1 cup (2 sticks) butter
1 cup light or dark brown sugar, firmly packed
Cooking oil spray
11 to 14 whole (double) graham crackers (see Box)
1 cup (4 ounces) already-chopped pecans

1. The oven should be already heated to 350°F.

2. Melt the butter, margarine, and brown sugar in a heavy 2-quart or larger saucepan over low heat, stirring from time to time. Meanwhile, spray the bottom and sides of a baking pan, preferably a 15 × 10-inch jelly-roll pan, with cooking oil spray. Line the pan with a single layer of graham crackers, using as many whole ones or pieces as you need to cover the pan bottom.

3. When the butter and margarine are melted, raise the heat to medium and bring the mixture to a boil. Boil 1 minute, stirring constantly. Reduce the heat to low and continue to cook, stirring constantly, for 1 minute more, until the mixture is well blended. Remove from the heat and continue to stir until the mixture stops bubbling. Stir in the chopped pecans.

4. Spoon the caramel mixture over the crackers. (Don't worry if all of the crackers are not completely covered. The caramel will spread during baking.) Bake for 8 minutes. Remove from the oven and cool for 15 minutes. Use a spatula to remove the cookies to a wire rack. (They should come apart in their original, whole shape.) Cut or break the pieces in half while still warm. Cool 5 minutes more (or until room temperature) and serve.

Makes about twenty-four 2½ × 2¼-inch cookies

These cookies taste like Louisiana pralines without the fuss. The recipe came from Kathleen Schwartz, an avid baker and former Raleigh, North Carolina, resident who now lives in upstate New York. She often whips them up for her grandchildren.

Be aware that the preparation and baking time takes 20 minutes, but you'll have to allow an extra 15 minutes for cooling. Whip them up before dinner, and by the time you're ready for dessert, the cookies will be ready, too. Leftovers are best stored in an air-tight tin with wax paper between the layers.

❋ We tested this recipe using Honey Maid brand graham crackers, and 12 of them fit exactly in a 15 × 10-inch jelly-roll pan. If your baking pan is not quite the same size, either larger or smaller, just use the number of crackers that fits. The caramel will spread to cover them during baking.

ORANGE BUTTER BALLS

½ cup (1 stick) butter
1 package (13½ ounces) graham cracker crumbs
2¼ cups confectioners' sugar
1 can (6 ounces) frozen orange juice concentrate
1 cup already-chopped pecans
1 package (7 ounces) sweetened flaked coconut (2⅔ cups)

1. Place the butter in a microwave-safe dish and microwave 10 seconds, uncovered, on high, to soften.

2. Combine the graham cracker crumbs and sugar in a 3-quart or larger bowl and stir well. Add the softened butter and orange juice concentrate and press into the dry mixture, using a fork. Continue until all the dry ingredients are moist and the mixture looks like coarse meal. Add the pecans and stir well.

3. Spread the coconut on a plate. Place a large storage container next to the plate.

4. Pinch off enough dough to make a ball the diameter of a quarter. Squeeze the dough in your fist and then roll it into a ball, using both hands. Place the ball on the coconut and repeat until about a dozen cookies are formed.

5. Rinse your hands and dry, then roll the balls in the coconut to coat. Remove them to the storage container and repeat until all of the cookies are formed and coated.

Makes about 6 dozen cookies

From Alicia:

This special cookie has always been a Christmas favorite for my family. But one Labor Day weekend, I pulled this recipe out and threw them together for a picnic. Because they're no-bake cookies, they are perfect for the hot summer months when heating up your kitchen is a definite turnoff. And because they're balls, they make great transportable food, one that actually makes it to the picnic looking the way it did when it left the house.

These delicious cookies are a favorite with kids of all ages—help make and to eat. The heat from your hands makes the dough stick together, so be sure to give each pinch of dough a good squeeze before rolling it into a ball. And yes, they're so quick, you *can* make 6 dozen in 20 minutes!

This fast and fabulous dessert features a homemade chocolate sauce that we're often tempted to eat with a spoon. But poured over a delicate angel food cake filled with creamy pudding, the sauce transforms humble supermarket ingredients into a dressed up version of Boston cream pie in only 20 minutes.

> ✳ *You may want to secure the layers with wooden picks to keep the cake steady. Remember to remove them, however, before serving.*

HEAVENLY CREAM CAKE

4 tablespoons (½ stick) butter
¼ cup skim or low-fat milk
2 tablespoons unsweetened cocoa powder
½ teaspoon vanilla extract
1½ cups confectioners' sugar
1 commercially prepared angel food cake (10 ounces)
3 snack-size cups or cans (3.5 ounces each) fat-free vanilla pudding

1. Melt the butter in a 1½-quart saucepan over medium-low heat. Add the milk, cocoa powder, and vanilla and stir briskly with a wire whisk until the mixture comes to a boil. Remove from the heat and whisk in the sugar. Continue to whisk for about 1 minute until the sauce is fairly smooth. (You will have a few small lumps.) Remove from the heat and set aside.

2. With a long, sharp, serrated knife, slice the cake into three equal horizontal layers. Gently remove the top two layers and set aside. Place the bottom layer, cut side up, on a cake plate. Spread the layer with 1⅔ containers of pudding. Place the second cake layer over the filling and spread with the remaining pudding. Top with the remaining cake layer (see Box).

3. Pour the chocolate sauce slowly over the cake, allowing it to run down the sides, covering the cake almost entirely. (There will be quite a bit of sauce on the plate.) Cover and refrigerate until ready to serve.

4. To serve, cut the cake into slices with a sharp, serrated knife, using a sawing motion. Serve extra sauce from the plate along with the slices, if desired.

Serves 8

THE DESPERATION ICE CREAM SOCIAL

An ice-cream sundae party is something we know everyone enjoys. Plus, it's easy. Here's how:

• Provide several flavors of ice cream and toppers, hot and cold, wet and dry, and let each person assemble his or her own sundae. Store-bought butter cookies are the only side dish you'll need.

• Topping ideas seem endless: Nuts, cherries, whipped cream, crushed peppermint candies, crushed pineapple, and crushed toffee bars are just a few.

• Entire supermarket shelves stock butterscotch, chocolate, and other ice-cream sauces. These will do in a pinch, but in less than 15 minutes (we promise), you can produce our rich sauces (this page to page 357), which will be the hit of the evening.

MANDARIN-RASPBERRY SUNDAE SAUCE

The zesty-sweet combination of raspberry and orange makes this a memorable sauce. If an alcohol-free sauce is preferred, substitute orange juice for the liqueur. Be sure to buy seedless jam. Leftovers if any, will keep, covered, in the refrigerator for up to 1 week.

1 jar (15¼ ounces) seedless, fruit-only raspberry jam
3 tablespoons orange-flavored liqueur, such as Triple Sec,
  or orange juice
1 can (11 ounces) mandarin oranges packed in light syrup

1. Place the jam in a 1-quart or larger bowl and whisk or stir until smooth. Stir in the liqueur.

2. Drain the mandarin oranges and discard the syrup. Gently stir the orange segments into the jam. Serve at once over ice cream.

Makes about 2¾ cups

Even those who think they don't like apricots fall for this ice-cream topper. And for those who love apricots, better make a double batch. It's perfect for just about any flavor of ice cream, from plain vanilla to double chocolate rocky road.

PINEAPPLE-APRICOT SUNDAE SAUCE

1 lemon
1 jar (12 ounces) apricot preserves
⅓ cup light or dark brown sugar, firmly packed
⅓ cup unsweetened pineapple juice

1. Grate enough zest from the lemon to make 1½ teaspoons. Reserve the remaining lemon for another use.

2. Combine the zest with the remaining ingredients in a 4-cup or larger microwave-safe bowl. Microwave 2 minutes, uncovered, on high. The preserves should be melted and the mixture warm throughout. Remove from the microwave and stir until the sugar is dissolved.

3. Serve immediately, or let the sauce rest and then serve it at room temperature. Leftovers will keep, refrigerated, for several weeks.

Makes about 2 cups

HOT CHOCOLATE DRIZZLE

1½ cups light corn syrup
⅓ cup unsweetened cocoa powder
¼ cup water
Pinch of salt
1 tablespoon butter
1 teaspoon vanilla extract

1. Combine the corn syrup, cocoa, water, and salt in a 4-cup or larger microwave-safe bowl. Microwave, uncovered, on high, for 3 minutes or until boiling. Remove from the microwave, add the butter and vanilla, and stir until the butter melts and the mixture is well blended.

2. Serve at once, or refrigerate, tightly covered. The drizzle will keep for up to several weeks. Before serving, reheat in the microwave for about 1 minute, stirring halfway through.

Makes about 2 cups

D on't be tempted to leave out the pinch of salt in this recipe—it's what gives it that old-fashioned ice-cream-parlor flair. Your children may not remember the delicious homemade chocolate sauce of the days before mass marketing, but for those of us who still crave that flavor, here it is. This chocolate drizzle will find you going back for seconds, and thirds, and maybe even just one more bite. . . .

THE ESSENTIAL SHOPPING LIST

The bottom line is you can't cook if you don't have any food in the house. So at some point, preferably when you're not desperate, make one initial extended shopping trip to get your groceries up to par. Then try to pinpoint a time in your schedule when regular shopping trips are easiest. Alicia catches the store on the way home from the gym in the very early morning or, on nights when her husband can be home, after tucking the kids into bed. Beverly, too, does a thorough shop once a week when she's not harried and can really concentrate. Like Alicia, she plans times to shop without children in tow.

THE BASICS

A Desperate cook always needs to keep a variety of canned goods on hand—beans (black, kidney, and others), broths (chicken, beef, and vegetable), and tomatoes (stewed and diced). You probably already have a couple of cans of tuna, but desperate cooks do well to add canned, white-meat-only chicken as well.

Stock assorted pasta of different shapes and flavors, and you'll be ready for a multitude of dinners without boredom. Quick-cooking rice (5- and 10-minute varieties) has improved vastly in the past few years (see the Box on page 59).

You'll want to have assorted oils and vinegars (see the Box on page 157 for specifics and substitutions) and general herbs and spices such as chili powder, garlic powder, onion powder, ground cumin, thyme, imported curry, oregano, salt, cayenne pepper, hot pepper flakes, and black pepper.

Frozen vegetables such as green peas and corn are best purchased in plastic bags rather than boxes (see freezer organization in the Organizing Your Pantry section on page 361).

DESPERATION CONVENIENCE ITEMS

The following list consists of ingredients that perhaps you've never noticed before or have never used. We call them Desperation Convenience Items, and when we have a brand preference, we've noted it. Many of these "convenience" items may be more expensive than their "regular" counterparts. But when you consider time and effort vs. extra expense on the Desperation scale, these handy helpers make all the difference. These convenience items are interchangeable with the "regular" ones if you can afford to spend slightly more then 20 minutes in the kitchen.

From the canned vegetable aisle:

- Stewed tomatoes (Mexican-style, Italian-style, and Cajun-style): Del Monte
- Diced, herb-flavored tomatoes ("Recipe Ready" pasta-style and salsa-style): Del Monte

From the ethnic foods aisle:

- Canned chopped green chilies: Old El Paso
- Salsa of heat-level choice

From the bread aisle:

- Bread crumbs, plain and Italian-style: Progresso
- Focaccia bread/pizza crusts: Boboli (sometimes stored near the refrigerated pizza dough)

From the dried herbs and spices aisle:

- Dried Italian seasoning blend

From the soup aisle:

- Low-sodium chicken bouillon crystals: Wylers
- Fish-flavored bouillon cubes: Knorr
- Vegetable-flavored bouillon cubes: Knorr

From the frozen foods aisle:

- Frozen concentrated lemon juice: Minute Maid (found in the freezer section, but store at home in the refrigerator)

- Frozen chopped onions (in plastic bags for easy measuring; see Box page 31)
- Frozen filled pastas: cheese-filled tortellini, cheese-filled ravioli, meat-filled ravioli
- Frozen red, yellow, and green bell pepper stir-fry mix: Birds Eye
- Frozen meatballs
- Frozen already-peeled shrimp (raw or cooked)
- Individually quick-frozen chicken breast halves or portions (sold in plastic bags, sometimes found near the frozen turkeys; see Box on IQF chicken on page 151)

From the dairy and refrigerated aisle:

- Already-shredded cheeses—especially bags of finely shredded sharp Cheddar (finely shredded melts faster), Montery Jack, Mexican blend, taco-style, grated and shredded Parmesan (freeze to prolong freshness; see the Box on page 245)
- Commercial pesto: Contadina (located near the fresh pastas; can be frozen for longer shelf life)
- Refrigerated biscuit and breadstick dough: Pillsbury
- Refrigerated prepared potatoes: Simply Potatoes

From the produce department:

- Already-peeled baby carrots
- Already-shredded cabbage coleslaw mix
- Already-shredded broccoli slaw mix
- Bags of prewashed and torn salad greens (blends of romaine, iceberg, green and red leaf, or spinach; see the Box on page 109)
- Already-sliced fresh mushrooms
- Bottled minced garlic (ask the produce manager if you don't see it; see the garlic Box on page 46)
- Bottled chopped ginger (ask the produce manager if you don't see it; see the ginger Box on page 287)
- Refrigerated fresh fruit such as mango strips and orange segments, in jars: SunFresh

ORGANIZING YOUR PANTRY

Desperation is something we don't plan, but we can count on it. The best offense is a defense. So, to avoid total panic when desperation strikes, you've got to have a plan. We've devised an organization system we call the Whole Kitchen Pantry Plan.

As we see it, the pantry is not just a few cupboard shelves, it's the refrigerator and freezer, too. With certain basic and "Desperation Convenience" ingredients in place and a system for finding and replacing them, you'll shave wasted minutes off of dinner prep time and never have to face the afterwork crowd at the checkout line again. (For more details, see our shopping list starting on page 358.)

Whether you follow our method or devise your own, there are two main reasons to make the initial time investment to set up The Whole Kitchen Pantry Plan:

1. The only way you can put dinner on the table in a flash is if you can find your ingredients.
2. With organized ingredients, you'll know in one glance what you can cook and what you need to buy.

You'll know you're truly hooked on the pantry way of life when, every time you open a can, jar, or bag, you write it on a shopping list for replacement.

ORDER IN THE PANTRY!

Organization is the key to keeping your pantry in working order. Even though our cupboard pantries are just narrow closets with shelves only 12 inches deep, in just a glance we can identify what we have and what we're missing.

Here's how we do it: Each shelf is divided into categories based on the way we cook. Nearly half of our recipes call for

"The only way you can put dinner on the table in a flash is if you can find your ingredients."

tomatoes, so half of one shelf contains nothing but tomatoes in every conceivable form—whole, diced, stewed, herb-flavored, sauce, and paste. Stacked as they are in rows, a quick reach snags the right can.

To the right of the tomatoes, we store the remainder of the canned vegetables, most noticeably every kind of bean we can buy. The second most important item in our pantries is broth, so we like to keep four cans of chicken broth and three cans each of beef, vegetable, and Oriental broths at all times.

The rest of the shelves look like this: half a shelf of rice and pasta products of various flavors and shapes. Another half-shelf is reserved for what we call exotics—ethnic foods, grouped by regions.

On the bottom shelf, we place little plastic baskets that hold our onions, potatoes, and fresh garlic.

KEEP THE FLAVOR NEAR THE STOVE

In a cabinet closer (but not too close) to our stovetop, we store oils, vinegars, dried herbs and spices, and other flavoring agents that are used over and over again. (Be aware that exposure to heat can affect the quality of oils and rob herbs and spices of their fresh flavors.)

The first time you sort through your existing cabinet, throw out all of the herbs and spices that have lost their aroma and write them on your shopping list to be replaced. When you've got them all together, group them and alphabetize the jars. (Beverly keeps hers on a twirling Lazy Susan–style rack. Alicia has a stair-step system.) To ensure freshness, buy seldom-used herbs and spices in the smallest possible quantities.

Store oils, vinegars, and other flavorings according to frequency of use. We keep olive oil, balsamic vinegar, and Worcestershire sauce front and center because we rely on them so often.

THE DESPERATION FREEZER SYSTEM

To organize the freezer, all you need is a big box of extra-large, freezer-weight, zipper-top plastic bags, such as the Ziploc brand.

Label one bag each for meat, cheese, and frozen vegetables. Next time you're left with half a bag of peas, close it with a twist-tie and stuff it into the vegetable zipper-top alongside the half-used bag of corn. If you tend to always have one bagel, one croissant, and one wheat roll left behind, mark a bag for bread. Add a bag for nuts. Frozen, they stay fresh practically forever.

The Desperation Freezer System is simple, but the change is quite dramatic. The big bags anchor on the freezer shelves better than a bunch of tiny, scattered ones, and we can easily spot things we used to scrounge for. Navigating gets easier still if you commit a particular shelf space to a specific food. Items we use daily go center and toward the front for easy reach. Fruit pops for the kids go on the bottom shelf, meat stays on the top.

THAT GOOD OLD FRIDGE

Organizing the refrigerator is easy, because most refrigerators have spaces designed for specific products. The key is to keep the ingredients in the same place day after day; this will speed you through preparing your shopping list or evaluating what's on hand to cook for dinner.

We suggest using the door space for small jars, bottles, and containers that easily get pushed to the back and forgotten. Eggs should be kept in their cartons and should not be stored in the door, since variations in temperature can affect their freshness.

The refrigerator can be a fantastic source of summertime meals when some of your favorite ingredients from the cupboard are stored, already chilled, in your fridge. (See the Box on page 119 for details.)

Once all three parts of your pantry are stocked with the basic and convenience items, you can slowly start to branch out and begin stocking more exotic and specialty items according to your personal preferences, and you'll think of your pantry as we think of ours—a collection of opportunities. Properly tended, it will serve you well.

"The refrigerator can be a fantastic source of summertime meals."

SHELF LIFE

Shelf life is as wonderful to the desperate cook as leftovers, and you should grab as much of it as you possibly can. If an ingredient keeps for a long time without spoiling, it simply means you have that much longer to rely on it. Shelf life eliminates a lot of time-consuming trips to the store.

An item's shelf-life isn't as big a mystery as you might think. Now that we're all looking more closely at the packaging for fat, cholesterol, calcium, and you-name-it breakdowns, it really isn't any harder to locate the stamped-on date. There are several types. "Use-by dates" and "expiration dates" refer to the last day you can safely use the product without freezing it (if it can be frozen). "Sell-by dates" list the last day the store should sell the item. Shelf life after the sell-by date of dairy products is about a week; meat should be a couple of days, but if you're in doubt about the quality of the food when you open it, discard it.

If the item is a packaged refrigerated or baked good, always check the date on several similar items on the grocery shelf before making a selection. We find the dates can vary from several days to a week. Of course, you'll always want to go for the best-tasting selection with the most distant date.

You'll find more information about shelf life scattered throughout this book. But here's a rundown on some of our favorite long-life ingredients that aren't always the first to come to mind.

Because ingredients that come in a can or jar will keep practically forever, you'll find recipes in this book that make good use of them, even some you've probably never thought about before. Canned chicken? You won't be able to tell the difference in Our Brunswick Stew or Easy Chicken Enchiladas (see the Index). We know it's difficult to believe. Until you try them, you'll just have to take our word for it!

We're always looking for meats that will keep practically forever—unfrozen. The best bets are cured meats such as turkey kielbasa and other sausages, ham, pepperoni, and Canadian bacon. A little goes a long way in adding flavor, so one or more of these is always in our fridges.

In the seafood realm, try these items found in the supermarket refrigerator case: smoked Nova Scotia salmon (or lox), other smoked fish, and imitation crab (surimi). From the canned goods aisle, look beyond the canned tuna and salmon to smoked mussles and smoked oysters.

Dairy products are another source of surprising shelf life. Ultra-pasteurized cheeses stay fresh, unopened, for weeks. For more details, see the Box on page 171.

The vegetable bin is always tricky. Your best bets for long-term storage are root vegetables, such as carrots and potatoes, and onions (we've always refrigerated ours but potatoes and onions can also be stored—separately—in a cool, dark, dry place). Most lemons and limes remain serviceable (if not quite as wonderful) for up to a month.

Finally, to make the best use of shelf life, pick at least one recipe from this book that relies mostly on long-term ingredients and always keep those items on hand. The following is a list of our favorites in this category (see the Index for page numbers). With these standbys and an organized Desperation Pantry, you can say good-bye to those five o'clock sprints through the fast lane forever.

Speedy Black Bean Soup
Minute Minestrone
Cuban Picadillo
Salsa Black Beans and Rice
Pasta with Smoked Salmon Cream
Pantry Pasta
Fancy Shrimp Fettuccine
Tuna with Red Beans and Aïoli
Sloppy Janes
Corny Chicken Casserole
Dinner Huevos in a Hurry

THE DESPERATE WEEK

From Beverly:

The desperate life comes in many forms, and some are worse than others. We can handle an isolated day, but how do you continue to put decent meals on the table when the desperation just doesn't let up? My three-week bout with pneumonia comes to mind. So does the aftermath of Hurricane Fran. And then there was emergency dental surgery followed by an unexpected and prolonged visit from my convalescing mother-in-law.

When life veers to the edge, I need more than one way to get a meal on the table quickly. When you've grown tired of cooking and weary of take-out, leftovers start to look a lot better, especially those that disguise themselves as something else.

Take our recipe for Two-for-One Noodles. It's ricotta noodles the first night, but later in the week the leftovers become Mock Spinach and Ricotta Lasagna. Both of these recipes take just 20 minutes start to finish. Likewise, make a big batch of Asian Rice Pilaf, and the leftovers can be whipped into Two-for-One Rice Salad with minimal work a few days later. Our recipes for Brunch Rice Burritos and Mediterranean Rice with Pita Points turn big batches of leftover rice into practically instant dinners. Scattered throughout this book, you'll find lots of other ways to make wise use of leftovers.

Then there's what we call "halfway cooking." That's when you buy part of the dinner and throw together the rest. One of my favorite secret weapons is a plain old roasted chicken. There they are—at the supermarket, the fast food outlet, and the take-out delicatessen—convenient and cheap. Buy one, head home, and dinner is done. Well, almost. What do you serve with a roasted chicken or, say, leftover meat loaf? You'll find everything you need to know about producing an array of speedy side dishes in our Quick Sides chapter, starting on page 306.

At Alicia's house and mine, here's what the dinners during a really desperate week might look like. We've given complete menus, but when things get really out of hand, you can eliminate the side dishes without suffering on Monday, Wednesday, Thursday, Friday, and Sunday. All the recipes listed appear in this book.

Monday: Two-for-One Noodles, Desperation Tossed Salad, and crusty store-bought bread.

Tuesday: Roasted chicken (store-bought), Mashed Potatoes with Onion and Basil, and Broccoli-Cheese Mini-Muffins.

Wednesday: Frenzied Fried Rice and Sweet-and-Sour Broccoli Slaw.

Thursday: Mock Spinach and Ricotta Lasagna (made with leftovers from Monday), iceberg lettuce wedges with My Vinaigrette, and crusty store-bought bread.

Friday: Pizza in a Panic and Sweet-and-Sour-Broccoli Slaw (left over from Wednesday) or Quick Carrot Salad.

Saturday: We deserve a splurge, so it's Pan-Seared Tenderloin with Béarnaise Sauce, Orzo with Mushrooms and Sun-Dried Tomatoes, and store-bought bread.

Sunday: It's time for comfort food, so I would choose Creamy Chipped Beef. At Alicia's house, it would be Grandma's Chicken Stew. Tutti-Frutti Salad is the perfect side for either one.

> *"When life veers to the edge, I need more than one way to get dinner on the table quickly."*

CONVERSION TABLE

U.S. Dry & Liquid Measures

The following equivalents are based on U.S. fluid measure, since in the U.S. measurements for dry ingredients, as well as for liquid, are by volume, not by weight.

1 pinch = less than ⅛ teaspoon (dry)

1 dash = 3 drops to scant ⅛ teaspoon (liquid)

3 teaspoons = 1 tablespoon (dry and liquid)

2 tablespoons = 1 ounce (liquid)

4 tablespoons = ¼ cup = 1 ounce (liquid)

5⅓ tablespoons = ⅓ cup (dry and liquid)

8 tablespoons = ½ cup = 4 ounces (liquid)

16 tablespoons = 1 cup = 8 ounces (liquid)

2 cups = 16 ounces (liquid) = 1 pint (liquid)

4 cups = 32 ounces (liquid) = 1 quart (liquid)

16 cups = 128 ounces (liquid) = 1 gallon (liquid)

Temperatures
°Fahrenheit (F) to °Celsius (C)

– 10°F = – 23.3°C (freezer storage)

   0°F = – 17.7°C

  32°F =   0°C (water freezes)

  50°F =   10°C

  68°F =   20°C (room temperature)

100°F =   37.7°C

150°F =   65.5°C

205°F =   96.1°C (water simmers)

212°F = 100°C (water boils)

300°F = 148.8°C

325°F = 162.8°C

350°F = 177°C (baking)

375°F = 190.5°C

400°F = 204.4°C (hot oven)

425°F = 218.3°C

450°F = 232°C (very hot oven)

475°F = 246.1°C

500°F = 260°C (broiling)

Approximate Equivalents

1 quart (liquid) = about 1 liter

1 stick butter = 8 tablespoons = 4 ounces = ½ cup

1 cup all-purpose presifted flour = 5 ounces

1 cup stone-ground yellow cornmeal = 4½ ounces

1 cup granulated sugar = 7 ounces

1 cup (packed) brown sugar = 6 ounces

1 cup confectioners' sugar = 4½ ounces

1 large egg = 2 ounces = about ¼ cup

1 egg yolk = about 1 tablespoon

1 egg white = about 2 tablespoons

Conversion Factors

If you need to convert measurements into their equivalents in another system, here's how to do it.

ounces to grams: multiply ounce figure by 28.35 to get number of grams

grams to ounces: multiply gram figure by .0353 to get number of ounces

pounds to grams: multiply pound figure by 453.59 to get number of grams

pounds to kilograms: multiply pound figure by 0.45 to get number of kilograms

ounces to milliliters: multiply ounce figure by 29.57 to get number of milliliters

cups to liters: multiply cup figure by 0.24 to get number of liters

Fahrenheit to Celsius: subtract 32 from the Fahrenheit figure, multiply by 5, then divide by 9 to get Celsius figure

Celsius to Fahrenheit: multiply Celsius figure by 9, divide by 5, then add 32 to get Fahrenheit figure

inches to centimeters: multiply inch figure by 2.54 to get number of centimeters

centimeters to inches: multiply centimeter figure by 0.39 to get number of inches

INDEX

A

Abbott, Melanie, 123
African chicken stew, 36-37
Aïoli, tuna with red beans and,
    118
Alicia's chicken with olives, 146-47
Angel biscuits with blueberries, 345
Angel food cake, heavenly cream,
    354
Angel hair pasta:
    cheesy ham casserole, 141-42
    creamy clams, 161
Antipasto, anti-stress, 104-5
Apollo's pasta, 185
Apple(s):
    English muffin "pub pie," 230-
    31
    a fall salad, 112
    -glazed burger steaks, 274-75
    harvest pork chops, 70-71
    tart, amazing, 348
    tutti-frutti salad, 314
Apricot-pineapple sundae sauce,
    356
Artichoke hearts:
    Apollo's pasta, 185
    Balsam Mountain Inn's fancy
        fettuccine, 173
    Greek-style brunch rice, 222-23
Asian-style dishes:
    drunken chicken, 75-76
    fish in a boat, 304-5
    pork chops, Misako's, 72-73
    pork hot pot, 16
    rice pilaf, 326
    see also Chinese-style dishes; stir-
        fries; Thai-style dishes
Asparagus:
    baked, Julie's best-ever, 316

Cinco de Mayo salad, 116-17
    smoked turkey roll-ups, 272-73
Aunt Flo's shrimp Creole, 95-96
Avocado:
    cool California bisque, 24
    salsa, 205

B

Back-to-Burgaw butter beans, 317
Bacon:
    Canadian, in English muffin
        "pub pie," 230-31
    and tomato pie, 219-20
Baked:
    asparagus, Julie's best-ever, 316
    chicken, flake, 266
    pork chops, miracle, 252
Balsamic vinegar, 14, 157
    lemon vinaigrette, 105
    maple glaze, ham with, 262
Balsam Mountain Inn's fancy
        fettuccine, 173
Barbecued:
    beef BBQ on corn muffins,
        193
    chicken, stovetop, 80-81
    shrimp on spicy rice, 92-93
    see also Grilled
Barringer-Willis, Margaret, 318
Basil:
    growing, 199
    mashed potatoes with onions
        and, 324
    summer's best pasta, 183
    see also Pesto
Bayou stroganoff, 65
BBQ:
    beef, on corn muffins, 193
    see also Barbecued

Bean(s):
    Blue Runners and rice, 99
    butter, back-to-Burgaw, 317
    French peasant supper, 68-69
    green, garlicky, 318
    and greens, 47
    minestrone, minute, 4-5
    red, in right-away beef penne, 130
    red, tuna with aïoli and, 118
    refried, in picante pizza, 209
    salsa, and rice, 98
    super chili, 40
    very vegetarian chili, 44-45
    white, and chicken chili, 34-35
    white, and lamb stew, 30-31
    see also Black bean(s)
Béarnaise, 236-37
Beef:
    already-cut, for quick cooking,
        28
    BBQ on corn muffins, 193
    chipped, creamy, 228
    confetti stuffed peppers, 249-50
    corned, in Reuben roll-ups with
        island cream sauce, 240-41
    curried, in pita bowls, 196-97
    curry, cravin', 50-51
    empanadas with chili-cheese
        sauce, 190-91
    fajitas in a flash, 53-54
    fiery Chinese, 63
    goulash, Hungarian, on rye
        toasts, 194-95
    ground, defrosting in
        microwave, 77, 243
    ground, freezing, 77
    hamburger steaks, Italian-style,
        248-49
    hamburger steak with mush-
        room gravy, 246-47

hamburger stroganoff in a hurry, 132-33
Jamaican macaroni, 140-41
kebabs, brown mustard, 297
lasagna, real-life, 134-35
meatballs and yellow squash, summer, 135-36
meat loaves, mini, Mom's, 242
moussaka in minutes, 60-61
and noodles with sour cream sauce, 138-39
penne, right-away, 130
picadillo, Cuban, 61-62
rib-eyes, Rio Grande, 295
rice and, heartland, 58-59
roast, roll-ups with horseradish cream, 238-29
salad with red-hot dressing, Thai, 102-3
shepherd's pie, skillet, 56-57
sloppy Janes, 192-93
steak and potatoes, pan- fried, Pop's, 234-35
steak on the spot, Chinese, 296
steak stew, 28
stir-fry, beat-the-clock, 52-53
tacos with so-simple salsa, 244-45
tenderloin, pan-seared, with béarnaise, 236-37
and white bean stew, 30
Beer-cheese veggie soup, 10
Beets, in beat-the-heat borscht, 23
Bennett, Liza, 18, 161, 198
Biscuit(s):
    angel, with blueberries, 345
    commercial mixes for, 329
    garlic cheese drop, 330
    refrigerator, doctoring up, 329
    sour cream, 331
    turnovers, 328
Bisque, cool California, 24
Black bean(s):
    burritos, 293
    and couscous Santa Fe style, 120-21
    jambalaya, flexible, 90
    and polenta, spicy, 292
    salsa beans and rice, 98
    soup, speedy, 13-14

southwestern chicken on the spot, 81-82
Blackened chicken (smokin' Cajun chicken), 264-65
Black-eyed peas, in vegetable Hoppin' John, 43
Blueberries:
    angel biscuits with, 345
    just peachy yogurt soup, 25
    tutti-frutti salad, 314
Blue Runners and rice, 99
Bob's famous fish, 279
Boiling water, 135, 147, 153
    salting and, 121
    symbol for, xviii
Borscht, beat-the-heat, 23
Bouillon, dried, 3
Bow tie pasta (farfalle), in tuxedo chicken, 152-53
Brady, Lynn, 130
Bread, food on, 188-211
    beef BBQ on corn muffins, 193
    chicken, creamy, on croissants, 202-3
    chicken casserole, corny, 201
    chicken tostadas with avocado salsa, 204-5
    eggplant and pita points, Middle Eastern, 210-11
    empanadas with chili-cheese sauce, 190-91
    goulash, Hungarian, on rye toasts, 194-95
    lamb, curried, in pita bowls, 196-97
    pizza, picante, 209
    pizza in a panic, 208
    seafood on the half shell, 198-99
    sloppy Janes, 192-93
    spanakopita in pastry cups, 206-7
    substitutions in, 191
    tuna melt, creamy, 200
Breads:
    biscuits, garlic cheese drop, 330
    biscuits, sour cream, 331
    biscuit turnovers, 328
    focaccia, fantastic, 336
    focaccia, feta, 337
    focaccia, mixed pepper, 338
    French, fabulous, 339

mini-corn muffins, cowboy, 335
mini-muffins, broccoli-cheese, 334
mini-muffins, Mexican, 333
pepper-Jack corn twirls, 332
pesto crescents, 340
tips for, 329
Breadsticks, Italian herb, 341
Breakfast for dinner, 212-31
    bacon and tomato pie, 219-20
    creamy chipped beef, 228
    eggs, company, 217
    English muffin "pub pie," 230-31
    French toast à l'orange, 229
    frittata, frantic, 216-17
    Greek-style brunch rice, 222-23
    hash brown casserole, 227
    huevos in a hurry, dinner, 218-19
    impostor grits and ham, 226
    omelet, easy, 215
    rice burritos, brunch, 221-22
    seaside eggs Benedict, 224-25
    tortilla, short-order, 214
Broccoli:
    cheese mini-muffins, 334
    cheese soup, PDQ, 11
    ravioli and, creamy, 177
    slaw, sweet-and-sour, 313
Broths:
    canned vs. homemade, 3
    Oriental-style, 16
    spiking with vinegar, 14
Brownies, magic, 349
Brown sugar, storing open boxes of, 131
Brunch rice burritos, 221-22
Brunswick stew, our, 38
Burger:
    steaks, apple-glazed, 274-75
    see also Hamburger(s)
Burnett, Sandra, 164
Burritos:
    black bean, 293
    brunch rice, 221-22
Butchers, 28, 195
Butter(ed):
    balls, orange, 353
    mustard sauce, 33
    rum-glazed ham, 261
Butter beans, back-to-Burgaw, 317

C

Cabbage:
  kielbasa, and potatoes, 32-33
  red, in beat-the-heat borscht, 23
  red, salad, 312
  scallop sauté, French, 96-97
Caesar salad:
  chicken, 108
  dressing for, 108-9
Cajun-style dishes:
  chicken, smokin', 264-65
  jambalaya, flexible, 90-91
  shrimp, barbecued, on spicy
    rice, 92-93
  stroganoff, bayou, 65
Cakes (savory), Cheddar corn, 319
Cakes (sweet):
  heavenly cream, 354
  pound, papaya and strawberry
    coulis over, 344
California bisque, cool, 24
Calorie cutting, 35
Canned foods, in refrigerator
    pantry, 119
Cannon, Susan, 186
Canola oil, 157
Cantaloupe, in tutti-frutti salad,
    314
Carolina crabcakes with creamy
    horseradish, 290-91
Carrot(s):
  salad, 312
  vegetable marinara, 166
Casadonte, Alicia and Frank, 146
Casseroles:
  cheesy ham, 141-42
  corny chicken, 201
  hash brown, 227
Cassoulet (French peasant supper),
    68-69
Cast-iron skillets, 55, 64
Cats (catfish), hot, with Fish Camp
    tartar sauce, 284-85
Cauliflower, in beer-cheese veggie
    soup, 10
Champagne vinegar, 14
Cheddar cheese:
  bacon and tomato pie, 219-20
  beer-cheese veggie soup, 10
  broccoli-cheese mini-muffins,
    334
  broccoli-cheese soup, PDQ, 11

corn cakes, 319
creamy tuna melt, 200
garlic cheese drop biscuits, 330
and ham casserole, 141
and ham pasta salad, 122
hash brown casserole, 227
impostor grits and ham, 226
potato soup, stress-free, 9
roast beef roll-ups with horse-
    radish cream, 238-39
Cheese:
  broccoli mini-muffins, 334
  broccoli soup, PDQ, 11
  brunch rice burritos, 221-22
  freezing, 245
  garlic drop biscuits, 330
  Parmesan, chicken fingers, 148-
    49
  Parmesan dressing, 311
  pepper-Jack corn twirls, 332
  Swiss, in Reuben roll-ups with
    island cream sauce, 240-41
  Swiss, in smoked turkey roll-
    ups, 272-73
  see also Cheddar cheese; Feta
    cheese
Chef salad, easy, 114
Cherries, dried, in ham with bal-
    samic maple glaze, 262
Chicken:
  barbecued, stovetop, 80-81
  breasts, defrosting in microwave,
    77, 243
  breasts, individually quick-
    frozen (IQF), 151
  breasts and halves, freezing, 77
  Brunswick stew, our, 38
  Caesar salad, 108
  casserole, corny, 201
  chili quesadillas, 271
  China in a pot, 18
  citrus, 78-79
  creamy, on croissants, 202-3
  drunken, 75-76
  enchiladas, easy, 269
  a fall salad, 112
  fingers Parmesan, 148-49
  flake baked, 266
  fried rice, frenzied, 83-84
  grilled, with mango salsa, 300-
    301
  hunter's, 154-55

lime-garlic, sauté, 267
lo mein, lazy, 84-85
Marsala, mind-the-clock, 156-
    57
mu-shu, mindless, 86-87
olé, 74-75
with olives, Alicia's, 146-47
pesto soup, presto, 19
piccata, lemony, 270-71
roasted, on greens, 110-11
schnitzel, sizzled, 268
smokin' Cajun, 264-65
spanakopita in pastry cups, 206-7
on the spot, southwestern, 81-
    82
stew, African, 36-37
stew, Grandma's, 39
stir-fry, beat-the-clock, 52-53
tetrazzini, oh-so-easy, 144-45
Thai, tempting, 88-89
tortilla soup, 17
tostadas with avocado salsa,
    204-5
tuxedo, 152-53
vegetable pasta, primo, 149-50
and white bean chili, 34-35
wild, skillet, 91
Children:
  names of new foods for, 169
  symbol for recipes friendly to,
    xviii
Chili:
  chicken quesadillas, 271
  super, 40
  very vegetarian, 44-45
  white bean and chicken, 34-35
China in a pot, 18
Chinese-style dishes:
  beef, fiery, 63
  fried rice, frenzied, 83-84
  lo mein, lazy, 84-85
  mu-shu, mindless, 86-87
  steak on the spot, 296
  stir-fry sauce, 85
Chocolate:
  brownies, magic, 349
  drizzle, hot, 357
Chowders:
  clam, almost-Dad's, 15
  corn, winter, 6-7
Cider vinegar, 14, 157
Cinco de Mayo salad, 116-17

Citrus chicken, 78-79
Clam(s):
  chowder, almost-Dad's, 15
  creamy, 161
  fritters, get-crazy, 289
  spaghetti, no-stress, 159
Clark-Brady, Lynn, 310
Coconut, in orange butter balls, 353
Company eggs, 217
Confetti stuffed peppers, 249-50
Cookies:
  orange butter balls, 353
  praline, presto, 352
Cool California bisque, 24
Corn:
  beef penne, right-away, 130
  cakes, Cheddar, 319
  chicken casserole with, 201
  chowder, winter, 6-7
  Mexican mini-muffins, 333
  mini-muffins, cowboy, 335
  muffins, beef BBQ on, 193
  twirls, pepper-Jack, 332
Corned beef, in Reuben roll-ups with island cream sauce, 240-41
Corn oil, 157
Cornstarch, storing open boxes of, 131
Coulis, papaya and strawberry, over pound cake, 344
Couscous, 36, 37
  basic, 37
  black beans and, Santa-Fe style, 120-21
  impostor grits and ham, 226
Cowboy mini-corn muffins, 335
Crab(meat):
  canned, pasteurized, 291
  Carolina crabcakes with creamy horseradish, 290-91
  seashore pasta salad, 123
Crabmeat, imitation (surimi):
  sailor's salad, 115
  seaside eggs Benedict, 224-25
Cream:
  horseradish, 239
  orange, 257
  sauce, island, 241
Creamy:
  chicken on croissants, 202-3

chipped beef, 228
clams, 161
Dijon dressing, 107
horseradish, 291
ravioli and broccoli, 177
tuna melt, 200
wild mushroom soup, 8-9
Creole shrimp, Aunt Flo's, 95-96
Crêpes, no-fail French, 351
Crescents, pesto, 340
Crisp, peach, practically perfect, 347
Croissants:
  creamy chicken on, 202-3
  seafood on the half shell, 198-99
Croquettes, gingered salmon, 286-87
Crowley's (Raleigh, N.C.), 156
Cuban-style dishes:
  chicken sauté, lime-garlic, 267
  picadillo, 61-62
Cucina Fresca (La Place and Kleiman), 181
Cucina Rapida (Wright), 160
Cucumbers:
  cool California bisque, 24
  gazpacho, Beverly's perfect, 20-21
Cup measures, 69
Curry(ied):
  beef, cravin', 50-51
  a fall salad, 112
  lamb in pita bowls, 196-97
  vegetables, Indonesian, 45-46
  yogurt mayonnaise, mahi mahi with, 283

D

Dairy products:
  expiration dates on, 171
  milk fat in, 153
  see also Cheese
Deceptively simple fish, 41
Deen, Denise, 349
Defrosting, in microwave, 77, 243
Desserts, 342-57
  angel biscuits with blueberries, 345
  apple tart, amazing, 348
  brownies, magic, 349

chocolate drizzle, hot, 357
cream cake, heavenly, 354
crêpes, no-fail French, 351
ice-cream sundae party, 355
lemon-ginger trifles, individual, 346
mandarin-raspberry sundae sauce, 355
orange butter balls, 353
papaya and strawberry coulis over pound cake, 344
peach crisp, practically perfect, 347
pineapple-apricot sundae sauce, 356
praline cookies, presto, 352
sopaipilla chips, so-sweet, 350
Dijon:
  dressing, creamy, 107
  dressing, sweet and savory, 310
  grilled shrimp, 303
Distilled white vinegar, 157
Dressings. *See* Salad dressings
Drunken chicken, 75-76

E

Ebanks, Reta, 140
Eggplant:
  moussaka in minutes, 60-61
  and pita points, Middle Eastern, 210-11
  ratatouille, summer's, 42
Eggs:
  bacon and tomato pie, 219-20
  Benedict, seaside, 224-25
  brunch rice burritos, 221-22
  company, 217
  French toast Ö l'orange, 229
  frittata, frantic, 216-17
  Greek-style brunch rice, 222-23
  hard-boiled, 124
  huevos in a hurry, dinner, 218-19
  omelet, easy, 215
  separating, 237
  shrimp salad, Ladies Lunch, 125
  tortilla, short-order, 214
Elbow macaroni. *See* Macaroni (elbow)
Electric stovetops, 235

Empanadas with chili-cheese sauce, 190-91
Enchiladas, easy chicken, 269
English muffin "pub pie," 230-31
Entrées, easy, 232-305
    beef, roast, roll-ups with horse-radish cream, 238-39
    beef kebabs, brown mustard, 297
    beef tacos with so-simple salsa, 244-45
    black bean burritos, 293
    black beans and polenta, spicy, 292
    burger steaks, apple-glazed, 274-75
    cats, hot, with Fish Camp tartar sauce, 284-85
    chicken, flake baked, 266
    chicken, grilled, with mango salsa, 300-301
    chicken, smokin' Cajun, 264-65
    chicken chili quesadillas, 271
    chicken enchiladas, 269
    chicken piccata, lemony, 270-71
    chicken sauté, lime-garlic, 267
    chicken schnitzel, sizzled, 268
    clam fritters, get-crazy, 289
    confetti stuffed peppers, 249-50
    crabcakes, Carolina, with creamy horseradish, 290-91
    fish, Bob's famous, 279
    fish fillets, flash-in-the-pan, 281
    fish fillets, golden fried, 275
    fish fillets, lemon-steamed, 278-79
    fish Florentine, 280
    fish in a boat, Asian style, 304-5
    fish in a boat, Italian style, 302-3
    ham, buttered rum-glazed, 261
    hamburger steaks, Italian-style, 248-49
    hamburger steak with mush-room gravy, 246-47
    ham roll-ups with orange cream, 256-57
    ham strips with orange mar-malade glaze, 263
    ham with balsamic maple glaze, 262
    mahi mahi with curry-yogurt mayonnaise, 283
    meat loaves, mini, Mom's, 242
    pork, grilled, with pretty pineapple salsa, 298-99
    pork au poivre, 255
    pork chops, miracle baked, 252
    pork chops, rice, and automatic gravy, 253
    pork loin, winter's warmest, 254
    Reuben roll-ups with island cream sauce, 240-41
    rib-eyes, Rio Grande, 295
    salmon, garlic-roasted, 282
    salmon croquettes, gingered, 286-87
    shrimp Dijon, grilled, 303
    shrimp-filled soft tacos, 288
    steak and potatoes, pan-fried, Pop's, 234-35
    steak on the spot, Chinese, 296
    tenderloin, pan-seared, with béarnaise, 236-37
    turkey, smoked, roll-ups, 272-73
    veal sofrito with fresh garlic, 251-52
    see also Bread, food on; Breakfast for dinner; Pasta; Salads, entrée; Skillet meals; Soups; Stews
Equipment:
    knife storage strips, 73
    measuring cups, 47
    measuring spoons, 69
    skillets, 55, 64
    vegetable peelers, 155
Expiration dates, 171

F
Fajitas in a flash, 53-54
A fall salad, 112
Farfalle (bow tie pasta), in tuxedo chicken, 152-53
Feta cheese:
    Apollo's pasta, 185
    focaccia, 337
    Greek pasta, 163
    Greek-style brunch rice, 222-23
    spanakopita in pastry cups, 206-7
Fettuccine:
    Alfredo (almost), 167
    Balsam Mountain Inn's fancy, 173
    with salmon cream, 162
    shrimp, fancy, 160
Fiery Chinese beef, 63
Fish:
    in a boat, Asian style, 304-5
    in a boat, Italian style, 302-3
    Bob's famous, 279
    cats, hot, with Fish Camp tartar sauce, 284-85
    deceptively simple, 41-42
    fillets, flash-in-the-pan, 281
    fillets, golden fried, 275
    fillets, lemon-steamed, 278-79
    Florentine, 280
    fresh, buying, 276-77
    grilled, Caesar salad, 108
    mahi mahi with curry-yogurt mayonnaise, 283
    salmon, garlic-roasted, 282
    salmon cream, pasta with, 162
    salmon croquettes, gingered, 286-87
    10-minute rule for, 282
    tuna and fusilli alfresco, 184
    tuna melt, creamy, 200
    tuna with red beans and aïoli, 118
    see also Shellfish; Shrimp
Fish Camp tartar sauce, 285
Flake baked chicken, 266
Focaccia:
    fantastic, 336
    feta, 337
    mixed pepper, 338
Fragrant rice pilaf, 325
Freezers:
    stocking cheese in, 245
    stocking meats in, 71, 77
French bread, fabulous, 339
French-style dishes:
    crêpes, no-fail, 351
    honeyed vinaigrette, 311
    onion soup, fast, 12-13
    peasant supper, 68-69
    pork au poivre, 255
    ratatouille, summer's, 42
    scallop sauté, 96-97
    vichyssoise, vite! vite!, 22
French toast à l'orange, 229

Fried:
cats, hot, with Fish Camp tartar sauce, 284-85
fillets, golden, 275
rice, frenzied, 83-84
Frittata, frantic, 216-17
Fritters, clam, get-crazy, 289
Fruit(s):
dressing, orange yogurt, 314
quick side dishes, 259
salad, tips for, 315
tutti-frutti salad, 314
see also specific fruits
Furr, Sandy, 200
Fusilli and tuna alfresco, 184

G

Garlic:
aïoli, tuna with red beans and, 118
bottled, 46
cheese drop biscuits, 330
green beans with, 318
lime chicken sauté, 267
potatoes and sausage with, 67
-roasted salmon, 282
Gas stovetops, 235
Gazpacho, Beverly's perfect, 20-21
Genoa orzo salad, 322
Ginger(ed):
bottled chopped, 287
lemon trifles, individual, 346
salmon croquettes, 286-87
Golden fried fillets, 275
Goodwin, Mary, 296
Goulash, Hungarian, on rye toasts, 194-95
Graham cracker(s):
crumbs, in orange butter balls, 353
presto praline cookies, 352
Grandma's chicken stew, 39
Grapes:
turkey salad with pecans and, 113
tutti-frutti salad, 314
Greek-style dishes:
Apollo's pasta, 185
brunch rice, 222-23
moussaka in minutes, 60-61
pasta, 163

spanakopita in pastry cups, 206-7
Green beans, garlicky, 318
Greens:
bagged, already-washed, 100, 109
beans and, 47
roasted chicken on, 110-11
Gressette, Felicia, 279
Grilled:
beef kebabs, brown mustard, 297
chicken with mango salsa, 300-301
fish in a boat, Asian style, 304-5
fish in a boat, Italian style, 302-3
pork with pretty pineapple salsa, 298-99
rib-eyes, Rio Grande, 295
shrimp Dijon, 303
steak on the spot, Chinese, 296
vegetable kebabs, great, 321
Grilling, 233, 294
Grits, impostor, and ham, 226

H

Ham:
with balsamic maple glaze, 262
buttered rum-glazed, 261
casserole, cheesy, 141-42
-cheese pasta salad, 122
frittata, frantic, 216-17
impostor grits and, 226
roll-ups with orange cream, 256-57
strips with orange marmalade glaze, 263
warm potato salad Dijon with, 106-7
Hamburger(s):
steaks, Italian-style, 248-49
steak with mushroom gravy, 246-47
stroganoff in a hurry, 132-33
Hart, Kathy, 290
Harvest dressing, southwestern, 117
Harvest pork chops, 70-71
Harvest vinaigrette, 310
Hash brown casserole, 227
Heartland rice and beef, 58-59

Heavenly cream cake, 354
Herb(s):
breadsticks, Italian, 341
growing, 199
see also specific herbs
Hicks, Sally, 47
Higham, Scott and Kathryn, 102-3
High heat, cooking over, 235
Hoisin sauce, 16
Hollandaise sauce, microwave, 225
Holland-glaze sauce, microwave, 273
Honeyed French vinaigrette, 311
Hoppin' John, vegetable, 43
Horseradish:
cream, 239
creamy, 291
Hot cats with Fish Camp tartar sauce, 284-85
Hot chocolate drizzle, 357
Hot sauces, 254
Huevos in a hurry, dinner, 218-19
Hungarian goulash on rye toasts, 194-95
Hunter's chicken, 154-55

I

Ice-cream sundaes:
hot chocolate drizzle for, 357
mandarin-raspberry sauce for, 355
as party fare, 355
pineapple-apricot sauce for, 356
Impostor grits and ham, 226
Indonesian curried vegetables, 45-46
Ingredients:
chicken breasts, individually quick-frozen (IQF), 151
dairy products, 153, 171
fish, fresh, 276-77
meat, frozen, 71, 77
oil, 157
orange segments, bottled, 78
refrigerator pantry and, 119
rice, "instant," 59
shrimp, 277
sour cream, reduced-fat, 139
vegetables, frozen, 57
vinegar, 157
Island cream sauce, 241

Islas de Canarias (Miami), 267

Italian-style dishes:

antipasto, anti-stress, 104-5

beans and greens, 47

chicken, hunter's, 154-55

chicken fingers Parmesan, 148-49

chicken Marsala, mind-the-clock, 156-57

chicken piccata, lemony, 270-71

chicken-vegetable pasta, primo, 149-50

clams, creamy, 161

feta focaccia, 337

fettuccine Alfredo (almost), 167

fish in a boat, 302-3

focaccia, fantastic, 336

focaccia, mixed pepper, 338

frittata, frantic, 216-17

hamburger steaks, 248-49

herb breadsticks, 341

lasagna, mock spinach and ricotta, 172

lasagna, real-life, 134-35

minestrone, minute, 4-5

orzo salad, Genoa, 322

pepperonata with penne and sausage, 142-43

pizza in a panic, 208

ravioli and broccoli, creamy, 177

ravioli with roasted red pepper cream, 178

rotini with fresh tomato sauce, 168

sausage and zucchini skillet, 66

shrimp and vegetables, 94-95

shrimp fettuccine, fancy, 160

spaghetti, no-stress, 159

spicy black beans and polenta, 292-93

tortellini, 174

vegetable marinara, 166

J

Jamaican-style dishes:

fish, deceptively simple, 41-42

macaroni, 140-41

Jambalaya, flexible, 90-91

Julie's best-ever baked asparagus, 316

Just peachy yogurt soup, 25

K

Kebabs:

beef, brown mustard, 297

grilled vegetable, great, 321

skewers for, 297

Kid-friendly recipes, symbol for, xviii

Kielbasa (turkey):

Blue Runners and rice, 99

cabbage, and potatoes, 32-33

French peasant supper, 68-69

jambalaya, flexible, 90-91

Kleiman, Evan, 181

Knives, storing on magnetic strip, 73

L

Ladies Lunch shrimp salad, 124

Lamb:

curried, in pita bowls, 196-97

cut for soup or stew, 195

and white bean stew, 30-31

La Place, Viana, 181

Lasagna:

mock spinach and ricotta, 172

real-life, 134-35

Latin-American style dishes:

chicken olé, 74-75

Cuban picadillo, 61-62

empanadas with chili-cheese sauce, 190-91

lime-garlic chicken sauté, 267

veal sofrito with fresh garlic, 251-52

see also Mexican-style dishes

Leftovers, as quick side dishes, 259

Lemon:

balsamic vinaigrette, 105

chicken piccata, 270-71

ginger trifles, individual, 346

juice, fresh vs. frozen, 285

-steamed fillets, 278-79

Lima beans, in back-to-Burgaw butter beans, 317

Lime-garlic chicken sauté, 267

Lofton, Sarah, 217

Lo mein, lazy, 84-85

M

Macaroni (elbow):

ham-cheese pasta salad, 122

Jamaican, 140-41

measuring, 131

minestrone, minute, 4-5

tetrazzini, oh-so-easy, 144-45

Magic brownies, 349

Mahi mahi with curry-yogurt mayonnaise, 283

Mandarin-raspberry sundae sauce, 355

Mango salsa, 301

Maple balsamic glaze, ham with, 262

Marinara, vegetable, 166

Market to Market (Service League of Hickory, N.C.), 224

Marsala, chicken, mind-the- clock, 156-57

Mashed potatoes with onion and basil, 324

Mayonnaise, curry-yogurt, mahi mahi with, 283

Measuring cups, 47

Measuring spoons, 69

Meat:

defrosting in microwave, 77, 243

stocking in freezer, 71, 77

see also Beef; Ham; Lamb; Pork; Sausage; Veal

Meatballs and yellow squash, summer, 135-36

Meat loaves, mini, Mom's, 242

Melt, creamy tuna, 200

Mexican-style dishes:

beef tacos with so-simple salsa, 244-45

black bean burritos, 293

brunch rice burritos, 221-22

chicken chili quesadillas, 271

chicken enchiladas, easy, 269

chicken tortilla soup, 17

chicken tostadas with avocado salsa, 204-5

Cinco de Mayo salad, 116-17

dinner huevos in a hurry, 218-19

mini-muffins, 333

salsa beans and rice, 98

shrimp-filled soft tacos, 288

Microwave, defrosting in, 77, 243
Middle Eastern eggplant and pita points, 210-11
Milk fat, 153
Mills, Dorothy, 158
Minestrone, minute, 4-5
Mini-muffins:
  broccoli-cheese, 334
  corn, cowboy, 335
  Mexican, 333
Misako's pork chops, 72-73
Mom's mini meat loaves, 242
Monterey Jack with jalapeños, in pepper-Jack corn twirls, 332
Moussaka in minutes, 60-61
Muffin(s):
  corn, beef BBQ on, 193
  corn, in corny chicken casserole, 201
  English, "pub pie," 230-31
  mini-, broccoli-cheese, 334
  mini-, Mexican, 333
  mini-corn, cowboy, 335
Mushroom(s):
  fettuccine, Balsam Mountain Inn's fancy, 173
  frittata, frantic, 216-17
  gravy, hamburger steak with, 246-47
  great grilled vegetable kebabs, 321
  orzo with sun-dried tomatoes and, 323
  pizza in a panic, 208
  vegetable marinara, 166
  wild, soup, creamy, 8-9
Mu-shu, mindless, 86-87
Mustard:
  brown, beef kebabs, 297
  butter sauce, 33
  Dijon, grilled shrimp, 303
  Dijon dressing, creamy, 107
  Dijon dressing, sweet and savory, 310

N

Names of new foods, for children, 169
New Orleans, dishes from:
  Blue Runners and rice, 99
  shrimp Creole, Aunt Flo's, 95-96
  see also Cajun-style dishes

Noodles:
  beefy, with sour cream sauce, 138-39
  chicken stew, Grandma's, 39
  hamburger stroganoff in a hurry, 132-33
  lo mein, lazy, 84-85
  pantry pasta, 169
  two-for-one, 170
  see also Pasta

O

O'Hara, Pam Smith, 120
Oil, 157
Olive oil, 157
Olives:
  chicken with, Alicia's, 146-47
  Greek-style brunch rice, 222-23
Omelet, easy, 215
Onion(s):
  chopping, 62
  cup measures for, 69
  flakes, dried, 31
  frozen chopped, 31
  great grilled vegetable kebabs, 321
  mashed potatoes with basil and, 324
  soup, fast French, 12-13
  vichyssoise, vite! vite!, 22
Orange:
  butter balls, 353
  citrus chicken, 78-79
  cream, 257
  French toast à l'orange, 229
  mandarin-raspberry sundae sauce, 355
  marmalade glaze, ham strips with, 263
  segments, bottled, 78
  yogurt fruit dressing, 314
Orzo:
  measuring, 131
  meatballs and yellow squash, summer, 136-37
  moussaka in minutes, 60-61
  with mushrooms and sun-dried tomatoes, 323
  salad, Genoa, 322
Oven, preheating, 233
  symbol for, xviii

Oyster, smoked, sauce, spaghettini with, 182

P

Pan-fried steak and potatoes, Pop's, 234-35
Pan-seared tenderloin with béarnaise, 236-37
Pantry:
  organizing, 362-65
  refrigerator as, 21, 119
Pantry pasta, 169
Papaya and strawberry coulis over pound cake, 344
Parmesan, 167
  broccoli-cheese soup, PDQ, 11
  chicken fingers, 148-49
  dressing, 311
  garlic cheese drop biscuits, 330
Parsley:
  fresh, storing, 184
  growing, 199
Pasta, 128-87
  Apollo's, 185
  beef penne, right-away, 130
  beefy noodles with sour cream sauce, 138-39
  boiling water for, 135, 147, 153
  cheesy ham casserole, 141-42
  chicken, hunter's, 154-55
  chicken, tuxedo, 152-53
  chicken fingers Parmesan, 148-49
  chicken Marsala, mind-the-clock, 156-57
  chicken-vegetable, primo, 149-50
  chicken with olives, Alicia's, 146-47
  clams, creamy, 161
  cooking vegetables in water with, 177
  fettuccine, Balsam Mountain Inn's fancy, 173
  fettuccine Alfredo (almost), 167
  Greek, 163
  hamburger stroganoff in a hurry, 132-33
  lasagna, mock spinach and ricotta, 172
  lasagna, real-life, 134-35

macaroni, Jamaican, 140-41
measuring, 131
meatballs and yellow squash,
summer, 135-36
no-cook sauces for, 179
orzo, in moussaka in minutes,
60-61
orzo, in summer meatballs and
yellow squash, 136-37
orzo salad, Genoa, 322
orzo with mushrooms and sun-
dried tomatoes, 323
pantry, 169
penne with summer sauce,
Sandra's, 164-65
pepperonata with penne and
sausage, 142-43
pesto, winter, 186-87
pizza, 180
ravioli and broccoli, creamy, 177
ravioli with roasted red pepper
cream, 178
rotini with fresh tomato sauce,
168
salad, ham-cheese, 122
salad, seashore, 123
salads, cold, 100-101
with salmon cream, 162
salting water for, 121
serving bowls for, 147
with shrimp, picnic, 126-27
shrimp fettuccine, fancy, 160
spaghetti, no-stress, 159
spaghetti, Topsail, 158-59
spaghettini with smoked oyster
sauce, 182
storing open boxes of, 131
stuffed, 175
summer's best, 183
tetrazzini, oh-so-easy, 144-45
tortellini, Italian-style, 174
tortellini with raisin butter, 176-
77
tuna and fusilli alfresco, 184
two-for-one noodles, 170
vegetable marinara, 166
ziti with basic no-cook sauce,
181
Pastry cups, spanakopita in, 206-7
Peach(es):
crisp, practically perfect, 347
tutti-frutti salad, 314

yogurt soup, 25
Peanut:
pantry pasta, 169
sauce, spicy, 89
Peanut oil, 157
Peas, in savory rice, 79
Peasant supper, French, 68-69
Pecans:
praline cookies, presto, 352
turkey salad with grapes and,
113
Peking sauce (hoisin sauce), 16
Penne:
beef, right-away, 130
pepperonata with sausage and,
142-43
with summer sauce, Sandra's,
164-65
two-for-one noodles, 170
Pepper (black), 255
pork au poivre, 255
Pepper(s):
beef penne, right-away, 130
confetti stuffed, 249-50
gazpacho, Beverly's perfect, 20-
21
great grilled vegetable kebabs,
321
huevos in a hurry, dinner, 218-
19
mixed, focaccia, 338
pepperonata with penne and
sausage, 142-43
pork hot pot, 16
red, roasted, cream, ravioli with,
178
Pepper-Jack corn twirls, 332
Pepperonata with penne and
sausage, 142-43
Pesto:
chicken soup, presto, 19
crescents, 340
French bread, fabulous, 339
pasta, winter, 186-87
penne with summer sauce,
Sandra's, 164-65
Picadillo, Cuban, 61-62
Picante pizza, 209
Picnic pasta with shrimp, 126-27
Pies (savory):
bacon and tomato, 219-20
shepherd's, skillet, 56-57

Pilafs, rice:
Asian, 326
fragrant, 325
savory, 79
spicy, 93
Pineapple:
apricot sundae sauce, 356
salsa, pretty, 299
Pita:
bowls, curried lamb in, 196-97
points and eggplant, Middle
Eastern, 210-11
Pizza:
in a panic, 208
pasta, 180
picante, 209
Planner, Desperate Week, 368-69
Polenta, spicy black beans and,
292
Pop's pan-fried steak and potatoes,
234-35
Pork:
chops, defrosting in microwave,
243
chops, harvest, 70-71
chops, miracle baked, 252
chops, Misako's, 72-73
chops, rice, and automatic gravy,
253
French peasant supper, 68-69
goulash, Hungarian, on rye
toasts, 194-95
grilled, with pretty pineapple
salsa, 298-99
hot pot, 16
loin, winter's warmest, 254
au poivre, 255
stroganoff, bayou, 65
see also Ham; Sausage
Portobello mushrooms, in creamy
wild mushroom soup, 8-9
Potato(es):
corn chowder, winter, 6-7
hash brown casserole, 227
kielbasa, and cabbage, 32-33
mashed, commercially prepared,
239
mashed, in roast beef roll-ups
with horseradish cream, 238-
39
mashed, with onion and basil,
324

pan-fried steak and, Pop's, 234-35

quick side dishes, 260

salad Dijon with ham, warm, 106-7

and sausage, garlicky, 67

shepherd's pie, skillet, 56-57

soup, stress-free, 9

tortilla, short-order, 214

vichyssoise, vite! vite!, 22

Pound cake, papaya and strawberry coulis over, 344

Praline cookies, presto, 352

Preheating oven, 233

symbol for, xviii

Prudhomme, Paul, 6

"Pub pie," English muffin, 230-31

Pyewacket (Chapel Hill, N.C.), 45

Q

Quesadillas, chicken chili, 271

R

Raisin(s):

butter, tortellini with, 176-77

a fall salad, 112

storing open boxes of, 131

Raspberry:

mandarin sundae sauce, 355

vinaigrette, 111

Ratatouille, summer's, 42

Ravioli, 175

and broccoli, creamy, 177

with roasted red pepper cream, 178

Ray, John, 156

Realon, Julie, 88, 176, 316

Red beans:

beef penne, right-away, 130

Blue Runners and rice, 99

minestrone, minute, 4-5

salsa beans and rice, 98

super chili, 40

tuna with aïoli and, 118

very vegetarian chili, 44-45

Red cabbage:

borscht, beat-the-heat, 23

salad, 312

Red-hot dressing, 103

Red wine vinegar, 14, 157

Refrigerator pantry, 21, 119

Reuben roll-ups with island cream sauce, 240-41

Rib-eyes, Rio Grande, 295

Rice:

and beef, heartland, 58-59

Blue Runners and, 99

burritos, brunch, 221-22

chicken olé, 74-75

confetti stuffed peppers, 249-50

fried, frenzied, 83-84

Greek-style brunch, 222-23

"instant," 59

jambalaya, flexible, 90-91

leftover, 223

pilaf, Asian, 326

pilaf, fragrant, 325

pork chops, and automatic gravy, 253

quick side dishes, 59, 260

salad, two-for-one, 327

salsa beans and, 98

savory, 79

shrimp Creole, Aunt Flo's, 95-96

southwestern chicken on the spot, 81-82

Spanish, speedy, 328

spicy, 93

storing open boxes of, 131

veal sofrito with fresh garlic, 251-52

vegetable Hoppin' John, 43

Rice wine vinegar, 14, 157

Ricotta:

and spinach lasagne, mock, 172

two-for-one noodles, 170

Rio Grande rib-eyes, 295

Roasted:

chicken on greens, 110-11

garlic-, salmon, 282

Roll-ups, 239

ham, with orange cream, 256-57

Reuben, with island cream sauce, 240-41

roast beef, with horseradish cream, 238-39

smoked turkey, 272-73

Rotini (corkscrew pasta):

Apollo's pasta, 185

chicken-vegetable pasta, primo, 149-50

with fresh tomato sauce, 168

picnic pasta with shrimp, 126-27

pizza pasta, 180

Rum-glazed buttered ham, 261

S

Safflower oil, 157

Sailor's salad, 115

Salad dressings, 308

Caesar, 108-9

Dijon, creamy, 107

Dijon, sweet and savory, 310

harvest vinaigrette, 310

honeyed French vinaigrette, 311

leftovers and, 312

lemon-balsamic vinaigrette, 105

my vinaigrette, 309

orange yogurt fruit, 314

Parmesan, 311

raspberry vinaigrette, 111

red-hot, 103

southwestern harvest, 117

sweet-and-sour, 127

Salad greens, bagged, already-washed, 100, 109

Salads, entrée, 100-127

antipasto, anti-stress, 104-5

beef, Thai, with red-hot dressing, 102-3

black beans and couscous Santa Fe style, 120-21

chef, easy, 114

chicken Caesar, 108

Cinco de Mayo, 116-17

a fall salad, 112

ham-cheese pasta, 122

pasta, cold, 100-101

pasta with shrimp, picnic, 126-27

potato, Dijon with ham, warm, 106-7

refrigerator pantry and, 119

rice salad with chicken, two-for-one, 327

sailor's, 115

seashore pasta, 123

shrimp, Ladies Lunch, 125

tuna with red beans and aïoli, 118

turkey, with grapes and pecans, 113

Salads, side-dish:
broccoli slaw, sweet-and- sour, 313
carrot, 312
fruit, tips for, 315
orzo, Genoa, 322
red cabbage, 312
rice, two-for-one, 327
tossed, desperation (recipe), 309
tossed, tips for, 308
tutti-frutti, 314
Salmon:
cream, pasta with, 162
croquettes, gingered, 286-87
garlic-roasted, 282
Salsa(s):
avocado, 205
beans and rice, 98
mango, 301
picante pizza, 209
pineapple, pretty, 299
so-simple, 245
Sandra's penne with summer sauce, 164-65
Sandwiches. *See* Bread, food on
Santa Fe style black beans and couscous, 120-21
Sauces (savory):
béarnaise, 236-37
-glaze, microwave Holland, 273
Hollandaise, microwave, 225
horseradish, creamy, 291
horseradish cream, 239
hot, 254
island cream, 241
mustard butter, 33
no-cook, for pasta, 179
orange cream, 257
peanut, spicy, 89
stir-fry, 85
tartar, Fish Camp, 285
see also Salsa(s)
Sauces (sweet):
hot chocolate drizzle, 357
mandarin-raspberry sundae, 355
papaya and strawberry coulis, 344
pineapple-apricot sundae, 356
Sauerkraut, in Reuben roll-ups with island cream sauce, 240-41

Sausage:
hash brown casserole, 227
jambalaya, flexible, 90-91
pepperonata with penne and, 142-43
potatoes and, garlicky, 67
and zucchini skillet, 66
see also Kielbasa (turkey)
Sauté, chicken, lime-garlic, 267
Scallop(s):
Greek pasta, 163
sauté, French, 96-97
seafood on the half shell, 198-99
Schnitzel, chicken, sizzled, 268
Schwartz, Kathleen, 352
Seafood:
on the half shell, 198-99
see also Fish; Shellfish; Shrimp
Seashore pasta salad, 123
Seaside eggs Benedict, 224-25
Seasoning cast-iron skillets, 64
Seasoning mixes:
for soup, 7
super, 265
Sell-by dates, 171, 366-67
Shelf-life, 366-67
of dairy products, 171
Shellfish:
clam chowder, almost-Dad's, 15
clam fritters, get-crazy, 289
clams, creamy, 161
clams, in no-stress spaghetti, 159
crabcakes, Carolina, with creamy horseradish, 290-91
sailor's salad, 115
scallop sauté, French, 96-97
seafood on the half shell, 198-99
sea scallops, in Greek pasta, 163
seashore pasta salad, 123
seaside eggs Benedict, 224-25
smoked oyster sauce, spaghettini with, 182
see also Shrimp
Shell pasta, in seashore pasta salad, 123
Shepherd's pie, skillet, 56-57
Sherry vinegar, 14
Shopping list, essential, 358-61

Shrimp:
barbecued, on spicy rice, 92-93
buying, 277
Caesar salad, 108
Cinco de Mayo salad, 116-17
Creole, Aunt Flo's, 95-96
fettuccine, fancy, 160
-filled soft tacos, 288
grilled, Dijon, 303
jambalaya, flexible, 90
pasta with, picnic, 126-27
salad, Ladies Lunch, 125
seafood on the half shell, 198-99
Topsail spaghetti, 158-59
and vegetables, Italian, 94-95
Side dishes, 306-41
asparagus, baked, Julie's best-ever, 316
biscuits, garlic cheese drop, 330
biscuits, sour cream, 331
biscuit turnovers, 328
breadsticks, Italian herb, 341
broccoli slaw, sweet-and- sour, 313
butter beans, back-to- Burgaw, 317
carrot salad, 312
Cheddar corn cakes, 319
focaccia, fantastic, 336
focaccia, feta, 337
focaccia, mixed pepper, 338
French bread, fabulous, 339
green beans, garlicky, 318
mini-corn muffins, cowboy, 335
mini-muffins, broccoli- cheese, 334
mini-muffins, Mexican, 333
orzo salad, Genoa, 322
orzo with mushrooms and sun-dried tomatoes, 323
pepper-Jack corn twirls, 332
pesto crescents, 340
potatoes, mashed, with onion and basil, 324
quick, 258-60
red cabbage salad, 312
rice, quick, 59
rice, savory, 79
rice, Spanish, speedy, 328
rice, spicy, 93
rice pilaf, Asian, 326

rice pilaf, fragrant, 325
rice salad, two-for-one, 327
summer squash medley, 320
tossed salad, desperation, 309
tutti-frutti salad, 314
vegetable kebabs, grilled, great, 321
Silver Palate Good Times Cookbook, The (Rosso and Lukins), 229
Sizzled chicken schnitzel, 268
Skewers, for kebabs, 297
Skillet meals, 48-99
beef, fiery Chinese, 63
beef curry, cravin', 50-51
chicken, citrus, 78-79
chicken, drunken, 75-76
chicken, stovetop barbecued, 80-81
chicken, Thai, tempting, 88-89
chicken olé, 74-75
chicken on the spot, south-western, 81-82
fajitas in a flash, 53-54
French peasant supper, 68-69
"instant" rice in, 59
jambalaya, flexible, 90-91
lo mein, lazy, 84-85
moussaka in minutes, 60-61
mu-shu, mindless, 86-87
picadillo, Cuban, 61-62
pork chops, harvest, 70-71
pork chops, Misako's, 72-73
potatoes and sausage, garlicky, 67
rice, fried, frenzied, 83-84
rice and beef, heartland, 58-59
salsa beans and rice, 98
sausage and zucchini, 66
shepherd's pie, 56-57
shrimp, barbecued, on spicy rice, 92-93
shrimp and vegetables, Italian, 94-95
shrimp Creole, Aunt Flo's, 95-96
stir-fry, beat-the-clock, 52-53
stroganoff, bayou, 65
wild turkey, 91
Skillets, 55
cast-iron, 55, 64
Slaw, sweet-and-sour broccoli, 313

Sloppy Janes, 192-93
Smokin' Cajun chicken, 264-65
Sofrito, veal, with fresh garlic, 251-52
Sopaipilla chips, so-sweet, 350
Soups, 2-25
seasoning mix for, 7
spiking with vinegar, 14
streamlined strategies for, 2-3
Soups, cold, 21
borscht, beat-the-heat, 23
California bisque, cool, 24
gazpacho, Beverly's perfect, 20-21
peachy yogurt, 25
refrigerator pantry and, 119
vichyssoise, vite! vite!, 22
Soups, hot:
beer-cheese veggie, 10
black bean, speedy, 13-14
broccoli-cheese, PDQ, 11
chicken tortilla, 17
China in a pot, 18
clam chowder, almost-Dad's, 15
corn chowder, winter, 6-7
minestrone, minute, 4-5
onion, fast French, 12-13
pesto chicken, presto, 19
pork hot pot, 16
potato, stress-free, 9
tomato, tangy, 5
veal or lamb cut for, 195
wild mushroom, creamy, 8-9
Sour cream:
biscuits, 331
fat content of, 139
sauce, beefy noodles with, 138-39
Southern-style dishes:
creamy chipped beef, 228
impostor grits and ham, 226
praline cookies, presto, 352
vegetable Hoppin' John, 43
white bean and chicken chili, 34-35
Southwestern-style dishes:
black beans and couscous Santa Fe style, 120-21
black bean soup, speedy, 13-14
chicken on the spot, 81-82
chili, super, 40
chili, very vegetarian, 44-45

fajitas in a flash, 53-54
harvest dressing, 117
rib-eyes, Rio Grande, 295
Soybean oil, 157
Spaghetti:
chicken fingers Parmesan, 148-49
chicken with olives, Alicia's, 146-47
hunter's chicken, 154-55
measuring, 131
no-stress, 159
Topsail, 158-59
winter pesto pasta, 186-87
Spaghettini with smoked oyster sauce, 182
Spanakopita in pastry cups, 206-7
Spanish-style dishes:
chicken olé, 74-75
gazpacho, Beverly's perfect, 20-21
picante pizza, 209
rice, speedy, 328
tortilla, short-order, 214
Spice jars, shaker tops of, 7
Spice level, 51
Spicy:
peanut sauce, 89
rice, 93
Spinach:
fancy shrimp fettuccine, 160
fish Florentine, 280
and ricotta lasagna, mock, 172
spanakopita in pastry cups, 206-7
winter pesto pasta, 186-87
Squash:
summer, medley, 320
yellow, meatballs and, summer, 135-36
see also Zucchini
Starches:
quick side dishes, 260
see also specific starches
Steak:
pan-fried potatoes and, Pop's, 234-35
on the spot, Chinese, 296
stew, 28
Stews, 26-47
beans and greens, 47
Brunswick, 38

chicken, African, 36-37
chicken, Grandma's, 39
chili, super, 40
chili, very vegetarian, 44-45
couscous as accompaniment for, 36
curried vegetables, Indonesian, 45-46
fish, deceptively simple, 41-42
kielbasa, cabbage, and potatoes, 32-33
lamb and white bean, 30-31
ratatouille, summer's, 42
steak, 28
veal or lamb cut for, 195
vegetable Hoppin' John, 43
vegetable veal, 29
white bean and chicken chili, 34-35
Stir-fries:
beat-the-clock, 52-53
beef, fiery Chinese, 65
chicken, Thai, tempting, 88-89
oil for, 157
sauce for, 85
Storing foods:
in open boxes, 131
pantry organization and, 362 -65
in refrigerator pantry, 21, 119
Stovetops, cooking over high heat on, 235
Strawberry and papaya coulis over pound cake, 344
Strickland, Florence Ann, 95, 320
Stroganoff:
bayou, 65
hamburger, in a hurry, 132-33
Summer meatballs and yellow squash, 135-36
Summer sauce, penne with, Sandra's, 164-65
Summer's best pasta, 183
Summer squash medley, 320
Summer's ratatouille, 42
Sundaes. See Ice-cream sundaes
Super seasoning mix, 265
Surimi (imitation crabmeat):
sailor's salad, 115
seaside eggs Benedict, 224-25
Sweet and savory Dijon dressing, 310

Sweet-and-sour:
broccoli slaw, 313
dressing, 127
Swiss cheese:
Reuben roll-ups with island cream sauce, 240-41
smoked turkey roll-ups, 272-73
Symbols, guide to, xviii

T

Tacos:
beef, with so-simple salsa, 244-45
soft, shrimp-filled, 288
Tangy tomato soup, 5
Tart, apple, amazing, 348
Tartar sauce, Fish Camp, 285
Teasley, Noell, 173
Tenderloin, pan-seared, with béarnaise, 236-37
Tetrazzini, oh-so-easy, 144-45
Thai House II (North Miami Beach, Fla.), 50
Thai-style dishes:
beef curry, cravin', 50-51
beef salad with red-hot dressing, 102-3
chicken, tempting, 88-89
spicy peanut sauce, 89
Time, efficient use of, 139
Tomato(es):
and bacon pie, 219-20
fresh, sauce, rotini with, 168
gazpacho, Beverly's perfect, 20-21
salsa, so-simple, 245
soup, tangy, 5
summer's best pasta, 183
sun-dried, in fantastic focaccia, 336
sun-dried, orzo with mushrooms and, 323
ziti with basic no-cook sauce, 181
Topsail spaghetti, 158-59
Tortellini, 175
Italian-style, 174
with raisin butter, 176-77
Tortilla(s):
chicken soup, 17
sopaipilla chips, so-sweet, 350

Tortilla, short-order, 214
Tossed salads:
desperation (recipe), 309
tips for, 308
Tostadas, chicken, with avocado salsa, 204-5
Trifles, individual lemon- ginger, 346
Tuna:
and fusilli alfresco, 184
melt, creamy, 200
with red beans and aãoli, 118
Turkey:
burger steaks, apple- glazed, 274-75
Caesar salad, 108
chef salad, easy, 114
chili, super, 40
ground, freezing and thawing, 77
salad with grapes and pecans, 113
smoked, roll-ups, 272-73
spanakopita in pastry cups, 206-7
tetrazzini, oh-so-easy, 145
wild, skillet, 91
Turkey kielbasa sausage:
Blue Runners and rice, 99
cabbage, and potatoes, 32-33
French peasant supper, 68-69
jambalaya, flexible, 90-91
Turnovers, biscuit, 328
Tutti-frutti salad, 314
Tuxedo chicken, 152-53
TVP (texturized vegetable protein), in very vegetarian chili, 44-45
Two-for-one noodles, 170
Two-for-one rice salad, 327

U

Use-by dates, 171, 366-67

V

Veal:
cut for soup or stew, 195
goulash, Hungarian, on rye toasts, 194-95
sofrito with fresh garlic, 251-52

vegetable stew, 29
Vegetable(s):
  beer-cheese veggie soup, 10
  chicken pasta, primo, 149-50
  cup measures for, 69
  curried, Indonesian, 45-46
  frozen, in bags vs. boxes, 57
  Hoppin' John, 43
  kebabs, grilled, great, 321
  marinara, 166
  quick side dishes, 259
  shrimp and, Italian, 94-95
  veal stew, 29
  see also specific vegetables
Vegetable oil, 157
Vegetable peelers, 155
Vegetarian entrées:
  beans and greens, 47
  black beans and couscous Santa
    Fe style, 120-21
  black beans and polenta, spicy,
    292-93
  chili, very vegetarian, 44-45
  curried vegetables, Indonesian,
    45-46
  eggs, company, 217
  fettuccine, Balsam Mountain
    Inn's fancy, 173
  fettuccine Alfredo (almost), 167
  French toast à l'orange, 229
  huevos in a hurry, dinner, 218-
    19
  omelet, easy, 215
  pasta, summer's best, 183
  penne with summer sauce,
    Sandra's, 164-65
  pesto pasta, winter, 186-87
  ratatouille, summer's, 42
  ravioli with roasted red pepper
    cream, 178
  rice, Greek-style brunch, 222-23
  rice burritos, brunch, 221-22

rotini with fresh tomato sauce,
  168
salsa beans and rice, 98
spanakopita in pastry cups,
  206-7
spinach and ricotta lasagna,
  mock, 172
vegetable Hoppin' John, 43
vegetable marinara, 166
ziti with basic no-cook sauce,
  181
Vegetarian soups, broth for, 3
Vermicelli, in Greek pasta,
  163
Vichyssoise, vite! vite!, 22
Vinaigrettes, 308
  harvest, 310
  honeyed French, 311
  lemon-balsamic, 105
  my, 309
  raspberry, 111
Vinegar, 157
  spiking broths and soups
    with, 14
Vitelli, Joanne, 108

W

Walnuts, in a fall salad, 112
Water, boiling, 135, 147, 153
  salting and, 121
  symbol for, xviii
Week of meal plans, 368-69
White bean(s):
  and chicken chili, 34-35
  French peasant supper,
    68-69
  and greens, 47
  jambalaya, flexible, 90
  and lamb stew, 30-31
  salsa beans and rice, 98
White vinegar, distilled, 157

Wild rice:
  quicker-cooking, 59
  turkey skillet, 91
Williams, Debi, 282
William Thomas House (Raleigh,
  N.C.), 217
Wine vinegars, 14, 157
Winslow, Rane, 110
Winter corn chowder, 6-7
Winter pesto pasta, 186-87
Winter's warmest pork loin, 254
Wright, Clifford, 160
Wynands, Marietta, 248

Y

Yellow squash:
  meatballs and, summer, 135-36
  summer squash medley, 320
  vegetable marinara, 166
Yogurt:
  curry mayonnaise, mahi mahi
    with, 283
  lemon-ginger trifles, individual,
    346
  orange fruit dressing, 314
  peach soup, 25

Z

Ziti:
  with basic no-cook sauce, 181
  beefy noodles with sour cream
    sauce, 138-39
  measuring, 131
  summer's best pasta, 183
  vegetable marinara, 166
Zucchini:
  great grilled vegetable kebabs,
    321
  and sausage skillet, 66
  summer squash medley, 320